THE ASHES CAPTAINS

The
ASHES CAPTAINS

GERRY COTTER

Foreword by SIR LEONARD HUTTON

The Crowood Press

First published in Great Britain by
The Crowood Press
Ramsbury, Marlborough,
Wiltshire SN8 2HE

British Library Cataloguing in Publication Data

Cotter, Gerry
The Ashes captains.
1. Cricket. English teams. Test matches
with Australian teams. Trophies: Ashes,
The, to 1988
I. Title
796.35′86′5
ISBN 1 85223 209 9

For Betty and Eric

Photographs 1938–1988 © Ken Kelly
Photograph of the author by Philip Miles

Typeset by Inforum Typesetting, Portsmouth
Printed in Great Britain by Butler & Tanner Ltd, Frome

Contents

Acknowledgements

A number of works have been invaluable aids in the writing of this book and I am happy to record my indebtedness to them. They are:

Bill Frindall, *The Wisden Book of Test Cricket* (Queen Anne Press).
Bill Frindall, *The Wisden Book of Cricket Records* (Queen Anne Press).
Alan Gibson, *The Cricket Captains of England* (Cassell).
Christopher Martin-Jenkins, *The Complete Who's Who of Test Cricketers* (Orbis).
Ray Robinson, *On Top Down Under* (Cassell Australia).
E.W. Swanton (ed.), *Barclays World of Cricket* (Collins).

Many other books have of course been referred to, and a bibliography appears at the end.

The bulk of the Statistical Highlights section is taken from David Frith's *England v Australia Test Match Records 1877–1985* (Collins) and I am very grateful to Mr Frith and to the publishers for permission to use material from the book.

My thanks to Mr Tuck of the John Rylands University Library of Manchester for his help in making available the library's cricket collection.

I am grateful to Ken Hathaway of The Crowood Press for greeting my idea enthusiastically and making suggestions which have been very beneficial to the end result.

I am especially grateful to Ken Kelly for the work he has put in – at short notice – in assembling the photographs.

I have browsed through many, many books in preparing this work, and if an author spots a statement, idea, opinion etc. of his which has gone unacknowledged, I hope he will be kind enough to forgive me.

Foreword

James Lillywhite to Mike Gatting, over a hundred years of Test cricket between England and Australia, what a feast of cricket between the old enemies. Gerry Cotter is to be congratulated on this outstanding book of cricket history, which will be welcomed by the likes of myself and thousands of cricket lovers in England and Australia.

In those hundred years of struggles between two countries, tempers have been lost, statements made and almost immediately regretted. Indeed, the 1932–3 tour of Australia was almost called off after the Adelaide Test: Douglas Jardine had become the most unpopular cricketer ever to visit Australia.

After the bodyline tour, the game was to change as the media realised that cricket could be news. Prior to 1932 the Press had sent few cricket writers on overseas tours, but radio then started to cover important games in both England and Australia and in the early 1950s television entered the world of cricket. The pitch has remained the same 22 yards, but changes in all other aspects of the game have been made – we like to think for the better, but in my opinion this is debatable.

When you become captain of England or Australia problems arise which you had no idea existed. When I was captain pitches were uncovered as they were in the days of W.G. Grace. I well remember looking out of the window at 3 a.m. in 1953 at Nottingham to see what the weather was doing; we were batting in a few hours on what *had been* a good wicket. Now, of course, all Test match pitches are covered, and so this is one problem which has been eliminated. But is the game more interesting? I doubt it.

Over the years we have seen some superb performances by batsmen and bowlers of both countries. Bradman's wonderful innings at Headingley when he made 334 (309 in one day) was a remarkable feat and his record is quite outstanding. When Bradman reached his century he then thought of a double century, and so on. Once he had reached ten runs he was almost impossible to get out on a good wicket. One thing that I noticed about Don was how keen he was to get off the mark; he took cheeky singles to get that dreadful '0' off the scoreboard.

On being made captain of Australia in 1936, Bradman lost the first two Tests, but then his batting returned to form and Australia won the last three Tests and so retained the Ashes. In 1938, when Don was again captain, I think Bill O'Reilly missed Clarrie Grimmett; four years earlier in England they had proved a match-winning pair, their accuracy was quite outstanding and together they were one of the best slow-bowling combinations that cricket has seen. Don made few mistakes but the omission of Clarrie was surely one.

I think he was very fortunate to have the sort of team a captain dreams about. On our arrival in Australia in 1946 under the captaincy of Walter Hammond, one little realised the talent which Australia possessed. Not only was there the power of Ray Lindwall and Keith Miller, but the class of Bill Johnston (first change) and the spinners, several of whom could not even make the team. The Australian Test teams of 1946–7, 1948 and 1950–1 were the finest teams I ever played against. Don Bradman was still the run-hungry cricketer who once made 452 not out for New South Wales, even if he was not the Bradman whom I had seen make 309 runs in one day sixteen years earlier. He was more sedate, nothing like so aggressive, but still a power in the land.

When you look through the imposing list of Ashes captains one wonders what these outstanding cricketers thought about apart from winning. I never really felt that the MCC were hell-bent on winning; they saw overseas tours as a way of spreading the 'Gospel of Cricket', and quite right too. Unfortunately not every cricketing board sees international cricket in the same way as the MCC.

Life could be very tough for me on my tour in 1954. In Brisbane I had put Australia in to bat hoping for a quick breakthrough but due to poor fielding Australia made a match-winning score. One evening as the match was drawing to its close, I took a cruise up the Brisbane River with George Duckworth to get away from the game, to have some sort of peace and quiet. The Brisbane River is not attractive, but that particular evening it was heaven. Duckworth and I talked over the match which was to end the following day with a defeat for England, a defeat by an innings and plenty. I was at rock bottom. I wanted to win in Australia as Douglas Jardine had over twenty years earlier, but I wanted to win without leaving an atmosphere.

Still, deep down, I had a feeling we could win, but how was I to give the players the confidence to recover from being one down? I had Brian Statham, Frank Tyson, plus the best wicket-keeper in the world, Godfrey Evans. The recovery was in the hands of those three; if Tyson or Statham broke down our chances would be almost eliminated. However, the run of the ball was with me, and the Ashes were retained – but only after a great struggle in the fourth Test on the delightful Adelaide Oval.

In 1953 I looked long and hard at the Australian team skippered by Lindsay Hassett. A good many of them had known outstanding success since 1946; Lindwall and Miller were still there, as was Bill Johnston. But the Don had gone; his departure must have placed added responsibility on the remaining players, particularly the newcomers.

At that time, we had had no success against Australia since 1932. Alec Bedser was still one of the finest bowlers in the world and had given great service to England and Surrey for several years and a young bowler who impressed me very much was Brian Statham. Cyril Washbrook had told me about him in 1950 in Australia and what he said proved correct; for several years Statham became a very reliable member of the England team, one of the finest cricketers to have played for his country. Fred Trueman was also showing great promise. He was young with all the qualities of a fine fast bowler and his inclusion at the Oval was the start of a fine Test match career.

In 1953 the English selection committee contained three former Ashes captains, including R.E.S. Wyatt, perhaps the most knowledgeable English Test cricketer alive today. During our selection meeting I listened carefully to his remarks; his memory was extremely good and his knowledge and love of cricket was unsurpassed.

Gerry Cotter gives the reader much information on the quality of Test cricket between England and Australia, along with many comments on the individual matches over a hundred years. I congratulate him on a fine book which will give much pleasure to all who read it.

Sir Leonard Hutton
1989

Preface

Captaincy of a cricket team is a complex business and a number of books have been written about it. My aim in this one has been to give some idea of the characters, abilities and leadership qualities of the men who have captained England and Australia against each other; they have been placed against their historical background, of course, but as I am not a social historian I have chosen to describe them in the context of their Test matches rather than in the social and political settings of their times. The latter would make a fascinating book, and if anyone wishes to write it I would guarantee them at least one sale.

One little problem was the tense with which I referred to players who are still alive. I adopted the compromise of past tense for those who have retired and present tense for those still playing, and if anyone feels put out to read of himself that 'he *was* a very friendly man' I can only hope that he will prove my usage wrong and demonstrate that he still is.

1

The Flame is Lighted

The original tours of Australia made by English cricket teams in the 1860s and 1870s were mainly financial ventures. A small group of sponsors guaranteed to pay the professional players a fixed sum for the trip, together with all travelling and hotel expenses, and then took their profits from the admission charges made at the grounds. It is hard to think of any other way in which international cricket could reasonably have begun, but the fact that the great and glorious tradition of Ashes Tests, with all the honour of playing for your country against the old enemy that they involve, actually had its origins in *money* seems somehow distasteful. One wants the Tests to have grown out of a desire by a group of romantically-inclined gentlemen that the cream of the players in each country should pit themselves against each other in honourable combat. One wants them to have *known* that they were setting in motion one of the greatest of all sporting traditions. Instead of which the first games were almost unpremeditated, and took place mainly so that a few individuals could make a profit. It's not fair.

It was on the fourth of these tours, led by James Lillywhite junior in 1876–7, that the two matches which came to be recognised as the first Tests were played. In the earlier tours the Englishmen had realised that the local players were steadily improving, especially the bowlers, and when Lillywhite's team lost twice to fifteen of New South Wales and once to fifteen of Melbourne the Australians felt that they would like to play them on equal terms. A match that had not been in the original schedule was therefore arranged to be played after the tourists returned from the New Zealand leg of their journey. Only later was it called the first Test match; it was described at the time as a Grand Combined Melbourne and Sydney XI v James Lillywhite's XI. The term Test match, incidentally, was not used until 1884 and first appeared in the *Melbourne Herald*.

Much was made of the distances which the England party had to travel in their 1986–7 tour of Australia, but they had it easy compared with Lillywhite's team. In New Zealand their coach got stuck in the flooded Otira Gorge one night, and they got soaked in pulling it out. Still in the same clothes they slept on the floor of a wooden hostel. Next morning they found

England's first captain, James Lillywhite jr, stands on the right of the picture, taken in 1870 or 1871. With him are, standing left to right, George Griffith, Tom Humphrey, Frank Silcock. Sitting, a young W.G. Grace, James Southerton. Front, Henry Jupp, Richard Humphrey. Jupp and Southerton played in the first two Tests.

their road blocked by a landslide and had to return to the hostel – where there was no food. When they finally arrived at their destination they began their game after only half an hour. After finishing in New Zealand they had six days of seasickness before they reached Melbourne, where the historic match started next day, 15 March 1877. One wonders how Gatting and Co. would have got on in such conditions.

James Lillywhite was one of a famous family of nineteenth-century cricketers, and along with Alfred Shaw and Arthur Shrewsbury he was to finance and organise four more tours, ultimately making a substantial loss because a separate tour took place at the same time. He was a medium-slow left arm bowler renowned for his great accuracy – much store was placed on nagging accuracy in those days – who took part in every Sussex match between 1862 and 1881; he could bat a bit, and was a good fielder. His cricketing skills were nothing exceptional, but he was a good organiser and was ready to learn from some of the mistakes that had been made on the earlier tours. To a considerable extent captaincy in those days centred on organisation, with little in the way of tactical planning, and within the limitations of the time he was efficient at the job. He is remembered as the England captain in the first two Tests, but his importance extends well beyond that; without his entrepreneurial skills the early years of Test cricket may well have been very different from what they were. He also published his *Cricketers' Companion*, which eventually became part of *James Lillywhite's Cricketers' Annual*. Happily he lived until 1929, and must have taken great pride in what he had helped to start.

Two former Surrey players, Charles Lawrence and William Caffyn, had done a great deal towards raising the standards of Australian cricket, and Caffyn had coached the man who was to be Australia's first Test captain, Dave Gregory. He was the first of the Gregory clan to achieve distinction; his brother Ned also played in the match (and recorded the first Test duck), two other brothers played for New South Wales, and he was the uncle of Syd and Jack Gregory who both had distinguished Test careers. The team was made up of six from Victoria and five from New South Wales, and it was the players themselves who chose him as captain.

At 6 feet 2 inches tall and with a full black beard he certainly looked the part, and he had a forceful personality that matched his appearance; he was an authoritarian, but not without some humour. There was nothing particularly stylish about his batting, but he was solid and determined and had a good defence – a useful attribute given some of the early wickets. Undoubtedly he was a shrewd captain who gave a good deal of thought to the game; during the Australians' 1878 tour of England, in which they did

'Handsome Dave' Gregory was Australia's first captain.

not play a Test, his captaincy came in for warm praise from the press. 'He changes the bowling with promptitude and excellent judgement and varies his field with a quick appreciation of the peculiarities of different batsmen,' said the *Standard*. Gregory is an important figure in the development of Australian cricket, for not only was he one of the instigators of this first challenge match, but in 1883 he became honorary secretary to the New South Wales Cricket Association, and gave much good service to his colony's cricketing affairs. He later became Paymaster of the Treasury and held the office with distinction. He also holds the record among Australian captains for producing the most children – sixteen of them, one more than Joe Darling.

Neither side pretended to be composed of the best eleven cricketers that its country could offer. Players such as the Graces, Hornby and Shrewsbury were back in England, and in addition Lillywhite had lost the services of his wicket-keeper Pooley who was in prison in New Zealand. In Christchurch, Pooley had tried the old trick of offering odds of twenty to one that he could forecast the individual scores of each of the local eighteen against his team. His offer was accepted by one Ralph Donkin, and he duly said that each man would score nought. Against a weak team this could hardly fail to bring him a profit, and when it did Donkin objected and a scuffle took place. Pooley and the English baggage man were arrested and spent six weeks waiting to go before the court. They were acquitted, and the local people, feeling that they had been hard done by, subscribed £50 for them and gave Pooley a gold watch. What a way to miss a Test match!

This was serious for Lillywhite, especially as his reserve keeper, Jupp, had eye trouble and could not keep wicket either, although he batted. In the end the opener Selby did the job, and lost runs and missed chances that Pooley would not have done. Gregory, for his part, lacked the services of three fine bowlers, Spofforth, Evans and Allan, and the *cognoscenti* in the crowd generally gave the home team little chance. The pitch, incidentally, was praised by the tourists as being quite up to English standards.

The hero of the match was Charles Bannerman, who had been born in Kent. His 165 was not only Test cricket's first century but the first one ever scored by an Australian against an English team, and it ended only when he retired hurt with a split finger. His innings represented 67.3 per cent of his team's total of 245, and quite remarkably this percentage has never been beaten in any Test match since. The English reply was 196, the highest score coming from Jupp, who made 63 despite his eye trouble, with Midwinter becoming the first bowler to take five wickets in a Test. In the second innings the home team could make only 104, but then the visitors fared little better and, with Kendall taking 7 for 55, fell 45 runs short of their target. The three thousand spectators were naturally delighted, but whether they set the precedent of invading the pitch is not recorded.

A return match was duly arranged, to start twelve days later. Spofforth came into the home team, as did Billy Murdoch who was soon to become the captain, but the Englishmen took their revenge. After dismissing Gregory's team for 122, four batsmen scored around the fifty mark, and they reached 261. In the second innings the home team came within two runs of this, leaving the tourists to lose six wickets in polishing off the runs needed. Yorkshire folk will be pleased to learn that of the 356 runs which the visitors scored with their bats, 329 of them came from their compatriots. Both games had been well fought and successful, but the feeling in Australia, quite justifiably, was that in future the visiting team should be as strong as possible.

Early in January 1879 the match that came to be regarded as the third Test took place. The Australian captain was still Gregory, but the touring team were led this time by an important figure in cricket history. Lord Harris was a good cricketer without being an outstanding one, a strong

Lord Harris, the first of the aristocrat Test captains and a great administrator.

attacking batsman, useful bowler and splendid fielder. A strong personality, the influence he exercised was usually for the good of the game, since he was a fair and just man noted for his sound judgement, a great supporter of the professionals and opponent of bowlers who 'threw', and a great upholder of the laws (which he always insisted were laws and not rules, since rules are made to be broken and laws are made to be kept). It was largely through his efforts that Kent's fortunes were revived after years in the doldrums, and he remained the central figure at Kent all his life. He also played an enormous role in the running of MCC, being President in 1895, a Trustee from 1906 to 1916, and Honorary Treasurer from 1916 to 1932. On top of this he was in his time Under-Secretary for India, Under-Secretary for War and Governor of Bombay. Moreover, he edited books about Kent and about Lord's, as well as writing his memoirs, *A Few Short Runs*, a curious title that suggests he had not always upheld the laws himself.

As a captain he insisted on high standards from his players, and those players who did not produce them tended to wish that they had. But the good players liked playing under him, knowing that if he praised them he really meant it and they had deserved it. Certainly he was autocratic, but he mellowed as he matured and his fairness meant that he was much respected. His friendly relations with the professionals (which not all the amateurs adopted) meant they were always ready to do their best for him, and he was perhaps the first of the tactician-captains who would often get batsmen out by playing on their weaknesses. Some of his players rated him the best captain who had ever lived, and maybe at the time they were right.

The match at Melbourne in January 1879 was, however, a disaster for the English, who did not have a strong team. On the morning of the match there was a thunderstorm, but Harris chose to bat all the same. Before long his team were 26 for 7, and only through himself and Absolom did the total reach 102. Spofforth achieved the first Test hat-trick – one wonders whether his colleagues hugged him in celebration – and took six wickets in all. The Australians then made 256, top scorer being Charles Bannerman's brother Alec, who put together a slow but sound (the standard epithets for his batting over many years) 73. In the tourists' second innings Spofforth went one better (finishing the match with 13 for 110) to bowl them out for 160, setting his team up for a ten-wicket victory. Harris himself batted well in both innings, but 'the Demon' had been too good for the Englishmen. It was not the only time that was the case.

A return game had been planned but it was cancelled after a fracas at Sydney. The crowd felt that one of the umpires was favouring the visitors, and when Dave Gregory lodged an objection to the umpire they invaded the

*W.L. Murdoch, sixteen times captain of Australia, who also played
once for England against South Africa.*

pitch. Harris was attacked by a larrikin with a stick, but was defended by Ulyett and Emmett, his professionals, and by Hornby. In the end peace was restored, but it created a great deal of ill feeling.

There had been an Australian tour of England in 1878, but no full representative match had been played. They had, though, seen off a fairly strong MCC team, putting them out for 33 and 19 and beating them by nine wickets in one day. The contretemps at Sydney, though, meant that when they toured in 1880 under Billy Murdoch many of the counties refused to entertain them and they had to go to the length of advertising for fixtures. The Surrey secretary, C.W. Alcock, however, felt that a representative match would be an excellent thing for cricket, and persuaded Harris towards conciliation. Harris agreed and collected together a team (not without difficulty as Ulyett, Emmett and Hornby, the three who had been at the centre of the storm in Sydney, refused to play). The first Test match in England began on 6 September 1880; fortunately for England Spofforth missed it through injury.

It was a notable game for a number of reasons. The Graces provided the first instance of three brothers playing together in Tests, and W.G.'s 152 was the first Test century for England. With Lucas he put on 120 for the second wicket, the first hundred partnership in Tests. England made 420 and then bowled the Australians out for 149, Morley taking five wickets. It was in this innings that one of cricket's most famous catches was taken: Bonnor hit one of the highest skiers ever seen, and the batsmen were on their third run when Fred Grace caught it. Poor Fred had only two weeks to live – he died of a chill caught from sleeping in a damp bed – and he made a pair in the match, but at least he has a kind of immortality for taking that catch. At one point in the follow-on the visitors were 14 for 3, but then Murdoch became the first captain to score a Test century as he exceeded W.G.'s score by one, and his team reached 327. The English then lost five wickets before getting the 57 they needed, giving the game an unexpectedly exciting climax. Murdoch had, incidentally, bet W.G. a sovereign that he would exceed his score, and he wore it ever after on his watch-chain. The final reconciliation with the Australians came when the Lord Mayor of London gave a banquet in their honour the day before they left.

Billy Murdoch went on to captain Australia sixteen times. A lawyer by profession, he had originally been a wicket-keeper, but he concentrated on his batting and became his country's first really outstanding batsman. He had very quick footwork and a wide range of strokes which he played with great style, being especially good on difficult wickets – as he had to be at the time. In his eighteen Tests he scored almost 900 runs at an average of 32, with two centuries. He was a genial and cheerful man, much loved by his players for the humour that he brought to the game, and his relaxed and friendly attitude meant that his team's dressing-room was a relaxed and friendly place. Tensions and bickerings within his team were banished, for the most part simply through the easiness of his personality. He led New South Wales from 1878–9 to 1889–90, and was renowned as a captain who was both a thinker and a leader by example.

By now the idea of representative England–Australia matches was firmly established, but the tours were still organised by sponsors on a commercial basis. The next England tour, in 1881–2, was arranged by Lillywhite and the two Notts players, Alfred Shaw and Arthur Shrewsbury, under Shaw's captaincy. Shaw was one of the great defensive medium-pace bowlers, whose accuracy – he never once delivered a wide – was so phenomenal that his career figures show that he conceded fewer runs than he bowled overs. Even allowing for the fact that many of those overs were only of four balls, that is a record which most bowlers would be proud to own. In one-day cricket he would have been invaluable. With his lovely easy action and mastery of control, his bowling was an artistic delight – and it brought him over 2,000 wickets. Having originally been considered an all-rounder he was a useful batsman and a fine slip fielder. In 1881 he and Shrewsbury organised a strike at Notts over the contract they were expected to sign, but the following year he was appointed county captain; he held the post for five years and Notts finished at the head of the Championship each time. He was an honest, friendly man who knew his cricket thoroughly, having joined Notts as an eighteen-year-old in 1864, and was a sound and sensible professional. When in his fifties he played for a while for Sussex and still continued to take wickets; he also coached Sussex and became a first-class umpire. In 1894 *The Times* recorded that 'the Earl of Sheffield and Alfred Shaw played cricket in August last at Spitzbergen, latitude 77 20, at midnight. This is the highest northern latitude in which cricket is recorded to have been played.' Somehow that second sentence seems rather superfluous.

Four representative games were played, and Australia had the better of things. The first one was a high-scoring draw, the first Test in which 1,000 runs were scored, and honours were about even at the end. The second Test was the first to be played at Sydney, and Australia won by five wickets thanks largely to the medium-paced spin of Palmer, who took eleven wickets. In the third game Palmer took another nine wickets, as did Garrett, but the victory was set up by an innings of 147 from McDonnell. He put on 199 with Alec Bannerman which remains, perhaps surprisingly, the highest

Alfred Shaw, captain of England against Australia in 1881–2.

The 1881–2 touring team to Australia and New Zealand. Standing, left to right, G. Ulyett, R. Pilling, James Lillywhite jr, J. Conway (Australian local manager), W.E. Midwinter (who also later played for Australia), W. Bates. Seated, left to right, A. Shrewsbury, A. Shaw (captain), T. Emmett, E. Peate. Front, left to right, R.G. Barlow, W.H. Scotton, J. Selby. Lillywhite, Shaw and Shrewsbury were England's only professional captains before Len Hutton, apart from one occasion when Jack Hobbs deputised during a match.

fourth-wicket partnership in England–Australia Tests made by either side in Australia. In the fourth match Ulyett scored 149 out of his team's 309, but Australia almost equalled that; the last day was then washed out, leaving this the last Test to be drawn in Australia until 1946–7, as until the Second World War they were all played to a finish.

If the English team had the worst of these encounters at least the organisers made a profit, but there was some unpleasantness when they returned home. Two of the players, Selby and Ulyett, were severely criticised in the press for, allegedly, taking bribes to throw a game against Victoria; for 'Happy Jack' Ulyett, at least, this would seem to be right out of character, but guilt or innocence was never proved and the matter died down. Selby, however, never played for England again, although he was probably past his best by this time anyway. The two defeats, followed by this piece of scandal, meant that the tour was not one of England's happiest.

And then came the historic match. Murdoch's team in 1882 played only one Test, at the Oval on 28 and 29 August, but it produced the first Australian victory over a full-strength English side in England. The England captain was Albert 'Monkey' Hornby, the Lancashire opener who came, with his partner Barlow, to be immortalised in verse by Francis Thompson. He was a small man (hence Monkey) who was an attacking batsman and a brilliant fielder, although in his six innings in Test cricket he totalled only 21 runs. Cardus saw him as a romantic, laughing, adventurous player who 'went after a ball rather as he went at a ditch in the hunting-field'. He also played nine times for England at Rugby football and was the first man to captain England at both sports. He led Lancashire from 1880 to 1891 and again in 1897 and 1898, winning the Championship outright twice and sharing it twice. He was an aggressive, sometimes rather truculent man, occasionally given to rashness, but who was a good competitor for all that. As a captain he was enthusiastic and kindly to his players, and as most of them felt that his better qualities outweighed his less attractive ones, he usually managed to get them to give their best for him.

In the match itself Australia batted first after two days of rain and were promptly bowled out for 63 by Peate and Barlow. England did not exactly press home this advantage, making only 101 as Spofforth took seven wickets. Australia's second innings is famous for the fact that Grace ran out Jones when he had left his crease to pat down the pitch. It produced 122, thanks mainly to Massie and Murdoch, leaving England only 85 to win. The story of how that innings stuttered, promised and then steadily collapsed has been told many times, with the inevitable references to the spectator who died of heart failure and the spectator who gnawed through his umbrella handle because of the tension. From 51 for 2 to 77 all out is pretty spectacular stuff, even if the pitch was drying, and Spofforth's second seven-wicket bag received all the praise it deserved. Almost half of the overs that the Australians bowled were maidens; twelve of them came in succession at one point to draw out the agony for everyone, and as the anxious crowd were almost totally silent and the weather was overcast the atmosphere must have been really eerie. What never seems to have been explained, though, is why Hornby kept back Studd until number ten; admittedly he had gone for nought in the first innings, but he had scored two centuries against the Australians that summer.

As every cricket lover knows, the following Saturday the *Sporting Times* published the mock obituary of English cricket which concluded with the

A.N. 'Monkey' Hornby, England captain in the Test which gave birth to the Ashes.

words 'The body will be cremated and the Ashes taken to Australia.' The man who wrote that obituary notice was a young journalist named Reginald Brooks (although *Wisden* mistakenly credited it to his father); it would have been pleasing to think that he looked back on it with a good deal of contentment as the years went by, knowing that he had created something immortal, but within six years, aged only thirty-four, he was dead.

1876–7	Melbourne	A 245, 104	E 196, 108	A 45 runs
	Melbourne	A 122, 259	E 261, 122–6	E 4 wkts
1878–9	Melbourne	E 113, 160	A 256, 19–0	A 10 wkts
1880	Oval	E 420, 57–5	A 149, 327	E 5 wkts
1881–2	Melbourne	E 294, 308	A 320, 127–3	Drawn
	Sydney	E 133, 232	A 197, 169–5	A 5 wkts
	Sydney	E 188, 134	A 260, 66–4	A 6 wkts
	Melbourne	E 309, 234–2	A 300	Drawn
1882	Oval	A 63, 122	E 101, 77	A 7 runs

1876–7

England

Batting	Innings	NO	HS	Runs	Average
A. Hill	4	2	49	101	50.50
G. Ulyett	4	0	63	149	37.25
A. Greenwood	4	0	49	77	19.25
T. Emmett	4	0	48	73	18.25
H. Jupp	4	0	63	68	17.00

Bowling	O	M	R	W	Average
J. Southerton	65.3	24	107	7	15.28
J. Lillywhite	84	37	126	8	15.75
G. Ulyett	77.1	32	123	7	17.57
A. Shaw	164	96	146	8	18.25
A. Hill	85	37	130	6	21.66

Australia

Batting	Innings	NO	HS	Runs	Average
C. Bannerman	4	1	165*	209	69.66
T.J.D. Kelly	2	0	35	54	27.00
N. Thompson	4	0	41	67	16.75
W.E. Midwinter	4	0	31	65	16.25
T.W. Garrett	4	1	18*	48	16.00

Bowling	O	M	R	W	Average
J.H. Hodges	34	9	84	6	14.00
T. Kendall	140.3	56	215	14	15.35
W.E. Midwinter	107.1	44	156	8	19.50
T.W. Garrett	26.1	12	48	2	24.00
F.R. Spofforth	44	9	113	4	28.25

Wicket-keepers: J.M. Blackham (A) 5 dismissals   J. Selby (E) 1 dismissal

Captains: D.W. Gregory – batting 1, 3; 1*, 43   bowling 0–9; did not bowl
J. Lillywhite – batting 10, 4; 2*   bowling 1–19, 1–1; 2–36, 4–70

C. Bannerman scored the first Test century, his 165* forming 67.3% of his team's total, a proportion that has never since been exceeded.

1878–9 Only Test

High scores: England – C.A. Absolom 52, Lord Harris 33, 36
Australia – A.C. Bannerman 73, F.R. Spofforth 39

Best bowling: England – T. Emmett 7–68
Australia – F.R. Spofforth 6–48, 7–62

Wicket-keepers: J.M. Blackham (A) 1 dismissal   L. Hone (E) 2 dismissals

Captains: D.W. Gregory – batting 12*
Lord Harris – batting 33, 36   bowling 0–14

F.R. Spofforth achieved the first Test hat-trick and became the first to take 13 wickets in a Test.

1880 Only Test

High scores: England – W.G. Grace 152, Lord Harris 52
Australia – W.L. Murdoch 153*, P.S. McDonnell 43

Best bowling: England – F. Morley 5–56, 3–90
Australia – W.H. Moule 3–23

Wicket-keepers: J.M. Blackham (A) 1 dismissal   A. Lyttelton (E) 0 dismissals

Captains: Lord Harris – batting 52
W.L. Murdoch – batting 0, 153*

W.G. Grace, whose two brothers also played, scored England's first Test century. Murdoch became the first Test captain to score a century.

1881–2

England

Batting	Innings	NO	HS	Runs	Average
G. Ulyett	8	0	149	438	54.75
J. Selby	8	1	70	202	28.85
W. Bates	8	1	58	192	27.42
A. Shrewsbury	7	0	82	186	26.57
W.H. Scotton	7	1	50*	158	26.33

Bowling	O	M	R	W	Average
W. Bates	241	121	334	16	20.87
G. Ulyett	99.2	37	180	8	22.50
E. Peate	232	117	258	11	23.45
W.E. Midwinter	194	79	272	10	27.20
A. Shaw	65	36	76	2	38.00

Australia

Batting	Innings	NO	HS	Runs	Average
S.P. Jones	4	3	37	63	63.00
P.S. McDonnell	7	1	147	302	50.33
W.L. Murdoch	7	1	85	215	35.83
T.P. Horan	7	1	124	212	35.33
A.C. Bannerman	5	0	70	167	33.40

Bowling	O	M	R	W	Average
T.W. Garrett	213.3	76	367	18	20.83
G.E. Palmer	365.2	145	522	24	21.75
W.H. Cooper	98.2	27	200	9	22.22
H.F. Boyle	107	47	135	6	22.50
G. Giffen	24.3	7	54	2	27.00

Wicket-keepers: J.M. Blackham (A) 10   R. Pilling (E) 7

Captains: W.L. Murdoch – batting 39, 22*; 10, 49; 6, 4; 85
            A. Shaw – batting 5, 40; 11, 30; 3, 6; 3   bowling 0–21; 1–12; 0–14; 1–29

In the third Test A.C. Bannerman and P.S. McDonnell's partnership of 199 remains the highest fourth-wicket partnership by either side in England v Australia Tests in Australia. In the fourth Test Ulyett's 149 was England's first Test century in Australia.

1882 Only Test

High scores: England – W.G. Grace 32, G. Ulyett 26
               Australia – H.H. Massie 55, W.L. Murdoch 29

Best bowling: England – E. Peate 4–31, 4–40, R.G. Barlow 5–19
                Australia – F.R. Spofforth 7–46, 7–44

Wicket-keepers: J.M. Blackham (A) 4 dismissals   A. Lyttelton (E) 0 dismissals

Captains: A.N. Hornby – batting 2, 9
            W.L. Murdoch – batting 13, 29

F.R. Spofforth became the first bowler to take 14 wickets in a Test. The Ashes came into being as a result of this match.

2

England's Only Lengthy Dominance Comes Early

The team that left for Australia on what was popularly described as a quest to recover the Ashes sailed from England before Murdoch's team did, only two weeks after the Oval Test, thereby showing a very commendable enthusiasm to restore their country's cricketing prominence as soon as possible. It could have ended in total disaster, for after having left Ceylon their ship was involved in a collision; no one was killed, but Morley broke a rib which kept him out of the team for part of the tour, and probably led to his death only four years later. They were led by The Honourable Ivo Bligh, later to become the eighth Lord Darnley, the central figure in the tale of the Ashes urn. He was only twenty-three at the time and remains the youngest captain in England–Australia matches. Standing 6 feet 4 inches tall, he was a handsome young man and a stylish batsman who had played regularly for Cambridge, captaining the University in his last year. He also played with distinction for Kent, but ill health meant that his career was short, for he retired in 1883. He did not distinguish himself in the four Tests in which he played, averaging only 10. He was very much the traditional amateur of his time, captain by virtue of his nobility rather than particular aptitude.

At first matters went Australia's way when they won the opening game easily. On a good pitch they made 291, then put England out for 177. Following on, England could make only another 169 and the home team won by nine wickets. England had now gone six Tests without a win. The next game, though, saw a reversal: England made 294, and dismissed Australia twice to record the first victory by an innings in Test cricket, Bates achieving England's first hat-trick. Only three matches had originally been planned, and the decider attracted about 50,000 people. England reached 247, and Australia then did well on a rain-affected pitch to make 218. By their second innings they needed 153, but, in fine weather, they were all out for 83 as Barlow took seven wickets. The Ashes had been recovered.

The Hon. Ivo Bligh's team that toured Australia in 1882–3.

The traditional story of what happened next is that a group of Melbourne ladies, one of whom was later to become Bligh's wife, burnt a bail, put the ashes in a small pottery urn, and presented it to the England captain. It remained Bligh's private property until his death in 1927, when he bequeathed it to the MCC, where it has been in the museum ever since (apart from its much-publicised trip to Australia in the company of the Prince of Wales at the time of their bicentenary). In his book *Cricket's Biggest Mystery: the Ashes*, Ronald Willis argues, however, that things may not have been as simple as that and that there is a good deal of uncertainty surrounding the urn. What is certain, however, is that the Australians asked for another match – which they won by four wickets despite a century from Steel – and then argued that they had not lost 'the Ashes' after all. The dispute lasted only until the next series since England won that 1–0, but once fancies that the entry in the record books under the 'Ashes held by' column, which says 'England' for that series, still sticks in a few Australian gullets. One oddity about this fourth match is that it saw Billy Midwinter playing for Australia once again. He had played for them in the first two Tests and then, as he had been born in Gloucestershire, played four times for England. He was now to play six more times for Australia. Several cricketers have played for more than one country, but he is the only man to have changed his allegiance twice.

For the next twenty years, as it happens, the idea of playing 'for the Ashes' seems to have dropped out of use. It was P.F. Warner who resurrected it when he announced before his 1903–4 tour that he was going to 'recover the Ashes'. Only after that did it catch the popular imagination.

In 1884 Murdoch brought another team to England. Lord Harris was scheduled to lead the home team but withdrew from the first Test because a Lancashire bowler named Crossland, whose action he considered illegal, was included. In the event Crossland did not play, but neither did Harris – and Hornby led the side in his last Test. This same match was Old Trafford's first Test and, surprise surprise, the first day was washed out.

England batted first on a wet pitch, and, had it not been for a fine innings from Shrewsbury, would have been in real trouble. As it was they managed to salvage a draw out of the three-day game. The second Test, the first to be played at Lord's, was notable for another fine century from Steel, and for the curious fact that the Australian player Scott, having helped put on 69 for the last wicket, was caught by his own captain; Murdoch was fielding as substitute for W.G., who had an injured finger. (There were a number of other occasions over the years when players were caught by their team-mates in simular circumstances; it would be hard to imagine that today.)

Steel's innings and seven wickets from Ulyett enabled England to win by an innings, and Harris was praised for the sound way he had handled his team.

The last Test at the Oval, the teams playing under the same captains on a dry, fast pitch, contained some interesting points for the statisticians. Australia's 551 (declarations were not allowed for another five years) contained three centuries, including Test cricket's first double-hundred from Murdoch. All eleven home players bowled in this innings, Grace keeping wicket while Lyttelton bowled his underarm lobs – and took 4 for 19 with them! England then had 8 wickets down for 181, when in marched Read, furious at being kept back till number ten. He promptly smashed 117 in even time, a performance which remains the highest Test innings by any number ten; his partnership with Scotton of 151 is still England's ninth-wicket record against Australia. The match was saved, and the Ashes were definitely England's, beginning a spell of England dominance that was to last until the next decade. It was also the last time Lord Harris was able to play for his country.

Once again it was only a few weeks after the last match that an all-professional party set off for another tour, promoted again by Lilly-white, Shaw and Shrewsbury. Before they left, however, there had been some unpleasantness when Shrewsbury and two other Notts players, Flowers and Barnes, who were now in the tour party, had declined to appear for the Players of England against the Australians at Sheffield as they felt the match fee offered was too low. This rankled with the Australians, and exacerbated the monetary problems that arose. One imagines that with all these fine, sporting, Victorian gentlemen around the early games must have been conducted in a noble spirit of great camaraderie, but one soon learns that human beings have not changed that much in the last hundred years.

Arthur Shrewsbury was the captain. Of the professional batsmen he reigned supreme, combining splendid defence with the ability to score plenty of runs, although on the whole he was more of a defensive than attacking batsman. He came into his own on bad wickets, adopting the policy of either going right forward or right back. Batting to him was an art that is perfectible, and he tried always to perform with that in mind, playing his shots neatly and precisely – epithets that reflect his own character very clearly, for he was quiet and serious and thought about the game a good deal. There is a famous story that in the days before tea intervals existed and if he were not out at lunch-time, he would ask the Trent Bridge attendant as he went back out to bat for 'a cup of tea at half-past four, please', and was usually there to receive it. Even more famous is W.G.'s reply, when asked

(Left) *'Give me Arthur' Shrewsbury.* (Right) *Irishman Tom Horan, one of the great characters of Australian cricket, both as a player and as a writer on the game under the name of Felix. Note the dark brown leather pads and the absence of batting gloves, which he never wore.*

who was the greatest batsman with whom he had been associated: 'Give me Arthur'. His 59 centuries included three in Tests, and he played many other very fine Test innings on pitches that a modern batsman, used to covered wickets, would encounter only in a nightmare. In his 23 Tests he scored 1277 runs at an average of 35.

He was captain of a team of professionals simply because he was the only one of the three organisers who was playing. He is not credited with any especial leadership skills, and was no doubt lucky to come up against a team beset with problems, but he seems to have made a good enough captain. As with Lillywhite and Shaw he was a good organiser, and that was important in the circumstances. For the most part the tours that the three men arranged were satisfactory to the other professionals, and they, having few complaints, were happy enough under his captaincy.

The 1884–5 series was the first in which five Tests were played. In the opening game, the first to be played at Adelaide, the Australian batsman

McDonnell, who was later to be captain, became the first man to score centuries in successive Test innings. England, however, took a good first innings lead with a hundred from Barnes (and a duck from Shrewsbury) and went on to win by eight wickets. The intention had been for Lillywhite to stand as umpire as he had done on an earlier tour, but Murdoch objected and he was replaced with a local man. This proved disastrous, but as most of his poor decisions went against the home team Murdoch had to fume in silence. Moreover, it did nothing to help the bad feeling brought on by Shrewsbury and the others dropping out of the Sheffield game the previous summer, and now, after a dispute about money with their own authorities, Murdoch and his team refused to take part in the next scheduled representative game at Melbourne – so they were promptly banned by the Victorian Cricket Association. As a result the XI for the second Test was totally different from the previous game, nine not having played in Tests before. Hardly surprisingly, England registered a ten-wicket win, with a century from Briggs and a fine 72 from the captain. It is worth noting in passing that after the first match an Adelaide newspaper criticised the Englishmen for 'appealing in chorus at every possible opportunity, presumably with the motive of discommoding the batsmen'. And we thought this was a modern problem.

In Murdoch's absence the Australians were led by Tom Horan, an Irishman who had already played in eleven Tests. He was a good attacking batsman and medium-pace bowler, but his Test record is not a distinguished one. He scored one century, and in this match produced a fighting captain's knock of 63, but he failed many times and finished with an average of under 19. One of his friends since childhood was Jack Blackham, one of the players now banned, so when Horan was asked to captain the side it must have been a difficult decision for him. He accepted because he felt that Test cricket was more important than individuals, and he believed anyway that the pay demand made by the rebel players – they wanted half the gate receipts of the Test – was excessive.

As a captain he understood the game well and was a sound assessor both of his own players and of the opposition's strengths and weaknesses. He did his best with limited resources – Graham Yallop would no doubt sympathise – but he was outplayed by a good professional team. His lasting achievement, however, was to become Australia's first player-turned-writer, for he wrote about cricket in *The Australasian* under the name of Felix for no less than thirty-seven years. Ready with praise when merited and realistic in his analysis of mistakes, his writings were highly respected. Only when he died did people discover the true identity of Felix.

Hugh Massie – victorious by six runs in his only Test as captain.

For the third game the home team was strengthened by the return of Bonnor, Bannerman and Spofforth, and the captaincy passed to Hugh Massie. Tall and powerful, he was a fine forcing batsman who in his first innings in England, at Oxford on the 1882 tour, had scored 100 before lunch and 206 before tea. He had gone on to gain his own little piece of immortality by scoring 55 in 45 minutes in the Ashes match at the Oval, a splendid and audacious knock that had set up his team's chance of victory.

The game itself was splendidly exciting. Australia batted first and made 181, thanks mainly to a tenth-wicket stand of 80 after a hailstorm at lunchtime had turned the ground white. When England batted Massie produced a stroke of genius by putting on Horan, the deposed captain, who was not exactly a front-line bowler; he enjoyed his big moment with the ball, taking 6 for 40 by pitching into Spofforth's foot-marks as England stumbled to 133 all out. Massie then put the big-hitting Bonnor in to open with Bannerman, but Shrewsbury inspired his men well to restrict Australia to 165, leaving England 214 to win. At 92 for 6 all was lost, but Flowers and Read put on 102 for the seventh wicket before falling just six runs short. An odd feature of the game was that Barnes, who took more wickets than anyone on the tour, apparently refused to bowl at all, despite being asked to by Shrewsbury. Since conditions would have suited him this may well have affected the result; his refusal has never been explained. Thus Massie gained a fine victory in his only Test as captain; it was in fact his last Test, for his professional career as a banker meant that he was not able to tour again. It was a very successful career, though, for he finished as General Manager of the Commercial Banking Company of Sydney.

For the fourth Test the captaincy changed hands yet again, this time to the wicket-keeper, Jack Blackham. Blackham is one of the great names of these early Tests, for he played in the first seventeen, his sequence only ending because of the dispute that saw all of Murdoch's team withdraw. In all, he played in thirty-five over a period of eighteen years, making eight tours to England. For a while he contested the title of 'the prince of wicket-keepers' with Dick Pilling of Lancashire, for both of them took their art to a standard never before seen, standing up to the stumps for even the fastest bowlers and so making stumpings that nowadays would be un-dreamed of – and on pitches that were considerably less true than they have become. Pilling's health failed, however, and he died young, leaving Blackham to gain the immortality.

Wearing thin pads and little gloves at which the modern keeper would either laugh or cry, his speed at gathering the ball and taking off the bails in one movement was legendary. Sometimes he stood back to Spofforth when the Demon was in particularly devilish mood, but usually he stood up and took many stumpings. He would stand with his feet splayed wider than most later keepers, and with his black beard bristling he must have been a menacing figure to a nervous batsman. As George Giffen put it, 'Woe betide the batsman who even so much as lifted the heel of his back foot as he played forward and missed the ball.'

He captained Victoria from 1882–3 to 1887–8, and led Australia in eight Tests, but his leadership skills do not appear to have matched those of his wicket-keeping. Behind the stumps he was calmness personified, but as a captain he was a worrier. He was as good as anyone at assessing his opponents, for his vantage point gave him the ideal opportunity for

Jack Blackham, the prince of wicket-keepers.

observing a batsman's strengths and weaknesses, and he was familiar enough with the opposition to know what tactics he ought best to adopt. However, when things were going wrong his nerves got the better of him, and he would pace around in an agony of misery; in England on the 1893 tour, when the home team won one match by an innings and had slightly the better of two draws, he lost a stone in weight. It is a curious fact that there have been so few outstanding wicket-keeper-captains over the years, no doubt because wicket-keeping is such a demanding business in its own right.

However, in this his first Test as captain he was successful. England had run up 269 and reduced Australia to 119 for 6 when Bonnor, all 6 feet 6 inches of him, came in. Two hours later he had scored 128 in a magnificent display of hitting, and Australia took a lead of 40. Rain then made the wicket difficult and England were bundled out for 77, allowing Blackham to record an eight-wicket victory and square the series. But he did not play in the last Test and the captaincy reverted to Horan, who must have wished afterwards that it hadn't. On a damp pitch Australia were dismissed for 163, whereupon Shrewsbury became the first England captain to score a century, albeit a very slow one. A total of 386 proved too much for the home team and they subsided a second time, giving England an innings victory. Very much in contrast to Australia, the same eleven English players had taken part in each game, and had retained the Ashes.

The Australian team touring England in 1886 was the first one to be sent from either country by an official body, the Melbourne Cricket Club. But it was without such leading players as Murdoch, Bannerman and McDonnell, and it became the victim of its own internal dissensions. It was led by Dr Henry 'Tup' Scott, while England's captain was Allan Steel of Lancashire.

In his day Steel was second only to W.G. as an all-rounder. As a very accurate slow bowler he was able to turn the ball either way, his leg-spin baffling many batsmen into defeat. As a batsman he was an attacking strokemaker, delighting in particular in the drive. He had captained Marlborough for two years, then at Cambridge he had been an outstanding player in an outstanding team, leading them to victory over Oxford, and later leading the Gentlemen to victory over the Players. As a barrister he was not able to play regularly for his county, but he did captain them on occasion. He was a gentleman in the best sense of the word, an intelligent and capable man who was popular everywhere for his skills and his sportsmanship. He was noted for his rather dandified way of dressing and like Hornby would sometimes miss a week or two's cricket to go up to Scotland and take pot shots at grouse. He scored exactly 600 runs in his 13

(Left)　*A.G. Steel, outstanding all-rounder, barrister and grouse shooter.*
(Right)　*Dr Henry 'Tup' Scott, captain of Australia in the unhappy 1886 series.*

Tests at the good average for those days of 35, and took 29 wickets at just under 21. He won all three games in this series, although the visitors were so troubled that he would have found it difficult to lose any. His other Test in charge two years later was less successful, but he was certainly a sound captain if not an outstanding one.

His opposite number, Henry 'Tup' Scott (the nickname derived from his fondness for riding round London on the top of twopenny buses), was a batsman noted for his good defence but who showed that he could score runs as well. Altogether on the tour he scored nearly 1300 but not many of them were in the Tests; two years earlier, though, he had averaged 74 in the three Tests, including a century. He was unable to quell the disputes that arose – apparently the players were physically fighting each other at one stage – and although he was respected by his team there is no doubt that he found the responsibility tough going, so that it affected both his performances and his judgement. *Wisden* said that he lacked the necessary authority and experience for captaincy, and others criticised the way he handled his bowlers, but he was severely depleted by injuries and loss of form by some key players. With such a small squad this meant that the manager and doctor had to play in some games.

The hero of the first Test was Barlow, he of whom Francis Thompson enthused when he referred to 'O my Hornby and my Barlow long ago'. Second-top score of 38 not out in the first innings and top score of 30 in the second, as well as 7 for 44 off 52 overs in Australia's second innings should have ensured a man-of-the-match award had such things been invented, and enabled England to get home by four wickets. The Lord's Test was notable for a wonderful innings from Shrewsbury on a wicked pitch. In just under seven hours he made 164, dealing with consummate skill with a ball that was utterly unpredictable in its movements, and his team reached 353. Briggs then produced match figures of 11 for 74, and England had won by an innings and 106 runs.

The Oval Test was even more emphatically won, although the weather went against the visitors to add to their other problems. So too did W.G., for he scored 170 as England clocked up 434. After the rain that then fell Lohmann and Briggs went through Australia for 68 and 149, Lohmann taking 12 wickets, and England won by an innings and 217 runs. To say that it was altogether a sad tour for the Australians is simply to state the obvious. Scott retired from first-class cricket after the tour but stayed in England to complete his medical studies; he then returned to Australia and became a country doctor, often travelling great distances over primitive roads to treat his patients. He was much loved and respected, and when he died of typhoid aged only fifty-one the people of his home town named their new hospital after him.

Financially, Shrewsbury and his colleagues made a loss on the next tour in 1886–7, although they won both Tests. Shrewsbury was again in charge of the Englishmen, while the Australians were led by Percy McDonnell, their only captain to have been born in England and their only captain who was also a Greek scholar. He was a very stylish batsman, a powerful hitter who loved to move forward and drive the ball on the rise. He was also a fine player on rain-affected wickets, perhaps second only to Shrewsbury. Since making his debut in 1880 he had some fine innings to his name, including three Test centuries and some very creditable series records. During his captaincy, though, his batting declined, and he was unlucky to come up against a strong England team – although he is still the captain who put England out for their lowest total in all Tests. He was an easy-going, warm-hearted man who was liked and respected by his players despite being younger than many of them; and although he won only one match of the six in which he was in charge, W.G. complimented him on the fine

(Left)   Percy McDonnell, Australian captain and Greek scholar.   (Right)
W.W. Read, captain of England only once, but with a one hundred per cent record.

judgement he had shown as captain and said it was no disgrace to him that his team should have lost.

In the opening Test at Sydney, McDonnell became the first Test captain to put in the opposition on winning the toss. The conditions were exactly right for bowling and he had two new bowlers who took full advantage of them. Turner and Ferris took a very short time to establish themselves as the first really good fast bowling partnership of Test cricket, dismissing England for 45, a figure that, as mentioned, remains their lowest, despite the attempt at the Oval in 1948 to reduce it. Australia could only reach 119, however, to which England replied with 184, the last three wickets producing 81. Needing 111 to win Australia didn't quite make it; Shrewsbury won praise for the way he controlled and inspired his team, and fine bowling and fielding saw the Englishmen home by 13 runs. This was Spofforth's last Test; in eighteen matches he had taken 94 wickets at 18, and sealed his name in cricket's history. In the second Test England were without Barnes for the glorious reason that he had had an argument with the Australian captain and in trying to hit him had punched a wall instead, damaging his hand so much that he missed most of the rest of the tour. Turner and Ferris again did the goods for Australia, but Lohmann did even better for England, becoming the first bowler to take eight wickets in a Test innings. His 8 for 35 is still the record for an English bowler in Australia, enabling England to win a low-scoring game by 71 runs.

The tour of 1887–8 saw Shrewsbury, Shaw and Lillywhite come a cropper and lose a good deal of money as another party, led by G.F. Vernon, were in Australia at the same time. This spelt the end of their adventures, and there were no Tests in Australia for four more years. In the event the two touring teams combined to play one match which is now regarded as a Test, but its claim to this distinction is a trifle dubious. McDonnell led the home team, while the compromise captain agreed upon by the two English parties was Walter Read. Read was an interesting character, a bluff and dashing extrovert who never worried about whom he upset. He was a very powerful batsman, especially off the front foot, and did a great deal to boost the fortunes of his county, Surrey, at a time when they were in the dumps. He was also a fearless close fielder who took many fine catches. His character is epitomised by his famous innings at the Oval in 1884, recorded above, when he struck 117 furious (and match-saving) runs because he was annoyed with Lord Harris at being left until number ten. He was an amateur, but one who needed to make some money out of the game since he was not over-endowed with wealth, and for several years was Surrey's assistant secretary whilst playing for them as well. His assertive personality had some merits as a captain and he knew his cricket well enough. With other more outstanding players about he was never going to lead England very often – in fact he had one other game in charge, one of the dubious early Tests against South Africa, which was won – but one has the feeling that he might have made quite a good captain had he had more opportunity.

To say that the Test itself was a low-scoring one would hardly begin to describe it. The wicket was spoilt by rain, and only Shrewsbury (inevitably) could cope at all; McDonnell could not emulate him, and Australia were all out for 42, a record which, unlike England's of the previous year, they did subsequently reduce. England's second innings posted 137, Turner and Ferris taking 18 wickets between them, but Peel and Lohmann took 19 as Australia went for 82 in their second innings. Spare a thought for the wicket-keepers in a game such as this, for their task is every bit as difficult as the batsman's. On a pitch that was utterly unpredictable and on which balls turned enormous distances, Pilling and Blackham were both able to give a very clear demonstration of why each was called 'the prince of wicket-keepers'.

1882–3	Melbourne	A 291, 58–1	E 177, 169	A 9 wkts
	Melbourne	E 294	A 114, 153	E inns 27 runs
	Sydney	E 247, 123	A 218, 83	E 69 runs
	Sydney	E 263, 197	A 262, 199–6	A 4 wkts
1884	Old Trafford	E 95, 180–9	A 182	Drawn
	Lord's	A 229, 145	E 379	E inns 5 runs
	Oval	A 551	E 346, 85–2	Drawn
1884–5	Adelaide	A 243, 191	E 369, 67–2	E 8 wkts
	Melbourne	E 401, 7–0	A 279, 126	E 10 wkts
	Sydney	A 181, 165	E 133, 207	A 6 runs
	Sydney	E 269, 77	A 309, 38–2	A 8 wkts
	Melbourne	A 163, 125	E 386	E inns 98 runs
1886	Old Trafford	A 205, 123	E 223, 107–6	E 4 wkts
	Lord's	E 353	A 121, 126	E inns 106 runs
	Oval	E 434	A 68, 149	E inns 217 runs
1886–7	Sydney	E 45, 184	A 119, 97	E 13 runs
	Sydney	E 151, 154	A 84, 150	E 71 runs
1887–8	Sydney	E 113, 137	A 42, 82	E 126 runs

1882–3

England

Batting	Innings	NO	HS	Runs	Average
A.G. Steel	7	1	135*	274	45.66
W.W. Read	7	0	75	228	32.57
W. Bates	7	1	55	172	28.66
C.T. Studd	7	0	48	160	22.88
E.F.S. Tylecote	7	0	66	142	20.28

Bowling	O	M	R	W	Average
C.F.H. Leslie	24	10	44	4	11.00
W. Bates	192.3	87	286	18	15.88
A.G. Steel	130	49	195	11	17.72
F. Morley	150	85	150	8	18.75
R.G. Barlow	244	124	343	16	21.43

Australia

Batting	Innings	NO	HS	Runs	Average
A.C. Bannerman	8	1	94	255	36.42
J.M. Blackham	7	1	58*	204	34.00
G.J. Bonnor	7	0	87	217	31.00
W.L. Murdoch	8	2	48	153	25.50
G. Giffen	7	0	41	162	23.14

Bowling	O	M	R	W	Average
T.P. Horan	38	16	63	5	12.60
A.C. Bannerman	11	2	17	1	17.00
H.F. Boyle	63	25	87	5	17.40
W.E. Midwinter	70	37	71	4	17.75
G.E. Palmer	270.1	114	397	21	18.90

Wicket-keepers: J.M. Blackham (A) 4 dismissals   E.F.S. Tylecote (E) 5 dismissals

Captains: W.L. Murdoch – batting 48,33*; 19*, 17; 19, 0; 0, 17
I.F.W. Bligh – batting 0, 3; 0; 13, 17*; 19, 10

In the second match W. Bates became the first Englishman to take a Test hat-trick and the first player to score a 50 and take 10 wickets. In the fourth match J.M. Blackham became the first wicket-keeper to score two fifties in a Test.

1884

England

Batting	Innings	NO	HS	Runs	Average
W.H. Scotton	1	0	90	90	90.00
W.W. Read	2	0	117	129	64.50
A.G. Steel	4	0	148	212	53.00
A.P. Lucas	3	1	28	67	33.50
A. Shrewsbury	5	0	43	142	28.40

Bowling	O	M	R	W	Average
A. Lyttelton	12	5	19	4	4.75
W.G. Grace	42	28	38	3	12.66
G. Ulyett	136.1	67	194	11	17.63
E. Peate	168	68	280	11	25.45
A.G. Steel	58	14	135	4	33.75

Australia

Batting	Innings	NO	HS	Runs	Average
H.J.H. Scott	4	1	102	220	73.33
W.L. Murdoch	4	0	211	266	66.50
P.S. McDonnell	4	0	103	159	39.75
G. Giffen	4	0	63	116	29.00
G.E. Palmer	4	2	14*	42	21.00

Bowling	O	M	R	W	Average
H.F. Boyle	77	28	141	9	15.66
G.E. Palmer	173	65	260	14	18.57
F.R. Spofforth	192.1	82	301	10	30.10
G.J. Bonnor	25	6	61	2	30.50
G. Giffen	84	33	147	4	36.75

Wicket-keepers: J.M. Blackham (A) 5 dismissals   R. Pilling (E) 1 dismissal
A. Lyttelton (E) 1 dismissal – and heading the bowling averages!

Captains: A.N. Hornby – batting 0, 4
Lord Harris – batting 4; 14, 6* bowling 0–15
W.L. Murdoch – batting 28; 10, 17; 211

In the third match W.L. Murdoch scored the first Test double-century.
W.W. Read's 117 is still the highest Test score by a number ten. In Australia's innings all eleven players bowled.

1884–5

England

Batting	Innings	NO	HS	Runs	Average
W. Barnes	8	1	134	369	52.71
A. Shrewsbury	9	3	105*	301	50.20
W. Bates	7	0	64	222	51.71
J. Briggs	7	0	121	177	25.28
J.M. Read	7	0	56	143	20.42

Bowling	O	M	R	W	Average
W. Bates	93.1	41	148	10	14.80
W. Barnes	206.2	97	292	19	15.36
G. Ulyett	178.2	86	295	14	21.07
R. Peel	390.2	193	451	21	21.47
W. Flowers	179.3	81	249	11	22.63

Australia

Batting	Innings	NO	HS	Runs	Average
P.S. McDonnell	4	0	124	230	57.50
J.M. Blackham	3	1	66	88	44.00
G.J. Bonnor	5	0	128	198	39.60
W. Bruce	4	1	45	98	32.66
T.W. Garrett	5	2	51*	94	31.33

Bowling	O	M	R	W	Average
T.P. Horan	55.1	29	80	6	13.33
S.P. Jones	43.2	16	80	5	16.00
F.R. Spofforth	194.1	84	306	19	16.10
G.E. Palmer	124.3	54	171	10	17.10
J.W. Trumble	89	41	112	5	22.40

Wicket-keepers: J.M. Blackham (A) 4 dismissals   A.H. Jarvis (A) 6 dismissals
J. Hunter (E) 11 dismissals

Captains: W.L. Murdoch – batting 5, 7
T.P. Horan – batting 63, 16; 0, 20   bowling 0–0; 0–5
H.H. Massie – batting 2, 21
J.M. Blackham – batting 11*
A. Shrewsbury – batting 0, 26*; 72, 0*; 18, 24; 40, 16; 105*

In the first match P.S. McDonnell became the first batsman to score centuries in successive Test innings.
In the last match A. Shrewsbury became the first England captain to score a Test century.

1886

England

Batting	Innings	NO	HS	Runs	Average
A. Shrewsbury	4	0	164	243	60.75
W.G. Grace	4	0	170	200	50.00
W.W. Read	4	0	94	176	44.00
W. Barnes	2	0	58	61	30.50
R.G. Barlow	4	1	38*	83	27.66

Bowling	O	M	R	W	Average
J. Briggs	134.1	75	132	17	7.76
R.G. Barlow	120	70	95	10	9.50
G. Ulyett	51	26	66	5	13.20
W. Barnes	31.3	16	53	4	13.25
G.A. Lohmann	116.2	55	191	13	14.69

Australia

Batting	Innings	NO	HS	Runs	Average
S.P. Jones	6	0	87	145	24.16
G.E. Palmer	6	0	48	130	21.66
A.H. Jarvis	4	1	45	63	21.00
H.J.H. Scott	6	0	47	110	18.33
J.W. Trumble	6	0	24	79	13.16

Bowling	O	M	R	W	Average
F.R. Spofforth	168.3	73	260	16	16.25
J.W. Trumble	61	18	110	5	22.00
T.W. Garrett	233	127	222	8	27.75
G.E. Palmer	109.2	43	177	5	35.40
G. Giffen	158	74	234	4	58.50

Wicket-keepers: R. Pilling (E) 2 dismissals   E.F.S. Tylecote (E) 5 dismissals
A.H. Jarvis (A) 3 dismissals   J.M. Blackham (A) 2 dismissals

Captains: A.G. Steel – batting 12, 19*; 5; 9 bowling 2–47, 1–9; 2–34, 0–14; 1–20
H.J.H. Scott – batting 21, 47; 30, 2; 6, 4

In the second match A. Shrewsbury made the record England Test score of 164. In the third match W.G. Grace took the record to 170.

1886–7

England

Batting	Innings	NO	HS	Runs	Average
M. Sherwin	4	3	21*	30	30.00
R.G. Barlow	4	1	42*	82	27.33
J. Briggs	4	0	33	71	17.75
W. Flowers	4	0	37	71	17.75
W. Bates	4	0	30	70	17.50

Bowling	O	M	R	W	Average
W. Barnes	68.1	45	47	8	5.87
G.A. Lohmann	110	51	137	16	8.56
W. Bates	64	33	53	5	10.60
W. Flowers	21	8	26	2	13.00
R.G. Barlow	57	31	57	3	19.00

Australia

Batting	Innings	NO	HS	Runs	Average
H. Moses	4	0	33	116	29.00
S.P. Jones	2	0	31	49	24.50
R.C. Allen	2	0	30	44	22.00
A.C. Bannerman	2	1	15*	19	19.00
P.S. McDonnell	4	0	35	59	14.75

Bowling	O	M	R	W	Average
T.W. Garrett	28	15	27	3	9.00
C.T.B. Turner	179.3	95	161	17	9.47
J.J. Ferris	183.3	86	243	18	13.50
F.R. Spofforth	12	3	17	1	17.00
W.E. Midwinter	13	5	21	1	21.00

Wicket keepers: J.M. Blackham (A) 0 dismissals   F.J. Burton (A) 1 dismissal
M. Sherwin (E) 5 dismissals

Captains: P.S. McDonnell – batting 14, 0; 10, 35
A. Shrewsbury – batting 2, 29; 9, 6

In the second match G.A. Lohmann became the first bowler to take 8 wickets in a Test innings; his 8–35 is still the England record in Australia.

1887–8 Only Test

High scores: Australia – J.M. Blackham 25*
England – A. Shrewsbury 44   J.M. Read 39

Best bowling: Australia – C.T.B. Turner 5–44, 7–43   J.J. Ferris 4–60, 2–43
England – R. Peel 5–18, 5–40   G.A. Lohmann 5–17, 4–35

Wicket-keepers: J.M. Blackham (A) 3 dismissals
R. Pilling (E) 3 dismissals

Captains: P.S. McDonnell 3, 6
W.W. Read 10, 8

3

The Years of the Champion

With the summer of 1888 we arrive at W.G. Grace's accession to the England captaincy. That, however, was not to be until the second Test, for Steel captained in the first, McDonnell continuing for Australia. If the Test the previous February in Sydney had been low-scoring, the one at Lord's exceeded it handsomely, producing only 291 runs in all, the record lowest aggregate for over forty years. In fact, of the ten innings in the three Tests that summer, six were of 81 or less. It was a muddy Lord's pitch that was responsible for the farce that occurred, and as it got steadily worse the second day produced no fewer than 27 wickets, Test cricket's biggest one-day tally. Australia went first and reached 116, and England, needing 37 to avoid the follow-on, were 26 for 7 before struggling to 53. The two second innings were 60 and 62 respectively, to give Australia victory by 61 runs. This was their only win between March 1885 and January 1892 (during which time England won 11) and was one of the few occasions on which Turner 'the Terror', for all his splendid bowling, finished on the winning side – and the only time that Ferris did.

And so to W.G. Only Sir Donald Bradman challenges Grace as the cricketer about whom most words have been written, and every cricket lover will be familiar with Grace's achievements during forty years of insatiable appetite for the game. His 54, 896 runs, had he been playing on the covered pitches of today, would probably have been 80,000 at least, for unlike so many successful sportspeople who have achieved all that their sport could offer and have no challenges left, he simply never lost the desire to keep playing cricket and keep scoring runs, and there is no reason to think that he would have done so if the pitches had presented less of a challenge. He set records that were unimaginable before he came along: the first to score 2,000 runs in a season; to do the double; to score 1,000 runs in May, achieved when almost forty-seven, after a period of apparent decline; to score a hundred centuries (which he did that same May); fifth in the overall list of run-scorers and sixth in the list of wicket-takers with 2,876.

The champion. W.G. Grace at the time of his last Test, aged nearly fifty-one, at Trent Bridge, 1899.

These are eloquent statistics, but there was just so very much more to the man. Easily the most famous private individual of Victorian England, he was not only admired for his deeds on the field but loved as well. Everyone knew he was not above adapting the laws from time to time, but such was his prowess that it merely made him liked all the more; of course he knew he was the champion (not that he was one for boasting about his deeds) and he knew the spectators had come to see him, so what did it matter in a minor match if he put the bails back on and continued with his innings? Had he not done enough for his sport and his country to be forgiven such little peccadilloes? Everyone knew that he made a great deal of money out of the game despite being an amateur; and everyone knew that he was generous with it too, as he was with his help for young players.

He was fortunate to have been born into a cricketing family, so that he was given much encouragement and coaching as a youngster. A natural athlete – the great figure of the pictures was once a willowy young man who was a fine hurdler – it was his speed of footwork, the sharpness of his eyesight, his remarkable hand–eye co-ordination, his great physical strength and his limitless concentration that were responsible for his batting success; those and a readiness to practise, a desire to keep on learning about the game, and a hunger for runs that was just never satisfied. He came on to the scene as a teenager and quickly asserted himself; overall, his most prolific years were from 1871 to 1876, during which time he scored 41 centuries, many of them enormous; in August 1876 he had consecutive innings of 344,177 and 318 not out, a case, if ever there was one, of 'running into a bit of form'. So massive are some of his feats that, confronted with a series of figures, the mind (as with Bradman) cannot properly take in the details of their grandeur and only a general impression of greatness is left. Moreover, all the time he was accumulating runs he was taking great quantities of wickets with his slow, teasing bowling – on seven occasions over a hundred in a season, three of which were over a hundred and fifty.

His colourful personality – and the fact that he did not suffer fools gladly – have produced the odd anecdote or two. Remarks, probably apocryphal, such as 'I don't like defensive strokes – you can only get three off 'em' are part of the lore of the game. So too is his remark, made after the 1884 Australians had complained that the English bats were wider than they should be and some of the English players had actually planed their own bats down, that he didn't care how much they shaved off his bat since 'All I want is the middle.' Soccer fans may amuse themselves by imagining the words spoken as Bill Shankly, the great Liverpool manager, might have spoken them.

Some leading amateurs of the day. Standing, left to right, W.M. Bradley, A.C. MacLaren, C.L. Townsend. Seated, left to right, Prince K.S. Ranjitsinhji, W.G. Grace. Front, C.B. Fry. MacLaren, Grace and Fry all captained England.

The stories, however, are just the seasoning that gives the dish its special flavour; the main course is his batting, for without him cricket may have taken much longer to reach the heights that it did. Earlier batsmen had tended to be predominantly either back-foot or front-foot players, and because Grace could play off either he had a correspondingly greater range of strokes. His batting was not particularly elegant, but it had a massiveness about it that enabled him to destroy even the best bowling, simply by hitting it along the ground with a straight bat. He was better against the quicker bowlers than the slower, although he claimed, of course, that he loved them all. C.B. Fry's oft-repeated words from Ranji's *The Jubilee Book of Cricket* will come to no harm for being given another airing:

'He revolutionized batting. He turned it from an accomplishment into a science. What W.G. did was to unite in his mighty self all the good points of all the players, and to make utility the criterion of style. I hold him to be not only the finest player born or unborn, but the maker of modern batting. He turned the old one-stringed instrument into a many-chorded lyre. Where a great man has led, many can go afterwards, but the honour is his who found and cut the path. The theory of modern batting is in all essentials the result of W.G.'s thinking and working on the game.'

Grace, then, is the Beethoven of cricket, bridging the old game and the modern just as Beethoven bridged the classical and romantic in music. Both were geniuses whose transforming influence was enormous, and whose achievements and place in history must keep them unchallenged on their respective pinnacles.*

Grace captained Gloucestershire from 1871 to 1898. Between 1873 and 1877 they won the Championship three times and shared it once, but that was the extent of their success. When he first captained England in 1888 he was, therefore, a very experienced leader; he had played nine Tests and a great many other 'big occasion' matches, and his capacity for rising to those big occasions was endless. Apart from his extensive knowledge of the game, perhaps his greatest quality as a captain was to instil his enormous enthusiasm and confidence into his troops. There were some who felt that he was not as good a captain as he might have been, but this was not a view shared by his successor, Archie MacLaren:

---

* I can't believe that no one has come up with this analogy before – Neville Cardus must surely have done – but I have not seen it anywhere. Extending it further, Bradman could be compared with Wagner, at least if we equate runs and notes. It fits well, for Grace and Beethoven were both all-rounders, while Bradman and Wagner were not. The analogy could no doubt be continued *ad tedium*.

'I could not have wished to serve under a more encouraging, sympathetic and appreciative captain. There was always the feeling of complete security, whenever I had the good fortune to be one of his team. The delight expressed by him on every occasion, at anything out of the ordinary, on the part of the fieldsmen, acted as an incentive to every man to produce his best. Indeed, I will go further   the winning atmosphere his presence created seemed to make everyone produce *more* than his best . . . In all the matches I played with or against him I can think of no occasion on which adverse criticism would have been justified.'

Having lost the first Test of 1888, England won the other two under Grace decisively. In those days the England team was chosen by the committee of the home club, and the Oval match was noted for including five Surrey players. The weather was fine and the pitch was good, but still Australia managed to get themselves all out for 80. England faltered at first but then got to 317, Grace's contribution being just 1. Then once again Australia batted badly and could reach only 100, a thoroughly disappointing performance. In the last Test at Old Trafford England were lucky with the weather. Heavy rain in the days before the match had left the pitch soft, and England made 172. But on the second day hot sun produced an appalling sticky wicket and the match was over before lunch, eighteen wickets, the all-time Test record, having fallen that morning. Australia's second innings lasted just one hour and nine minutes, their briefest ever. It was the shortest completed Test match that has ever been played in England.

The following winter England were in South Africa, and played two matches that were subsequently designated Tests. The fact that at the time the first one was played it was not even regarded as first class makes their status as Tests just a trifle questionable, but they are in the books as such. 'Proper' Test cricket resumed in 1890 when Murdoch, his differences behind him, brought a team to do battle with Grace and his men. Two matches were played, at Lord's and the Oval, the one scheduled for Old Trafford being completely washed out. The number of balls per over was increased to five in this series, the figure at which it remained for the rest of the decade in England. Australia's team for the first contained five débutants; these included Syd Gregory and Hugh Trumble, who were later (much later in Gregory's case) to captain the team. Lyons started the game off in remarkable style, reaching 50 in 36 minutes, a record that has been equalled but not beaten, but the innings fell away and his team were all out for 132. Grace was then out second ball and Lyons continued his performance with 5 for 30, but England reached 173. Barrett, another débutant, then became the first man to carry his bat through a completed innings in England–Australia Tests (Tancred had done it for South Africa in the second match there) as he scored 67 out of 176. Grace atoned for his lapse, however, scoring 75 in what were admittedly the best batting conditions of the game, and England were home by seven wickets.

Rain before the next game caused another crop of low scores, all four of them finishing within ten runs of each other. The hero for England was 'Nutty' Martin who, on his début, took six wickets in each innings – and then played only one more Test, against South Africa. To Australia's 92 England replied with 100, with another duck from Grace. 102 from the visitors meant that England had to get 95 on a pitch that was still very far from easy. They were 32 for 4 before J.M. Read and Cranston took the score to 83, but then four more wickets fell for only ten runs. The ninth-wicket pair of Sharpe and MacGregor groped and missed for several overs, got a single to level the scores, and then stranded themselves in the middle of the pitch going for the winning run – only for Barrett, the bat-carrying hero of the previous match, to throw wide, leaving England victorious by two wickets.

That marked the end of Billy Murdoch's Test career for Australia but, having settled in England, he (with J.J. Ferris) toured South Africa with England in the winter of 1891–2. Both played in the only Test, which England won massively, Murdoch displaying his wicket-keeping skills in the second innings. From 1893 to 1899 Murdoch played for and captained Sussex; he and W.G. remained great friends and he also played for Grace's London County team for some years. In 1911 he died of a stroke whilst watching Australia v South Africa in Melbourne; had he lived two more days he would have seen the team he had once led win by 530 runs. Australia's first truly high-class batsman was embalmed and brought to England to be buried, where, during his funeral, play was suspended on all the county grounds.

Grace's first Tests in Australia came in 1891–2, when he captained on the tour led by Lord Sheffield. This was perhaps the most important tour ever made to Australia, for their team's recent lack of success had led to a waning of interest from the Australian crowds. Lord Sheffield therefore persuaded Grace to take out a strong team and do his best to generate interest. As a result of this the Sheffield Shield came into being. The interest proved to be enormous, Lord Sheffield donated 150 guineas for the furtherance of cricket in Australia and the newly-formed Australian Cricket Council set up the Shield for competition among Victoria, South Australia and New South Wales, which began the following season. Blackham, having had one successful Test as captain seven years earlier, led the Australians. After a number of years in which England had had the stronger team, the two sides for once were fairly evenly matched; England lacked Shrewsbury and Australia were without Murdoch, but there were some good players on view. This series also saw the beginning of the six-ball over in Australia.

The home team made a good start when they won the first Test by 54 runs. The second Test at Sydney then proved a remarkable game. Australia batted first and made only 145 as Lohmann took 8 for 58. England replied with 307 as Abel became the first Englishman to carry his bat through a Test innings, so that at the end of the second day the home team were deeply in the mire. Lyons then scored a fine century and Bannerman an extremely slow 91 (three boundaries in seven-and-a-half hours, and a comment in *Wisden* that 'invaluable as it was, however, it would in a match of less interest have thoroughly tired out the spectators') and they managed to reach a total of 391. Moses was not able to bat in this innings because of a leg injury, and Grace incurred the crowd's wrath by refusing him a runner in the first innings and not allowing a substitute on the field until late in the match because Blackham had known about the injury beforehand. His uncharitableness backfired on him when it rained and England, needing 230 to win, slumped to 11 for 3 at the close; he came in for a good deal of criticism for not sending in nightwatchmen and not saving himself until conditions improved. Only Stoddart then lived up to his reputation with a fine 69, as Turner and Giffen gave Australia victory by 72 runs, provoking what *Wisden* called 'a scene of almost indescribable enthusiasm'. England did get a thumping consolation victory in the last match, running up 499 before rain ruined the pitch and Australia were bowled out twice for 100 and 169; but the Ashes were Australia's.

Blackham brought his team to England again in 1893. It was an experienced team as most of them had played in the previous series, and once again the balance was about even. The Australians, however, were full of factions and apparently bent on their own destruction; on one occasion after a train journey to Brighton porters found that a compartment was spattered with blood. No doubt it was because of such problems that the cares of captaincy seemed to affect Blackham even more in England than they did at home, for this was the series in which he lost a stone in weight.

England's captain, on the other hand, was unlikely to be affected by the cares of captaincy, having usually lapped up the responsibility – and even less likely to lose a stone in weight. Grace was injured for the first Test, however, and the captaincy went to Andrew Stoddart, another of those great sporting all-rounders which the Victorian era seemed to produce so

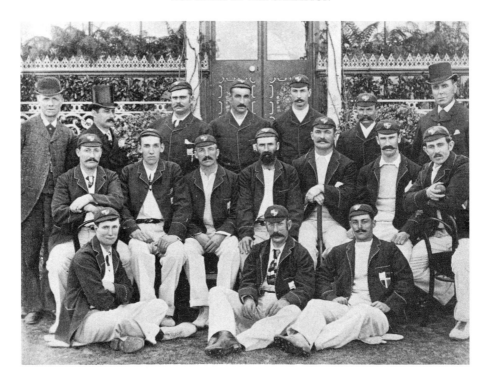

*The 1893 Australian touring team. Standing, left to right, R Carpenter
(umpire), V. Cohen (manager), A.H. Jarvis, W.F. Giffen, W. Bruce,
A.C. Bannerman, R.A. Thoms (umpire). Seated, left to right,
G.H.S. Trott, H. Trumble, G. Giffen. J.M. Blackham (captain),
J.J. Lyons, R.W. McLeod, C.T.B. Turner. Front, left to right,
H. Graham, A. Coningham, S.E. Gregory. As well as Blackham,
G. Giffen, Trott, Trumble and Gregory all went on to captain their
country.*

easily; he also played for England at Rugby football. He was a very stylish,
stroke-playing batsman whose career with Middlesex culminated in a
farewell performance in 1900 that can hardly ever have been surpassed –
221, his highest score, in his very last innings for the county. He also held
the record for the highest score ever made at the time in any class of cricket,
having compiled 485 for Hampstead against, very appropriately, the Stoics.
He had played four Tests before this series, and in the last Test on the
previous tour had made a fine century.

As the son of a well-to-do merchant he did not have the public school–
university background of many of the amateurs, but he liked to think of
himself as a young 'blood'. This may not sound an ideal attribute for the
business of captaincy, but he took his responsibility very seriously and

A.E. Stoddart, captain of a triumphant tour of Australia and a disastrous one.

showed himself most able to command the liking and respect of his team. They meant a great deal to him, and more than one writer speaks of him 'coaxing' his players, humouring them when humouring was required and being firm when necessary – an early exponent of the psychological approach. He had an impulsive nature, and although not all of his impulsive moves came off, his friendliness meant that the mistakes were not held against him. He made two tours to Australia, the first successful, the second quite the opposite. After the first he was very highly regarded for his captaincy and his sportsmanship, while after the second, in which he criticised the crowds for their frequent barracking, his popularity took a nosedive. When things began to go wrong on that second tour (starting, soon after his arrival in Australia, with the death of his mother, to whom he was very close) his captaincy became pedestrian and uninspiring, whereas on the first tour it had been an important element in England's success. He had fostered a happy atmosphere and it had brought its own rewards.

The first Test contained a significant milestone for Arthur Shrewsbury as he became the first man to score 1,000 runs in Tests; his century also meant that he was the first to score three hundreds for England. He and F.S. Jackson were primarily responsible for taking the score to 334, and Australia were in deep trouble before Harry Graham, on his début, scored their first Test century at Lord's to save the match. On the third day Stoddart became the first Test captain to declare, but as it happened it was meaningless as the rest of the match was rained off. The decisive game was played in a heatwave at the Oval. Grace returned as captain and six England batsmen scored over 50, Jackson topping the lot with a century. Tiredness as much as anything led the visitors to collapse for 91, a mere 392 behind. Their second innings of 349 was more respectable, but not enough to avert an innings defeat.

At Old Trafford England again had the edge, a century from Billy Gunn (the first in an Old Trafford Test) helping them to a first innings lead of 39. At the end of Australia's second innings Turner and Blackham put on 36 invaluable runs, ensuring that England's run-chase was altogether too tall an order. During the course of the partnership Turner dislocated a finger; it will be recalled that the England captain was a doctor, and he duly pulled it back into place so that Turner could continue. Cricket never has been a game for the squeamish, after all.

For 1894–5 Stoddart organised his first, successful, tour. Both sides showed a number of changes, and England were without the likes of Grace and Shrewsbury. Perhaps on paper Australia had slightly the stronger team, but there was not a lot between them.

Soon after the start of the first Test at Sydney, Australia were 21 for 3. By the end of their innings they had reached 586, thanks mainly to 161 from Giffen and 201 from Gregory; the latter and Blackham put on 154 in 73 minutes, the captain's 74 being his highest Test score in his last match. This is still the record ninth-wicket partnership in Ashes Tests. In reply England made 325, with nearly everyone making a contribution of some sort. Ward top-scored with 75, and when England followed on he improved on this to the tune of 117. Again, with the aid of a number of dropped catches and an easy pitch nearly everyone made some runs, but with England only just ahead the seventh-wicket stand of 89 between Ford and Briggs proved crucial. Giffen became the only player in Ashes history to score two hundred runs and take eight wickets in one match, but England still reached 437, setting Australia 177 to win. At the end of the fifth day they had made 113 for 2, but that night the weather broke. In bright sunshine Peel (who arrived late after a night of sorrow-drowning since the game seemed lost) and Briggs worked their way through. The closing stages were desperate as the batsmen tried to squeeze every run they could, but when Blackham was last man in they still needed fifteen – and he was batting with a thumb injury that had happened in England's first innings. But he could produce no heroics, and his team fell ten short. Winning a Test after following on has happened on only one other occasion, and few readers will need to be told when or where that was, or who the England heroes were.

Back in 1886, when the Australians were planning their tour to England, many people felt that the captaincy should have been given to George Giffen. Now that the injury to Blackham's thumb spelt the end of his career, Giffen was the obvious leader to replace him. Blackham retired from the game altogether and returned to the Melbourne bank where he worked, much loved by his countrymen. He lived until he was almost eighty, and for all the glorious wicket-keepers that Test cricket has since seen there have been few to challenge his princely rank.

George Giffen was the great all-rounder of his era, the W.G. of Australia. He was an attacking, determined batsman with plenty of strokes, especially powerful in the drive, and a very sound defence to back it all up. As a very accurate slow-medium off-break bowler, he took many wickets through skilful variations of flight and pace. One particular delivery, a slow ball given plenty of height, brought him a good many caught-and-bowled victims. He toured England five times, although most of his great deeds were performed at home, some of which have never been equalled: he is the only man to have taken sixteen wickets in a match five times, and on one of those occasions he scored no fewer than 271 runs in one innings as well, a performance that seems unlikely to be equalled. Over a period of twelve years he scored one-third of South Australia's runs and took five-eighths of the wickets. The story went that parents in Adelaide taught their children to say 'God bless Mummy and Daddy and George Giffen', an accolade that not even the great doctor is reported to have received. He played on into his forties and remains the only Australian to score 10,000 runs and take 1,000 wickets without having been in English county cricket.

He captained South Australia from 1886–7 to 1897–8, during which time they won the Sheffield Shield the year after it was instituted. His obituary in *The Times*, however, stated that 'his merits as a leader were not commensurate with his merits as a player'. It is, of course, one of the unwritten rules of the game that as far as the critics are concerned a bowler-captain will invariably either under-bowl or over-bowl himself – he can never get it right. Giffen, said the critics, was guilty of the latter, and it counted against him when his captaincy was analysed afterwards. In his first Test as captain, in which he bowled 78.2 overs in England's second innings, Hugh Trumble, the vice-captain, told the story that several players urged him to ask Giffen to take himself off. When Trumble at last agreed and suggested a change to Giffen, the captain replied 'Yes, I think I'll go on at the other end.' He did, and finished with six wickets.

Giffen's first morning as captain saw him winning the toss, inserting the opposition and supervising his bowlers as they put them out for 75. Coningham, playing in what was his only Test, took MacLaren's wicket with the first ball of the match. But Australia could reply with only 123, and on a good pitch England batted with great determination to run up 475. The backbone of this was 173 from Stoddart, which remained the highest score by an England captain in Australia until Denness beat it in 1974–5. Faced with such a hefty score Giffen's batsmen were never really in the hunt, and England gained a second victory that at one stage had seemed very unlikely.

Two Tests later the Australians were level. In intense heat at Adelaide, Iredale's 140 in Australia's second innings and Albert Trott's 110 without losing his wicket and 8 for 43 in England's second innings – on his début – were remarkable performances. Trott became an instant national hero as the home team won by 382 runs. In the fourth Test Stoddart put Australia in on an unpleasant pitch, but Harry Graham and Albert Trott saw them to 284, before rain left the pitch a quagmire. England subsided twice in one day and lost by an innings and 147 runs. In this match Briggs became the first bowler to take a hundred Test wickets, closely followed by Turner (in eight fewer matches) who was playing in what proved to be his last Test.

(Left) *Harry Trott, the postman whose intelligent captaincy transformed Australian cricket.* (Right) *George Giffen, Australia's answer to W.G.*

Rumour had it that even Queen Victoria was interested in the decider. It was billed as the match of the century, and watched by an enormous crowd. Solid batting from almost everyone saw Australia to 414, but England were not to be outdone and MacLaren's maiden Test century, with 73 from Peel after four consecutive Test ducks, saw them only 29 behind. Good bowling by Richardson and Peel then left England to get 297 to win. At 28 for 2 and with the sky becoming steadily greyer, enter Jack Brown. Twenty-eight minutes later he had fifty to his name, still the fastest half-century in Test cricket. After 95 minutes he had his century, going on to 140 and with Albert Ward, who scored 93, putting on 210 for the third wicket. Mac-Laren and Peel polished off the rest, to round off a splendid series with a memorable victory.

Another exciting three-match series followed in 1896, for again the teams were well-balanced. W.G. was back in charge for England and had the likes of Tom Richardson and F.S. Jackson in the team, with Dick Lilley beginning his illustrious career behind the stumps, while for Australia Clem Hill was making his début (admittedly quietly) and Ernie Jones (the man who bowled a ball through W.G.'s beard) was bowling at great speed. They were led by Harry Trott, the elder brother of Albert, a man with a special place in the history of Australian cricket. He was a useful all-rounder, a batsman who could defend or attack with equal ease and no little elegance. As well as being a fine close fielder he was also a good leg-spin bowler, who once astonished everyone by opening the bowling in a Test and taking the wickets of Grace and Stoddart cheaply. He led Victoria from 1892–3 to 1903–4, winning the Sheffield Shield in its first year and on four other occasions; but more important was the way he brought to the national team a quality that it had needed very badly for some years – discipline.

Harry Trott had had little in the way of education and had worked as a postman. However, he was simply one of those men who commands respect for the best reasons; for his ability as a player, for his great shrewdness and intelligence as a tactician, for his steadiness in a crisis, for his fairness and sportsmanship and for his friendliness and readiness to listen to grievances. He knew he had a strong team and that it would be stronger if the internal problems that had arisen so often before could be eliminated, so he made it his task to do just that. He achieved it as much as anything through the warmth of his personality, without having to lay down the law and without upsetting anyone. He was a shrewd judge of character who carefully watched his men (many of them higher up the social ladder than he was) and saw how to get the best out of them. He noted their problems, sympathised with them and suggested remedies, and they readily responded to his good sense and friendliness. In a match he was always ready to be flexible, always ready to act on intuition, a characteristic that upset some of the English professionals and led them to criticise his captaincy because they liked the captain to have a settled plan! He always showed a deep understanding of his bowlers' problems and made sure that they were not over-bowled, and he had the priceless knack of sensing which bowler would be best for the conditions. For Clem Hill he was simply the best captain under whom he played:

'Harry was quick to grasp a situation. He saw an opponent's weakness in a second. He knew in a moment when a crack bowler was having an off-day. Time and again he got a champion batsman's wicket by putting on a bowler whom he knew the batsman did not like.'

Although Australia lost this 1896 series 2–1 Grace admitted that England had been lucky, and it was not long before Trott put things right.

Australia lost the first Test on the opening morning, when Richardson took six wickets to skittle them out for 53. Grace then completed his 1,000 runs in Tests as England took a big lead, but there followed a captain's century from Trott as he and Gregory put on 221 in only 160 minutes. Rain made the pitch difficult for England as they chased 109, but they lost only four wickets in making it. This was Lohmann's last Test; no bowler since has ever achieved a better striking rate than his wicket every 34 balls.

The second Test saw the arrival of Prince Ranjitsinhji on the international scene – thanks to Trott and his team manager agreeing happily that he play for England – a début which he duly marked with a beautiful undefeated century, although little support from his fellow batsmen meant that it was in vain. Australia opened with 412, but England could not match this and followed on. After Ranji's effort, which included the first Test century before lunch, the Australians needed 125 to win. Richardson, having taken seven wickets in the first innings, bowled with great spirit to take six more and nearly produce an upset, but the visitors achieved their target. Trott, not normally prone to nerves but having been dismissed for 2, found the tension so overpowering that he left the ground and drove round Manchester in a cab until it was over. There was a landmark for Giffen when he became the first player to record 1,000 runs and 100 wickets in Test cricket.

Whether Queen Victoria took an interest in the deciding game of this series does not appear to be recorded. What is recorded, however, is that before the game at the Oval five professionals – Abel, Richardson, Hayward, Lohmann and Gunn, the first four of them Surrey players – wrote to the Surrey committee requesting match fees of £20 each, despite having accepted £10 for the first two games. This proved ill-advised, and three of them later withdrew their request and played. Lohmann and Gunn held out, although Lohmann subsequently apologised. Unfortunately the match was badly affected by rain and was very low-scoring; England managed a first-innings lead of 26, and then set Australia 111 to win on an appalling pitch. Their highest scorer was the number eleven, McKibbin, who made 16 of their 44, Peel finishing his Test career with 6 for 23. The pitch was never easy for anyone, but Australia undoubtedly had the worst of it; a good example of a closely-contested series really being decided by the toss.

The last day of the second Test had seen W.G.'s forty-eighth birthday. An era was approaching its end, but it had a little while yet to run; in that season of 1896 he scored over 2,000 runs, and there were more still to come. The problem was his mobility; he could still take some good catches, but when he finally dropped out of Test cricket he said it was because 'the ground is getting a bit too far away'. This, though, was not until after the first match of the next home series, by which time he was almost fifty-one. His Test record always seems unremarkable – 1,098 runs at 32 in

22 matches – but this underlines better than anything the way in which conditions have changed over the years and, anyway, his best years in the early 1870s preceded the Test matches. He played many fine innings on rain-affected pitches in low-scoring games, and for good measure he took no fewer than 39 catches in 22 games. But the series just ended marked the end of England's early dominance; the Ashes were about to change hands for a few years.

1888	Lord's	A 116, 60	E 53, 62	A 61 runs
	Oval	A 80, 100	E 317	E inns 137 runs
	Old Trafford	E 172	A 81, 70	E inns 21 runs
1890	Lord's	A 132, 176	E 173, 137–3	E 7 wkts
	Oval	A 92, 102	E 100, 95–8	E 2 wkts
1891–2	Melbourne	A 240, 236	E 264, 158	A 54 runs
	Sydney	A 145, 391	E 307, 157	A 72 runs
	Adelaide	E 499	A 100, 169	E inns 230 runs
1893	Lord's	E 334, 234–8d	A 269	Drawn
	Oval	E 483	A 91, 349	E inns 43 runs
	Old Trafford	A 204, 236	E 243, 118–4	Drawn
1894–5	Sydney	A 586, 166	E 325, 437	E 10 runs
	Melbourne	E 75, 475	A 123, 333	E 94 runs
	Adelaide	A 238, 411	E 124, 143	A 382 runs
	Sydney	A 284	E 65, 72	A inns 147 runs
	Melbourne	A 414, 267	E 385, 298–4	E 6 wkts
1896	Lord's	A 53, 347	E 292, 111–4	E 6 wkts
	Old Trafford	A 412, 125–7	E 231, 305	A 3 wkts
	Oval	E 145, 84	A 119, 44	E 66 runs

1888

England

Batting	Innings	NO	HS	Runs	Average
J. Shuter	1	0	28	28	28.00
F.H. Sugg	2	0	31	55	27.50
W. Barnes	4	0	62	90	22.50
G.A. Lohmann	4	1	62*	64	21.33
R. Abel	4	0	70	81	20.25

Bowling	O	M	R	W	Average
A.G. Steel	4.2	3	4	1	4.00
R. Peel	110.2	48	181	24	7.54
J. Briggs	84.1	42	94	12	7.83
W. Barnes	51	25	67	7	9.57
G.A. Lohmann	94.3	50	144	11	13.09

Australia

Batting	Innings	NO	HS	Runs	Average
J.J. Lyons	2	0	32	54	27.00
J.J. Ferris	6	3	20*	66	22.00
P.S. McDonnell	6	0	32	70	11.66
C.T.B. Turner	6	0	26	59	9.83
J.D. Edwards	6	1	26	48	9.60

Bowling	O	M	R	W	Average
C.T.B. Turner	164	62	261	21	12.42
J.J. Ferris	119.2	59	167	11	15.18
S.M.J. Woods	54.1	18	121	5	24.20

Wicket-keepers: J.M. Blackham (A) 6 dismissals   M. Sherwin (E) 2 dismissals
H. Wood (E) 2 dismissals   R. Pilling (E) 1 dismissal

Captains: A.G. Steel – batting 3, 10* bowling 1–4, 0–0
W.G. Grace – batting 1; 38
P.S. McDonnell – batting 22, 1; 0, 32; 15, 0

1890

(Over increased to 5 balls in England)

England

Batting	Innings	NO	HS	Runs	Average
G. Ulyett	1	0	74	74	74.00
W.G. Grace	4	1	75*	91	30.33
J.M. Read	4	1	35	90	30.00
W. Gunn	4	0	34	81	20.25
R. Peel	1	0	16	16	16.00

Bowling	O	M	R	W	Average
W.G. Grace	14	10	12	2	6.00
F. Martin	57.2	21	102	12	8.50
J.W. Sharpe	15	8	18	2	9.00
G. Ulyett	9	5	11	1	11.00
W. Barnes	12	5	26	2	13.00

Australia

Batting	Innings	NO	HS	Runs	Average
J.J. Lyons	4	0	55	122	30.50
J.E. Barrett	4	1	67*	80	26.66
G.H.S. Trott	4	0	39	76	19.00
E.J.K. Burn	4	0	19	41	10.25
C.T.B. Turner	4	0	24	38	9.50

Bowling	O	M	R	W	Average
P.C. Charlton	9	1	24	3	8.00
J.J. Ferris	113	50	171	13	13.15
J.J. Lyons	40.1	13	73	5	14.60
H. Trumble	22	7	45	2	22.50
C.T.B. Turner	104	50	159	6	26.50

Wicket-keepers: J.M. Blackham (A) 3 dismissals   G. MacGregor (E) 5 dismissals

Captains: W.G. Grace – batting 0, 75*; 0, 16 bowling 2–12
W.L. Murdoch – batting 9, 19; 2, 6

In the first match J.E. Barrett (A) became the first player to carry his bat through a completed innings in England v Australia Tests. In the second match F. Martin became the first bowler to take 12 wickets on Test début.

1891–2

(Over increased to 6 balls in Australia)

England

Batting	Innings	NO	HS	Runs	Average
R. Abel	5	1	132*	217	54.25
A.E. Stoddart	5	0	134	265	53.00
W.G. Grace	5	0	58	164	32.80
R. Peel	5	0	83	134	26.80
J.M. Read	5	0	57	131	26.20

Bowling	O	M	R	W	Average
J. Briggs	116.3	31	268	17	15.76
G.A. Lohmann	188.2	71	289	16	18.06
R. Peel	94.5	43	128	6	21.33
W. Attewell	193.1	97	216	8	27.00
J.W. Sharpe	150	53	287	9	31.88

Australia

Batting	Innings	NO	HS	Runs	Average
J.J. Lyons	6	0	134	287	47.83
W. Bruce	6	0	72	226	37.66
A.C. Bannerman	6	0	91	202	33.66
H. Moses	3	0	29	67	22.33
R.W. McLeod	6	0	31	126	21.00

Bowling	O	M	R	W	Average
C.T.B. Turner	155.4	52	338	16	21.12
J.J. Lyons	5	0	22	1	22.00
R.W. McLeod	110.4	37	227	10	22.70
G. Giffen	130.3	35	397	15	26.46
G.H.S. Trott	60	7	210	6	35.00

Wicket-keepers: J.M. Blackham (A) 7 dismissals G. MacGregor (E) 3 dismissals
H. Philipson (E) 1 dismissal

Captains: J.M. Blackham – batting 4*, 0; 3*, 0; 7*, 9
W.G. Grace – batting 50, 25; 26, 5; 58 bowling 0–34

In the second match R. Abel became the first England player to carry his bat through a completed Test innings.

1893

England

Batting	Innings	NO	HS	Runs	Average
A. Shrewsbury	5	1	106	284	71.00
F.S. Jackson	3	0	103	199	66.33
W. Gunn	5	1	102*	208	52.00
W.G. Grace	3	0	68	153	51.00
A.E. Stoddart	5	0	83	162	32.40

Bowling	O	M	R	W	Average
W.H. Lockwood	93	27	234	14	15.28
T. Richardson	57.4	20	156	10	15.60
J. Briggs	120.1	40	293	16	18.31
W. Flowers	11	3	21	1	21.00
A.W. Mold	98.1	32	234	7	23.42

Australia

Batting	Innings	NO	HS	Runs	Average
W. Bruce	5	1	68	159	39.75
H. Graham	5	0	107	170	34.00
A.C. Bannerman	5	0	60	161	32.20
G.H.S. Trott	5	0	92	146	29.20
J.J. Lyons	5	0	33	117	23.40

Bowling	O	M	R	W	Average
G. Giffen	171.4	59	342	16	21.37
C.T.B. Turner	175	72	315	11	28.63
W. Bruce	71	23	156	5	31.20
H. Trumble	135.2	30	234	6	39.00
R.W. McLeod	85	30	157	2	78.50

Wicket-keepers: G. MacGregor (E) 9 dismissals   J.M. Blackham (A) 4 dismissals

Captains: A.E. Stoddart – batting 24, 13
          W.G. Grace – batting 68; 40, 45
          J.M. Blackham – batting 2; 17, 2*; 0*, 23*

In the first match A. Shrewsbury became the first man to score 1,000 runs in Tests. In the second match A.C. Bannerman became the first Australian to do the same thing.

1894–5

England

Batting	Innings	NO	HS	Runs	Average
J.T. Brown	10	2	140	343	42.87
A. Ward	10	0	117	419	41.90
A.E. Stoddart	10	1	173	352	39.11
A.C. MacLaren	10	1	120	240	26.66
R. Peel	9	0	48	168	18.66

Bowling	O	M	R	W	Average
T. Richardson	309.1	63	849	32	26.53
R. Peel	325.1	77	721	27	26.70
J. Briggs	150.3	29	435	15	29.00
A.E. Stoddart	3	0	31	1	31.00
W. Brockwell	77	26	238	5	47.60

Australia

Batting	Innings	NO	HS	Runs	Average
A.E. Trott	5	3	86*	206	103.00
G. Giffen	9	0	161	475	52.88
H. Graham	3	0	105	121	40.33
S.E. Gregory	9	0	201	362	40.22
F.A. Iredale	9	0	140	337	38.44

Bowling	O	M	R	W	Average
S.A. Callaway	33.3	14	56	5	11.20
C.T.B. Turner	187.1	76	349	18	19.38
A.E. Trott	79	17	192	9	21.33
J.C. Reedman	9.3	2	24	1	24.00
G. Giffen	343.2	111	820	34	24.11

Wicket keepers: J.M. Blackham (A) 2 dismissals   A.H. Jarvis (A) 8 dismissals
               L.H. Gay (E) 4 dismissals   H. Philipson (E) 10 dismissals

Captains: J.M. Blackham – batting 74, 2
G. Giffen – batting 32, 43; 58, 24; 8; 57, 51
bowling 6–155; 5–76, 2–74; 3–14, 5–26; 4–130, 1–106
A.E. Stoddart – batting 12, 36; 10, 173; 1, 34*; 7, 0; 68, 11
bowling 1–31

In the first match G. Giffen became the only player to score 200 runs and take 8 wickets in England v Australia Tests. A.E. Stoddart's 173 in the second match was the highest score by an England captain in Australia until 1974–5. In the third match A.E. Trott, on début, scored 110 runs and took 8–43. In the fourth match J. Briggs became the first bowler to take 100 Test wickets. In the fifth match J.T. Brown scored his first 50 in 28 minutes, still the fastest 50 in Tests. G. Giffen's all-round performance in the rubber has never been equalled – 475 runs and 34 wickets.

1896

England

Batting	Innings	NO	HS	Runs	Average
K.S. Ranjitsinhji	4	1	154*	235	78.33
W. Gunn	2	1	25*	38	38.00
A.E. Stoddart	4	1	41	103	34.33
R. Abel	6	0	94	184	30.66
A.F.A. Lilley	5	1	65*	92	23.00

Bowling	O	M	R	W	Average
R. Peel	32	14	53	8	6.62
J.T. Hearne	127.1	56	211	15	14.06
G.A. Lohmann	33	12	52	3	17.33
T. Richardson	175	58	439	24	18.29
A.F.A. Lilley	5	1	23	1	23.00

Australia

Batting	Innings	NO	HS	Runs	Average
F.A. Iredale	4	0	108	152	38.00
G.H.S. Trott	6	0	143	206	34.33
S.E. Gregory	6	0	103	182	30.33
J.J. Kelly	6	3	27	72	24.00
T.R. McKibbin	3	1	28*	44	22.00

Bowling	O	M	R	W	Average
T.R. McKibbin	69.3	20	162	11	14.72
C.J. Eady	32	12	69	4	17.25
H. Trumble	170.1	58	339	18	18.38
G.H.S. Trott	25	3	80	4	20.00
G. Giffen	95	21	285	9	31.66

Wicket-keepers: A.F.A. Lilley (E) 9 dismissals   J.J. Kelly (A) 9 dismissals

Captains: W.G. Grace – batting 66, 7; 2, 11; 24, 9 bowling 0–14; 0–11
G.H.S. Trott – batting 0, 143; 53, 2; 5, 3 bowling 2–13, 0–4; 2–46, 0–17

In the second match 'Ranji' became the first Indian to play Test cricket and scored a century on début. G. Giffen, in his 30th match, became the first to make 1,000 runs and take 100 wickets.

4

The Captain Becomes a Tactician

It was round about the middle of the 1890s that the role of the captain began to change. Before then the job had usually been done by the leading, or perhaps most aristocratic, amateur, and his role had primarily been to inspire and encourage his men by word and deed. Some of them, such as Harris and Grace, tried to assess the strengths and weaknesses of the opposition and would do their best to exploit any known weaknesses. But it was all fairly elementary, for tactical thinking as it is now understood and practised was in its infancy. The men who, more than any others, took it out of its infancy at least into its youth were Harry Trott and Joe Darling of Australia and, under their influence, Archie MacLaren of England.

Strange as it may now seem, bowlers would, by and large, simply bowl; they did not usually analyse the batsmen carefully and plan their attack accordingly. Grateful batsmen would often score more runs than they should have done simply because the bowler did not perceive that he would do better if he did not put the ball where the batsman most liked it. Trott and Darling made their bowlers think much more about their craft, prospering greatly as a result – and on pitches which had improved considerably in recent years. They also thought more about field settings than previous captains had done, observing the way in which a batsman was playing and adjusting their field to deal with it. They would, too, vary their batting order if changing conditions suggested greater flexibility. Not surprisingly, this intelligent approach paid off.

In 1897–8 Stoddart again organised and led a tour to Australia. He was, though, without some important players from the previous tour, and their replacements did not do too well. MacLaren and Ranji batted splendidly, but for Australia a powerful team was coming together under Harry Trott; Hill began to show his class, Noble made his début in the second Test and took wickets immediately, and some other good players were coming to their peak. When, soon after his arrival, Stoddart heard that his mother had died he withdrew and the captaincy went to Archie MacLaren.

A.C. MacLaren, England captain a record twenty-two times against Australia, but never won the Ashes.

Anyone who has read the writings of Sir Neville Cardus is likely to know that MacLaren was Cardus's great hero, the man he referred to as 'the noblest Roman'; MacLaren's majestic batting and patrician appearance and character inspired him to some of his deepest purple prose. In an age of glorious batsmen he was fit to hold his own with any of them, and he was to captain his country against Australia more times than any other player. Yet of the twenty-two Tests, spread over five series, in which he was captain, only four were won, and he never once won the Ashes. Opinions vary over his quality as a captain, some claiming that he was one of England's finest and others being much less effusive. There would seem little doubt that he was often on the wrong end of some rough luck, and was unfortunate to coincide with the strongest teams that Australia had thus far produced – and the best captains.

As a schoolboy he had made his mark with Harrow, and in 1890 he made his début as an eighteen-year-old for Lancashire. A number of fine innings saw him into the England team on Stoddart's previous tour, where his century in the final Test was crucial to England's taking the rubber. Then in July 1895, having missed a number of games because of a teaching commitment, he went to Somerset and scored 424. Admittedly it was against a fairly weak team, but it was an astonishing feat and took only 470 minutes. It has since been passed six times abroad, but until Graeme Hick scored 405 not out in 1988 – also at Taunton – it remained the only score over 400 ever made in English first-class cricket. It did rather help to cement his place in the England team. His batting was based on positive, decisive movement, either going well forward or well back and rarely being caught in no man's land. This made him a fine player on sticky wickets, just as it had Shrewsbury. One feature that attracted attention was his very high backlift as he waited to receive the ball, so that the full swing of the bat helped convey the impression of majesty.

The splendour of his batting, his handsome appearance and aristocratic mien made him popular with the public as well as with Cardus, but the man himself was full of contradictions. For all his aristocratic bearing his father was a Manchester businessman rather than a peer of the realm, and Michael Down, in his biography of MacLaren, suggests that in adopting the attitudes he did he was possibly over-correcting for a feeling of inferiority. Unlike most other amateurs he was normally short of money, and for several seasons missed a number of games because he had to take a teaching job, hardly a proper state of affairs for a county captain. He would borrow from anyone he could, including his own professionals, and was even at one point threatened with expulsion from MCC because he had not paid his subscription; yet whenever he did have money he was very generous with it. When he wanted to be, he was a warm and charming companion and an excellent raconteur, but he could change very quickly. He could be tactless, bloody-minded and thoroughly unpleasant, often for little apparent reason. John Arlott summed him up thus: 'It was MacLaren's tragedy that all his virtues bred their own faults. He was strong but inflexible, intelligent but intolerant: single-minded but humourless: impressive on the field but often disappointingly petty off it.'

As a captain he had his admirers and his detractors. The critics – Warner in particular – claimed that he was too pessimistic, and that when his team was up against it he tended to criticise rather than encourage. Certainly he was serious and strict on discipline, but some of the men who played under him denied that he was prone to depression. Michael Down suggests that his complex personality produced different reactions in different people, so that what has been called his pessimism might perhaps be seen as too inflexible an approach to the people around him. Admittedly he was pessimistic about his luck, but he had good reason to be. Few captains before him had been concerned with the psychology of the game, but in MacLaren's case it is important. He was excellent at producing a feeling of inferiority in the other team, but unfortunately he could produce the same effect in his own players. His imperious nature created a feeling of hostility about many matches, and some of his players found this difficult to take. C.B. Fry described him as 'an iron and joyless captain . . . under him you entered every game bowed down with the Herculean labour of a cricket match against Australia; you went as in a trance to your doom.' Down notes wryly that 'this "iron and joyless" attitude would be regarded as competitive and professional today.'

There have been few critics, though, of his tactical expertise. The greatest of his contemporaries rated him unsurpassed as a tactician. Monty Noble called him 'a wonderful judge of the game and a master of field placing. He could estimate an opponent's strength and ferret out his weakness with great accuracy, and, what is more, he knew the right kind of bowler to put on to take advantage of his knowlege.' Fry said that when playing Lancashire you felt as if you were playing against a brain, and that MacLaren played his cricket as a kind of athletic chess; and Lancashire did win the Championship under his leadership. He gave a great deal of thought to his field placings, taking great care to study a batsman's favourite strokes and do his best to block them. If he was inflexible in some things, he was very flexible in his field placings, for he would frequently make changes to deal with an altering situation in a way that was not all that common at the time.

He was occasionally criticised for using his main bowler for too long, but Down defends this as a genuine tactic on his part since he believed that even a tiring strike bowler was more likely to take wickets than a fresh change bowler as he was a higher-class player. Sometimes he was proved disastrously wrong, sometimes vindicated.

On that 1897–8 tour he captained England in the first two Tests and the last. Sydney was always his favourite ground, and he duly scored a century there, with Ranji making 175 (despite having been ill with tonsillitis until just before the game) as England reached 551. Australia were made to follow on, during the course of which McLeod, who was deaf, was run out when he left his ground after being bowled by a no-ball, not having heard the umpire's call. Apologies were later made, but it was an unpleasant incident. Darling became the first left-hander to score a Test century, but the match had been lost on the first innings, and England recorded a nine-wicket win. The defeat seemed to inspire the home team, and in great heat they won the next match by an innings. McLeod scored what must have been a very satisfying century as Australia made 520, then bowled England out twice. The pitch broke up and MacLaren's criticisms of it were not well received in the press.

Stoddart returned as captain for the next two Tests, but Trott was now inspiring his team as no Australian team had ever been inspired before. The third Test followed the pattern of the second, with Darling scoring 178 out of his team's 573 and becoming the first batsman to score two hundreds in a rubber. MacLaren emulated him in the second innings, but it was another innings defeat for England. The pattern was almost repeated in the fourth Test; out of Australia's 323 Hill made 188, which has never been beaten by a player under twenty-one in Ashes Tests. When England batted, the air was full of smoke from bush fires, leading Ranji to observe that Australians must be the only people who would set fire to their country to win a cricket match. Again they had to follow on and managed to set Australia a target of 115, but they ran up an eight-wicket victory. MacLaren and Ranji were going well in the second innings when MacLaren apparently got a fly in his eye and gave a catch as a result. Ranji ill-advisedly said that this cost England the game, and the press had great fun.

For the last Test Stoddart again dropped out and MacLaren took over. England made 335 before Tom Richardson, playing his final Test, took eight wickets to restrict the home team to 239. However, England were then dismissed cheaply with MacLaren going first ball, and Darling scored his third century of the series in ninety-one minutes (Australia's fastest ever against England) to set up a six-wicket win. With the old enemy comprehensively beaten by four to one Australia naturally rejoiced. It was a time of much political discussion over the creation of a federation out of the various colonies, and word had it that the fine victories of this series were much more influential towards that end than any number of conferences would ever have been.

Stoddart had played his last Test. It had been a wretched tour for him and he could hardly wait to get home. He continued to play until 1900, but once he left the game his fortunes and his health declined. He got into monetary difficulties, had a nervous breakdown and became very depressed. In the end it all became too much for him and in 1915, just a few months before W.G. died, he shot himself. He was not the only cricketer, nor even the only England captain, to take his own life around this time: Albert Trott had shot himself the previous year, and so too, in 1903, had Arthur Shrewsbury, believing that he was suffering from an incurable illness. They were not the only Test cricketers who would end their own lives.

It was the last Test, too, for Harry Trott, although he continued to play for Victoria for another ten years. His great achievement as a captain was to ensure that the up-and-coming talents were not dissipated as some earlier ones had been, and, fortunately for Australia, he was succeeded by a man who was able to continue the work he had begun. Sadly, an illness that puzzled the doctors led to his having mental breakdowns, and his last years were spent as a semi-invalid. He outlived Stoddart by only two years, and even in the depths of 1917 his passing was mourned throughout Australia.

The man whom the players chose to replace him as captain was The Honourable Joseph Darling. His father had sat on the Legislative Assembly of South Australia, and had been very influential in setting up the Adelaide Oval. By a happy chance (was it just chance?) it was there that fourteen-year-old Joe made 252 for his school and there too that he made his highest Test score of 178 in the series just finished. That series, in which he scored 537 runs at 67 with three centuries, was the peak of his Test run-getting, but he was to play many fine and crucial innings for his country in the years ahead. He was, too, to captain Australia eighteen times against England, a figure exceeded only by Bradman. He had made his début in the 1894–5 series, played in every subsequent Test and had taken over as captain of South Australia in 1898–9; he was to lead them for eight years, but without winning the Sheffield Shield.

He was one of the first of the fine Australian left-handers, a powerfully-built man of medium height with a powerful personality to match. He was an opener, and like all the best openers he could defend solidly or he could force the pace along, depending on the state of the game. As a captain he

Joe Darling, Australian captain who carried on the good work started by Harry Trott.

was a disciplinarian, and his Presbyterian background meant that he would not tolerate drunkenness or theatricality, nor behaviour that threatened the unity of the team. He was a very hard worker who insisted that his team follow his example, and while this meant that they were all very fit it also meant that he expected his bowlers to do more than a bowler-captain would have asked of them. But his players all respected and liked him for his batting and his fighting qualities, for his firmness, resoluteness and fairness, and for the confidence he himself showed and made them feel in themselves. In particular they knew that he was always likely to be in control of any situation, and that with his tactical acumen he would know the best way to deal with it. He tended to discuss tactics only with someone whom he thought understood the game as well as he did, but the complete trust that his players had in him meant that they would follow his orders unhesitatingly, and they pulled out the stops not just for themselves or their country but for their captain.

MacLaren missed the opening Test of the 1899 series, the first to be played at Trent Bridge, because of his teaching commitment. Australia made 252, to which England, captained by Grace, replied with 193; Grace and Fry put on 75 for the first wicket, despite W.G. no longer exactly relishing the pace of Jones. Australia then declared at 230, leaving England to survive for four hours; that they did so, after four wickets had gone for 19, was due to an unbeaten 93 from Ranji, supported by Hayward. This was a historic match for England, for it was Grace's last Test. C.B. Fry told how he went to the selection meeting for the second Test and as he walked in was asked by Grace whether he thought MacLaren ought to play. He said he did, whereupon W.G. said 'That settles it.' Only then did Fry realise that it would be in W.G.'s place. Sad as it was, the decision was the right one, and the Old Man himself thought it was time to quit because of his lack of mobility. All England knew that a poignant moment had arrived, and in retrospect it is a little surprising that, despite suggestions from *The Times* and *Punch*, he was not knighted. People have been honoured for much less.

For the second Test MacLaren returned to the captaincy, and held the position for the rest of the series and the two following. But it was in this match that a young man named Victor Trumper made his first impression on Test cricket and showed people what sublimely beautiful batting could look like. Jones took seven wickets to dismiss England for 206, whereupon Hill and Trumper each scored 135 to see their team to 421. England managed to make Australia bat again, but only just, and a ten-wicket win was recorded. It was to be the only match of the series to see a result, although England had the better of the other games.

Headingley's maiden Test was preceded by rain, and when Australia batted their first three wickets fell without a run on the board. They reached 172, to which England replied with 220. Hearne achieved a hat-trick in Australia's second innings, after which England needed 177 to win – and it rained. On the first evening of the match Johnny Briggs had suffered a violent fit and played no more cricket that season. The following summer he did play again for a while, but was then confined to an asylum and by 1902 he was dead. The story has it that he believed he was bowling in his ward and each day would tell the nurses and doctors his bowling figures.

The fourth Test brought about a change in the follow-on law, which until then was compulsory after a deficit of 120 runs, but now became optional as it was realised that it could penalise the team that was on top. England batted first and made 372 thanks mainly to a hundred from Hayward. Bradley then took a wicket with his first ball in Test cricket, and took four more as the visitors were all out for 196. MacLaren had over-bowled him, however, and the Australians were able to put up a grim fight and hold on, Noble being the mainstay as he became the only batsman to score two separate fifties on the same day of a Test. The Oval Test saw a glut of runs on a perfect pitch. Jackson and Hayward both opened with centuries and England reached 576, a figure they were not to exceed in a Test at home until 1930. Australia had little trouble saving the game, despite 7 for 71 from Lockwood in their first innings, and when he had to go off in their second innings they were able to bat through and so record their first series win in England.

So to a new century. Cricket's Golden Age was gleaming brightly, with legendary batsmen playing glorious strokes. There were many fine bowlers too, but as it was still the custom for most balls to be of a good length directed at the off stump, and as the pitches very much favoured the batsmen, the bowlers tended to play the supporting role in the entertainment, especially as most were professionals while the top batsmen were mostly amateurs. With such high standards the game was tremendously popular; maybe a little of the early innocence had been lost, and maybe the sun did not shine all the time, but the professionals earned a reasonable wage, the amateurs were able to enjoy themselves, and the spectators were able to feast themselves. Perhaps the glories have been embellished with the passage of the years, perhaps the harshness of world war has made us look back with anything but anger to the days before cynicism was invented. Perhaps, too, we seethe at the feudal idea that the amateurs took the field through the main gate in front of the pavilion while the professionals went on through a side entrance, and perhaps we are annoyed that in every anecdote the professional always speaks in broad dialect. But for all that it *was* a good time.

It had been the intention that the first tour of the new century to Australia should be the first to be organised by the MCC, but they were not able to assemble a representative side. The Australians therefore asked MacLaren to get a team together for the 1901–2 season, and he duly did so. The leading amateurs, such as Ranji, Fry and Jackson, were unavailable, as were some of the best professional bowlers, since Yorkshire refused to allow Hirst and Rhodes to tour because of a monetary dispute. Thus his team, which was to encounter a very fine Australian side under Darling, was some way from being the best that England could offer; yet he did have some players with him who were to go on to great things – Jessop, Braund, Blythe and Sydney Barnes. The inclusion of Barnes was one of MacLaren's great triumphs, for he was very inexperienced at first-class level but had much impressed MacLaren in a match for Lancashire. In the first two Tests he took nineteen wickets, but then sustained an injury that put him out of the rest of the tour and tipped the balance very much the way of the home side. The Australians rated him the finest bowler ever to come from England.

As with the previous series England got off to a good start, with MacLaren scoring yet another century at Sydney. Australia fell almost 300 short of England's innings and then subsided a second time to give England a big win. Barnes, Braund and Blythe all took wickets on their début, but England flattered to deceive. The second Test was affected by rain and after Australia had scored 112 England were shot out for just 61. For his second innings Darling showed his tactical skill by almost reversing his batting order, saving his better players in the hope that the pitch would improve – a ploy almost unthinkable a few years before. It worked so well that Duff, on his début, remains the only number ten to hit a century against England, as his team reached 353. Noble and Trumble then shot England out for an easy victory. Both Noble and Barnes took thirteen wickets.

What was probably the decisive moment in the series occurred in the third Test when the new spikes in Barnes's boots caused him to twist his knee. England had scored 388 in their first innings and Barnes had bowled only seven overs, so that the England attack was severely weakened. Australia replied with 321, and by the time of their second innings needed 315 to win. No team had ever scored over 300 in the fourth innings to win a Test but Australia did so now; Hill, having recorded the first 99 in Tests in the previous match, continued in this one with 98 and 97, a sequence that remains unrivalled, but there seems to be general agreement that had Barnes not been injured it would have been England's match.

Hugh Trumble, a great bowler who won his two Tests as captain.

Because of business commitments Darling did not play in the last two Tests and Australia were captained by Hugh Trumble. Trumble was one of the great medium-pace bowlers, whose tally of 141 wickets in Ashes Tests has been passed only by Lillee and Botham. He gained his success by bowling medium-pace off-spin of a consistently good length, getting some turn even on the hardest pitches and a great deal more on the responsive ones. It was said that his accuracy was such that by dropping the ball repeatedly on the same spot he could wear the pitch enough to make his off-spin bite. At 6 feet 4 inches tall, he used his height to good effect, and brought a very intelligent cricketing brain to his art; many of his victims were fine batsmen who were simply out-thought. Naturally he would attack a batsman's weaknesses, but he realised too the value of playing to his strengths, and buying his wicket by feeding him his favourite stroke once too often – although 'buying' is hardly the right word for a bowler whose

Test average is under 22 and whose career average is under 19. He was also a very useful batsman with some good innings to his name and an outstanding slip fielder. He was renowned as a chivalrous sportsman who was a delightful, humorous companion noted for his gentle practical jokes.

He led Victoria from 1899–1900 to 1903–4, taking the Sheffield Shield once, and was a very experienced Test player. His captaincy in these two matches was admirable, as he handled his bowlers well and exhorted his players to great efforts when it looked as though England might pile up a big score in the first innings of the fourth Test. From 179 for 2 they were all out for 317 thanks to some determined play from the Australians, who then replied with 299. England's second innings then collapsed for 99 as Noble and Saunders took five wickets apiece, backed up by some fine fielding orchestrated by Trumble, and Australia won easily. Saunders took nine wickets on his début – and was then left out of the last match. That last Test was played on a pitch which took several showers during the game, and the scores reflected it. To Australia's 144 England replied with 189, and Australia then set them 211 to win. Perhaps they would have done it if Jessop had not run out MacLaren when he had made 49; as it was they fell to Noble and Trumble and finished 32 short. Australia had repeated their 4–1 margin of the previous series.

England's problem had been the lack of depth in bowling once Barnes had been injured, for they did not have a reserve bowler. With a little more luck it could have been a very different story; MacLaren would have been a hero indeed had he beaten that fine Australian team with his limited resources. It had been a well-fought series enjoyed by all, but the next one was to produce two all-time classics.

MacLaren and Darling led their teams throughout this 1902 series. Nineteen years later, when his players were steam-rolling all before them, Armstrong insisted that the 1902 team had been a stronger one, and some of the writers of the time agreed with him. The first game saw Edgbaston's introduction to Test cricket, marked by England playing what is usually reckoned to be the strongest batting line-up they have ever fielded. Amongst this galaxy it was Johnny Tyldesley who shone with 138 as England made 376 and then, on a pitch that had been affected by rain, but which was not all that bad, Hirst and Rhodes bowled Australia out for 36, their lowest Test score of all time. By the time play started on the third day after more rain, though, the pitch was dead and the visitors were able to bat out time. Three days later against Yorkshire the Australians were put out for 23. The second Test was then largely washed out, while the third, the only Test ever played in Sheffield – the smoke from nearby factories (the English equivalent of bush fires) made the light so bad at times that it was considered unsuitable for further Test cricket – was won by Australia thanks mainly to an aggressive century from Hill and eleven wickets from Noble on a pitch that was wearing. And so to Old Trafford.

Australia batted first, and by lunch had reached 173 for 1, Trumper recording the first century before lunch on the first day in Test cricket. Eventually, though, Rhodes and Lockwood managed to keep the score to 299. England's 262, after being 44 for 5, centred on a century from Jackson with support from Braund on a pitch that was distinctly unpleasant. When Australia batted again they were soon in trouble, only Gregory and Darling getting any runs – Darling only doing so because Fred Tate, playing in his only Test and fielding at deep square leg, dropped a catch off Braund's bowling.

Australia managed to reach 86, with Lockwood taking eleven wickets, setting England 124. The first wicket made 44 and the score stood at 72 for 2 when MacLaren was caught in the deep trying to score the runs before the rains came. The story has it that he returned to the dressing-room, threw his bat across the room and said that he had 'thrown away the match and the bloody rubber' – not guaranteed to improve the confidence of those waiting to go in. Sure enough Trumble and Saunders then went through the order, and when the last pair, Rhodes and Tate, came together 8 more runs were needed – at which point a shower held up play for 45 minutes. When play restarted Tate edged a four and the tension grew even greater. Then Saunders bowled him, and Australia had gained one of the most famous of all victories.

Poor Tate lived with that match for the rest of his life and one hopes that the Chairman of Selectors, Lord Hawke, did too, for it was at his insistence that Tate was in the twelve. Having unaccountably dropped Jessop, the selectors had planned to include Haigh of Yorkshire. Hawke, though, was reluctant to see his Yorkshire team depleted any further – Jackson, Rhodes and Hirst were already in the team – and so stood out for Tate. MacLaren, by no means Hawke's greatest admirer, did not want Tate, but responded by making Hirst twelfth man in order to spite Hawke – astonishing goings-on in which the Chairman of Selectors and the captain of England put their personal feelings before the job of winning a Test match. The only consolation was that it led to an historic match, but it also meant that Australia had retained the Ashes.

Jessop and Hirst were back in the team for the final game. Australia batted first and made 324, and when England replied Trumble took 8 for 65 on a wet pitch. The follow-on deficit was increased to 150 in this series, and

England just managed to avoid it. Australia's second innings got off to a bad start when Trumper was run out, and it did not really recover, but England still needed 263 when they began their reply. Before long they were 48 for 5 and the match seemed over when Jessop came to the crease. Seventy-five minutes later, on an improving pitch and to scenes of enormous excitement, he had scored the fastest Test century ever.

For all that the game was transformed, there were still 76 wanted when he was out, and now the hour belonged to Hirst. With Lilley's help he slowly approached the target, but at 248 the ninth wicket fell and he was joined by Rhodes. According to one of English cricket's most endearing and enduring legends Hirst said to Rhodes 'We'll get 'em in singles, Wilfred.' Maybe he did and maybe he didn't, but as they chipped away at those runs the crowd could hardly bear the tension. In fact nine of the fifteen were made in singles, the two Yorkshiremen being undoubtedly the calmest people in the ground, and when Rhodes made the winning hit the crowd went berserk. Ever since it has been known as 'Jessop's match', but it was every bit as much Hirst's match: 5 for 77 in Australia's first innings, top score in England's first innings with 43 to save the follow-on, and now 58 not out to win the match. Very rarely has Test cricket produced two such exciting finishes in the space of three weeks. Had the team for the fourth Test not been the subject of a feud between the Chairman of Selectors and the captain, England might even have won back the Ashes.

1897–8	Sydney	E 551, 96–1	A 237, 408	E 9 wkts
	Melbourne	A 520	E 315, 150	A inns 55 runs
	Adelaide	A 573	E 278, 282	A inns 13 runs
	Melbourne	A 323, 115–2	E 174, 263	A 8 wkts
	Sydney	E 335, 178	A 239, 276–4	A 6 wkts
1899	Trent Bridge	A 252, 230–8d	E 193, 155–7	Drawn
	Lord's	E 206, 240	A 421, 28–0	A 10 wkts
	Headingley	A 172, 224	E 220, 19–0	Drawn
	Old Trafford	E 372, 94–3	A 196, 346–7d	Drawn
	Oval	E 576	A 352, 254–5	Drawn
1901–2	Sydney	E 464	A 168, 172	E inns 124 runs
	Melbourne	A 112, 353	E 61, 175	A 229 runs
	Adelaide	E 388, 247	A 321, 315–6	A 4 wkts
	Sydney	E 317, 99	A 299, 121–3	A 7 wkts
	Melbourne	A 144, 255	E 189, 178	A 32 runs
1902	Edgbaston	E 376–9d	A 36, 42–2	Drawn
	Lord's	E 102–2	A —	Drawn
	Sheffield	A 194, 289	E 145, 195	A 143 runs
	Old Trafford	A 299, 86	E 262, 120	A 3 runs
	Oval	A 324, 121	E 183, 263–9	E 1 wkt

1897–8

England

Batting	Innings	NO	HS	Runs	Average
A.C. MacLaren	10	1	124	488	54.22
K.S. Ranjitsinhji	10	1	175	457	50.77
T.W. Hayward	9	0	72	336	37.33
G.H. Hirst	7	0	85	207	29.57
N.F. Druce	9	0	64	252	28.00

Bowling	O	M	R	W	Average
J.T. Hearne	217	66	538	20	26.90
A.E. Stoddart	10	2	32	1	32.00
T. Richardson	255.5	50	776	22	35.27
T.W. Hayward	52	15	164	4	41.00
J. Briggs	190	56	485	9	53.88

Australia

Batting	Innings	NO	HS	Runs	Average
J. Darling	8	0	178	537	67.12
C.E. McLeod	8	2	112	352	58.66
C. Hill	8	0	188	452	56.50
S.E. Gregory	8	2	71	264	44.00
J. Worrall	2	0	62	88	44.00

Bowling	O	M	R	W	Average
M.A. Noble	150.5	33	385	19	20.29
C.E. McLeod	116.2	48	236	10	23.60
E. Jones	198.2	32	553	22	25.13
H. Trumble	232.3	57	535	19	28.15
W.P. Howell	163.1	66	284	9	31.55

Wicket-keepers: J.J. Kelly (A) 4 dismissals   W. Storer (E) 11 dismissals

Captains: G.H.S. Trott – batting 10, 27; 79; 3; 7; 18
  bowling 1–78; 1–49, 0–17; 0–14, 0–18; 2–33, 1–39; 2–56, 0–12
  A.C. MacLaren – batting 109, 50*; 35, 38; 65, 0
  A.E. Stoddart – batting 15, 24; 17, 25 bowling 1–10; 0–22

The 188 scored by C. Hill in the fourth match is still the highest score by a batsman under 21 in England v Australia Tests. The century scored by J. Darling in the fifth match is still the fastest (91 minutes) for Australia in England v Australia Tests. He became the first batsman to score three hundreds in a rubber and the first to score 500 runs in a rubber.

1899

England

Batting	Innings	NO	HS	Runs	Average
T.W. Hayward	7	1	137	413	68.83
K.S. Ranjitsinhji	8	2	93*	278	46.33
A.F.A. Lilley	5	1	58	181	45.25
F.S. Jackson	8	1	118	303	43.28
J.T. Brown	2	1	27	41	41.00

Bowling	O	M	R	W	Average
W.H. Lockwood	65.3	24	104	7	14.85
J. Briggs	30	11	53	3	17.66
H.I. Young	110.1	39	262	12	21.83
J.T. Hearne	199.3	87	321	13	24.69
C.L. Townsend	28	5	75	3	25.00

Australia

Batting	Innings	NO	HS	Runs	Average
C.L. McLeod	2	1	77	108	108.00
C. Hill	5	0	135	301	60.20
M.A. Noble	9	2	89	367	52.42
J. Worrall	8	1	76	318	45.42
H. Trumble	9	3	56	232	38.66

Bowling	O	M	R	W	Average
F. Laver	32	7	70	4	17.50
H. Trumble	192.3	78	375	15	25.00
E. Jones	255.1	73	657	26	25.26
M.A. Noble	170.3	73	406	13	31.23
W.P. Howell	164	61	346	8	43.25

Wicket-keepers: W. Storer (E) 0 dismissals   A.F.A. Lilley (E) 14 dismissals
J.J. Kelly (A) 5 dismissals

Captains: W.G. Grace – batting 28, 1 bowling 0–31, 0–6
A.C. MacLaren – batting 4, 88*; 9; 8, 6; 49
J. Darling – batting 47, 14; 9, 17*; 9, 16; 4, 39; 71, 6

In the fourth match M.A. Noble became the only batsman to score two separate 50s on the same day in a Test.

1901–2

England

Batting	Innings	NO	HS	Runs	Average
A.C. MacLaren	9	0	116	412	45.77
L.C. Braund	9	2	103*	256	36.57
T.W. Hayward	9	0	90	305	33.88
J.T. Tyldesley	9	0	79	232	25.77
A.F.A. Lilley	9	0	84	211	23.44

Bowling	O	M	R	W	Average
S.F. Barnes	138.2	33	323	19	17.00
J.R. Gunn	144.3	52	360	17	21.17
T.W. Hayward	46	13	113	5	22.60
C. Blythe	175	63	470	18	26.11
L.C. Braund	278.7	76	738	21	35.14

Australia

Batting	Innings	NO	HS	Runs	Average
W.W. Armstrong	7	4	55*	159	53.00
C. Hill	10	0	99	521	52.10
R.A. Duff	8	1	104	311	44.42
S.E. Gregory	10	1	55	269	29.88
J. Darling	6	0	69	154	25.66

Bowling	O	M	R	W	Average
J.P.F. Travers	8	2	14	1	14.00
C.J. Eady	10.3	2	43	3	14.33
J.V. Saunders	67.1	19	162	9	18.00
M.A. Noble	230	68	608	32	19.00
F. Laver	17	6	39	2	19.50
H. Trumble	267.2	93	561	28	20.03

Wicket-keepers: J.J. Kelly (A) 16 dismissals   A.F.A. Lilley (E) 14 dismissals

Captains: J. Darling – batting 39, 3; 19, 23; 1, 69
H. Trumble – batting 6; 3, 22 bowling 3–65; 5–62, 3–64
A.C. MacLaren – batting 116; 13, 1; 67, 44; 92, 5; 25, 49

In the second and third matches C. Hill scored 99, 98 and 97 in consecutive innings. In the fourth match J.J. Kelly became the first wicket-keeper to make 8 dismissals in a Test.

1902

(Over increased to 6 balls in England)

England

Batting	Innings	NO	HS	Runs	Average
W. Rhodes	7	6	38*	67	67.00
F.S. Jackson	8	1	128	308	44.42
G.H. Hirst	5	1	58*	157	39.25
G.L. Jessop	5	0	104	190	38.00
J.T. Tyldesley	7	0	138	245	35.00

Bowling	O	M	R	W	Average
W.H. Lockwood	81.1	18	206	17	12.11
S.F. Barnes	32	13	99	7	14.14
W. Rhodes	140.5	38	336	22	15.27
G.H. Hirst	79	18	208	9	23.11
F.W. Tate	16	4	51	2	25.50

Australia

Batting	Innings	NO	HS	Runs	Average
C. Hill	8	1	119	258	36.85
V.T. Trumper	8	0	104	247	30.88
H. Trumble	6	2	64*	107	26.75
A.J.Y. Hopkins	7	1	40*	117	19.50
M.A. Noble	7	0	52	129	18.42

Bowling	O	M	R	W	Average
H. Trumble	172.4	55	371	26	14.26
M.A. Noble	127	41	307	14	21.92
A.J.Y. Hopkins	17	5	49	2	24.50
J.V. Saunders	131.1	23	473	18	26.27
E. Jones	39	13	107	3	35.66

Wicket-keepers: A.F.A. Lilley (E) 12 dismissals   J.J. Kelly (A) 6 dismissals

Captains: A.C. MacLaren: batting – 9; 47*; 31, 63; 1, 35; 10, 2
J. Darling: batting – 3; dnb; 0, 0; 51, 37; 3, 15

In the fourth match V.T. Trumper became the first batsman to score a century before lunch on the first morning of a Test, and with R.A. Duff he put on the fastest century opening stand in England v Australia Tests (57 minutes). In the fifth match G.L. Jessop scored a century in 75 minutes, then a record.

5

Edwardian Fortunes

The tour to Australia in 1903–4 was the first to be arranged by the MCC, and MacLaren (surprise, surprise) was at the centre of a controversy about it. He had planned his own tour for that English winter, but because he felt that England's bowling strength was not good enough he had written to Melbourne requesting a delay of a year. Melbourne promptly wrote to MCC asking them to organise a tour, which they did. When it was announced that it was to be captained by Pelham Warner, MacLaren was mightily affronted, and the controversy simmered away for weeks. He did not go, and neither did several other of the leading amateurs. Clearly, then, the batting was not as strong as it might have been, but England had a useful team all the same. Encouraged by Warner's captaincy on his crusade to 'recover the Ashes', some of the players had some very inspired days. Australia too had a new captain for the series; Darling was unavailable, and the leadership of what was still a very good team passed to Monty Noble. For two relatively inexperienced captains they were to prove themselves distinctly adept at the job.

'Plum' Warner is remembered as one of cricket's greatest servants. Perhaps in some people's minds his administrative work may have slightly obscured his achievement as a captain, but in his playing days he was as highly regarded for his leadership qualities as anyone. When he was called on to lead England his experience of captaincy was limited, and his years in charge of Middlesex still lay ahead (from 1908 to 1920 when, for the most part, the county finished near the top of the table, and in his final season a dramatic late surge brought them the Championship). His Test experience was limited, too, for he had played only twice, on both occasions in South Africa; in the first match his century set up England's victory. His batting was neat, balanced, skilful and determined, and though a slightly-built man he was always ready to take on the real quickies. His 29,000 runs included 60 centuries, and if his Test average is not in the front rank he played some fine innings during this tour.

His captaincy was founded on a natural understanding of the fact that even cricketers have problems and disappointments, and his friendly,

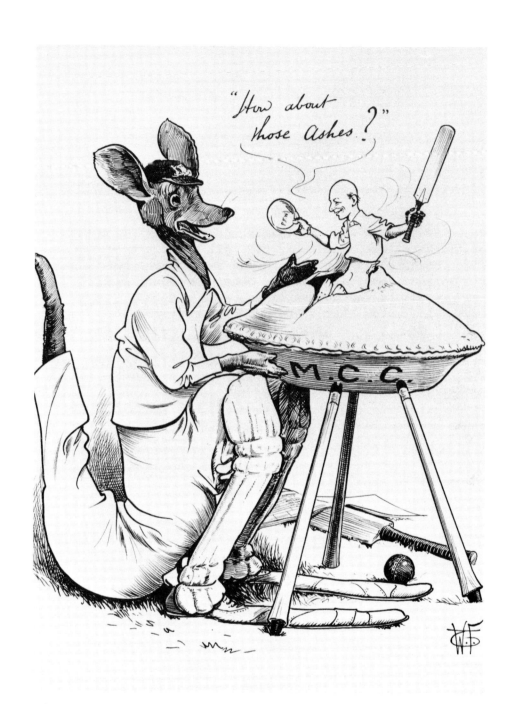

'Plum Pie'. It was Warner who revived the idea of the Ashes, after twenty years in which the term had hardly been mentioned. This cartoon is by William T. Fletcher from the Bystander of 16 December 1904.

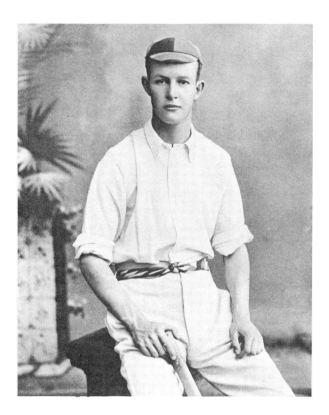

A youthful P.F. Warner, later to become one of cricket's senior statesmen.

fatherly approach brought the best out of his players. Unusually for that period he was a democratic leader, the first touring captain to have his professionals staying in the same hotel as the amateurs. He had been in first-class cricket for nearly ten years and his grasp of tactics was both sound and shrewd. In particular he would pay great attention to detail; opponents were studied carefully, weaknesses and idiosyncrasies noted and exploited – and he was not above listening to good advice when it was offered.

Monty Noble's stature in Australia is no less than Warner's is in England, for his combination of all-round skills and leadership ability has only ever been equalled by Richie Benaud. He worked as a young man in a bank but turned to studying dentistry as he felt it would give him more time to play cricket. Few other sportsmen, one suspects, have returned from an overseas tour with a supply of ready-made dentures and a machine for shaping them to a patient's mouth. A tall, powerful man, he was an orthodox, beautifully controlled batsman with a relaxed stance and enormous powers of concentration who could bat for hours to save a game, as in 1899 when he had the

Old Trafford crowd chanting the Dead March. He could play with great spirit, as thirty-seven centuries – seven of them doubles – showed. Four times he headed the batting averages in Australia, and with Warwick Armstrong he is still the holder of Australia's sixth-wicket record, 428 against Sussex in 1902, of which his share was 284. He found that the softer English wickets made his forward play more risky so he became much more of a back-foot player, drawing praise from *Wisden* by the way he made the change without its affecting his run-flow. He bowled off-spin at a pace that varied from slow to medium, always with great accuracy and skilful control of flight and with a late-swing that brought him many wickets. In 42 Tests he finished just three runs short of 2,000 and took 121 wickets as well as many fine catches, especially at point; and he had that priceless ability to be exactly the man for a crisis.

Monty Noble. Great all-rounder and great captain.

However, it was his captaincy that took him to greatness. He led New South Wales from 1902–3 to 1909–10, a period which saw them very dominant, winning the Sheffield Shield six times. He was made captain of Australia only on the morning of the first Test of the 1903–4 series, and responded to the honour by scoring his only Test century. His first two Tests were lost (and with them the Ashes) but he went on to lead his country fifteen times and win the Ashes twice. In the view of C.B. Fry he was the man to captain an Earth team against Mars. His knowledge of the game was profound, and his faith in his own judgement was usually so well-placed that his men would accept all his decisions, however detrimental to themselves, without demur, knowing that they were unquestionably for the good of the team. As a bowler-captain he was able, like Harry Trott, to emphathise with his bowlers and not overwork the main strikers, who said that his intense determination and great confidence rubbed off on them and moved them to great things. He took the art of field-placing to a level not seen before, developing the ploy of leaving a gap on the off-side to invite a drive at a ball that, if the bowler got it right, could well end up in gully's hands.

Only the highest standards were good enough, and his players under-stood this very well. He had enormous strength of character – his word was law – but he was a disciplinarian only when someone had allowed their standards to slide; he was a kind, fair-minded and tolerant man who enjoyed a joke as much as anyone. He treated his players as sensible and responsible men and expected them to behave as good ambassadors for their country. His magnetic personality and his great cricketing ability meant that he was always popular with them and greatly respected by all his opponents, especially as his standards of fair play were second to none. Ray Robinson tells of Noble's principles, beliefs that would no doubt make some modern players laugh in derision were they to recall them as they yell and wave frantically at the umpire; 'Any member of his side who appealed without justification would be given a reproving look and sometimes a spoken rebuke. As soon as he realised an instinctive appeal was unwar-ranted he would say "No, not out." ' Robinson also tells the story that as Noble was born a military band passed his parents' house, and his mother, hearing the music, prophesied that her son would become famous.

The first Test of the series completed the hat-trick of glorious matches. Arnold took Trumper's wicket with his first ball in Test cricket, and the Australian innings of 285 was then built around the captain's century. At 118 for 4 Braund and Foster – R.E. or 'Tip' of the Foster brotherhood in his maiden Test innings – came together in difficult batting conditions and took the score to 243 overnight. Next day conditions were better and Foster blossomed. Braund got his century, wickets fell cheaply and then Foster put on 115 for the ninth wicket with Relf and 130 for the tenth wicket with Rhodes in just 66 minutes. He was finally out for 287, having set several records including the highest score in Test cricket (lasting for twenty-six years) by which time England had made 577. As if one great innings in a match was not enough, Trumper then produced perhaps the best of all his efforts; and his 185 not out, with a century in just 94 minutes, took Australia to 485 and a lead of 193. There was an unpleasant moment when Hill was judged run out after making 51 and the crowd expressed their displeasure to such an extent that Warner threatened to take his team off the field. Noble persuaded him not to, and the match continued. When England began their second innings, the pitch was wearing and 194 was far from a foregone conclusion, but Hayward and Hirst saw them home with five wickets in hand. If it did not have quite the nerve-shattering tension of the previous two matches the game did at least contain some of the most memorable batting in Test history.

England won the second Test mainly because they won the toss, and after the first day rain made the pitch difficult. Their first innings totalled 315, to which the home team replied with 122. Tyldesley followed 97 in the first innings with 62 in the second as England scraped to 103, batting without the sick Foster. Rhodes then followed 7 for 56 with 8 for 68 to become the first man to take 15 wickets in an Ashes Test – and he had eight catches dropped! England won by 185 runs. This was the low-point of Noble's captaincy; in the next Test the corner was turned. Hill became the first batsman to 2,000 Test runs, Trumper scored yet another century and Australia made 388. With only four specialist batsmen England could make only 245, to which Australia replied with a century from Gregory and a total of 351. England never got anywhere near what was asked of them.

The fourth Test was significant in that it was the first one to be won by an important contribution from a googly bowler. Rain kept the scores low, Noble taking seven wickets in England's 249, to which Australia replied with 131. Another 210 from England left Australia with a target of 329 on an improved pitch, but Bosanquet struck with six wickets, including 5 for 12 at one stage, and the Ashes had returned to England. The last Test followed a similar pattern with the sides reversed: 247 to Australia, with eight wickets to Braund, to which England replied on a rain-affected pitch with the princely total of 61, Cotter taking six wickets in his second Test with some hostile bowling. By their second innings England needed over 300 and were never in contention, but the happy ending was provided by

Hugh Trumble. Playing in his last first-class match he took 7 for 28 including a hat-trick, while Noble emulated Giffen and completed the Test double.

Thus Warner won the Ashes in his only series as captain. He had shown great tactical skill and was widely praised for the way in which he had inspired his men. In 1911–12 he again went to Australia as captain only to fall ill soon after arrival and miss the rest of the tour – but it is for his work with the MCC that he is mostly remembered. He sat on the committee for nearly sixty years, was Deputy Secretary during the war, was elected President in 1950 and two years before his death he became the first life Vice-President in the club's history. He served as Chairman of Selectors and was the manager on one tour to Australia during which he and the captain, a chap named Jardine, did not always see eye to eye. He founded the *Cricketer* and edited it for many years, was cricket correspondent of the *Morning Post*, and in his spare time he wrote or edited about twenty books on the game. The Warner Stand at Lord's is a memorial to the man Christopher Martin-Jenkins called 'the very reverend dean of Cricket's Cathedral'.

For the 1905 visit by the Australians there were three candidates for the England captaincy – Warner, MacLaren and Jackson. Jackson had been first choice for the previous tour, but had been unable to go (in fact he played all his Tests at home) but as he was now available, and as the selectors were always glad of the opportunity to put one over on MacLaren, Jackson was appointed. There were some dissenting voices, but with Providence smiling benignly throughout, Jackson delivered the goods – with a vengeance.

Most of the great Edwardian amateurs were batsmen but The Honourable Francis Stanley Jackson – 'Jacker' to many people – was a genuine all-rounder of very high class. He played for Harrow (where his fag was a lad named Churchill) at Lord's when only fifteen, captained Cambridge for two seasons and began playing for Yorkshire while still at university. In seventeen years with Yorkshire he was only able to play one full season, but when he did he scored over 1500 runs and took over 100 wickets. While still at Cambridge he played twice for England and scored 91 and 103 (he should have played three times, but he withdrew to play in a crucial match for Yorkshire and help them win their first Championship, a decision that did not endear him to everybody) and over the years he scored a total of five Test centuries to finish with an average of nearly 49.

In style his batting was fit to rank beside any of his great contemporaries, those products of the public schools and universities where batsmanship

Hon. F.S. Jackson, the radiant gleam in England's Golden Age.

was refined and polished until it was brought to a perfection of beauty. Timing the ball sweetly he would drive and cut with much grace and strength, but as ever with these batsmen the attacking stroke-play was founded on classical defence so that he could cope just as well with a treacherous pitch as a true one. Renowned as one of the most adaptable and confident of batsmen he meticulously put into practice the old saw about playing each ball on its merits. He bowled fast-medium with a naturally easy, flowing action and took many wickets with his ability to spin the ball in from the off and vary his pace with great subtlety. Almost six feet tall and with a fine physique he looked every inch an outstanding athlete.

He had played in fifteen Tests before this series, but, apart from the small matter of leading his men during the Boer War, he had not had a great deal of captaincy experience. However, he proved himself to be a natural leader of the best kind, with a good temperament, sound judgement and the precious ability to rise to the occasion. Allied to his cricketing skills was a fine brain that gave him a good grasp of tactics, an ability to inspire his men to play to their best, and a belief which he communicated to all that cricket is meant to be enjoyed. Being fully aware of the dangers that can spring from dissension in the ranks he made sure that MacLaren played an active role in the leadership, always taking him with him to inspect the wicket and consulting him over any number of matters – and he publicly expressed his gratitude to MacLaren afterwards. His generous, friendly nature meant that it was easy for his team to be a contented unit, and a number of the players wrote that they looked back on that series as an especially happy one.

England had a strong team that was similar to that of the previous rubber, but the Australians were weaker than they had been for some time. Darling returned to resume the captaincy – by a remarkable coincidence both captains had been born on 21 November 1870 – but he was without Trumble, who had retired, and such bowlers as Saunders and Jones, both of whom had a question mark against their action. The two main batsmen, Trumper and Hill, both struggled for form and to round off their misfortunes Jackson won all five tosses and was lucky with the weather.

Jackson began his captaincy with a duck as England, on a decent wicket, could do no better than 196. He atoned, though, by taking 5 for 52 and restricting Australia to 221 with the help of an injury to Trumper. He atoned even further in the second innings by scoring 82 not out to go with MacLaren's century as England rattled up 426, Darling being reduced to telling Armstrong to bowl leg-theory to try and contain the runs. Jackson's declaration gave Australia, minus Trumper, five hours to survive, but the

A postcard of the 1905 Australian touring team. Top row, left to right, C. Hill, C.E. McLeod, J.J. Kelly, D.R.A. Gehrs. Middle row, left to right, R.A. Duff, S.E. Gregory, J. Darling (captain), M.A. Noble, V. Trumper. Bottom row, left to right, A.J. Hopkins, P.M. Newland, W.P. Howell, W.W. Armstrong, A. Cotter, F. Laver. Between them, Darling, Noble, Hill, Gregory and Armstrong led Australia in fifty-one Ashes Tests.

day belonged to Bosanquet. He produced his finest Test figures – 8 for 107 – but it is important to note that as the wickets were falling McLeod ran to the pavilion to ask Darling if he should appeal against the light, an appeal that would almost certainly have been successful. Darling said no; his team had been outplayed and should pay the penalty.

The Lord's Test was washed out on the third day with England on top. In the next match Jackson scored the first Test century at Headingley, his home ground, but after England led by over 100 on first innings he possibly delayed his second innings declaration rather too long as Armstrong again tried to contain the score with his slow leg-side bowling. Australia lost seven wickets but were able to hold on for a draw.

Old Trafford then saw more England fortune with the weather. Batting first on a dead pitch Jackson scored another hundred as his team made 446, but overnight rain made the wicket difficult. Even so Australia did themselves no favours by attacking the bowling with gusto, and duly got themselves out for only 197. Following on on a pitch that was even worse they seemed not to learn from their first innings mistakes and fell for 169 by lunch on the third day. Since it rained shortly after the match had finished they must have regretted not digging in for a draw. The final Test then took on the same pattern as the third. On a lovely pitch Fry scored a beautiful century and England made 430, whereupon Duff did the same in fine style for Australia as they made 363. Then it was Tyldesley's turn for a hundred, but the visitors were able to hang on for their draw. Having lost the toss in all five Tests and again in the MCC match, Darling greeted Jackson at the Scarborough Festival stripped to the waist and suggested a wrestling match for choice of innings. Jackson replied that he would depute Hirst to represent his country, Darling thought better of it, and when the toss was made Jackson did not even look at the coin. He won, of course.

He also topped the batting aggregates and averages and the bowling averages, so it could be said that he finished his Test career with something of a flourish. His public career, however, was far from over: for eleven years he sat in parliament, he became President of MCC, served as Chairman of Selectors and became Governor of Bengal, where he narrowly escaped being assassinated. Cricket was never more than a very pleasurable sideline amongst what he considered the more important aspects of life, and he no doubt felt that overseeing the peace and prosperity of Bengal was rather more important than hitting a ball with a piece of wood. One suspects that there will always be some people who will disagree with him.

His funeral in 1947 produced one of cricket's gentlest anecdotes. The Bishop of Knaresborough said afterwards that there were hundreds of cricketers present 'and as I gazed down on the rapt faces of that vast congregation, I could see how they revered him . . . how they reverenced him as though he were the Almighty, though, of course, infinitely stronger on the leg-side.'

Darling played on in Australia for a little longer and then retired to his sheep farm in Tasmania. At the age of fifty he was elected to Tasmania's parliament as an Independent, and stayed there for the rest of his life, a much respected figure who had led his country to some of her finest victories. When he wasn't scoring runs or farming sheep he was bringing up children – fifteen of them.

If the Australian team for that series had been rather below strength, so too was the England team for the next one. They were without the likes of Hayward, Hirst, MacLaren, Tyldesley and Lilley – and the man who was to be their most successful batsman, George Gunn, was not originally in the team but happened to be in Australia for health reasons. Australia, captained once again by Noble, showed some changes from the previous series but were undoubtedly favourites to win since the English batting was not reckoned to be over-strong. England's appointed captain was Arthur Jones, but shortly before the first Test he went down with a severe chest infection and the leadership passed to a rather reluctant Frederick Fane.

Fane, from Ireland, was an attractive batsman with a good range of strokes who played mostly off the front foot. If his star shines but dimly now we should remember the others who were there to eclipse him; in another age he might well have achieved greater prominence. He played for Essex on and off for nearly thirty years, captaining them from 1904 to 1906, and scoring twenty-five centuries in his career. Leadership did not come naturally to him, though, and, strange as it may seem to an outsider who has no real idea of the problems and pressures involved, he never had any desire to captain his country. This says much for his integrity as he must

F.L. Fane, the Irishman who deputised a little reluctantly for A.O. Jones during the 1907–8 tour.

have realised that he lacked some of the attributes for the job, but as he won two out of the five Tests he captained (including those against South Africa) he obviously had some skills at it. However, his captaincy did suffer from the fact that his best fielding positions were in the deep; although a very good outfielder, the boundary is hardly the best place from which to control your team's fortunes.

Some Ashes series, such as in 1902, have been savoured by posterity for the quality or the excitement of some of the matches. The 1907–8 series contained two matches of nail-shredding tension, but in England at least they are rarely mentioned, perhaps because the last three Tests ended with distinct advantages to Australia or perhaps because none of the great Edwardian amateurs took part. The series is noteworthy as the one in which Jack Hobbs made his début, it contained one remarkable partnership and, with a bit more luck for England and some better captaincy, the result might even have been different.

Gunn was called in to make his début in the first Test after Jones had been taken ill, and responded by making a century. The decision to bring him in had been Fane's, but he made another that probably cost him the match; he played the reserve wicket-keeper Young, the first to wear spectacles in a Test, instead of the first choice Humphries, since he was supposed to be a better batsman and had kept well in a recent game. Young was to have a poor match and make some mistakes that were crucial in a close game. England's first innings made 273 and Australia replied with 300. Gunn again top-scored for England as they too scored 300, leaving the non-mathematicians with an easy task for once. Overnight rain then turned a good pitch into a dead one, and Australia struggled towards their target. The seventh wicket fell with 89 still needed, the eighth with 55 needed. Hazlitt joined Cotter and, not without alarms, they approached ever nearer to 274. There were some hectic scramblings, and more than once they nearly ran themselves out, but they finally made it and Australia won by two wickets. Fane's principal error, without doubt, was to under-bowl Rhodes and Crawford; Rhodes had taken 177 wickets the previous summer and was given only twelve overs in the match, while Crawford had only thirteen. At one point in the Australian first innings Hill asked Rhodes why he was in the side, and was told 'I'm in, I suppose, for my singing, Clem.' It was a match that England really should have won.

Fate then decreed that in the second match the same situation should apply in reverse. Australia led off with 266 with Crawford, given a decent bowl, taking five wickets. England replied with 382 thanks to a century from Hutchings and 83 from Hobbs on his début. Several of the Australians then put together good scores and they reached 397, setting a target of 282. Everyone except Gunn contributed some runs, Fane top-scoring with 50, but wickets fell steadily and 39 were still wanted when the ninth wicket went, leaving Barnes and Fielder at the crease. Like Hazlitt and Cotter before them, they chipped away at the target and reached it, but when the scores were level they got the winning run only because Hazlitt threw at the stumps and missed; had he thrown to the keeper, Test cricket's first tie would have happened much earlier than it did.

The third Test was played in intense Adelaide heat. Australia made 285 and England replied with 363, Gunn's 65 being made despite blisters that formed on his hands and then broke in the heat. By around lunchtime on the fourth day Australia were 180 for 7, only 102 runs on, when Hartigan, playing in his first Test, and Hill, who had been suffering from influenza, came together. Hill was so weak that at times he seemed hardly able to stand up, and he vomited frequently, but Hartigan helped him on and with the aid of three spilled catches (before many runs had been scored) the partnership began to unfold. When it was broken the following morning it had put on 243, a figure that remains Australia's highest eighth-wicket stand in all Tests; Hill finished with 160 and Hartigan with 116. Faced with having to score 429 England capitulated and lost by 245 runs.

A.O. Jones was sufficiently recovered to lead the side for the first time in the fourth Test. Fane dropped out to accommodate him, but although he proved to be a more inspiring captain, especially in Australia's first innings, he could make little difference to the result. Jones was normally an opening batsman who was, on his day, quite brilliant, but who was also noted for having a streak of impetuosity. He played in twelve Tests but never did himself justice, never managing a higher innings than 34. He was a useful leg-break bowler, but more importantly was an extremely fine all-round fielder – perhaps the best England produced before 1914 – who in his school-days had invented the gully position. He had been the captain of Nottinghamshire since 1900, leading them to the Championship the previous summer, and was widely regarded as one of the best of the county captains. His illness meant, of course, that he didn't get a proper crack at this series, but he seems to have been something of a worrier, an indecisive man who would get bogged down in administrative details, at least on tour. He was not the ideal leader to inspire a recovery from 2–1 down with two to play.

Yet he made a good enough start. In that fourth Test England suffered the frustration of putting out Australia for 214 on an excellent pitch, well handled and inspired by Jones, only to have their own innings ruined by

A.O. Jones. Little success as Test batsman or captain, but perhaps the greatest fielder before the First World War.

rain. Hobbs gave a brilliant display of wet-wicket batting but he was on his own; the last seven wickets could accumulate no more than 17 runs, and England were all out for 105. At 77 for 5 Australia were not much better off, but Armstrong came to the rescue with his first Test century and they eventually reached 385. Once again England lost heart in the face of a large target, and Australia won by 308 runs. Similarly in the fifth Test England seemed to be on top after they had put Australia in, dismissed them for 137 and then scored 281 themselves, with another century from Gunn. The big Australian disappointment of the series had been Trumper – a succession of low scores had even included a 'pair' – but now, unfortunately for England, he at last came good. Dropped when he had scored only one, he went on to add a further 165, helping to take his team to 422, their fourth consecutive substantial second innings score. Needing 279 England watched the rain fall yet again and were soon reduced to 87 for 6; the tail wagged a bit, but they finished 49 short. If they had had all the luck of the 1905 series, things had evened out a little after this one.

The team which Noble brought for the 1909 tour appeared before the series to be rather a weak one, lacking the batting of Darling and Hill and apparently not over-blessed with bowlers. Macartney, Bardsley and Ransford were all new to English crowds, but they made sure they would be remembered. England, perhaps surprisingly, made MacLaren captain after Jackson had said he would not be available – surprisingly because he had not been in any great batting form and had not been in the best of health either, with recurring rheumatic problems. However, he was still regarded as the best captain in the country, and there was no opposition to his appointment. Except for a famous happening in the final Test, his captaincy was generally praised.

England's team for the first Test was a strong one, and Australia were not helped by having had many of their early matches affected by rain. Most of the first day was lost to rain but then on a pitch that was not really difficult Blythe and Hirst put Australia out for 74. England could manage only 121 in reply, but then clever field placings and some marvellous catching kept the visitors down to 151, Blythe and Hirst taking all twenty wickets. With 105 wanted MacLaren dropped down the order and sent out Hobbs and Fry, both of whom had been out first ball the day before. A typical MacLaren move, it paid off as England won by ten wickets.

For a variety of reasons – illness, injury, selectoral obtuseness and so forth – England's team for the Lord's Test was much changed, and the bowling in particular was very unbalanced with four medium-pacers and little else. Noble won the toss and put England in, and had it not been for King, playing in his only Test, their 269 would have been quite a lot less. Ransford then scored his only Test century thanks to being dropped three times, and Australia took a lead of 81. Needing to bat for most of the last day to ensure a draw, England promptly collapsed to 41 for 6, and struggled to 121. Australia soon polished off the deficit. MacLaren offered to resign after this defeat but was persuaded to carry on, managing to ensure some rather more sensible selections for the next game. 'We can and will beat them with ordinary luck,' he wrote.

He never was all that lucky, MacLaren. Hardly an hour had passed before Jessop, in throwing the ball awkwardly, ruptured some of his back muscles so badly that he played no more cricket till next season. He was badly missed, for England's batting was in woeful shape. Having dismissed Australia for 188 they failed by six runs to reach the same figure. A score of 207 from Australia should not have left England with an impossible target, but they managed to set the record for their lowest ever score at Headingley, 87. Probably not even Jessop would have made that much difference. The fourth game was then drawn but it did contain one notable statistic. Ask an enthusiast which overseas bowler has the best innings analysis for a Test in England and it is likely to be some time before the name Frank Laver is mentioned. After Australia had scored 147 Laver took 8 for 31 and held England, without Jessop and Hobbs, to 119. A good deal of time was lost to rain, though, and Noble batted on through much of the last day, leaving England no chance of forcing a win. Since this ensured that he retained the Ashes it was perfectly justifiable – but this of course was Edwardian England, and he was criticised for not 'playing the game'. One can, without too much trouble, imagine his private response.

Because of his occasional high-handedness and his imperious, abrasive character, controversy had followed MacLaren throughout his career. Almost inevitably it reached something of a zenith in his last Test, as though the press and everyone else realised that this would be their last chance to have a go at him. The bowling attack, for which he was held responsible, lacked a fast bowler but included D.W. Carr, a googly bowler who had only just made his first-class début at the age of 37. The plan was that he should act as a secret weapon – and he did. After seven overs he had taken 3 for 19, but as he lacked another strike bowler MacLaren kept him on – and on – and on. With the aid of some dropped catches, including a straightforward chance to MacLaren, Bardsley made 136, Australia made 325 and Carr's figures were 5 for 146. England actually exceeded that, but when Australia batted again Bardsley became the first man to score a century in each innings of a Test. Once again Carr was over-bowled, and he finished his only Test with 7 for 282 off 69 overs. The match petered out into a draw, but MacLaren was pilloried for his use of Carr. It was a sad end for the old warrior.

Some of the team selections, admittedly, had been quite astonishing, but Noble had emulated Jackson in winning the toss all five times and very little had gone right for MacLaren after the first match, often through no fault of his own. The fact that his captaincy ended in a hail of criticism must have hurt such a proud man very deeply, and it is pleasing to recall that fourteen years later he achieved a famous victory over Armstrong's team with a group of amateurs who had not played in any of the summer's Tests – and that he was able to say, along with a well-known singer, that he did it his way. After so many vicissitudes he deserved one glowing triumph.

It was the end of the Test line too for Monty Noble. Having won eight of his fifteen Tests as captain and taken the Ashes twice he was able to look back at the record books with rather more satisfaction than MacLaren. Both did some journalism in their time, and were also involved in radio broadcasting at a time when this was a rarity. Both died during the Second World War, by which time Test cricket had long since shed any last vestiges of the innocence of its early years and was well advanced along its path to becoming the grim business that it can so often be today.

By this time Australia had won three series by the margin of four Tests to one, a feat England were yet to achieve. Their captain when they did so was a man who had not played Test cricket before, and who led the side only because the appointed captain fell ill early in the tour. The hero of this particular *Boys' Own* story is Johnny Douglas, the setting is Australia 1911–12.

Pelham Warner was the appointed captain, and he took with him a team that was short on amateur players but long on cricketing talent. The only other amateurs were Douglas and Frank Foster, but there were some very fine professional players in both batting and bowling departments. Australia were more or less the same team that had won in England two years earlier, except that they had lost Noble and Macartney did not play until the last match. They were led by the very experienced Clem Hill, playing in what would be his last series.

Clem Hill, legendary batsman for whom things went very wrong as an Ashes captain.

Warner had been unwell on the boat journey but played in the first match and scored 151, which proved to be his only innings in Australia. No vice-captain had been appointed, and so when he was taken ill he had to decide who should take over. Both Douglas and Foster (not one of the Fostershire brotherhood) had captained their counties for the first time the previous summer, and Foster had done so well that he led Warwickshire to their first Championship after years in the doldrums. But he was only twenty-two, whereas Douglas was twenty-nine and considerably more experienced – and he too had moved Essex several places up the table. Douglas, therefore, got the vote.

His Test career was to fall into two very distinct parts in a way that perhaps no other captain's ever has. His initials were J.W.H.T. and it was during this tour that a spectator christened him 'Johnny Won't Hit Today'. It was appropriate for a good deal of his batting, for if the situation demanded it he could be the dourest of blockers; unfortunately, he also had a habit of blocking pretty dourly when the occasion didn't demand it. Yet he could hit out too, and although he was not the master of every stroke in

J.W.H.T. Douglas. Few captains have been so well acquainted with the 'twin impostors' of triumph and disaster.

the book, and was not all that attractive a player to watch, he didn't score 24,500 runs, including 26 centuries, by blocking dourly all the time. It never seems to have occurred to anyone, though, to apply the 'Johnny Won't Hit Today' to his fast-medium bowling; with his enormous stamina he could bowl for very long periods without losing speed or accuracy, and his bowling was widely respected. Almost 1900 wickets at 23 apiece tell their own story, and show that Douglas was a very fine all-round cricketer. In fact he was a very fine all-round sportsman, for he not only played for England as an amateur footballer but he won the Olympic middleweight boxing gold medal in 1908. The boxing connection showed through in that he was one of cricket's really great fighters, a man who would never stint his effort no matter how bleak the situation. He expected his men to do the same.

There is a famous head-and-shoulders photograph of Douglas in which he is gazing piercingly at the viewer, everything about him, from the black hair parted down the middle to the firm mouth and the square jaw, suggesting toughness and determination; a man with whom one argument would be more than enough. Certainly the men who played under him tended to agree, for he was a strong authoritarian whose word was law and who would brook no misdemeanour, but he was also friendly, kind and humorous with it, and it didn't matter if a player was not producing results so long as he was trying his hardest. With such a strong personality his occasional moments of tactlessness or insensitivity alienated him from a few players, but the great majority of them found him a fine leader, fair, honest and, as long as they had given their all for him, loyal and supportive to them. He had a habit of testing people's attitudes and commitment in various ways, and if they measured up to his expectations he would prove a staunch ally. If, however, they were not quite on his wavelength and did not respond in the way he expected, he seemed to be unable to understand that their way might be just as good as his. This was a definite flaw in his leadership qualities, and it cost him good relations with a number of players. He was noted, though, as an excellent tutor and encourager of young players who showed him that they really wanted to succeed, and there were many prominent players who were only too pleased to acknowledge their debt to him.

If Douglas still had his reputation to make, Clem Hill had made his years ago. Apart from missing the 1909 tour to England he had been a fixture in the Australian team since 1897–8, and was undoubtedly one of the greatest of all left-handers; his Test record was even slightly better than Victor Trumper's, and he held the record for the most Test runs until Jack Hobbs beat it in 1926. His stance at the wicket was not noted for its beauty as he held the bat low down on the handle, but he was very fleet of foot, strong all round the wicket and loved to punish short bowling. Like any stroke-maker what he wanted to do was attack, but he also relished a good backs-to-the-wall situation and saved his team on any number of occasions. He had captained South Australia since 1901–2 and recently won the Sheffield Shield, and had led the national team the previous season at home to South Africa, winning the series 4–1 – but Hill's last rubber was to be an unhappy one.

Like other great players he was to find that the responsibility of captaincy was a heavy burden, but unlike some of them he was not blamed by his team for the defeats that they suffered. Hill was a cheerful character liked by almost everyone, and his men had great faith in his ability, experience and knowledge of the game. He had, after all, played under Trott, Darling and Noble, and a good deal of their wisdom should have rubbed off. No doubt it had, but somehow he was not able to follow in their footsteps. Against a background of strikes which threatened problems for the Melbourne ground, there were other unpleasant events taking place behind the scenes in Australian cricketing politics, and they must have unsettled him greatly.

Yet for the first game the problems were Douglas's. Having lost the toss Douglas upset Barnes by not giving him the new ball but taking it himself, so that the sensitive Barnes felt put out and did not bowl well. With a hundred from Trumper Australia made 447 and England responded with 318, the captain not troubling the scorers. More solid batting from Australia left England with 438 for victory, and they fell well short. The Australian hero was Hordern, the googly bowler playing in his first Test against England, who took twelve wickets. Warner, who was not able to see the match but wrote a report based on what he was told by the players, said that Douglas was not in control of the side, despite having had several games to become familiar with them; in particular it was felt that his field-placings had been none too perceptive. He kept the captaincy for the next Test only after a lengthy discussion.

And then suddenly everything went England's way, thanks mainly to the most famous opening spell of bowling in Ashes Tests. Despite having felt unwell before the game, Sydney Barnes took three wickets in his first over, described by Hill as the most torrid he had ever witnessed. After nine overs he had taken four wickets for three runs, after eleven overs five wickets for six runs. Australia did manage to get to 184, but England had turned the corner. Hearne became the youngest century-maker for England against Australia as they made 265. Foster and Barnes then dismissed Australia to give England a target of 219. Hobbs's first hundred against Australia ensured a comfortable victory. In the next Test more fine bowling from Foster and Barnes, who put Australia out for 133 on a good pitch, and fine batting from Hobbs, who made 187 to help England to 501, combined to set up another victory. Australia came back well, with 98 from Hill (his fifth score between 96 and 99 against England) helping them to 476, but again the runs were comfortably polished off.

When the Australian selectors met to pick the team for the fourth Test one of them, Peter McAlister, was very critical of Hill's captaincy. After he persisted in his insults Hill hit him, and the two men had a fight – hardly ideal preparation for a captain trying to get back into a Test series. We can never know the real effect that it had on Hill, but it cannot have done much good for his confidence. Because of the strikes it was not even certain that the ground would be available, so this must have been a worrying time all round. Hill was not helped by the fact that Douglas's stock had soared, and there was much praise for the way in which he was inspiring his men and handling his bowling and field-placings.

On winning the toss for the first time in the series Douglas put Australia in and Barnes and Foster bowled them out. Hobbs and Rhodes then exceeded Australia's 191 by a considerable margin, putting on what is still the highest opening stand in Ashes Tests of 323, and setting England on course for 589. The great partnership was not a chanceless one, but it was scored in only 268 minutes. Overnight rain then spiced the wicket up a bit and Douglas took advantage of it, putting himself on early and taking 5 for 46, his best Test figures. Fittingly it was he who took the wicket which gave England the Ashes, and the subsequent celebrations included winning the final Test as well.

England took a good first innings lead and set Australia 363 to win, but they fell 70 short. Woolley's hundred in the first innings was notable as the first by an English left-hander against Australia; it is remarkable that it should have taken well over thirty years. The real English heroes of the series, though, were Barnes and Foster, with thirty-four and thirty-two wickets respectively in conditions that often favoured the batsmen, Foster also contributing 226 runs into the bargain. Their bowling in this rubber has gone down as some of the finest ever seen from a touring team in Australia. Douglas's fifteen wickets had given them invaluable support, and he returned home a hero praised by everyone for his performances, his astute captaincy, his sound judgement and his excellent rapport with his players. He insisted that he had had much help from Warner and the senior players – and Warner has certainly received plenty of kudos for the way he controlled affairs and advised Douglas from his sick-bed – but he pulled off a splendid achievement nonetheless.

That this was Hill's and Trumper's last series was due to the internal political manoeuvrings of the men who would control Australian cricket. A Board of Control had been set up in 1905 and in its early years appears not to have distinguished itself by its integrity. A rather convoluted story boils down to the fact that in the past the touring team's manager had been selected by the players themselves from their squads, whereas the Board now wanted to send an external manager and to pay him out of tour takings that would otherwise have gone to the players. A group of six players therefore wrote to the Board, pointing out that under the regulations this was illegal, and if the Board persisted in its course they would withdraw from the trip to England in 1912. The six were Hill, Trumper, Armstrong, Cotter, Ransford and Carter, very much the backbone of the team, and as neither side would back down, the team that went to England was a very weak one. It meant a sad end to Hill's Test career after so much glory. He went on playing until 1922–3, after which much of his later life was devoted to horse-racing in various official capacities. He died at the age of 68 as a result of falling from a Melbourne tram.

The year 1912 saw Test cricket's one and only triangular tournament, a good idea that fell horribly flat partly because of the weather and partly because the Australian and South African teams were well below full strength. The fact that Douglas was not only passed over for the England captaincy but was not even in the team shows how cricket was conducted at the time. English touring teams were very rarely composed of the best players in the country as several of the best amateurs would have other commitments which prevented them from touring. Over the years there were a number of players who had a good tour, yet could not find a place in the next home series, but none did it as spectacularly as Douglas. The captaincy was given for the first time to C.B. Fry; the leadership of Australia, meanwhile, had passed to Syd Gregory.

Fry is one of the most legendary of British sportsmen, and it seems surprising that he captained England in only this one season. Apart from being a brilliant classical scholar at Oxford, he held the world long jump record for 21 years and played soccer for England. In 1902 he played for Southampton in the FA Cup Final (which they lost) and then, two days later, scored 82 at the Oval. Altogether a striking character, Fry was a razor-sharp talker who could dominate any discussion (one wonders what it must have been like when he and MacLaren were in full flow together). He was the writer of a number of cricket books and the editor of *C.B. Fry's*

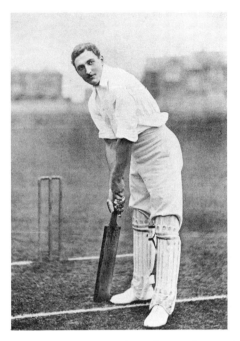 

(Left)   C.B. Fry. He achieved many things in his life, even if the throne of Albania did elude him.   (Right)   Syd Gregory. Captaincy of a weak Australian team in 1912 meant a sad end to a fine career.

Magazine, stood as a Liberal candidate for Parliament and worked with Ranji on the League of Nations. Most important of all for him, he commanded the training ship TS *Mercury* on the Hamble for nearly forty years. The famous legend has it, too, that he was offered the crown of Albania, but the truth of this seems to be that during a session of the League of Nations an Albanian bishop visited Ranji and Fry and made it known that anyone, preferably English, who would be willing to give £10,000 a year to his country could well find himself as its monarch. Fry, of course, had no such sum; Ranji probably did, but he didn't want to lose Fry's help as his adviser in the League of Nations, and so the idea fizzled out. But the biographical note that finishes with the words 'he was also offered the throne of Albania' has an impact that is pretty hard to beat.

As a batsman, he was more of a scientist than an artist, applying an academic mind to the technique needed to reach the top; his splendid fitness and great powers of concentration enabled him to score nearly 31,000 runs in his career at an average of 50, finishing with 94 centuries. In 1901 six of those centuries were in consecutive innings, a record that has been equalled but never exceeded. He finished top of the English batting averages six times, but his Test record does not really match up to this. He scored two splendid centuries but had a good many failures too, and finished with a Test average of 'only' 32. He played for Sussex alongside the great Ranji – from whom he was happy to admit that he learned a lot – forming perhaps the most glistering of all the Golden Age's combinations. No doubt there were days when the gleam was dulled, but it is a harmless enough pastime for us to look back (through spectacles tinged with soft mellow sunlight) and try to imagine what it must have been like to see the two of them in their glory, the classical Fry at one end and the romantic Ranji at the other.

In 1904 Fry took over the captaincy from Ranji and held it for five seasons, until his work on the *Mercury* caused him to move to Hampshire. During this time the county enjoyed mixed fortunes, and for all his sporting prowess he has not gone down as one of the great captains. He was appointed for only the first match of the tournament but told the selectors that it would have to be all or nothing, and they duly made it all. He was not without his critics as the matches progressed, especially during the rain-reduced first game against Australia when he hardly bowled Woolley at all. *Wisden* found this unintelligible, but Fry, realising that the game could not be won, held Woolley back for later in the series to use as a surprise weapon, a policy that paid off very well in the last match.

Syd Gregory has various claims to fame. One is that he was born in a cottage on the site of the present Sydney Cricket Ground; another that he was the first Australian to follow his father into Test cricket, his father Ned having played in the original Test (and also built the first proper scoreboard at Sydney). Other claims to fame are that at 5 feet 5 inches he was one of the shortest players Australia has ever had; his fifty-eight Test appearances remained a record for forty-four years and fifty-two Ashes Tests remain a record still; he was almost certainly the best cover fieldsman to come out of Australia before the First World War and he was a rather useful batsman with four very fine Test centuries to his name. He had first played against England twenty-two years earlier, barely missing any Tests since, and with the 1912 tour he equalled Blackham's record of eight visits to England. As a batsman his speedy footwork and strong wrists more than made up for any lack of inches, and he was noted as one of the best hookers of his day. With a full range of strokes his style was one of text-book orthodoxy, unostentatious and neat – to match his appearance. He was a modest, kind and friendly man, an easy companion who enjoyed a social evening.

Yet fortune did not always smile on him. His income from cricket enabled him to buy a shop in Sydney, but a succession of incompetent and dishonest partners meant that while he was on tour the business went bankrupt and he had to take a clerical job. Towards the end of his playing days the rift between the leading players and the Board meant that his career ended on a note of defeat and sadness. Admittedly it also meant that he at last achieved the captaincy of his country, but for all his qualities he was not really a leader and the tour was a big disappointment. The team was so weakened by the loss of the six leading players that it would have taken a very fine captain to salvage much from the wreckage.

He tried to lead by example but his form in the Tests was wretched, and although his experience meant that he had all the tactical knowledge, his easy-going nature meant that he was unable to instil the discipline that many of the players needed; there were reports of excessive drinking and general bad behaviour reminiscent of the years before Trott had taken over. His lack of control meant that he would allow a situation to drift away from him all too easily, sometimes continuing with bowlers who were not taking wickets simply because he hoped that their luck would change. When these various points are combined with the fact that Australia were simply short on Test-level playing ability, one hopes they were grateful to the South Africans for sending an even weaker team.

Australia started the tournament well enough by beating South Africa by an innings, a match notable for containing Test cricket's only double hat-trick. Matthews took three wickets in each innings on the same afternoon, all of them without assistance. England then also beat South Africa by an innings, after which the first England–Australia game was spoiled by the weather. The second round of matches paralleled the first, Australia and England both beating South Africa and then losing much of their game to rain. For the third Australia–South Africa game the weather again intervened, making it the only game South Africa did not lose. England then beat South Africa in a low-scoring match on a wet pitch, after which it was announced that the last game would be a 'timeless' one, the first such Test in England. Because of a wet pitch Fry refused to start the game on time and so was barracked when he came in to bat. England made 245, mainly thanks to Hobbs and Woolley, and in their reply Australia went from 90 for 2 to 111 all out on a drying pitch. Fry then scored a splendid 79 on a pitch that was still difficult to help set Australia a target of 310. Woolley took another five wickets to finish with 10 for 49 to add to his first innings 62, as the visitors were all out for 65. Because of the barracking Fry refused to go out on the balcony to receive the cheers, and when Ranji said 'Now, Charles, be your noble self,' he replied 'This is not one of my noble days.' It was his last gesture in Test cricket.

There was something almost prophetic in the way the Golden Age drew towards its end in an ill-fated tournament that was ruined by the weather at a time when, according to popular mythology, the sun always shone. There would be precious little sunshine for English cricket for a long time to come.

1903–4	Sydney	A 285, 485	E 577, 194–5	E 5 wkts
	Melbourne	E 315, 103	A 122, 111	E 185 runs
	Adelaide	A 388, 351	E 245, 278	A 216 runs
	Sydney	E 249, 210	A 131, 171	E 157 runs
	Melbourne	A 247, 133	E 61, 101	A 218 runs
1905	Trent Bridge	E 196, 426–5d	A 221, 188	E 213 runs
	Lord's	E 282, 151–5	A 181	Drawn
	Headingley	E 301, 295–5d	A 195, 224–7	Drawn
	Old Trafford	E 446	A 197, 169	E inns 80 runs
	Oval	E 430, 261–6d	A 363, 124–4	Drawn
1907–8	Sydney	E 273, 300	A 300, 275–8	A 2 wkts
	Melbourne	A 266, 397	E 382, 282–9	E 1 wkt
	Adelaide	A 285, 506	E 363, 183	A 245 runs
	Melbourne	A 214, 385	E 105, 186	A 308 runs
	Sydney	A 137, 422	E 281, 229	A 49 runs
1909	Edgbaston	A 74, 151	E 121, 105–0	E 10 wkts
	Lord's	E 269, 121	A 350, 41–1	A 9 wkts
	Headingley	A 188, 207	E 182, 87	A 126 runs
	Old Trafford	A 147, 279–9d	E 119, 108–3	Drawn
	Oval	A 325, 339–5d	E 352, 104–3	Drawn
1911–12	Sydney	A 447, 308	E 318, 291	A 146 runs
	Melbourne	A 184, 299	E 265, 219–2	E 8 wkts
	Adelaide	A 133, 476	E 501, 112–3	E 7 wkts
	Melbourne	A 191, 173	E 589	E inns 225 runs
	Sydney	E 324, 214	A 176, 292	E 70 runs
1912	Lord's	E 310–7d	A 282–7	Drawn
	Old Trafford	E 203	A 14–0	Drawn
	Oval	E 245, 175	A 111, 65	E 244 runs

1903–4

England

Batting	Innings	NO	HS	Runs	Average
R.E. Foster	9	1	287	486	60.75
A.E. Relf	3	2	31	44	44.00
T.W. Hayward	9	0	91	321	36.66
J.T. Tyldesley	10	0	97	277	27.70
P.F. Warner	10	1	79	249	27.66

Bowling	O	M	R	W	Average
W. Rhodes	172	36	488	31	15.74
B.J.T. Bosanquet	104.1	7	403	16	25.18
E.G. Arnold	158.3	32	475	18	26.38
L.C. Braund	129.3	30	359	13	27.61
G.H. Hirst	163.2	29	451	15	30.06

Australia

Batting	Innings	NO	HS	Runs	Average
V.T. Trumper	10	1	185*	574	63.77
M.A. Noble	10	3	133	417	59.57
R.A. Duff	10	0	84	304	30.40
C. Hill	10	0	88	276	27.60
S.E. Gregory	8	0	112	189	23.62

Bowling	O	M	R	W	Average
A. Cotter	52.5	6	150	11	13.63
H. Trumble	199.4	60	398	24	16.58
M.A. Noble	136.1	41	330	16	20.62
W.P. Howell	137.5	51	296	14	21.14
A.J.Y. Hopkins	107.1	26	295	11	26.81

Wicket-keepers: J.J. Kelly (A) 10 dismissals A.F.A. Lilley (E) 16 dismissals

Captains: M.A. Noble – batting 133, 22; 0, 31*; 59, 65; 6*, 53*; 29, 19
bowling 3–99, 0–37; 0–4; 1–10; 7–100, 1–40; 4–19, 0–19
P.F. Warner – batting 0, 8; 68, 3; 48, 79; 0, 31; 1, 11

In the first match R.E. Foster's 287 was the highest score in Tests and is still the highest score on Test début and the highest for England in Australia. In the second match W. Rhodes took 15–124. In the third match C. Hill became the first batsman to score 2,000 Test runs.

1905

England

Batting	Innings	NO	HS	Runs	Average
F.S. Jackson	9	2	144*	492	70.28
C.B. Fry	7	1	144	348	58.00
J.T. Tyldesley	9	1	112*	424	53.00
W. Rhodes	5	2	39*	146	48.66
R.H. Spooner	3	0	79	131	43.66

Bowling	O	M	R	W	Average
F.S. Jackson	67.5	8	201	13	15.46
A. Warren	39.2	9	113	6	18.83
G.L. Jessop	8	2	19	1	19.00
C. Blythe	32	11	77	4	19.25
W. Brearley	73.1	16	277	14	19.78

Australia

Batting	Innings	NO	HS	Runs	Average
R.A. Duff	8	0	146	335	41.87
W.W. Armstrong	9	1	66	252	31.50
J. Darling	9	1	73	230	28.75
J.J. Kelly	7	4	42	73	24.33
S.E. Gregory	5	1	51	94	23.50

Bowling	O	M	R	W	Average
R.A. Duff	30	8	85	4	21.25
A.J.Y. Hopkins	38	10	115	4	28.75
F. Laver	189.3	55	510	16	31.87
A. Cotter	127	13	427	13	32.84
W.W. Armstrong	280.3	94	538	16	33.62

Wicket-keepers: A.F.A. Lilley (E) 8 dismissals   J.J. Kelly (A) 6 dismissals
Captains: F.S. Jackson – batting 0, 82*; 29, 0; 144*, 17; 113; 76, 31
                      bowling 5–52, 0–6; 4–50; 1–10, 0–10; 2–26, 0–20; 1–27
            J. Darling – batting 0, 40; 41; 5, 2; 73, 0; 57, 12*

In the fourth match F.S. Jackson became the only player to score five centuries against Australia in England.

1907–8

England

Batting	Innings	NO	HS	Runs	Average
G. Gunn	10	1	122*	462	51.33
J.B. Hobbs	8	1	83	302	43.14
J. Hardstaff (sr)	10	0	72	311	31.10
K.L. Hutchings	10	0	126	273	27.30
L.C. Braund	10	1	49	233	25.88

Bowling	O	M	R	W	Average
J.N. Crawford	237.4	36	742	30	24.73
A. Fielder	216.3	31	627	25	25.08
S.F. Barnes	273.2	74	626	24	26.08
W. Rhodes	157.4	42	421	7	60.14
K.L. Hutchings	11	1	63	1	63.00

Australia

Batting	Innings	NO	HS	Runs	Average
W.W. Armstrong	10	1	133*	410	45.55
H. Carter	10	3	66	300	42.85
R.J. Hartigan	4	0	116	170	42.50
M.A. Noble	10	0	65	396	39.60
C. Hill	10	0	160	360	36.00

Bowling	O	M	R	W	Average
J.V. Saunders	267.1	52	716	31	23.09
J.A. O'Connor	107	21	300	12	25.00
W.W. Armstrong	180.1	63	361	14	25.78
C.G. Macartney	102.1	20	266	10	26.60
M.A. Noble	147	42	299	11	27.18

Wicket-keepers: H. Carter (A) 11 dismissals   R.A. Young (E) 5 dismissals
                  J. Humphries (E) 7 dismissals
Captains: M.A. Noble – batting 37, 27; 61, 64; 15, 65; 48, 10; 35, 34
                      bowling 0–14, 2–23; 0–26, 2–41; 0–38, 0–14; 3–11, 1–14; 1–62, 2–56
            F.L. Fane – batting 2, 33; 13, 50; 48, 0
            A.O. Jones – batting 3, 31; 0, 34

In the third match R.J. Hartigan, on début, and C. Hill, suffering from influenza, put on 243 for the eighth wicket, which remains the Australian record for that wicket in all Tests. Hill's 160 is the highest by a number nine batsman in Tests.

1909

England

Batting	Innings	NO	HS	Runs	Average
J. Sharp	6	2	105	188	47.00
A.F.A. Lilley	7	4	47	106	35.33
C.B. Fry	6	2	62	140	35.00
K.L. Hutchings	2	0	59	68	34.00
W. Rhodes	7	2	66	168	33.60

Bowling	O	M	R	W	Average
C. Blythe	91.3	19	242	18	13.44
A.E. Relf	52.4	18	94	6	15.66
S.F. Barnes	155.3	54	340	17	20.00
G.H. Hirst	143.4	27	348	16	21.75
W. Rhodes	79	8	242	11	22.00

Australia

Batting	Innings	NO	HS	Runs	Average
V.S. Ransford	9	3	143*	353	58.83
W. Bardsley	10	0	136	396	39.60
V.T. Trumper	9	1	73	211	26.37
S.E. Gregory	10	1	74	222	24.66
W.W. Armstrong	9	1	45	189	23.62

Bowling	O	M	R	W	Average
F. Laver	108.2	38	189	14	13.50
C.G. Macartney	127.2	33	258	16	16.12
W.W. Armstrong	140.2	51	293	14	20.92
A. Cotter	122.4	10	365	17	21.47
M.A. Noble	59.2	18	118	4	29.50

Wicket-keepers: A.F.A. Lilley (E) 10 dismissals H. Carter (A) 10 dismissals

Captains: A.C. MacLaren – batting 5; 7, 24; 17, 1; 16; 15
M.A. Noble – batting 15, 11; 32; 3, 31; 17, 13; 2, 55
bowling 0–2; 3–42, 1–12; 0–22; 0–11; 0–29

In the fourth match F. Laver's 8–31 is the best analysis by an overseas bowler in a Test in England. In the fifth match W. Bardsley became the first batsman to score a century in each innings of a Test.

1911–12

England

Batting	Innings	NO	HS	Runs	Average
J.B. Hobbs	9	1	187	662	82.75
W. Rhodes	9	1	179	463	57.87
F.E. Woolley	7	1	133*	289	48.16
J. Vine	3	2	36	46	46.00
G. Gunn	9	0	75	381	42.33

Bowling	O	M	R	W	Average
F.R. Foster	275.4	58	692	32	21.62
S.F. Barnes	297	64	778	34	22.88
J.W.H.T. Douglas	139.5	30	355	15	23.66
F.E. Woolley	68.1	12	209	8	26.12
J.W. Hitch	40	2	183	5	36.60

Australia

Batting	Innings	NO	HS	Runs	Average
S.E. Gregory	2	0	40	72	36.00
W.W. Armstrong	10	0	90	324	32.40
V.S. Ransford	10	2	43	252	31.50
R.B. Minnett	10	0	90	305	30.50
C. Hill	10	0	98	274	27.40

Bowling	O	M	R	W	Average
H.V. Hordern	272.2	43	780	32	24.37
G.R. Hazlitt	43	7	127	4	31.75
R.B. Minnett	59	12	179	5	35.80
W.W. Armstrong	149.3	39	334	9	37.11
C. Kelleway	113.5	24	249	6	41.50

Wicket-keepers: H. Carter (A) 9 dismissals   H. Strudwick (E) 2 dismissals
E.J. Smith (E) 8 dismissals

Captains: C. Hill – batting 46, 65; 4, 0; 0, 98; 22, 11; 20, 8
J.W.H.T. Douglas – batting 0, 32; 9; 35; 0; 18, 8
bowling 1–62, 4–50; 1–33, 0–38; 1–7, 2–71; 5–46; 1–14, 0–34

In the fourth match the opening partnership of 323 between J.B. Hobbs and W. Rhodes is still the highest opening stand by either side in England v Australia Tests and is the highest by England for any wicket in Australia. S.F. Barnes took 34 wickets in the rubber for a new England record, and F.R. Foster's 226 runs and 32 wickets remained the best English all-round performance until I.T. Botham's in 1981.

1912

England

Batting	Innings	NO	HS	Runs	Average
J.B. Hobbs	4	0	107	224	56.00
W. Rhodes	4	0	92	204	51.00
C.B. Fry	4	0	79	145	36.25
F.E. Woolley	4	0	62	99	24.75
J.W.H.T. Douglas	2	0	24	42	21.00

Bowling	O	M	R	W	Average
F.E. Woolley	23.2	7	55	10	5.50
H. Dean	54	19	97	6	16.16
W. Rhodes	21.2	6	60	3	20.00
S.F. Barnes	62	26	122	5	24.40
F.R. Foster	39	18	50	2	25.00

Australia

Batting	Innings	NO	HS	Runs	Average
C.G. Macartney	3	0	99	133	44.33
C. Kelleway	4	1	61	107	35.66
W. Bardsley	3	0	30	51	17.00
D.B.M. Smith	3	1	24*	30	15.00
C.B. Jennings	4	1	21	44	14.66

Bowling	O	M	R	W	Average
R.B. Minnett	10.1	3	34	4	8.50
G.R. Hazlitt	113.3	36	218	12	18.16
W.J. Whitty	110	42	252	12	21.00
S.H. Emery	19	2	68	2	34.00
C.G. Macartney	48	12	78	2	39.00

Wicket-keepers: E.J. Smith (E) 3 dismissals   W. Carkeek (A) 2 dismissals

Captains: C.B. Fry – batting 42; 19; 5, 79
S.E. Gregory – batting 10; dnb; 1, 1

6

From the Big Ship to the Young Hero

It was two years after the war before Test cricket restarted with England's visit to Australia in 1920–1. Johnny Douglas, so successful on his previous tour, led England once more, and Warwick Armstrong, coming to the peak of his achievement, captained Australia.

Armstrong's record as captain is one of the most impressive in Test history – eight consecutive victories and two draws in ten matches. The reservation that is usually made is that he was in charge of one of the strongest teams of all time, and came up against a weak England team; in other words, he was lucky to be in the right place at the right time and other people could have done the job just as well. Not only is that unkind, it is altogether too simplistic.

Apart from considerable cricketing ability, two things about Armstrong stood out. One was his physical size, for he towered some 6 feet 3 inches and by the end of his career weighed twenty-two stone. The young man who had made his Test début twenty years earlier had been a great deal slimmer, but now, with a girth to rival that of W.G., he was known as the 'Big Ship'. The other was his dominating, abrasive personality. Intent on getting his way at all times he never bothered whom he might upset, speaking his mind and sometimes, it seemed, actually looking for trouble. However, he always believed it to be in the interest of his team, and writers never fail to point out that the gruffness concealed a kind and generous nature.

He had toured England three times previously as an all-rounder, one of the few Australians to make 10,000 runs and take 500 wickets. What his batting lacked in grace it made up for in strength, assurance and confidence; Edmund Blunden said of an innings against Somerset that Armstrong made the bat look like a teaspoon and the bowling weak tea. In 1902 he and Monty Noble set the Australian sixth-wicket record of 428 against Sussex, and on the 1905 tour he scored 2,000 runs at 48 (including a triple century), also taking 130 wickets at 17. As a slow bowler he had enormous stamina, despite taking a long run-up, and on a favourable pitch he could make his

Warwick Armstrong leads his Australian team on to the field at Trent Bridge in the first Test of 1921. Behind him, left to right, are Gregory, Taylor, Collins, Pellew, Carter and Andrews.

accurate and controlled leg-breaks turn sharply. He was a containing bowler rather than an attacking one, but even when over forty he still took wickets; by that age he was no longer able to get the turn from leg that he had earlier, but as Ray Robinson put it: 'He got as many wickets as ever by fooling batsmen into thinking that every one of his "straight breaks" was an intentional part of an artful scheme.' Right to the end, when he weighed twenty-two stone, his bowling action remained tidy and well-balanced.

By the time Armstrong came to the captaincy his long experience had taught him a great deal about strategy and tactics, and he was an excellent judge of a player's abilities. Add these to his combative, aggressive nature, his fierce determination to succeed, his refusal to be dominated by anyone and the respect he commanded from his players and you have a formidable captain. Had the teams been more equally matched in his two series as captain, one cannot help feeling that his leadership qualities would still have seen Australia victorious, maybe quite convincingly. He insisted on strict discipline from his team – even to the extent of making them go to bed at eleven o'clock on the evening before a Test and then staying out himself until one – and he rivals Jardine for the title of number one autocrat among the Ashes captains. To say that his players regarded him with great affection would be some way from the truth, but he knew how to get the best out of them. He had the killer instinct, playing hard and not believing in conciliatory gestures; he was stubborn and iron-willed, but he was also a man of strong principles and he played the game fairly. Off the field he smoked an enormous pipe at all times, even when going out to toss, and he could be very affable when he wanted.

His team for that first Test contained seven new caps (England's had four) and some of them were outstanding cricketers. Of the batsmen, Macartney, Bardsley and Kelleway were still there from earlier days, and during the series they all contributed good runs. They were joined by Collins, Pellew and Johnny Taylor who all scored well; in all the Australians scored ten centuries to England's four, and simply put together many more runs throughout.

Of those seven débutants two bowlers made a particular impact on the series. Arthur Mailey, the leg-spinner who was no doubt the only man in history to have been notified of international selection whilst cleaning a water meter under a coolibar tree, took thirty-six wickets at 26. This is still the Australian record for a five-match series and is made more impressive by the fact that in one match he didn't bowl. While Mailey was weaving his spells at one end, Jack Gregory was charging in at the other, taking twenty-three wickets from sheer pace. He was also accumulating the small matter of 442 runs at 73, including a century in the second Test when batting at number nine, and taking fifteen catches into the bargain, the record for a non-wicket-keeper in a Test rubber. Ted McDonald, it should be noted, did not make his début until the third Test and took only six wickets in this series; next summer it would be a different story.

Tactically, Armstrong was always willing to make changes to meet any situation that might arise. For instance, in most of the matches under his leadership in which Australia were called upon to bat for any length of time in the second innings, the order in that innings was different from the first. Too much switching about is not usually a good idea, but somehow he seemed to sense who was the right man for the moment; certainly Australia amassed some substantial scores. Being forthright by nature, he always tried to take the game to the opposition and not give them the chance to get into the driving seat, which admittedly was not difficult with the players he had. But if the situation required defensive play he would pack his leg-side field and bowl at leg stump, the run-saving ploy that really came into its own with the advent of one-day cricket. He also delighted in the occasional surprise move, such as the one he made in the first Test at Sydney. When Australia took the field, instead of opening with his fast man, Gregory, he gave the ball to the medium-paced Kelleway – who promptly added the name of C.A.G. Russell to those who have been out first ball on début.

England were simply never in contention. Douglas was a dogged enough fighter, but he did not have the troops with which to fight. True the Australians had more débutants in the first Test than England, but the Great War had taken its toll of English cricketers. Nor did they help their cause by dropping plenty of catches, but perhaps the writing was on the wall when Australia made a record second innings score of 581 in the first match, of which Armstrong made 158. England, faced with scoring 659 to win, were demoralised from the outset. In the second Test – in which Gregory scored a century and took eight wickets – two factors brought about England's downfall: an eighth-wicket partnership of 173 and the weather. It rained heavily on the Sunday and the sun then produced a real sticky. Hobbs made a century but England lost by an innings. Strangely, Armstrong used seven bowlers, including two specialist batsmen, without giving Mailey a bowl, and when the selectors picked him for the third match they instructed the captain to make sure he was used. Armstrong complied and Mailey took ten wickets to establish himself firmly in the team.

That third Test was the nearest England got to victory. They took a first innings lead of 93, but Australia then surpassed by one run their record second innings score of the first game (Armstrong getting 121), and their total of 582 still stands as the highest second innings score in Ashes Tests. (The match aggregate of 1,753 runs is also still an Ashes record.) Another Hobbs century helped England to their highest score of the series, but they were still 119 runs short. In the fourth Test Mailey took 9–121, still the only time an Australian bowler has taken nine wickets in a Test innings; England's Makepeace, aged 39 years 173 days, became the oldest player to score a maiden Test hundred, and Armstrong scored his third century of the rubber – whilst suffering from malaria. He had picked up the disease in New Guinea during the war, and felt an attack coming on whilst waiting to go in to bat. The story goes that he sent for two whiskies, drank them neat, and scored 123 not out. It gave his team a first innings lead of 105 and ultimately an eight-wicket victory. Throughout the rubber Armstrong led by example, failing with the bat only in the last game; but then Macartney scored a chanceless 170 to set up Australia for a nine-wicket win and the whitewash.

Douglas took all the blame, of course, but the following summer he was still there to preside over a further English nightmare. Injury and illness deprived them of Hobbs for virtually the entire series, and in their despair the selectors tried no fewer than thirty players, the record for any Test rubber. But without Hobbs the batting, at least in the first three games, was mostly dismal, Woolley's two 90s in the second Test standing out like a beacon. McDonald and Gregory were simply too fast for them, McDonald finishing with 27 wickets at 24 and Gregory with 19 at 29. The first game, the hundredth between the countries, lasted less than two days as England collapsed twice, the two fast men taking sixteen wickets between them. The second Test, thanks to Woolley and Tennyson, was more of a contest; but the England bowlers could match Australia's neither for speed nor for containment. Of 30 overs that Armstrong bowled in the match 18 were maidens and only 28 runs were conceded, the sort of economy that can decide a three-day match.

Part of the 1920–1 Australian team. Standing, left to right, C. Kelleway, J.M. Gregory, J Ryder. Seated, left to right, W. Bardsley, W.W. Armstrong, C.G. Macartney. Ryder and Bardsley also led Australia in Ashes Tests.

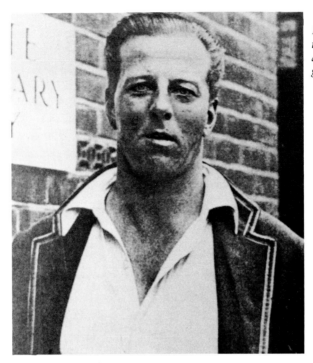

Hon. Lionel Tennyson, the third Baron Tennyson. His appointment cost one rash gambler £1,000.

For the third Test England replaced Douglas with The Honourable Lionel Tennyson as captain, although Douglas kept his place in the team. Having played five times against South Africa before the war without much success, Tennyson was brought back for the second Test of 1921; he launched himself at the bowlers with great fire for 74 not out, and although the game was lost he so impressed the selectors that they decided he was the leader to reverse the run of defeats. In 1920 a friend of his had laid 1,000 to 1 against his captaining England, a little story which ought to contain a moral somewhere.

Tennyson had captained Hampshire since 1919, and was to do so until 1933, never finishing higher than sixth in the Championship. In his early days he had been a fast bowler but then concentrated on batting with a good deal of success. As a large, very strong man he loved to take on the fast bowlers and hit the ball off his front foot, although, to his annoyance, he was much less sure against the slower men. Ian Peebles says of him that even at a time when there was plenty of individuality he was an outsize personality, something of a throw-back to the age of the Regency buck, boisterous and whole-hearted, incessantly mixing triumph and disaster — rather different from his Poet Laureate grandfather.

Tennyson's first game as captain was the third Test at Headingley, and England, in their desperation, made seven changes from the previous match. Hobbs returned after missing the first two games through injury, but then went down with appendicitis on the first day and didn't play again all season. That was only one of England's misfortunes; Tennyson split a hand trying to stop a blistering drive from Macartney and had to go off, Douglas taking over again while England fielded. Australia piled up 407 and then reduced England to 67 for 5, although Douglas and Brown, on his début, stopped the rot. Then came the heroics from Tennyson; batting virtually one-handed he scored 63 and just saved the follow-on as England scraped to 259. He was helped by Douglas who scored 75, during which he had his thumb driven inwards by Gregory. Cardus relates that 'when he got back to the pavilion he could hardly get his glove off, and the thumb was horrible to look at. No hint all day did Douglas give on the field of the pain martyrising him.' To no avail, though – England's second innings could manage only 202 (with another one-handed 36 from Tennyson) and they lost by 219 runs.

It was in the fourth Test that England at long last got on top, though as the first day had been washed out there was never much chance of a result. The match is notable for an unwittingly illegal declaration by Tennyson; he declared at 5.50 p.m., but Australia's wicket-keeper Carter told Armstrong that under the laws a declaration was not allowed in a two-day match unless there were 100 minutes left for the other side to bat. By the time this had been sorted out – and then explained to the crowd, who thought Armstrong was pulling a fast one and booed him accordingly – 25 minutes had been lost and then, to cap it all, Armstrong bowled the next over despite having bowled the one before the break. England declared overnight at 362 for 4 but on an easy pitch they had batted too slowly. Next day Collins stayed nearly five hours for 40 to save the game – prompting the suggestion from the crowd 'Hey, Tennyson, lad, read him some of thy grandad's poems' – and although they were all out for 175 there was no time left for England to press home their advantage.

Again rain interrupted the first day of the final Test, but on the second day Mead reached 182 not out as England declared on 403. But there was to be no Australian collapse, and they finished only just short of England's total. On the third day no fewer than 471 runs were scored, but there was never any chance of a result and the game petered out. Towards the end Armstrong instructed four of his batsmen to share the bowling for the rest of the match. He then wandered out to the boundary and stayed there – and took a fine running catch – his aim being to make his feelings on three-day

Tests clear for all to see. When a newspaper blew towards him he picked it up and began reading it; asked afterwards why he had done so, he said that he had wondered who they were playing and wanted to find out. Like Fry refusing to go out on to the balcony, he left Test cricket with something akin to a 'V sign'.

At least Tennyson could claim that he had put the brake on the steam-roller, and with better luck from the weather in the fourth Test he might even have recorded a win. Some of the players who were brought in when he took over, such as Russell, Mead and Brown, scored well – and in his three Tests as captain he himself scored 150 at an average of 50 – so that at least England were able to avoid the earlier collapses that gave games away. He was a purposeful captain who led by example and enjoyed the challenges of the game, a cheerful character rather than a profound thinker. However, he knew what he was about for all that; witness the time in 1922 when Hampshire, having been bowled out by Warwickshire for 15, went on to win the match by 155 runs and Tennyson's winnings were reputed to be quite substantial. (For a glorious piece on this of which P.G. Wodehouse would have been proud, the reader is recommended to turn to 'Long Odds at Edgbaston' by Kenneth Gregory in his delightful collection *In Celebration of Cricket*.) Ian Peebles says that perhaps the aptest comment on Tennyson was made by someone who observed that whenever he entered the room everyone smiled. It was something that would never have been said of his grandfather.

Armstrong's autocratic manner made him less than popular with the English crowds, not that that would have bothered him. He was roundly criticised in the game against Kent for not making the home team follow on when almost 500 adrift on first innings. But his argument was sound enough: 'There's a Test coming on and I'm not overworking my bowlers for anybody.' The decision caused a furore, and after the game the Kent president, Lord Harris, remarked that the club would be happy to see ten of the Australian team again. Armstrong was unmoved.

He was not to go through the tour undefeated, however. Archie Mac-Laren came out of retirement to prove his claim that the Australians were not invincible, and did so at Eastbourne with an all-amateur team of whom none had played in that summer's Tests. Cardus insists that, having disposed of the England XI for 43 in the first innings, any suggestion of casualness by the Australians was very short-lived. Armstrong desperately wanted to remain unbeaten, and Cardus's description of him in the closing stages, as his team failed by 28 runs to reach the 196 they needed for victory, has considerable poignancy: 'This afternoon Armstrong's face as he witnessed the breaking of Andrews's wicket – which was a certain omen of the end – had a profoundly sombre expression. Gone the old affability! Where were his quips and oddities now?' Poor Armstrong. He had been a fine captain, and one can almost feel sorry for him. Almost.

During the tour a chance meeting with a whisky merchant in Glasgow shaped the rest of his life, for when he retired after this series he went into the business himself. It goes without saying that he prospered; when he died his estate was worth £90,000. He was, simply, one of those fortunate individuals who are successful at whatever they do.

Of Douglas, Neville Cardus wrote that 'While our pointed tongues chastised him there was not one of us who did not know in his heart that Douglas was the noblest Roman, the one English cricketer tough and big enough to stand face to face with Armstrong as our leader. Why, to choose as we did the gay and amenable Tennyson for our main counter to Armstrong was like placing a velvet glove into a grip of iron.' Maybe, but the results suggest that the velvet glove did not do too badly. Douglas played twice more for England, called in as captain against South Africa in 1924 when Arthur Gilligan was injured, only for the match to be washed out on the first afternoon, and then playing his last game against Australia on Gilligan's tour. In 1928 he became a Test selector, but only two years later, at the age of forty-eight, he was drowned while on a business trip with his father. Their ship was in a collision in thick fog in the Kattegat; a survivor said that Douglas could have saved himself but went below to try and rescue his father. He was not seen again.

If Armstrong takes the credit for captaining his great team, the man who must take much of the credit for putting it together is Herbie Collins. In 1919 he was asked to lead the Australian Imperial Forces side, a team made up of Australian servicemen still in England after the war which played against many county and private teams. He found he had some very good players in his squad, and was able to nurture the likes of Jack Gregory and Bertie Oldfield, helping them become the outstanding players they were. He made a successful début in the first Test after the war and scored centuries in his first and third games; in England in 1921 he was less happy, but on the way home Australia played three Tests against South Africa, whereupon Armstrong handed over the captaincy to him. He scored a double century in the second match and led his team to victory in the third to take the rubber 1–0. Unthinkably by today's standards Australia played no Test cricket for three years, but when England toured in 1924–5 Collins was the obvious leader. He also captained a strong New South Wales side from 1919–20 to 1925–6, leading them to four Sheffield Shield titles.

In his earlier days he had been a bookmaker, and apparently he sometimes played poker to prepare himself mentally for a Test match – although he was not a captain to take a gamble. He had a variety of nicknames such as Poker Face (inevitably), Nutty, Lucky and Horseshoe, the last two reflecting his luck (skill?) with the toss. Ray Robinson describes him as a Bohemian who was very fond of opera. His batting was based on determination and concentration rather than glorious and memorable strokeplay, but was good enough to bring him 1,350 runs at 45 in his 19 Tests.

His success as captain was founded on an ability to observe closely the temperament of each of his team and then treat them accordingly. Quietly spoken, thoughtful and a good friend to his players, he was a very shrewd and knowledgeable cricketer who studied the opposition thoroughly. He was a born fighter who always played the game hard but fairly, and although it might sound corny to say it nowadays, in the 1920s a cricket team took inspiration from his style of leadership. His way of moving a fieldsman was typical of the man – no arm-waving, just a nod, a quick hand movement or pointing with the finger was enough. He was dour rather than humorous, but he had his lighter moments; Robinson tells how once in an inter-district match in Sydney his slow bowler was hit for several sixes in a few overs and asked to be taken off. 'No fear,' said Collins, 'I haven't enjoyed anything like this for years.'

His team at the end of 1924 was strong on all-rounders, but the crucial difference between the two sides was that the England bowling was markedly weak. They had Maurice Tate, who bowled his heart out – and must have brought enormous joy and pride to his father Fred after his own Test experience – but very little other penetration. Arthur Gilligan, the England captain, had been badly hit above the heart whilst batting the previous summer and was no longer the force he had been as a fast bowler, while none of the others emerged as a striking partner for Tate. Tate, at his peak, laboured gloriously throughout, sending down almost twice as many overs as any of his team-mates and taking more than twice as many wickets, and at the lowest average. His thirty-eight wickets remain the record for an England bowler in Australia, and thirty of them were batsmen of high calibre. For much of the time it was a case of Tate attacking and the other bowler containing; it didn't take the Australians long to realise that their best approach was to defend against Tate until he tired and concentrate on scoring against the rest. Happily the batsmen were rather better matched, especially as Hobbs and Sutcliffe played together against Australia for the first time and scored prodigiously, with three hundreds from Hobbs and four from his partner.

*Arthur Gilligan watches
Herbie Collins toss the coin
at Adelaide in the 1924–5
series.*

Few captains have been as popular as Arthur Gilligan. Appointed captain of Sussex in 1922, he made them into one of the best-liked teams in the country and an outstandingly good fielding side. It has to be said, though, that he did not achieve any great impact on the Championship, for the highest they finished under his leadership was fourth in 1929, his last year as captain. He was an amateur leader in the classical mould, for whom the revered traditions of sportsmanship and grace in defeat were of paramount importance. He had a good combative streak in him that made him a determined opponent, but he played cricket as the happy game it should be.

He was primarily a fast bowler, and a very accurate one at that, but he was a good enough batsman to notch up twelve first-class centuries. The first of these was scored when batting at number eleven, one of the few times this has ever happened, and by coincidence it was for Cambridge University against Sussex. Sadly, though, his injury drastically curtailed his bowling; the doctors told him he must never bowl fast again, and although he did his best to take no notice he was forced to concede that they were right. He never regained the penetration that he once had, and was no longer really up to Test standard. Had he been able to give Tate his full support the result of that series may well have been different, for it was more closely contested than the margin of 4–1 might suggest.

Gilligan had made his Test début in the 1922–3 tour of South Africa, and was then appointed captain for the home series against that country in 1924. The first three games were won convincingly and the last two ruined by the weather (although he missed the fourth Test). The first match saw Tate's début, and between them Gilligan and Tate bowled out the visitors for 30 in 12.3 overs. Gilligan took 6 for 7, following this up with 5 for 83 in the second innings when South Africa made 390; as England won by an innings it was the peak of his Test career. Admittedly South Africa at that time were much weaker than the Australians, but those three victories had been so comprehensive that Gilligan was the obvious leader for the 1924–5 tour.

The 1924–5 MCC team to tour Australia. Standing, left to right, H. Howell, R.K. Tyldesly, A.P.F. Chapman, F.C. Toone (manager), M.W. Tate, W.W. Whysall, J.L. Bryan. Seated, left to right, F.E. Woolley, J.W. Hearne, J.W.H.T. Douglas, A.E.R. Gilligan (captain), J.B. Hobbs, E.H. Hendren, H. Strudwick. Front, left to right, R. Kilner, A.P. Freeman, H. Sutcliffe, A. Sandham. Douglas and Chapman also led England against Australia.

The first morning's play of the first Test of that tour set the pattern for the series. Collins won the toss and batted, whereupon Tate bowled with great fire but little luck. Ponsford, on his début, was almost bowled three times in his first over from Tate. Collins, despite by his own admission being turned inside out by Tate, shielded him and as the bowler tired both went on to make centuries. Jack Fingleton relates that Collins told him that Clem Hill went to the dressing-room during lunch and said 'Well, that's the toughest bowling I've ever seen. If Tate had had any luck your whole team would have been out twice before lunch.' He did in fact take eleven wickets, but the other bowlers came in for punishment and Australia totalled 902 runs in their two innings. Crucially, Mailey featured in tenth-wicket stands of 62 and 127 (the latter, in which Taylor scored a hundred despite suffering from a boil behind the knee, is still a record against England) which tipped the scales, England failing by 193 to reach their target.

In the next game the home team compiled a record score of 600, despite having been 47 for 3. Ponsford became the first player to score a century in his first two Tests, while Hobbs and Sutcliffe became the first partnership in Test history to bat throughout a full day. But the rest of the batting fell away and England were all out for 479. Tate and Woolley then bowled Australia out for 250, Tate taking 6 for 99, but England again fell short of their target, despite a third consecutive century from Sutcliffe which made him the first Englishman to score three successive centuries in Tests and to score a century in each innings of an Australian Test. Once again the match had been lost because the bowling, at least in the first innings, lacked penetration.

In these two matches England had simply been outplayed; now Fortune took against them as well. In the third Test, having reduced Australia to 119 for 6, they lost three bowlers to injury, including Tate. Woolley and Kilner had to do a great deal of work, but Ryder scored 201 not out and his team reached 489. England responded with 365 and then, with Woolley and Kilner again doing most of the work, bowled Australia out for 250. Chasing 375 to win, England fell an agonising 11 runs short. It was in this match that Gilligan, having lost the toss for the third time, went down on his hands and knees to examine the coin, a piece of clowning that the crowd enjoyed. Four years later, also at Adelaide, England were to get their revenge as Australia, chasing 349, fell 12 short.

Collins's ability to win the toss was one of the legends of Australian cricket at the time. Throughout this series winning the toss led to victory, and Gilligan called wrongly four times. But in the fourth Test it was Gilligan's turn to get it right, and this time Fortune favoured England. In the first innings they put together 548, with six of the first seven batsmen scoring 40 or more. Thereafter the match was interrupted by frequent showers which did enough to the pitch to make life difficult for the Australian batsmen, and England were able to record their first post-war win over the old enemy by an innings and 29 runs. Even the Australians agreed that it was about time some of the luck went England's way. By an odd coincidence, for the third match running Australia's second innings totalled exactly 250. England might have known that Collins would come out fighting after such a defeat, and sure enough they were overwhelmed in the last Test. Hobbs and Sutcliffe had a rare double failure, but the matchwinner was Clarrie Grimmett. He announced himself on his début with 11 for 82, bowling England out cheaply twice, to give Australia a 307-run victory and make a sad end to Gilligan's Test career. There is no doubt that Australia was the stronger team, but maybe Collins was flattered by a winning margin of 4–1.

One could suggest, perhaps, that Gilligan was one of those captains who are too 'nice' and that a tougher attitude might have brought more success, but that is to fail to understand the way he played the game. His easy-going approach gave him a good rapport with his players, and had he been luckier with the toss and less hampered by injuries at crucial moments, the series may well have taken a different turn. Happily, the players were well received when they returned to England as there was general agreement that they had put up a good fight, without any luck, against a stronger team. The Australians remembered Gilligan as a fine sportsman and a graceful loser, and his habit of referring to the professionals as 'Mr', instead of simply by their surnames as was usually the custom in England, made him well-liked. In later years he became heavily involved in the administration of the game, becoming president of Sussex and, in 1967, president of MCC. He also became a radio commentator and wrote a number of cricketing books. His brother Alfred captained England in the inaugural Tests against New Zealand, making them the only brothers to lead England.

The team which Collins led to England in 1926 was still a good one, although beginning to decline from the heights. Macartney was playing what proved to be his final series and went out gloriously, scoring three centuries, and Woodfull, in his first series, scored two. But none of the bowlers really imposed themselves, and the pendulum began to swing back towards England. Arthur Carr had been chosen as the tough leader who would give Collins as good as he received, and he had some useful players under him. For the first time in many years the teams were fairly well matched.

England captains 1880 to 1912. Top row, left to right: Lord Harris,
A. Shrewsbury, W.G. Grace, W.W. Read. Middle row: A.E. Stoddart,
A.C. MacLaren. Bottom row: P.F. Warner, A.O. Jones, Hon. F.S. Jackson,
C.B. Fry. The badges are England (left) and MCC Touring Teams.

England captains 1920–1 to 1948. Top row, left to right: Hon. L.H. Tennyson, J.C. White, D.R. Jardine, G.O.B. Allen. Middle row: R.E.S. Wyatt, A.E.R. Gilligan, P.F. Chapman, C.F. Walters. Bottom row: W.R. Hammond, J.W.H.T. Douglas, A.W. Carr, N.W.D. Yardley.

Australian captains. Top row, left to right: W. Bardsley, J. Ryder,
H.L. Collins. Centre: W.L. Murdoch. Bottom row: D.G. Bradman,
W.M. Woodfull, A.L. Hassett.

First day cover of the 1977 Melbourne Centenary Test.

First day cover of the 1977 Centenary series. The captains are J.M. Brearley and G.S. Chappell and the signatures, appropriately for the Leeds Test, are of Herbert Sutcliffe, Sir Leonard Hutton and Geoffrey Boycott. It was in this match that Boycott scored his hundredth hundred.

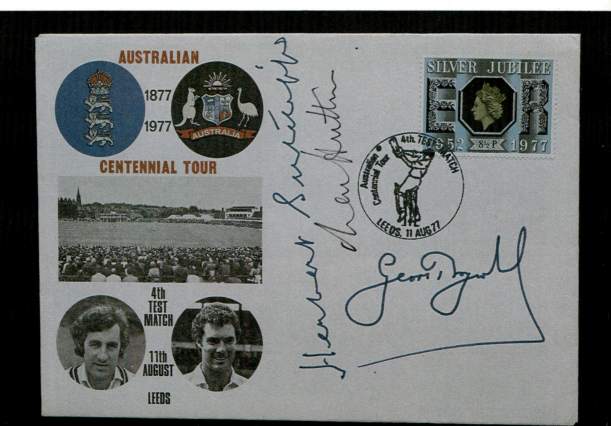

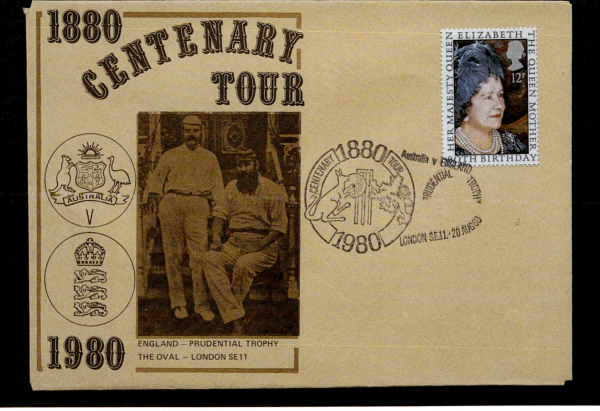

First day cover from the 1980 Centenary Tour. W.L. Murdoch and W.G. Grace are shown, although the England captain was Lord Harris.

First day cover of the 1980 Lord's Centenary Test.

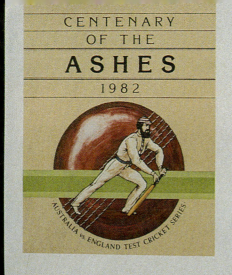

First day cover celebrating the centenary of the Ashes. The date of 30 August is in fact incorrect – the match finished on 29 August but the obituary was not published until 2 September.

Mike Smith demonstrates stylish batsmanship, but for the coaching manual rather than the spectators.

(Previous page) England and Australia Test players and officials past and present before the Centenary Test at Lord's in 1980.

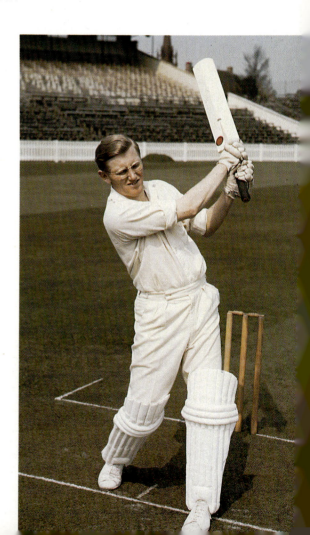

(Left)   *A.W. Carr, England captain remembered by posterity for one dropped catch.*   (Right)   *Warren Bardsley. Dismissed first ball in his first Test as captain, he had scored 193 not out in his previous Test innings.*

Arthur Carr is one of those unfortunate players (like Fred Tate) remembered not so much for cricketing skills as for one dropped catch. His skills were considerable, in fact, for he was a strong, attacking batsman, an excellent fielder and a formidable county captain who led Nottinghamshire from 1919 to 1934. There was something of the bulldog about him, both in appearance and attitude. His first games for England had been in the 1922–3 series in South Africa, but it was his bad luck that the one year when he was most successful with the bat there was no touring side; in 1925 he scored 2,338 runs at almost 52, and had there been international competition his Test record would no doubt have been better than it is. Lady Luck was not exactly his boon companion when he played for his country.

As a result of his good season in 1925 he was seen by many as the best man to lead England against Australia in 1926. There was some support for the more experienced Percy Fender; he was an excellent county captain, and has good claim to the title of best captain never to lead England, but Carr's toughness was felt to be an important factor. People remembered Armstrong's aggressive captaincy and decided that this was what was needed from England, and Carr was by some way the most aggressive of the county captains. Indeed, his character was quite similar to Armstrong's, for not only did he not try to avoid controversy but sometimes appeared to be looking for it. He had been moulding together a useful side at Trent Bridge that three years later was to wrest the Championship from the Lancashire and Yorkshire domination, and his players loved him.

Rain washed out the first Test after no more than fifty minutes, but it was in the second Test that signs of an England revival began. Australia scored 383, Bardsley carrying his bat for 193, and England replied with 475 for 3 declared, including centuries from Hobbs and Hendren. But with Tests in England still limited to three days (this was the last series against Australia in which they were) the match was drawn. Carr's captaincy was praised; he had fielded well, handled his bowlers and field-placings cleverly, and generally inspired his team.

Unfortunately Collins then went down with neuritis and missed the next two Tests, handing over the captaincy to Warren Bardsley. Bardsley is remembered not as a captain but as a very fine left-handed batsman, usually an opener. He captained New South Wales for two years before the war, winning the Sheffield Shield in his first year, but led Australia only in these two matches. Cardus describes him as playing with an exemplary straight bat, as having very quick and shrewd footwork and a wide range of strokes, and as an excellent outfielder. His description of Bardsley's attitude towards a bouncer is delightful: 'He would toss his head backwards at a bumping ball with a sniff of the nose, a sign of contempt, letting it fly past a yard or so from the nose aforesaid, entirely unmoved.' One wonders what he would have made of Holding, Marshall and Co.

In his first tour of England in 1909 Bardsley had become the first player to score a hundred in each innings of a Test, making 136 and 130 at the Oval. He toured regularly after that and seemed to find English conditions much to his liking, averaging almost 50 in all matches there. He was a permanent fixture in Armstrong's triumphant team. His highest score was the 193 not out mentioned earlier, which made him, at the age of 43, the oldest Australian to score a century against England; this is also the highest score made by a batsman over 40 in England–Australia Tests. In the following game at Headingley, proudly leading his country for the first time, he lost the toss, was put in to bat, and was out first ball.

For Arthur Carr this was the game when things began to go wrong. Having won the toss he made two crucial mistakes. The previous day there had been a storm, and now that the sun was shining he felt that the wicket would become sticky and so put Australia in. It was one of the more spectacularly misjudged insertions, for the wicket proved easy and Australia reached 494. For years afterwards George Geary maintained that Carr's mistake was to take two batsmen with him to inspect the wicket instead of two bowlers. Things started well enough as Bardsley fell to the opening ball, but England's joy was short-lived. Macartney came in and hit two, then edged his fourth ball to Carr's left at third slip. He got both hands to the ball, but dropped it. Macartney went on to score 151, of which 112 came before lunch, and with Woodfull grinding away at the other end Australia reached 235 before the second wicket fell. Carr appeared badly affected by the dropped catch, giving the impression to many people that he had lost control of his team. By the second day he seemed recovered but, in David Lemmon's words, 'a ghost was with him for the rest of the summer'. Bardsley then became the first Australian captain to lead an attack which contained two googly bowlers, Grimmett and Mailey. Grimmett took 5 for 88 as England were all out for 294, Geary and Macaulay putting on 108 for the ninth wicket. England duly followed on, but in a three-day match Hobbs and Sutcliffe saw them to safety with an opening stand of 156. Bardsley tried seven bowlers but still couldn't press home his advantage.

Carr's misfortune continued in the fourth Test at Old Trafford. Because of the weather hardly any play was possible on the first day, and then Carr went down with tonsillitis. Jack Hobbs led the team in his absence, the first professional to do so since Arthur Shrewsbury, making this one of the few Tests in which both teams were led by acting captains. But a two-day match was unlikely to be anything other than a draw. Bardsley failed again, but Australia made 335; once again Bardsley used seven bowlers, but there was no great penetration and England reached 305 for 5. Gregory, incidentally, sent down 72 overs in those first four Tests without taking a wicket. Hobbs's captaincy, as one would expect, was greatly praised, but as a professional it was unthinkable that he might be appointed instead of Carr for the final Test.

By the time of the English selection meeting for the final Test Carr claimed that he was perfectly fit. He was astonished, therefore, to find himself dropped and the captaincy given to Percy Chapman. The selectors issued a statement saying that in view of his recent poor health he had generously offered to resign his place, but Carr refuted it and claimed he had been sacked. There was uproar among the Press and public. As it turned

Percy Chapman, cavalier batsman, close fielder extraordinary and one of England's most successful captains.

out, the gods were smiling on Chapman at this time and all went well for him, but one wonders what mixed feelings Carr must have had at the ecstatic acclaim that the young hero received after the match was won. That is something that never seems to get a mention when the story of 'How the Ashes were Regained' is told.

Carr played for England twice more, taking over the captaincy from Jack White for the last two Tests against South Africa in 1929. He won the first game by an innings and drew the second, so that England took the series 2–0. By 1935, though, his career was ended through his support for Larwood and Voce and for bodyline bowling. Never one to worry about whom he upset, he advocated fast leg-theory in an uncompromising way that made him very unpopular, and when it was declared illegal by MCC it spelt his end. If his England appearances had not been marked by the best of fortune his county career had been a fine one, and it was sad that it ended on such a controversial note.

Of the players in MacLaren's team that spoiled Armstrong's unbeaten record in 1921, the one who was destined for the greatest cricketing triumphs was Percy Chapman. His contribution to that match had been modest enough, but it presaged what was to be one of the most successful careers that an England captain has had in matches against the old enemy.

There is a strong element of the *Boys' Own* hero about Percy Chapman, although he spoiled the image by drinking excessively when things went wrong later in life. Over six feet tall and with curly blond hair, the same words recur in everything you read about him: his manner was 'debonair', his face was 'cherubic', his presence was 'towering'. His batting was attacking and flamboyant, his close fielding and catching were dazzlingly brilliant. Cricket for him was a game to be enjoyed, a challenge to be relished, a straightforward business to be played in a sporting and carefree spirit.

When he found himself entrusted with the captaincy for the crucial final Test he was still three weeks away from his twenty-sixth birthday; only two Englishmen, Bligh and Botham, and one Australian, Murdoch, have held the office in these matches at an earlier age. The critics said that he was too young, that he had little captaincy experience, and that when in charge of the Kent team he had not shown any great aptitude. There was, in fact, very little support for him from anyone – except the person who mattered most, the Chairman of Selectors. Pelham Warner made the point that Pitt was Prime Minister at twenty-five just as Chapman was now captain, and both of them had attended Pembroke College, Cambridge. Obviously an ideal qualification for regaining the Ashes.

Chapman's England début had come in 1924 against South Africa, and he had played nine Tests before he was made captain, without any outstanding innings to this name. He batted left-handed, in the dashing, polished manner of the great Edwardian stroke-makers, always ready to take the attack to the bowlers. He was especially fond of lofting the ball deep into the outfield, with, as Ian Peebles recalls, the occasional surprising result, such as a six high over third man – the kind of buccaneer stroke that epitomises his approach. His close fielding was, if anything, even more spectacular, for his reflexes were quite extraordinary and his hands were huge, a combination which meant that little passed him by. He made the gully his speciality and dominated many batsmen by the threat of his presence.

The Oval Test was to be played to a finish and Chapman, having won the toss, duly batted. Incredible as it may now seem, Grimmett, with his slow leg-breaks, was one of Australia's opening bowlers; true, it was not long before he was replaced, but by Mailey, the other leg-spinner. Mailey, in fact, took six wickets in the first innings and nine in the match. When Chapman came in after lunch the score was 108 for 3, and he immediately went for the bowling, scoring 49 in quick time. In the context of a timeless Test it wasn't the dour, responsible innings that the captain might be supposed to play, but the crowd enjoyed it. Only Sutcliffe, with 76, scored more and England were all out for 280. Australia's first innings bettered that by 22 runs, and by the close on the second day Hobbs and Sutcliffe were unbeaten on 49. That night there was a violent storm and the ground was drenched. As the game restarted the sun came out and began to dry the wicket; Mailey and Grimmett must have drooled with anticipation. But, in one of the very finest feats of batsmanship, Hobbs and Sutcliffe stood firm that morning, putting on no less than 172 for the first wicket, nearly fifty more than the Australian second innings could manage in total. Hobbs made 100 and Sutcliffe 161, to set up a total of 436. Australia needed 415 to win, and the wicket was crumbling. They fell 289 runs short.

There were over twenty thousand in the Oval for that last day, and they witnessed an inspired England performance. The bowling gave nothing away, brilliant catches were taken and Chapman's captaincy was determined and imaginative. He was not too proud to ask advice from his senior professionals, Hobbs and Rhodes, but there was no doubt who was in charge. (A.A. Thomson records that he once asked Rhodes who was the best captain he had played for. 'Mr Chapman,' he said, 'he always did what me and Jack told him.') He even, when the end was in sight, took off Rhodes and Larwood, who had taken seven wickets between them, so that all his bowlers could try to take a wicket, which they duly did. Rhodes was less than amused, but it was one of those gestures which show the spirit in which Chapman played his cricket. The scenes that greeted the victory had never been known at a cricket match in England; twenty thousand fortunate souls roaring adulation of their heroes. It must have been a heady moment for a young man.

Collins may have been impeded by the after-effects of his neuritis, although he scored 61 in his first innings, but he came in for some criticism for his handling of his bowlers during the Hobbs and Sutcliffe stand. Monty Noble, for instance, suggested that Richardson was bowled for too long, since Hobbs was only pretending to be in trouble against him in the hope that Collins would keep him on instead of putting on someone more dangerous such as Gregory. One of Collins's problems was that Macartney, his left-hander, was unable to get much turn, perhaps feeling his years at the end of a hard season. If Noble was right it is a good illustration of how difficult captaincy can be, although many Australians felt that Armstrong would not have let them get away with it.

In later years, like many another player, Collins wrote for a newspaper. Unlike most other players, however, he dared to criticise Don Bradman; he did not like the 'feeling' that came into the game at the time of Jardine and Bradman. He himself played the game hard, but always in good spirit. Fingleton tells how Collins saw Bradman after the poor Test at Adelaide in the 1946–7 series when the home team had obviously played for a draw. Collins told him that he had written an article for his paper about him. 'In case they don't print it in full I'll tell you the theme of it,' he said. 'I've suggested that cricket would be a better game now if you got out of it.' Fingleton records laconically that 'Bradman passed on'.

Dudley Carew, writing in 1926, summed up Collins thus: 'Collins withdrew deeper and deeper into the hard shell of his dour and invincible spirit. Cromwell would have welcomed him as one of his lieutenants; he knows how to watch and how to fight.'

1920–1	Sydney	A 267, 581	E 190, 281	A 377 runs
	Melbourne	A 499	E 251, 157	A inns 91 runs
	Adelaide	A 354, 582	E 447, 370	A 119 runs
	Melbourne	E 284, 315	A 389, 211–2	A 8 wkts
	Sydney	E 204, 280	A 392, 93–1	A 9 wkts
1921	Trent Bridge	E 112, 147	A 232, 30–0	A 10 wkts
	Lord's	E 187, 283	A 342, 131–2	A 8 wkts
	Headingley	A 407, 273–7d	E 259, 202	A 219 runs
	Old Trafford	E 362–4d, 44–1	A 175	Drawn
	Oval	E 403–8d; 244–2	A 389	Drawn
1924–5	Sydney	A 450, 452	E 298, 411	A 193 runs
	Melbourne	A 600, 250	E 479, 290	A 81 runs
	Adelaide	A 489, 250	E 365, 363	A 11 runs
	Melbourne	E 548	A 269, 250	E inns 29 runs
	Sydney	A 295, 325	E 167, 146	A 307 runs
1926	Trent Bridge	E 32–0	A —	Drawn
	Lord's	A 383, 194–5	E 475–3d	Drawn
	Headingley	A 494	E 294, 254–3	Drawn
	Old Trafford	A 335	E 305–5	Drawn
	Oval	E 280, 436	A 302, 125	E 289 runs

1920–1

England

Batting	Innings	NO	HS	Runs	Average
J.B. Hobbs	10	0	123	505	50.50
J.W.H.T. Douglas	10	1	68	354	39.33
C.A.G. Russell	8	1	135*	258	36.85
J.W. Hearne	2	0	57	71	35.50
J.W.H. Makepeace	8	0	117	279	34.87

Bowling	O	M	R	W	Average
E.R. Wilson	21	5	36	3	12.00
P.G.H. Fender	100.2	7	410	12	34.16
C.H. Parkin	212.2	28	670	16	41.87
J.W.H.T. Douglas	121	13	420	8	52.50
F.E. Woolley	217	58	530	9	58.88

Australia

Batting	Innings	NO	HS	Runs	Average
C.G. Macartney	4	1	170	260	86.66
W.W. Armstrong	7	1	158	464	77.33
J.M. Gregory	8	2	100	442	73.66
H.L. Collins	9	0	162	557	61.88
C.E. Pellew	6	0	116	319	53.16

Bowling	O	M	R	W	Average
C. Kelleway	146.5	32	315	15	21.00
W.W. Armstrong	102.5	26	204	9	22.66
J.M. Gregory	208.1	30	556	23	24.17
A.A. Mailey	243.5	27	946	36	26.27
H.L. Collins	26	5	84	2	42.00

Wicket-keepers: W.A.S. Oldfield (A) 7 dismissals   H. Carter (A) 11 dismissals
H. Strudwick (E) 14 dismissals   A. Dolphin (E) 1 dismissal

Captains: W.W. Armstrong – batting 12, 158; 39; 11, 121; 123*; 0
bowling 0–2, 1–21; 2–50, 4–26; 1–29, 0–41; 0–9; 1–26
J.W.H.T. Douglas – batting 21, 7; 15, 9; 60, 32; 50, 60; 32*, 68
bowling 0–14, 2–79; 2–83; 2–69, 0–61; 0–17, 0–13; 2–84

In the first match W. Rhodes became the first player to score 2,000 runs and take 100 wickets for England. A.A. Mailey's 9–121 in the fourth match is still the only instance of nine wickets in an innings for Australia, and his 36 wickets in the series is still the most for Australia v England in a five-match series. J.M. Gregory took 15 catches in the series, still a record for a fielder in any Test series.

1921

England

Batting	Innings	NO	HS	Runs	Average
C.P. Mead	2	1	182*	229	229.00
C.A.G. Russell	3	1	102*	216	108.00
J.W. Hitch	2	1	51*	69	69.00
L.H. Tennyson	5	1	74*	229	57.25
G. Brown	5	0	84	250	50.00

Bowling	O	M	R	W	Average
C.W.L. Parker	28	16	32	2	16.00
W. Rhodes	13	3	33	2	16.50
C.H. Parkin	121.5	21	420	16	26.25
F.J. Durston	33.4	2	136	5	27.20
V.W.C. Jupp	39.1	4	142	5	28.40

Australia

Batting	Innings	NO	HS	Runs	Average
W. Bardsley	8	2	88	281	46.83
E.A. McDonald	5	3	36	92	46.00
C.G. Macartney	8	1	115	300	42.85
T.J.E. Andrews	7	0	94	275	39.28
H. Carter	5	0	47	160	32.00

Bowling	O	M	R	W	Average
E.A. McDonald	205.5	32	668	27	24.74
W.W. Armstrong	127	50	212	8	26.50
J.M. Gregory	182.2	35	552	19	29.05
A.A. Mailey	124.4	18	398	12	33.16
H.S.T.L. Hendry	52	11	135	3	45.00

Wicket-keepers: H. Strudwick (E) 2 dismissals   G. Brown (E) 4 dismissals
H. Carter (A) 11 dismissals   W.A.S. Oldfield (A) 1 dismissal

Captains: J.W.H.T. Douglas – batting 11, 13; 34, 14; bowling 2–34; 2–53, 0–23
L.H. Tennyson – batting 63, 36; dnb; 51
W.W. Armstrong – batting 11; 0; 77, 28*; 17; 19
bowling 0–1, 0–33; 1–9, 0–19; 2–44, 2–6; 2–57; 0–44

1924–5

(Over increased to 8 balls in Australia)

England

Batting	Innings	NO	HS	Runs	Average
H. Sutcliffe	9	0	176	734	81.55
J.B. Hobbs	9	0	154	573	63.66
A.P. Freeman	4	2	50*	80	40.00
E.H. Hendren	9	1	92	314	39.25
W.W. Whysall	5	0	76	186	37.20

Bowling	O	M	R	W	Average
M.W. Tate	316	62	881	38	23.18
R. Kilner	169.1	32	375	16	23.43
E.E. Hendren	5.1	0	27	1	27.00
F.E. Woolley	120	14	399	9	43.88
J.W. Hearne	147.3	12	539	11	49.00

Australia

Batting	Innings	NO	HS	Runs	Average
J. Ryder	6	1	201*	363	72.60
J.M. Taylor	10	0	108	541	54.10
W.H. Ponsford	10	0	128	468	46.80
W.A.S. Oldfield	10	3	65*	291	41.57
A.E.V. Hartkopf	2	0	80	80	40.00

Bowling	O	M	R	W	Average
C.V. Grimmett	31.3	5	82	11	7.45
H.S.T.L. Hendry	15.7	3	41	3	13.66
C. Kelleway	171	39	413	14	29.50
A.J. Richardson	114	34	248	8	31.00
J. Ryder	40	7	133	4	33.25
J.M. Gregory	208.4	22	816	22	37.09
A.A. Mailey	244	21	999	24	41.62

Wicket-keepers: W.A.S. Oldfield (A) 18 dismissals
H. Strudwick (E) 18 dismissals

Captains: H.L. Collins – batting 114, 60; 9, 30; 3, 26; 22, 1; 1, 28
bowling dnb; 0–10; 0–19, 0–19; 0–18; 1–36
A.E.R. Gilligan – batting 1, 1; 17*, 0; 9, 31; 0; 5, 0*
bowling 1–92, 2–114; 3–114, 0–40; 1–17; 0–24, 1–26; 1–46, 1–46

In the first match the tenth-wicket stand of 127 between J.M. Taylor and A.A. Mailey remains the Australian record for that wicket against England. In the second match W.H. Ponsford became the first batsman to score a century in each of his first two Tests. J.B. Hobbs and H. Sutcliffe batted throughout the third day, the first time this had been achieved in a Test. In the fourth match Sutcliffe became the first batsman to score four centuries in a Test series, and W.A.S. Oldfield became the first wicket-keeper to make either five dismissals or four stumpings in a Test innings. In the fifth match C.V. Grimmett took 11–82 on début. Sutcliffe scored a record 734 runs in the series, and M.W. Tate's 38 wickets is still the record for an English bowler in Australia.

1926

England

Batting	Innings	NO	HS	Runs	Average
J.B. Hobbs	7	1	119	486	81.00
G.E. Tyldesley	1	0	81	81	81.00
H. Sutcliffe	7	1	161	472	78.66
G.G. Macaulay	1	0	76	76	76.00
E.H. Hendren	6	3	127*	186	62.00

Bowling	O	M	R	W	Average
W. Rhodes	45	24	79	6	13.16
C.F. Root	107	47	194	8	24.25
H. Larwood	95	19	252	9	28.00
M.W. Tate	208.3	64	388	13	29.84
G.T.S. Stevens	64	7	184	5	36.80

Australia

Batting	Innings	NO	HS	Runs	Average
C.G. Macartney	6	1	151	473	94.60
W. Bardsley	5	1	193*	231	57.75
W.M. Woodfull	6	0	141	306	51.00
A.J. Richardson	5	0	100	155	31.00
W.A.S. Oldfield	6	2	33*	112	28.00

Bowling	O	M	R	W	Average
C.V. Grimmett	204	59	414	13	31.84
A.A. Mailey	172.4	25	592	14	42.28
C.G. Macartney	126.2	48	215	4	53.75
A.J. Richardson	150	57	273	4	68.25
J.M. Gregory	105	20	298	3	99.33

Wicket-keepers: H. Strudwick (E) 6 dismissals
W.A.S. Oldfield (A) 6 dismissals

Captains: A.W. Carr – batting dnb; dnb; 13; dnb
A.P.F. Chapman – batting 49, 19
H.L. Collins – batting dnb; 1, 24; 61, 4
W. Bardsley – batting 0; 15

W. Bardsley's 193* in the second match is the highest score by a player aged over 40 in England v Australia Tests, and he is the oldest batsman to score a century for Australia against England. In the third match C.G. Macartney, having been dropped fourth ball, scored a century before lunch, and his second-wicket partnership of 235 with W.M. Woodfull was then the record for any wicket by either side in England. J.B. Hobbs overtook C. Hill's record 2,660 runs in England v Australia Tests. In the second innings of the fifth Test the opening stand of 172 between Hobbs and H. Sutcliffe, which turned the match England's way, was achieved after overnight rain had made the pitch extremely difficult for batting.

7

The Wormkiller and the Autocrat

For most of the period between the wars Australian teams tended to be stronger than English teams, winning twenty-two Tests to England's fifteen. Jack Ryder, however, drew the short straw, being made captain for the 1928–9 series at a time when the Australians were in transition. Many of the fine players of earlier in the decade had gone, and there were some strange selections to replace them. At thirty-nine and with fifteen Tests to his name Ryder hardly lacked experience and he captained the team soundly and sensibly, although Percy Chapman and some bad luck early on proved too much for him. Few captains could have made much of the first two Tests, given the strengths of the teams and the influence of Chapman, and it says much for Ryder that he dragged his side back into the series.

In his early days Ryder had been a fast-medium bowler, but after the Great War he concentrated on batting and became an attacking batsman with a drive that Ray Robinson compared to a slamming gate. As well as two Test centuries he once made 295 runs in 245 minutes when Victoria compiled their world record score of 1,107 against New South Wales in 1926, the match in which Arthur Mailey complained that a man in the crowd had dropped Ryder twice off his bowling. Throughout the 1928–9 series he batted well, making more runs than anyone else – 492 at an average of 54. His Test average, in fact, was a fine 51, some seven points more than his career average. As a captain, he certainly led by example.

Everything went against Australia in the opening Test, the first to be staged in Brisbane, when they lost by the record margin of runs in Test history. Gregory broke down in England's first innings and took no further part in the match while Kelleway was unable to bowl in England's second innings as he had ptomaine poisoning; neither played Test cricket again. England batted first and made 521, with a century from Hendren; Australia replied with 122. One significant moment occurred early in the Australian innings when Chapman took a magnificent catch in the gully to dismiss Woodfull for 0; from that moment on, many of the home batsmen seemed

J. S. RYDER

(Left) *Jack Ryder. He had the misfortune to captain the only weak Australian side between the wars.* (Right) *Jack White, Somerset farmer and England captain.*

to be restrained by Chapman's presence close to the wicket and unable to play their natural game. As Tests in Australia were still being played to a finish, Chapman chose to bat again. England reached 342 for 8 before he became the first captain to declare in a Test in Australia. Batting two short, Australia were all out for 66, and England won by 675 runs. It was the kind of nightmare that is probably best simply forgotten.

The twenty-year-old Bradman made his début in the match, batting at number seven, but scored only 18 and 1. For the second Test he was dropped, the only time that it ever happened. This time the batsmen put up a better account of themselves, Woodfull and Hendry scoring centuries in the second innings, but England made hay against a weak bowling attack and every batsman got into double figures, Hammond making 251. The bad luck continued when Ponsford, having scored only 5 in his first innings, had a bone in his hand broken by a ball from Larwood that put him out for the rest of the season. There was also some controversy over Kippax's first innings dismissal; he had scored only 9 when a ball from Geary, having hit him on the pad, trickled on to his wicket and dislodged a bail. He stood his ground and only left when the square leg umpire confirmed he was out. The crowd thought Duckworth had knocked the bail off and, in best Sydney Hillite fashion, suggested alternative ways in which he could be passing his time. It could have become unpleasant but Chapman managed to smooth things over. England won easily by eight wickets, although it should have been by ten wickets as they needed only 15 runs in their second innings, and Chapman sent in two bowlers who promptly got out.

The next two Tests were tense, close games that Australia came near to winning, England's margin of victory getting smaller in each match, just as Australia's had done four years earlier. At Melbourne Bradman announced himself in earnest, scoring 79 and 112, and Kippax, Ryder and Woodfull all scored centuries. England, however, had Hammond scoring his second consecutive double century – and then had Hobbs and Sutcliffe to see them through a bad time in the second innings on a real 'sticky'. No captain, however wily, could do much against these two in this mood; they brought all their skill and experience to bear in staying while the pitch eased off, allowing England to achieve an unlikely three-wicket victory. Ryder was much criticised for allowing victory to slip away, but he had neither a really fast bowler nor a left-arm spinner, either of whom could have made a big difference. In the fourth Test Hammond scored two more centuries and Jardine made 98, but Australia produced another batting prodigy in the nineteen-year-old Archie Jackson. He made 164 in his maiden Test innings; four years later he died of tuberculosis. Chasing 349 to win, Australia looked as though they would do it; but Chapman took a blinding catch and then Hobbs ran out Bradman, and they fell just short – just as England had done four years earlier at Adelaide when Ryder scored his 201. Chapman's bowling changes and field-placings had been exactly right, and it seemed he could do no wrong.

But complete revenge for the 1921 whitewash was not to be; for reasons that have never been precisely explained Chapman stood down from the final Test, and England lost. Officially it was because he had been ill with influenza, but possibly he stood down because he had not been batting well or because he wanted to give someone else a chance. The captaincy went to Jack White. A slow left-arm bowler, he spun the ball very little but picked up wickets by constantly varying his flight and pace – no fewer than 2,356 of them in all, at an average of only 18. He was the most successful bowler of the series, taking 25 wickets at 30 on what were mostly batsmen's pitches. A short run and easy action enabled him to wheel away for hours; at Adelaide he bowled 124.5 overs in scorching heat, 37 of them maidens, taking 13 for 256. Monty Noble said that his bowling was every bit as important for England as Hammond's record 905 runs.

White, a cheerful, unflappable character was known as 'Farmer' partly because this actually was his occupation and partly because, with his sturdy build and rosy cheeks, he was the epitome of the Somerset countryman. This was the only time he led England against Australia, but he was captain for the first three Tests at home to South Africa the following summer, winning one and drawing two. He was one of very few spin bowlers to captain England, and as he played fourteen of his fifteen Tests after the age of thirty-seven he was very experienced when he did so. He had captained Somerset in the previous two summers, a shrewd operator who did his best with rather limited resources, but at Melbourne he inevitably suffered by comparison with Chapman and was simply unable to inspire his men in the way that Chapman had done. The game was a very slow affair which went into an eighth day, at the time the longest ever played, and England contrived to lose despite scoring 519 in their first innings. Hobbs's 142, at the age of forty-six, was his last Test century, and he is likely to remain the oldest man to score one; he also became the first to 5,000 Test runs.

Australia's reply of 491 was scored at less than two runs an over, but three young players, Fairfax, Wall and Hornibrook, all playing in their first Test match, did well, and in the second innings England could manage only 257. Maybe Chapman could have engineered something – another blinding catch that sent the adrenalin racing through his team, perhaps – and stopped the home team reaching the 286 they needed. In any case, White could not and Australia cruised home by five wickets. Ryder must have enjoyed being there at the end, not out on 57, in his last Test.

Ryder's captaincy was based on orthodoxy. He was a quiet, slow-spoken man, scrupulously fair, not given to experiments or fancy stuff, but very sound on fundamentals; he inspired respect and liking and had an easy, natural relationship with his players. To come up against Hammond scoring 905 runs, though, is rank bad luck, especially as all the other England batsmen got runs too. Since the England attack was also markedly better than Australia's, and the team was led and inspired by Chapman at his peak, we should remember that with a little more luck Australia could have won the series 3–2. Ryder has gone down in the record books as a loser, but after the first two crushing defeats he came very close to being a national hero. He was a Test selector for many years, and was noted as a great helper of young players. At the Centenary Test in 1977, at the age of 87, he was very proud to lead the parade of old Australian Test players. Just three weeks later he died.

It was the inspiration that Chapman provided and which was missing from the last Test that must be the key to his success. He was a very friendly and sociable man, always ready for a drink and a chat, and very popular as a result. Off the field he carried out the duties of a touring captain with much distinction. His team loved him, and blossomed under his old-fashioned idea that the game was meant to be enjoyed; even the Australian public took him to their hearts (which was more than they did to the next England captain they saw). His cavalier approach meant that he was not a great tactical analyst, but he was a very perceptive judge of a cricket match; his bowling changes and field placings were successful far too often for a critic to say he was just lucky. David Lemmon, in his biography of Chapman, sums up his captaincy as a blend of cheerfulness, shrewdness and confidence that attracted good fortune.

He was made captain again for the 1930 series, although he had put on a lot of weight and was now over fifteen stone. His opposite number was Bill Woodfull, captaining Australia for the first time.

Woodfull was to lead his country in three full Ashes series, winning five Tests and losing four – but those four were all against Jardine and his bodyline tactics, while the five included regaining the Ashes twice. Since he also beat West Indies by four Tests to one and South Africa by five to nil, his overall record is excellent. By profession he was a mathematics teacher, so that the mind he brought to the job of leading his country was a disciplined one. He was also renowned for his straightforwardness and common sense, his tolerance and consideration to others.

As a leader he was very democratic and very courageous, taking much more bodyline punishment from Larwood and Voce than anyone else and never shirking what he saw as his duty to his team. Not surprisingly his players were utterly loyal to him. He was one of the most unspectacular and unostentatious of captains, preferring a patient and firm approach rather than Chapman's cavalier one. In fact he was criticised for the predictable way in which he would wheel away endlessly with his main bowlers. Ray Robinson comments that 'he did seem to overplay his trump cards, Grimmett and O'Reilly, yet when either was given a spell you could almost hear the batsmen sigh with relief. He never committed the error of leaving them off too long.' His caution was such that he often went into a Test with only three front-line bowlers so that his batting was as strong as possible, an approach which brought him the criticism it deserves. Not a man for issuing commands, his method was to outline his strategy to his team and leave it to them to use their own means of carrying this out. Perhaps this will only work successfully when the team is a strong one, but Woodfull was lucky in that; had he been in Ryder's place at the beginning of the previous series his attitude may well have been different.

His batting was legendary for the imperturbable, patient way in which he would build an innings. His backlift was minimal and what small movement there was was almost vertical, so that his strokes, according to Ian Peebles, had an air of the guillotine. So few chances were given, so many balls played along the ground, that he came to be called 'Old Steadfast' and the 'Unbowlable' and, surely one of cricket's most splendid nicknames, the 'Wormkiller'. He had plenty of those strokes, however, and scored 49 centuries in 245 innings, a ratio exceeded only by Bradman. From the time he made his Test début in 1926 he was a permanent fixture in the team, and finished with an average of 46. He led Victoria from 1926–7 to 1933–4, taking them to four Sheffield Shield titles.

When the series started Chapman found that his magic touch had not deserted him. In the first Test he batted well and fielded brilliantly, to inspire his depleted team – Larwood missed the last day through illness – to a 93 run victory. It was his ninth win in nine Tests as captain, including six against Australia, an unparalleled record. There his winning run ended, but not his personal triumphs. In the second game he scored his only Test century, making 121. He also took an astonishing catch to dismiss Bradman, famously described by Neville Cardus:

'When Bradman made the stroke, Chapman bent down, picked the ball up half-an-inch from the grass, threw up a catch beyond belief, and assumed his usual stance in the "gulley" – legs apart, arms folded. The roar of the crowd expressed amazement and joy. As Bradman was departing for the Pavilion, maybe the most astounded man of all, I was watching the game in front of the Tavern with Sir James Barrie. "Why is he going away?" asked Barrie, as Bradman left the crease. "But surely," I said, "surely, Sir James, you saw that marvellous catch by Chapman?" "Oh yes," replied Barrie, "I saw it all right. But what evidence have we that the ball which Chapman threw up in the air is the same ball that left Bradman's bat?"'

As it happened, in the first innings Bradman had scored 254 and Woodfull 155 to set up Australia's highest total against England, 729 (also the highest in any match at Lord's). England lost by seven wickets, but there was no criticism of Chapman's captaincy; the selectors, as usual, took the stick.

The third and fourth Tests were both affected by the weather and drawn, with Australia having the better of things in both. The third was notable for Bradman's 334, which included 309 scored on the first day, a record which seems unlikely to be beaten. And then came the thunderbolt – Chapman was dropped and Bob Wyatt appointed in his place. The newspapers were beside themselves, the public was in uproar, even the Australians were furious. It was uncannily similar to what had happened four years earlier, except that Chapman's success had been vastly greater than Carr's. There was to be no fairy story for Wyatt, though; the scales now contained Bradman, and were weighted towards Australia.

For all the furore over the dropping of Chapman, Wyatt was given a warm reception; he was always popular, and everyone realised he was not to blame for the loss of the great hero. When he went in England were in trouble at 197 for 5, but he put on 170 with Sutcliffe and the total reached 405. This, however, was the series in which Bradman scored his record 974

Bob Wyatt replaced Chapman just as Chapman had replaced Carr, but couldn't work the same magic.

'*The Exile. Napoleon Chapman on board the* Ballyroughluck.*' A cartoon by Strube from the* Daily Express *of 16 August 1930 after Chapman had been deposed from the captaincy.*

runs, and it was his fourth-wicket partnership of 243 with Jackson that proved decisive, enabling his team to reach 695. In their second innings England could manage no more than 251 as Hornibrook, with 7 for 92, enjoyed his moment in the limelight. Defeat by an innings and 39 runs was particularly sad for Hobbs, as it was his final Test and he scored only 9 in his last visit to the crease, but particularly pleasurable for Woodfull as he regained the Ashes on his thirty-third birthday.

Thereafter Percy Chapman's career went into steady decline. He had been named as captain for the tour to South Africa before being dropped for the last Test, but that series was lost 1–0 and he never played for England again. Because of his weight he became increasingly immobile, and his batting, never noted for its great technique, deteriorated rapidly. He captained Kent frequently and continued to bring the same sense of enjoyment to his cricket as he had always done, but the old magic had gone. After 1936 he played only a few times, finally retiring in 1939.

Even at the height of his career he was sowing the seeds of his own destruction. For his success depended, at least in part, on his sociable nature which brought out such an enthusiastic response from his team, and in that sociable nature drinking featured very prominently. As he got older he became more and more alcoholic. His wife left him, people who once had cheered him now avoided him, and he became a very sad and lonely man. Arthritis set in, and the last years of his life were years of pain and great unhappiness. As David Lemmon points out, there is a strong element of Greek tragedy in Chapman's story. In his youth the gods blessed him with gifts that made him a national hero, but also within him was the fatal flaw that would destroy him. His problem was that he remained forever in spirit a young man, unable and certainly unwilling to adapt to the change that came over the climate of Test cricket. He was one of the last of the cavalier captains, whose misfortune was to overlap with the roundheads who turned Test cricket into a war of attrition. Since cricket for him was primarily about enjoyment, about swinging the bat lustily and entertaining the spectactors, he could never understand the win-at-all costs attitude. It is a measure of the prevalence of that attitude today that he seems to be spoken of only little, despite being one of cricket's most successful captains. There is something slightly unreal about him, as though we cannot quite believe that such a friendly and debonair gentleman who gave such pleasure to so many could have been so triumphant at the rather dour game that cricket has now often become. Robertson-Glasgow wrote that 'my own idea of a cricket match is to bowl on a fast pitch with damp on top and to have Chapman, as captain, in the gully.' Chapman, we may be sure, would have enjoyed every moment of it.

So many words have been written about the bodyline tour of 1932–3 that what follows can do little more than repeat the story for the nth time. Whether you believe it is a story worth repeating yet again may well depend upon your nationality.

Fast leg-theory bowling, as it is properly called – 'bodyline' was a term coined by Australian journalists – was the strategy which Douglas Jardine decided was the best way to overcoming a strong Australian batting line-up headed by Don Bradman. It involved the fast bowlers bowling frequent short-pitched balls at the leg stump – and as this is the one which generally has the batsman's body in front of it there were plenty of bruises sustained before the series was over. A ring of fielders close in on the leg side meant that from a defensive back-stroke to a short-pitched ball there was a good chance of being caught, while most aggressive strokes were more of a dangerous undertaking than usual. It was all within the laws of the time, but

W. M. WOODFULL

(Left) *Douglas Jardine. Not the most popular man ever to visit Australia.* (Right) *Bill Woodfull, 'The Wormkiller' who twice won the Ashes on his birthday.*

it is difficult to argue with those who felt it was contrary to the spirit of the game. Bowling at the leg stump had been used as a defensive ploy for decades but this was different.

Jardine himself is usually thought of as a cold, dispassionate man who was intent on winning at all costs, but, as so often, his present-day reputation has become distorted. Certainly he was highly intelligent and shrewd, and if his patrician manner made him aloof he also had qualities which inspired fierce loyalty from his players. He insisted that they did exactly what he said, and if they didn't obey him they were out, although once mutual respect had been reached he was a staunch ally. An addition to his obituary in *The Times* spoke of him as gentle and diffident, at least in his later years, and as being concerned with ethical and religious problems. His particular interest was Hindu philosophy; for Christianity he had no time at all, dismissing it as 'rewards and fairies'. It is not hard to imagine the response of most of the aggrieved spectators at the Adelaide Test, had they been told that the England captain often pondered problems of ethics.

He had been an outstanding batsman for Winchester and Oxford before joining Surrey in 1921, and invariably wore his Harlequins cap when batting. He played for them until 1933, becoming captain in the last two years, and had played seven Tests, including the 1928–9 tour of Australia, before he was appointed captain against New Zealand in 1931. When confirmed as leader for the Australian tour he planned his campaign almost on military lines, making it his main objective to curb Bradman's run-scoring. Having watched Bradman he believed him to have a weakness against very fast bowling directed at his leg stump, and he knew that he had, in Harold Larwood, the ideal bowler to exploit this. Not only was he extremely fast, he was also remarkably accurate and, for a short man, able to extract plenty of bounce, all of which were essential to Jardine's plan. John Arlott has written that 'Without Larwood Bodyline *might* not have come as and when it did. Without Bradman it *might* not have been considered necessary. Without Larwood it would *never* have won a series of Tests, and might have passed almost unnoticed.' Voce and Bowes also bowled leg-theory, although with less pace, but Allen insisted on bowling in an orthodox manner.

Having decided on his plan, Jardine stuck to it unswervingly, perhaps foolishly so at times, for in the second Test Larwood had to continue to bowl after he had torn his boot, risking an injury. In the final Test, with the Ashes already won, Larwood again had to go on bowling, in short spells, for as long as Bradman was in, despite the fact that he had a splintered bone in his left foot. As soon as Bradman was out he left the field – and never returned to the Test arena. For all his forcefulness, though, Jardine could sometimes be rattled. Ray Robinson records that on two occasions when the Australians were standing up to the bowling and he feared they might get on top, he became panicky; 'He shifted fieldsmen about every couple of balls, and wherever the last four was hit he sent a man, in a way otherwise seen only in under-13 house matches. That caused the Australians to regret that his captaincy was never put to the test against them in straight cricket.'

Perhaps, too, he was fortunate to come up against Bill Woodfull as the captain – not because Woodfull lacked the courage to take him on, which he assuredly did not, but because he refused to retaliate with similar tactics as he was often urged, maintaining that 'the game is too good to be spoilt'. Maybe a full-scale retaliation from Australia would have brought a truce, maybe not, but many have wondered how Jardine would have fared against Warwick Armstrong.

Bradman in fact missed the first Test as he had been advised to rest. It was McCabe, however, who produced one of the great innings, 187 not out, against ferocious leg-theory bowling. Australia made 360, but England, with Sutcliffe, Hammond and Pataudi getting centuries, reached 524. The lead of 164 proved to be the exact figure of Australia's second innings, Larwood taking his second five-wicket haul, and England managed to score the one run they needed without loss. Chapman, of course, would have sent in two bowlers to get that run; Jardine never. The second Test, though, was a different story. Bradman returned, but suffered his only first-ball dismissal in Tests when he played on to Bowes, and Australia could manage only 228. England, though, having started the match without a specialist slow bowler, were overturned by O'Reilly for just 169; and when Bradman scored a courageous century in the second innings England were left needing 251 to win. They never came near it, as O'Reilly took ten wickets in the match to give the home team victory by 111 runs.

However, it was the third Test at Adelaide that was the real cauldron. At one point in their first innings England were 30 for 4, but Leyland, Wyatt and Paynter saw them to 341. On the second day, early in the Australian innings, Larwood was bowling to Woodfull with an orthodox slip field when the last ball of an over struck him over the heart. He took some time to recover, and then, as he prepared to face Larwood's next over, Jardine signalled to his fielders to pack the leg trap. The crowd erupted, booing Jardine and Larwood mercilessly. When Pelham Warner, the MCC manager who deplored Jardine's tactics, went to the Australian dressing-room to enquire after Woodfull, the Australian captain produced what is perhaps the most famous line of all cricket's stories: 'There's two teams out there and only one of them's playing cricket.'

There was uproar again the following day when Oldfield edged a short ball from Larwood on to his temple, and was unable to take further part in that game or the next. *Wisden* called it probably the most unpleasant Test ever played and said that the whole atmosphere was a disgrace to cricket. England won by 338 runs, but it is worth noting that Allen, with his orthodox bowling, took eight wickets, although whether he would have done so had the batsmen not been so unsettled is another matter. The Australian Board of Control cabled MCC complaining bitterly about the unsporting behaviour, but since MCC were unaware of what was really happening they replied haughtily that they had full confidence that their captain, team and manager would do nothing to infringe the laws or the spirit of the game. For a while there was the possibility that the tour might be called off, but while cables were going back and forth the matches continued to be played and Jardine continued to employ the same tactics.

England regained the Ashes in the fourth Test thanks mainly to an innings from Paynter that has become part of cricket's folklore. After the match had started he had gone down with tonsillitis and been taken to a nursing home with a temperature of 102. When England then fell 124 behind with only four first innings wickets left Jardine ordered Voce to go and smuggle Paynter out. He survived for an hour and a half that day and returned next morning to make 83, giving England a small lead. In the second innings Australia collapsed for 175 and Jardine had achieved his objective; as it happened, on the day that the Ashes were regained, Archie Jackson died aged 23. The final Test followed a similar pattern, England taking a small first innings lead and then bowling Australia out for 182 to win by eight wickets. Larwood, annoyed at being sent in as nightwatchman, made his highest Test score of 98 in his last innings, and was warmly applauded by the crowd. Jardine, however, made himself even more unpopular, if that were possible, by continuing to employ leg-theory tactics even when the Ashes had been won.

Jardine, in fact, did not distinguish himself with the bat in that series, although his overall Test average was 48. The following summer he scored a splendid 127 against West Indian fast bowlers who were also using fast leg-theory, which ought to have muted the Australian critics somewhat. Ray Robinson claims that his handling of England's batting was uninspiring, and that 'under his command the Englishmen laboured along in low gear for most of the time'. On the other hand, Jack Fingleton described him as a canny, astute captain who 'was as artful a skipper as you would meet in a day's walk in smelling out the weakness of batsmen' – and although one of the most autocratic captains ever to lead a team on to a cricket field, he had the support of most of his players in what he was doing. At times he could be very negative in his play, at others very forceful, and there are endless stories which show him in contradictory lights. One of the best, though, concerns his popularity with Australians; during one match he brushed a fly from his face only for someone in the crowd to tell him to mind what he was doing as 'the flies are the only friends you've got'.

That Jardine felt the need to adopt such tactics against the menace of Bradman must remain the highest compliment ever paid to a cricketer, apart from a knighthood. That the following winter he chose to adopt similar tactics against the fledgling Indians in their first home series was inexcusable. Perhaps the Australians, not surprisingly, have tended to exaggerate the evil of bodyline, but Jardine undoubtedly alienated vast numbers of people and seemed to remain unmoved by the outrage he caused. For all that, a number of English writers have seen his achievement as good enough to rank him among the great captains; few of their overseas colleagues have agreed with them.

1928–9	Brisbane	E 521, 342–8d	A 122, 66	E 675 runs
	Sydney	A 253, 397	E 636, 16–2	E 8 wkts
	Melbourne	A 397, 351	E 417, 332–7	E 3 wkts
	Adelaide	E 334, 383	A 369, 336	E 12 runs
	Melbourne	E 519, 257	A 491, 287–5	A 5 wkts
1930	Trent Bridge	E 270, 302	A 144, 335	E 93 runs
	Lord's	E 425, 375	A 729–6d, 72–3	A 7 wkts
	Headingley	A 566	E 391, 95–3	Drawn
	Old Trafford	A 345	E 251–8	Drawn
	Oval	E 405, 251	A 695	A inns 39 runs
1932–3	Sydney	A 360, 164	E 524, 1–0	E 10 wkts
	Melbourne	A 228, 191	E 169, 139	A 111 runs
	Adelaide	E 341, 412	E 222, 193	E 338 runs
	Brisbane	A 340, 175	E 356, 162–4	E 6 wkts
	Sydney	A 435, 182	E 454, 168–2	E 8 wkts

1928–9

(Over reduced to 6 balls in Australia)

England

Batting	Innings	NO	HS	Runs	Average
M. Leyland	2	1	137	190	190.00
W.R. Hammond	9	1	251	905	113.12
E.H. Hendren	9	0	169	472	52.44
H. Sutcliffe	7	0	135	355	50.71
J.B. Hobbs	9	0	142	451	50.11

Bowling	O	M	R	W	Average
G. Geary	240.3	70	477	19	25.10
J.C. White	406.4	134	760	25	30.40
H. Larwood	259.1	41	728	18	40.44
M.W. Tate	371	122	693	17	40.76
W.R. Hammond	119	30	287	5	57.40

Australia

Batting	Innings	NO	HS	Runs	Average
A.A. Jackson	4	0	164	276	69.00
D.G. Bradman	8	1	123	468	66.85
A.G. Fairfax	1	0	65	65	65.00
J. Ryder	10	1	112	492	54.66
W.M. Woodfull	10	1	111	491	54.55

Bowling	O	M	R	W	Average
T.W. Wall	75	13	189	8	23.62
J. Ryder	68.5	16	180	5	36.00
H.S.T.L. Hendry	165.1	51	328	8	41.00
C.V. Grimmett	398.2	96	1024	23	44.52
J.M. Gregory	41	2	142	3	47.33

Wicket-keepers: W.A.S. Oldfield (A) 10 dismissals
                  G. Duckworth (E) 14 dismissals

Captains: J. Ryder – batting 33, 1; 25, 79; 112, 5; 63, 87; 30, 57*
                  bowling 0–23, 0–43; 0–22; 0–14; 1–16; 1–20, 1–13; 2–29;
          A.P.F. Chapman – batting 50, 27; 20; 24, 5; 39, 0
          J.C. White – batting 9*, 4 bowling 2–136, 0–28

In the first match W.A.S. Oldfield did not concede a bye in England's match total of 863 runs. In the third match W.R. Hammond became the first batsman to score double centuries in consecutive Test innings. In the fourth match A.A. Jackson, on début, became the youngest century-maker in England v Australia Tests. H. Sutcliffe and D.R. Jardine's 262 for the third wicket is still the England record for that wicket against Australia. In the fifth match J.B. Hobbs became the oldest man to score a Test century at 46 years 82 days and the first to score 5,000 runs in Tests. Hammond set a new series aggregate record of 905 runs.

1930

England

Batting	Innings	NO	HS	Runs	Average
H. Sutcliffe	7	2	161	436	87.20
K.S. Duleepsinhji	7	0	173	416	59.42
A.P.F. Chapman	6	0	121	259	43.16
R.E.S. Wyatt	2	0	64	71	35.50
R.W.V. Robins	4	2	50*	70	35.00

Bowling	O	M	R	W	Average
M.S. Nichols	21	5	33	2	16.50
T.W.J. Goddard	32.1	14	49	2	24.50
R.K. Tyldesley	89	23	234	7	33.42
R.W.V. Robins	85.2	7	338	10	33.80
M.W. Tate	280.1	82	574	15	38.26

Australia

Batting	Innings	NO	HS	Runs	Average
D.G. Bradman	7	0	334	974	139.14
W.M. Woodfull	7	1	155	345	57.50
W.H. Ponsford	6	0	110	330	55.00
A.F. Kippax	7	1	83	329	54.83
A.G. Fairfax	5	2	53*	150	50.00

Bowling	O	M	R	W	Average
S.J. McCabe	87	21	221	8	27.62
A.G. Fairfax	134.2	34	335	12	27.91
C.V. Grimmett	349.4	78	925	29	31.89
P.M. Hornibrook	196.1	50	471	13	36.23
T.W. Wall	229.4	44	593	13	45.61

Wicket-keepers: G. Duckworth (E) 12 dismissals
                  W.A.S. Oldfield (A) 15 dismissals

Captains: A.P.F. Chapman – batting 52, 29; 11; 121; 45; 1
          R.E.S. Wyatt – batting 64, 7 bowling 1–58
          W.M. Woodfull – batting 2, 4; 155, 26*; 50; 54; 54

In the second Test Australia's 729 remains the highest total in any match at Lord's and their highest score against England. D.G. Bradman's 254 is the highest Test innings at Lord's. In the third match Bradman scored 309 runs on the first day, still a Test record, and his 334 was the highest Test score at the time. At 214 minutes his double-century is still the fastest in Tests. His 974 runs at 139.14 has never been passed.

1932–3

England

Batting	Innings	NO	HS	Runs	Average
E. Paynter	5	2	83	184	61.33
W.R. Hammond	9	1	112	440	55.00
H. Sutcliffe	9	1	194	440	55.00
R.E.S. Wyatt	9	2	78	327	46.71
Nawab of Pataudi	3	0	102	122	40.66

Bowling	O	M	R	W	Average
H. Larwood	220	42	644	33	19.51
T.B. Mitchell	21	5	60	3	20.00
H. Verity	135	54	271	11	24.63
W. Voce	133.3	23	407	15	27.13
G.O.B. Allen	170.6	29	593	21	28.23

Australia

Batting	Innings	NO	HS	Runs	Average
D.G. Bradman	8	1	103*	396	56.57
S.J. McCabe	10	1	187*	385	42.77
L.S. Darling	4	0	85	148	37.00
W.M. Woodfull	10	1	73*	305	33.88
P.K. Lee	2	0	42	57	28.50

Bowling	O	M	R	W	Average
T.W. Wall	160.1	33	409	16	25.56
W.J. O'Reilly	383.4	144	724	27	26.81
H. Ironmonger	245.1	96	405	15	27.00
P.K. Lee	52.4	13	163	4	40.75
D.G. Bradman	12	1	44	1	44.00

Wicket-keepers: W.A.S. Oldfield (A) 7 dismissals   H.S.B. Love (A) 1 dismissal
L.E.G. Ames (E) 10 dismissals

Captains: W.M. Woodfull – batting 7, 0; 10, 26; 22, 73*; 67, 19; 14, 67
D.R. Jardine – batting 27; 1, 0; 3, 56; 46, 24; 18, 24

In the fourth Test E. Paynter, suffering from severe tonsillitis, left a sick-bed to score 83 and turn the match England's way.

8

The Artist as Machine (or Vice Versa)

After the acrimony of bodyline the 1934 tour by the Australians was an important one for restoring damaged friendships; Bob Wyatt, who had never approved of the leg-theory tactics, can take much credit for making it successful. As captain of England, however, Wyatt somehow contrived to be almost permanently unlucky. A man who was as good a cricketer and as thorough a student of the game as he should not lose the Ashes twice. He was unlucky enough to take over, both in 1930 and in 1934, from a successful captain, and the fact that these two predecessors were so different in character must have made it hard for him. Both of them, in their separate ways, were rather larger than life, and it is fair to say that with Wyatt we return to something nearer normality.

He was a solid batsman with a full range of strokes, who usually played in the middle order but was also an opener. In a career that lasted from 1923 to 1957 he scored over 39,000 runs at an average of 40, with 85 centuries, although his Test average was under 32. He was also a medium-pace swing bowler good enough to take just over 900 wickets. He captained Warwickshire from 1930 to 1937, Worcestershire from 1949 to 1951, and led England against New Zealand (drawing his only match as captain), West Indies (helping to win one rubber but losing another) and South Africa (losing a rubber), as well as his Ashes matches. In all he played in forty Tests, and was described by R.L. Arrowsmith as being indispensable to England at a time when English cricket was strong. Unfortunately, he was also prone to injury, suffering no fewer than twelve broken bones in fourteen years.

His method of captaincy was to analyse the opposition's strengths and weaknesses carefully and to evolve a masterplan to beat them. Most Test captains, at least from the 1930s onward, have been analysts and strategists, but the successful ones have possessed other qualities as well. Somehow Wyatt didn't seem able to produce these extras. More often than not he won the toss, but was then unable to press home the advantage this gave him. On

THE ARTIST AS MACHINE

the other hand, almost every time he lost the toss he went on to lose the game, and the rubber. His captaincy is epitomised by one Test against the West Indies, when the last English batsman was out to the penultimate possible ball of the match. True he came up against an Australian team that was stronger than England – in three of his five Tests as captain, including the 1930 Oval Match, Bradman and Ponsford scored massively – but England were by no means weak. In Bill Woodfull, too, he was opposed by an experienced leader who was determined to regain the Ashes which he felt had been taken from him in a travesty of cricket.

As it happened Wyatt missed the first Test because of a fractured thumb. The captaincy was given to Cyril Walters, who had played in six previous Tests with good success. He had captained a weak Worcestershire team since 1931, so he knew what he was about. Walters, the first Welshman to captain England, was an elegant, stylish right-handed batsman who

Cyril Walters (right) became the first Welshman to lead England after Bob Wyatt broke a thumb before the first Test of 1934 Here he opens the innings with the great Herbert Sutcliffe.

finished with an average of 52 from his eleven Tests, before poor health and domestic commitments caused a premature retirement during the 1935 season. Informed opinion said that had he not retired he could have been one of the great captains of England.

Between Bradman's début and the war Australia beat England ten times, and this was the only victory in which he did not score a century. It was also notable for two début performances: Farnes, the Essex fast bowler who replaced Larwood, took five wickets in each innings, and for the visitors Chipperfield became the first batsman to score 99 in his first Test. Australia's first innings made 374, England replied with 268, and when, on the fourth morning, Australia had reached 273 for 8 Woodfull declared, giving England four and three-quarter hours in which to score 380 – or to survive. It proved to be the most finely judged of declarations. England started well enough, but then wickets began to fall to Grimmett and O'Reilly. Their figures bear witness to a superb piece of bowling to win a match against a team defending desperately: Grimmett 47–28–39–3, O'Reilly 41.4–24–54–7. England, simply, were not allowed to save the game because the bowling was too good for them. But as the minutes ticked away and still the batsmen stonewalled the tension for the crowd was unbearable. There were ten minutes left when the last wicket fell.

So Walters's only experience of Test leadership ended in defeat, but by no means disgrace. He himself had top-scored with 46 in the second innings, and in the series scored 401 at an average of 50. At least he had captained his country in what Cardus called 'one of the grandest Test matches ever fought and won and lost'. Somehow it was typical of Wyatt's bad luck that, when he came to win one match and lose one, he should go down in the records as an Ashes-losing captain because of a defeat in which he had not been able to play any part. Having said that, in the drawn fourth Test England were thoroughly outplayed and were saved only by the weather.

The second Test was Verity's match. On the only occasion since 1896 when England have beaten Australia at Lord's, the Yorkshire left-arm spinner took 15 for 104 (14 of them in one day, so setting a record in England–Australia Tests which has never been beaten). After England had scored 440 with hundreds from Leyland and Ames (the only century by a wicket-keeper in Ashes Tests until Alan Knott's at Adelaide in 1975), Australia reached 192 for 2 by the Saturday evening and a draw seemed inevitable. But on the Sunday evening it rained heavily, creating a pitch which Verity exploited to the full. Wyatt was criticised by Cardus for switching his bowling when the Australians were struggling, but he realised his errors quickly enough and England bowled them out just seven runs away from avoiding the follow-on. Verity followed his 7 for 61 with 8 for 43 as Australia were all out for 118, and England won by an innings in three days.

At Old Trafford a beautiful pitch, glorious weather and the last two Australian batsmen combined to ensure a high-scoring draw. The match is remembered for two particular overs: one from O'Reilly in which he took the wickets of Walters, Wyatt and Hammond in four balls, and the first one from Allen, which contained three wides and four no-balls. England scored 627 despite O'Reilly's efforts, and then got Australia to 454 for 9, still 24 away from the follow-on. O'Reilly and Wall took the score to 491, however, and saved the match.

The Headingley Test was a different story. England batted miserably to scrape to 200, but then reduced the visitors to 39 for 3 at the end of the first day. At the end of the second day they were 494 for 4, Bradman and Ponsford having put on 388. Bradman finished with 304 and Ponsford with 181; the next highest score was McCabe's 27. Needing 384 to avoid an innings defeat England struggled to 229 for 6 before rain came to their rescue at lunch-time on the last day.

The timeless Oval Test produced Australia's biggest victory by a runs margin. Bradman and Ponsford, playing in his last Test, exceeded the heights of Headingley and averaged over 80 runs an hour as they put on 451 for the second wicket, still a Test record for any wicket, although it was equalled in 1983. Remarkably, in both matches Ponsford was out hit wicket. England's reply to Australia's 701 was 321, and they also lost the services of Ames through severe lumbago. Australia batted again and made 327, during the course of which Woolley, recalled at the age of 47, deputised behind the stumps and conceded 37 byes, still a record for a Test innings. This was the last appearance by a pre-1914 Test player, but it was not a happy one; he scored 4 and 0. England then subsided for 145, and Australia won by 562 runs. Once again, in one of those neat curiosities that cricket throws up, the victory that regained the Ashes was achieved on Woodfull's birthday.

Poor fielding was one reason for England's failure; Ponsford in particular was missed a number a times. On paper Wyatt had a strong team, but the batsmen too often collapsed and the bowlers and fielders too often performed indifferently; inevitably the captain must take his share of responsibility for that. Even the one win was helped by the weather and was thanks to an inspired performance by one player, and he seemed unable to mould his players into a cohesive unit. For all that, he has remained a highly respected figure, and in later years he became a Test selector and wrote widely about cricket.

G.O.B. 'Gubby' Allen, now Sir George Allen, England captain against
Australia 1936–7. A lifelong servant of the game, both as player and
administrator, here he presents the ICC Associate World Cup to
Duncan Fletcher, captain of Zimbabwe, in 1982.

Woodfull, now aged 37, retired at the height of his success and returned
to teaching, becoming headmaster of Melbourne High School and ultimately being awarded an OBE for his services to education. He died in what many
people would consider an ideal way – of a heart attack while playing golf.

For the series at home to India in 1936 the selectors appointed 'Gubby'
Allen as captain, with a view to giving him some experience before the trip
to Australia that winter. Since his opposing captain was going to be Don
Bradman he clearly needed all the experience he could get. In fact he took
twenty wickets and won the three-match series 2–0, so that he was able to
set off for Australia with some confidence.

Allen was primarily a fast bowler, but he was a strong and correct
batsman good enough to notch up eleven centuries, including one against
New Zealand. Being an excellent close fielder, he was a fine all-rounder. His
bowling action was rhythmic and classical, beautifully described by Cardus
as 'sideways on, left shoulder seen momentarily by the batsman, then a
strong urgent swing over, after a run to attack that was sturdy and
galloping, and not too long'. He is the only England captain to have been
born in Australia (he also had an uncle, Reginald Allen, who played once

for Australia in 1886–7), but Eton and Cambridge confirm his nationality. He first played for Middlesex in 1921, although business commitments meant that he was rarely able to play regularly and that he was never captain. When he was given the England leadership his experience was therefore very limited.

Allen had made his debut against Australia in 1930 and played in the three Tests against New Zealand in 1931, once taking 5 for 14, but there was criticism when he was selected for Jardine's tour of Australia. He responded by bowling very well and taking twenty-one wickets. He would have nothing to do with bodyline but he must have benefited from the apprehension that it caused the batsmen. The 1934 series had restored friendly relations, but if there was any worry that the Australian public still harboured grudges Allen soon dispelled it with his friendliness and sportsmanship. His approach was to study the Australian strengths and weaknesses very carefully and to work out a field-setting for each batsman; to McCabe, for instance, he posted a deep, wide mid-on for the lifted hook. And when a batsman arrived at the crease the bowler whom he seemed to like the least was quickly in action against him. For the first two Tests all went well, but as the series steadily went sour on him and his batsmen lost confidence, his enthusiasm never waned and he strove as hard as he knew to lead his team back into contention.

It happened that he was confronted by a captain who, despite scoring two ducks early on, managed to score 810 runs in the series, still a record by a captain in any Test rubber. Bradman's batting deeds are so legendary as to need little amplification here; those twenty-nine Test centuries, many of them double or triple-hundreds, at an average of 99.94, place him far above everyone else. He was the most superbly organised batsman the game has known, a man who allied perfect technique and the ability to play any stroke to any ball with limitless concentration, an abundance of self-confidence and an insatiable desire both to score runs and to win. Some people felt that he batted like a ruthless machine, but they overlooked the variety of strokes which his innings usually contained and the way in which he so often scored his runs at a tempo appropriate to the state of the match. Neville Cardus's view was that he was tired of hearing him referred to as a run-making machine: 'When does a batsman who commands all the strokes and plays them rapidly and scores 300 in a day in a Test match, when does he cease to be an artist and degenerate into a "machine"?' Cardus adds: 'And for all the rare organisation of his technique, nature is in it always. Bradman has not allowed enormous skill to ruin the salt touch of his original self. The *gamin* comes out in a sudden cross-bat solecism.'

The incomparable Sir Donald Bradman during his triumphant 1948 tour. The supply of superlatives needed to describe his batting has long since run out – and his captaincy was pretty successful too.

The one qualification that might be made is to say that he was the world's best batsman 'on good wickets', for many of his failures were on rain-affected pitches when he would often get out to a rash stroke. Ray Robinson suggested that, having grown up in Australia where they were encountered less often than in England, his cricketing education had that gap in it, so that when he had to bat on a real 'sticky' he changed his normal methods too much and brought about his own downfall. That seems a fair assessment, and the criticism should not be laboured since he produced some fine wet-wicket knocks. Every cricket lover knows of Bradman's phenomenal record, and it helps to understand him better if we remind ourselves that he was, occasionally, mortal.

What, though, of Bradman the captain? Keith Miller said that 'to understand Don Bradman you have to appreciate that in everything he undertook, he wanted, indeed had, to win.' Norman Yardley said that there was only one thing he enjoyed more than beating you by an innings and two hundred runs and that was beating you by an innings and three hundred runs. For many people this merciless passion for victory that fires sporting champions is an unattractive quality, and Bradman's relentless efficiency in achieving his aims meant that he was not always the most popular of people – although in his last tour of England the crowds flocked in great numbers to see him. In the words of Lindsay Hassett, 'Don got just about what he deserved to get out of cricket – a lot of runs, a lot of money and very few friends.' He had his critics who saw him as the captain whose obsession with victory furthered, to the detriment of the game, the win-at-all-costs attitude favoured by Jardine; others took a less extreme view and saw him simply as a highly competitive man for whom winning was, quite rightly, very important. Others felt that he was not above using his power to settle old scores. The dropping of Grimmett seemed to many to fall into this category, Bradman's arguments in favour of Ward, his replacement, appearing rather weak. Ward duly failed and some eminent people never forgave Bradman for it.

When he took over, Bradman was not an experienced leader, and was more prone to direct his bowlers' field-placings than any other captain of the time except Jardine, even to the extent of disrupting the placings of someone like O'Reilly. He would sometimes, too, give directions to his batting partners, even doing it by pantomime in full public view. But as he settled into the job, his field-setting became very sophisticated and his captaincy grew to match his stature as a batsman. In twenty-four Tests in charge he won fifteen and lost only three, two of which were his first two games; in four rubbers against England and one against India he won four and drew one. Obviously he was helped by having a strong team but there have been plenty of apparently strong teams that have not done themselves justice, and he must take much of the credit for ensuring that his sides played to their full potential. It was the smoothness of their performance that was often so impressive, for he ran them like the proverbial well-oiled machine, with only the occasional hiccup such as over using bowlers. He was a very astute man who gave much thought to his tactics, knew how to motivate his men and, more than anyone else, could lead by example. Without being a strict disciplinarian he managed to have the players completely under his control; they in their turn knew just what was expected of them, knew the standards they had to maintain and knew that if they fell below them they would be out. He was not much of a socialiser, preferring to unwind on his own with a cup of tea rather than join in the general merriment, but his players had such respect and liking for him that this caused little resentment.

Don Bradman's was a complex character that mingled pitilessness with kindness. Some of the older players felt that the spirit in which they had played the game had been more cordial and that cricket had been more enjoyable for everyone than it now was under Bradman; but there are many people only too happy to testify to his sportsmanship, his thoughtfulness and his generosity. There must be few who would not agree that he was a great and influential captain.

The 1936–7 series was a remarkable one, partly because only one Test was unaffected by rain. In the first match England batted first, and Worthington was out first ball. McCormick soon had 3 for 17, but then had to go off with lumbago, and a century from Leyland enabled England to reach 358. Fingleton scored exactly 100 to become the first player to score centuries in four successive Test innings – and was out first ball next time. Voce, bowling without a suggestion of leg-theory, took 6 for 41 on an easy pitch to dismiss the home team for 234. In England's second innings the aforementioned Ward had his one moment of glory as he took 6 for 102, but Australia were left needing 381 for victory. Overnight rain made the pitch so sticky that Allen and Voce went through them for 58, their lowest home total of the century. Just before the game, it should be noted, Bradman had suffered a tragedy with the death of a new-born son.

In the second game Hammond scored the fourth of his double-centuries against Australia to help England reach 426. This took two days, and on the third morning a thunderstorm again came to England's aid as Australia were all out for 80 and lost by an innings. England two up! Much rejoicing back home. And then the luck, not unreasonably, turned. At Melbourne

Australia batted first, and on a pitch that rain had turned into a gluepot, Bradman declared at 200 for 9. Hammond and Leyland managed to put on 42, Hammond's innings often described as one of the best of his life. Allen declared at 76 for 9, making this the first Test in which both sides declared their first innings, but many felt that he should have done so earlier and put Australia in on that horror of a pitch. He could not know, of course, that the sun was about to return, allowing Bradman to score 270. England lost by 375 runs and the series had turned its corner. It was in this game that Allen and Walter Robins planned that, at a given signal, Allen would drop a ball short to Bradman; Robins, a fine sprinter, would already be running from square leg to long leg, Bradman would hook and Robins would catch him. Bradman played his part and hooked, but Robins dropped him. 'Hell, Gubby, I'm sorry,' he said. 'Don't give it a thought, Walter,' came the reply. 'It has probably cost us the rubber, but don't give it a thought.'

At Adelaide Allen performed the highly unusual feat of talking Bradman out. He was on 26 when he covered up and let a couple of balls go by. 'Why don't you hit 'em?' said Allen jokingly. Bradman promptly lashed out and was bowled. On a comfortable wicket England took a first innings lead, but then Bradman scored another double-century and Fleetwood-Smith took a ten-wicket haul to give Australia victory by 148 runs. Back at Melbourne for the final match, Australia became the first team to win a rubber after losing the opening two games. Bradman, McCabe and Badcock all scored centuries as they reached 604, aided by several dropped catches, and then England subsided twice to lose by an innings and 200 runs. The matches were watched by a total of 943,513 spectators, the record for any Test series.

'Gubby' Allen captained England against West Indies in three Tests after the war at the age of 45, but lost that rubber 2–0. Back in 1935 he had joined the MCC Committee; from 1955 to 1962 he was Chairman of Selectors; in 1963 he served as President of MCC and from 1964 to 1976 as its Treasurer, a period that saw the voluntary transfer of power from the MCC to the Cricket Council, the TCCB and the National Cricket Association. In 1986, to the surprise of no one, he was knighted for the enormous service he had given to the game.

If that series had contained some very short innings, the one that followed it in 1938 more than made up for it. England were led this time by Walter Hammond, who, not without many qualms, had turned amateur in the hope of being offered the captaincy. He was by such a wide margin the outstanding English cricketer of his day that he was the obvious choice as leader, even if his captaincy experience was limited.

*The immortal Walter Hammond, most majestic of batsmen. This
painting hangs in Gloucestershire's Bristol clubroom.*

His immortality is every bit as great as Bradman's, for he was one of the most complete of all-rounders; he complemented his prodigious batting skills – over 50,000 runs with 167 centuries, including a Test total of 7,249 at 58 with 22 centuries – with fine medium-fast bowling and slip fielding which has hardly ever been equalled – 110 catches in 85 Tests. Many writers say that it was a privilege just to watch him walk out to bat, for grace and dignity marked everything he did, and his batting combined splendour, power and artistry to an unrivalled extent; his offside driving was such stuff as dreams are made on. He had been in the team since 1927, although he had sometimes been disappointing at home, especially in 1934.

It seemed that he saw an Ashes Test as a duel between himself and Bradman, each their country's great champion, and he sometimes batted as though he carried the whole burden of his team's score; undoubtedly he played much more freely and enjoyably for Gloucestershire than he normally did for England, although having said that his career average was slightly lower than his Test average. It was a duel in which Bradman usually had the edge, the difference between them, according to Cardus, being that Hammond could be kept quiet but Bradman never could. Cardus wrote that Hammond 'belongs, in his method, to the Golden Age, the pre-war period when we did not consider it criminal for a player to get caught at long-on in a Test match for less than two hundred.'

Ronald Mason, in his book on Hammond, suggests that England approached the 1938 series in a defensive frame of mind which arose from the repeated punishment handed out by Bradman over the years, so that throughout the series Hammond played with the intention of making enough runs to avoid defeat even if Bradman could not be kept completely in control – a plan that was helped by winning every toss. As it happened, Hammond's captaincy was generally well received by the critics; *Wisden* called him sagacious and inspiring. His approach was to give his players credit for being intelligent cricketers and not impose detailed orders on them. His thorough knowledge of the game enabled him to assess each of his opponents carefully and set the best field to the right bowler. Generally his tactics worked well, and England had rather the better of a drawn series in which one match was lost to rain. Ray Robinson, in fact, voted Hammond the best captain England had between the wars. Given Chapman's record that seems surprising, and in the first series after the war, when he was in his forties and had plenty of personal problems, his captaincy was a disaster. But that is a later story.

Evidence for Hammond's desire to pile up the runs comes in the first Test. Barnett and Hutton scored centuries, and Paynter and Compton then put

In the Old Trafford Test of 1926 England were led by Jack Hobbs when A.W. Carr went down with tonsillitis after the first day. Alongside him here are some of the finest English players of the early 1930s. Standing, left to right, George Duckworth, Bill Voce, Frank Woolley, Maurice Tate, Harold Larwood. Seated, left to right, Patsy Hendren, Jack Hobbs, Walter Hammond, 'Tich' Freeman.

on 206 in 138 minutes, Paynter going on to a double-century. When Compton was out for 102, having become England's youngest century-maker at twenty years and nineteen days, he was reprimanded by Hammond because he had told him to play himself in again after reaching his hundred and go on to amass a really big score. As it was England reached 658. Australia's reply centred on McCabe, whose 232 caused Bradman to tell his team to 'come and watch this, you'll never see the like again', and they made 411. Following on, though, they had no trouble in saving the match on a wicket that was so good for batting that almost 1500 runs were scored in four days. Brown and Bradman scored centuries, making this the only Ashes Test to contain seven hundreds. In Mason's graphic words, the match 'capsized with an overload of runs'.

At Lord's Hammond made a magnificent 240, the highest score by an England captain against Australia. England totalled 494, but Brown then carried his bat for 206 in Australia's reply of 422. When Hammond declared his second innings closed Australia were 314 behind with only 165 minutes left, surely an unduly cautious decision by a captain who had to win to regain the Ashes; the draw was inevitable. The Old Trafford Test was then washed out completely. At Headingley poor batsmanship and difficult conditions enabled the ball to dominate the bat for once. Only Hammond stood firm as O'Reilly and Fleetwood-Smith hustled England out for 223. The second day was very dark and the pitch damp, but Bradman told his players not to appeal because he felt they would make more runs in those conditions than after the rain that looked imminent had actually arrived. He manoeuvred the strike himself as much as possible, scoring yet another century in one of his finest innings, and gave Australia a slight lead. The spinners, O'Reilly in particular, then went through England for 123, Hammond falling first ball, and Australia just got home by five wickets before the rains arrived. The Ashes had been retained.

So to the ludicrous events on an Oval pitch that had been vastly over-prepared for a timeless Test. It is said that McCabe, opening the bowling to Hutton and seeing it played firmly back to him, remarked to the umpire 'They'll make a thousand.' As every cricket lover knows, they declared at 903 for 7. There were records aplenty, most of them to Hutton: the highest Test innings (364), the longest first-class innings (797 minutes) (both since exceeded), the highest England partnership against Australia (382 with Leyland for the second wicket) and batting while 770 runs were being scored. It was also, rather neatly, the hundredth English century against Australia. And his batting was so monumentally solid throughout that he gave only one chance, a possible stumping at 40. Fleetwood-Smith, poor man, gained his own record – of 298 runs conceded in a Test innings. To cap it all, with the England score at over 800 Bradman decided to bowl himself, and in his third over he caught his foot in a pothole and chipped a bone. Even many Australians felt that this was the best thing that could have happened, for had he batted on that pitch the match might have outlasted the scheduled close of the season the following month. As it was, with Fingleton also injured, Australia batted two short and were dismissed for 201 and 123. It was perhaps the most nonsensical match ever played, and very few people can actually have enjoyed it. Bradman asked for trouble by going into the game without his fast bowler McCormick, while Hammond's remorseless insistence on the accumulation of ever more runs scarcely enhanced the game as a spectacle. Throughout the dark wartime days ahead many cricket lovers must have looked back and regretted that they did not have something more stirring to cheer them as their most recent memory of Ashes Tests.

1934	Trent Bridge	A 374, 273–8d	E 268, 141	A 238 runs
	Lord's	E 440	A 284, 118	E inns 38 runs
	Old Trafford	E 627–9d, 123–0d	A 491, 66–1	Drawn
	Headingley	E 200, 229–6	A 584	Drawn
	Oval	A 701, 327	E 321, 145	A 562 runs
1936–7	Brisbane	E 358, 256	A 234, 58	E 322 runs
	Sydney	E 426–6d	A 80, 324	E inns 22 runs
	Melbourne	A 200–9d, 564	E 76–9d, 323	A 365 runs
	Adelaide	A 288, 433	E 330, 243	A 148 runs
	Melbourne	A 604	E 239, 165	A inns 200 runs
1938	Trent Bridge	E 658–8d	A 411, 427–6	Drawn
	Lord's	E 494, 242–8d	A 422, 204–6	Drawn
	Headingley	E 223, 123	A 242, 107–5	A 5 wkts
	Old Trafford	Abandoned through rain		
	Oval	E 903–7d	A 201, 123	E inns 579 runs

1934

England

Batting	Innings	NO	HS	Runs	Average
M. Leyland	8	1	153	478	68.28
H. Sutcliffe	7	1	69*	304	50.66
C.F. Walters	9	1	82	401	50.12
E.H. Hendren	6	0	132	298	49.66
L.E.G. Ames	7	1	120	261	43.50

Bowling	O	M	R	W	Average
K. Farnes	81.2	18	228	10	22.80
H. Verity	271.2	93	576	24	24.00
W.E. Bowes	144.3	27	483	19	25.42
E.W. Clark	101.2	15	324	8	40.50
G. Geary	88	17	203	4	50.75

Australia

Batting	Innings	NO	HS	Runs	Average
W.H. Ponsford	7	1	266	569	94.83
D.G. Bradman	8	0	304	758	94.75
S.J. McCabe	9	1	137	483	60.37
W.A. Brown	9	0	105	300	33.33
A.G. Chipperfield	8	1	99	200	28.57

Bowling	O	M	R	W	Average
W.J. O'Reilly	333.4	128	698	28	24.92
C.V. Grimmett	396.3	148	668	25	26.72
H.I. Ebeling	31	9	89	3	29.66
A.G. Chipperfield	79	19	222	5	44.40
S.J. McCabe	92	22	219	4	54.75

Wicket-keepers: L.E.G. Ames (E) 10 dismissals
                  W.A.S. Oldfield (A) 14 dismissals

Captains: C.F. Walters – batting 17, 46
            R.E.S. Wyatt – batting 33; 0; 19, 44; 17, 22
                           bowling dnb; dnb; dnb; 0–28
            W.M. Woodfull – batting 26, 2; 22, 43; 73; 0; 49, 13

In the first match A.G. Chipperfield became the first player to score 99 on début. In the second match H. Verity took 15 for 104, 14 of them in one day, still the record number of wickets in one day in England v Australia Tests. L.E.G. Ames became the first wicket-keeper to score a century in England v Australia Tests, and W.A.S. Oldfield became the first wicket-keeper to make 100 dismissals. In the fourth match D.G. Bradman and W.H. Ponsford scored 388 for the fourth wicket, still the fourth-wicket record. In the fifth Test they scored 451 for the second wicket, still the record for any wicket in Test cricket.

1936–7

(Over increased to 8 balls)

England

Batting	Innings	NO	HS	Runs	Average
W.R. Hammond	9	1	231*	468	58.50
M. Leyland	9	1	126	441	55.12
C.J. Barnett	9	0	129	395	43.88
J. Hardstaff (jr)	9	0	83	256	28.44
R.E.S. Wyatt	4	0	50	100	25.00

Bowling	O	M	R	W	Average
W. Voce	162.1	20	560	26	21.53
K. Farnes	73.3	8	256	11	23.27
W.R. Hammond	88.4	8	301	12	25.08
G.O.B. Allen	128.7	12	526	17	30.94
H. Verity	195.7	57	455	10	45.50

Australia

Batting	Innings	NO	HS	Runs	Average
D.G. Bradman	9	0	270	810	90.00
S.J. McCabe	9	0	112	491	54.55
R.G. Gregory	3	0	80	153	51.00
J.H. Fingleton	9	0	136	398	44.22
A.G. Chipperfield	6	2	57*	155	38.75

Bowling	O	M	R	W	Average
M.W. Sievers	75.2	25	161	9	17.88
L.J. Nash	24.5	2	104	5	20.80
W.J. O'Reilly	247.6	89	555	25	22.20
L. O'B. Fleetwood-Smith	131.4	20	463	19	24.36
E.L. McCormick	84	6	316	11	28.72

Wicket-keepers: W.A.S. Oldfield (A) 8 dismissals
                  L.E.G. Ames (E) 15 dismissals

Captains: D.G. Bradman – batting 38, 0; 0, 82; 13, 270; 26, 212; 169
            G.O.B. Allen – batting 35, 68; 9; 0*, 11; 11, 9; 0, 7
                           bowling 3–71, 5–36; 3–19, 1–61; 1–35, 2–84; 2–60, 0–61; 0–99

In the first match J.H. Fingleton became the first batsman to score four centuries in successive Test innings. In the third match he and D.G. Bradman put on 346 for the sixth wicket, still a Test record for that wicket. Bradman's 270 is the highest second-innings score in England v Australia Tests and the highest by a number seven Test batsman. He batted down the order as he had a severe chill. His total of 810 runs is the best for any captain in a Test rubber.

1938

England

Batting	Innings	NO	HS	Runs	Average
M. Leyland	1	0	187	187	187.00
L. Hutton	4	0	364	473	118.25
E. Paynter	6	2	216*	407	101.75
J. Hardstaff (jr)	3	1	169*	184	92.00
W.R. Hammond	6	0	240	403	67.16

Bowling	O	M	R	W	Average
W.E. Bowes	75.4	12	188	10	18.80
H. Verity	154.1	53	354	14	25.28
M. Leyland	8.1	0	30	1	30.00
K. Farnes	179.4	32	581	17	34.17
W.J. Edrich	35.2	6	139	4	34.75

Australia

Batting	Innings	NO	HS	Runs	Average
D.G. Bradman	6	2	144*	434	108.50
W.A. Brown	8	1	206*	512	73.14
S.J. McCabe	8	0	232	362	45.25
S.G. Barnes	2	0	41	74	37.00
B.A. Barnett	8	1	57	195	27.85

Bowling	O	M	R	W	Average
W.J. O'Reilly	263	78	610	22	27.72
E.L. McCormick	114	20	345	10	34.50
L. O'B. Fleetwood-Smith	217.5	34	727	14	51.92
S.G. Barnes	38	3	84	1	84.00
S.J. McCabe	103	19	293	2	146.50

Wicket-keepers: L.E.G. Ames (E) 2 dismissals   W.F.F. Price (E) 2 dismissals
               A. Wood (E) 3 dismissals
               B.A. Barnett (A) 5 dismissals

Captains: W.R. Hammond – batting 26; 240, 2; 76, 0; 59
                        bowling – 44, 0–15; dnb; dnb; 0–8
           D.G. Bradman – batting 51, 144*; 18, 102*; 103, 16; dnb
                        bowling dnb; dnb; dnb; 0–6

In the first match D.C.S. Compton became England's youngest century-maker. In the second match W.R. Hammond made the highest score by an England captain in England v Australia Tests. W.A. Brown carried his bat for 206, the total of 422 being the highest in which anyone has carried his bat in Tests. In the last game L. Hutton's 364 was then the highest Test score. His 13 hours 17 minutes is the longest England innings, and he was at the crease while a record 770 runs were scored. His partnership of 382 for the second wicket with M. Leyland is the best for any England wicket against Australia.

9

England versus History

By the 1946–7 series Hammond was forty-three and Bradman was thirty-eight. Bradman had been suffering for years from fibrositis and there was a rumour (no more) that if he failed in the first Test he might call it a day. For Hammond it was the last challenge, the final chance to overcome the man who had stood between him and the accolade of 'the world's best batsman'; he had, after all, done well in the unofficial 'Victory Tests' when he had led England, and in the 1946 season he topped the batting averages by a street.

However, it was all to go very wrong for him – and to a large extent he brought about his own downfall. There cannot have been many successful touring captains who did not have a good rapport with their players, sympathise with them when the strains were taking their toll, and do their best to help and encourage them. By that yardstick Hammond was doomed as a touring captain; he had his personal problems, ranging from, by coincidence, his own fibrositis to an impending divorce, and he let them prey upon him so that he was often moody and irritable.

He seemed unable to descend to the level of his men and understand their troubles, remaining detached for much of the time; when the team went on long, hot train journeys he and the manager would travel by road, usually in a Jaguar – a practice that might have been acceptable before the First World War but was unlikely to improve team relations after World War Two. He even complained when they drank with the 'enemy' and he made the mistake of trying to get the players to do things his way; advice would have been all well and good but he went in more for orders. Denis Compton was a prime sufferer here, being criticised for moving out to the slow bowlers instead of staying in his crease, as Hammond believed they should be played in Australia. Compton felt that the captain wanted him to play in a way that was alien to him, and inevitably it affected his performances, at least for the first three Tests.

England also had to contend with 'history repeating itself', a major headache for any captain. As at the end of the previous conflict Australia found that a whole string of top-line players – Miller, Lindwall, Tallon, Morris, Toshack, McCool – had emerged from the hostilities, and although

England had found some good newcomers, too, they had also lost some fine ones, Verity and Farnes in particular. Most of the England team had played before the war; Evans, Bedser and Ikin were the only regular newcomers. Most crucially of all England had no real fast bowler, while Australia had found one of the great combinations – and of course there was Bradman, who may have had health problems before the series but still managed to score 680 runs at an average of 97. Perhaps England felt relieved that they restricted him to only one double-century. E.W. Swanton wrote that at the start of the tour he rated England's chances at fifty–fifty after it was announced that O'Reilly had retired, and that seemed to be the general opinion. How could anyone know that arguably the greatest cricket team of all time was about to come together?

Early in the first Test there was an incident which may have affected that 'greatest team' profoundly. Bradman had made 28 when he was caught at chest height by Ikin at second slip. It seemed so clear-cut that England did not even appeal, but Bradman stayed his ground. When the appeal was made it was turned down, both the umpire and Bradman feeling that the catch had been made from a bump-ball. At the end of the over Hammond said to Bradman, 'That's a bloody fine way to start a series.' There was no love lost between them for the rest of the rubber. (Hammond did afterwards say that he thought it was a catch but that he may have been wrong.) Bradman went on to make 187 out of Australia's 645, and any thoughts of retirement were deferred; he was still to bring much pleasure to many people, both English and Australian, before he did so. For the third wicket here he put on 276 with Hassett, still an Ashes record for that wicket. England then had to bat twice after heavy rain and storms, during which enormous hailstones fell and the covers and stumps floated away. In the circumstances they were not totally disgraced, although an innings and 332 runs represents Australia's biggest ever victory. It is curious that each team's largest win should come in consecutive Tests, even if they were eight years apart.

In the second Test, however, England simply batted poorly on a good wicket and could make only 255. In reply Barnes scored what was then the slowest double-century in all first-class cricket, while Bradman batted with his left leg strapped up because of a torn muscle (and also with the after-effects of gastritis). Both of them scored 234, Barnes in ten and three-quarter hours, Bradman, playing exclusively off the back foot, in six and a half. Their fifth-wicket 405 has never been bettered in first-class cricket. Evans, in his first game against Australia, did not concede a bye as the total reached 659, still the highest score not to include a bye. England managed 371 with a century from Edrich, but it was another innings defeat. The spinners Johnson and McCool took sixteen wickets between them as the English batsmen followed their captain's orders and stayed in the crease.

It had been agreed that the Tests would be limited to six days, which meant that the third match became the first one to be drawn in Australia for almost 63 years. After the first innings both sides were nearly all square, but Australia then ran up 536 with big scores from Morris, Lindwall and Tallon, the last two putting on 154 in 88 minutes. England had only three wickets left at the end, benefiting from a break for rain. The fourth Test was also a high-scoring draw, both Compton and Morris making a century in each innings. It is famous as the match in which Godfrey Evans took 97 minutes to get off the mark (easily a Test record) as Compton tried to keep the strike and set a decent target for the bowlers to aim at. But with the pitch playing easily this was never on anyway, and at the end the home team were nearer to victory than the visitors.

This was Hammond's last match against Australia as his fibrositis was causing him great problems; he did have one more Test against New Zealand, where he got the warmest of receptions and top-scored for his team in a rain-affected draw. Thereafter his career drifted quietly and sadly to its close, and although he still had some eighteen years to live they were mostly melancholy ones, spent in South Africa. The end was hastened when he was badly injured in a road accident. After he died, Cardus wrote in *Wisden* that 'his cricket was, I think, his only way of self-realization'; certainly it seemed that the meaning went out of his life with the decline of his career. How could anyone who had achieved such deeds be anything but mightily proud of them? Easily, it would seem, since he also had the knowledge that he had so often come off second best to his arch-rival. Apparently that distressed him more than we ordinary mortals could ever understand.

The contrast between Hammond's gloomy disposition and the cheery one of his successor could hardly have been more marked. Norman Yardley came to the England captaincy at precisely the wrong time, yet he was rarely heard to complain about it. Having served in the same battalion as Hedley Verity and having played alongside him in his last match, he no doubt felt that there were more important things to complain about than Miller and Lindwall skittling your team out. He was an all-rounder who, if not quite out of the top drawer, was still a good Test cricketer. On this present tour he had put together some useful scores at least one of which saved his team from defeat, and he had taken good wickets with his gentle medium-pace,

Norman Yardley (left) chose an unfortunate time to come to the England captaincy. With him here is Hedley Verity, the great Yorkshire left-arm spinner who died in Italy in 1943.

including Bradman three times. His batting was sound if unspectacular, and he could attack with a good range of strokes when the mood was upon him. He was not a strike bowler by any means, but like many another seemingly innocuous medium-pacer he was a noted partnership-breaker. A fine all-round athlete, he was six times North of England squash champion.

Yardley was the first Yorkshireman to captain England since F.S. Jackson, and he did so before he led his county. His misfortune persisted even here, for although he managed to share one Championship with Middlesex his reign from 1948 to 1955 coincided with the great Surrey team that swept all before them. Playing against reasonable opposition he could captain his side to victory well enough – he just had a habit of stepping in front of juggernauts. He was widely regarded as the most tactically shrewd of the county captains of his day with a very thorough knowledge of the game; he would weigh up the risks involved in any move, and without doing anything too unreasonable would see that some chances are very much worth taking. One of his favourite ploys was to try and block a batsman's strongest scoring shots, a tactic he knew could change the course of an innings.

He was also greatly liked by all his players as a naturally friendly man, easy to talk to and responsive to their problems. In fact some critics have said that one reason for his lack of success was that he was 'too nice', that he lacked toughness. It was true, as J.M. Kilburn said, that he did not enjoy fighting for its own sake, but the problem with the 'too nice' argument is that there have been successful captains in the same mould. More pertinent would seem to be Alan Gibson's comment that ' "nice" is a word with various meanings, and if in Yardley's case we interpret it as "fastidious", we are perhaps getting somewhere near him.' His style of captaincy would have been better suited to the 1920s, for his approach had something of Percy Chapman's – a successful 'nice' captain – about it even if he lacked some of Chapman's flair for the job; certainly he was not happy with the way in which Test cricket was becoming ever more cynical.

His captaincy began well in the final game of the series. A century from Hutton helped England to 280, after which Wright took seven wickets as Australia were dismissed for 253. Yardley says in his autobiography, *Cricket Campaigns*, that this was one of those days when nothing would go wrong for him and every move he made came off; it's good to know that this happened to him sometimes, for one tends to think that nothing ever went right for him in Ashes Tests. In their second innings, however, England were without Hutton (down with tonsillitis) and only Compton could put up a decent score, so that Australia's target was no more than 214. The pitch was taking spin and Yardley felt they could still do it – until Edrich, who had hardly missed a catch all tour, dropped Bradman off a relatively easy chance at 2. Needless to say he had made the match safe before he gave another one, and Australia took the rubber 3–0.

Yardley had a successful summer at home to the South Africans in 1947, and was then made captain against Australia in 1948, the series in which Tests in England finally became five-day matches. He relates that this was the first time that the players had all got together before a Test to analyse the opposition and plan their tactics. Some of the plans they worked out duly came off, but they soon realised that the Australians had been doing some scheming of their own, as the first eight English wickets for 74 runs in the first Test clearly showed. In fairness it should be said that the weather turned against England almost as soon as they began to bat, favoured Australia, then went against England once more. Australia replied with 509. By the time England batted again the light was very bad, and Miller upset the crowd by bowling many short-pitched deliveries. England had to make a big score to get a draw, and Compton came up with one of the greatest of innings; with no fewer than nine interruptions for bad light, rain and the scheduled intervals his 184 runs were spread over three days. England reached 441, but Australia polished off the deficit comfortably as rain fell all around Trent Bridge but not on the ground itself.

The Lord's game was the 150th England–Australia Test, but it was hardly a worthy landmark. Australia made 350 with the aid of some tail-wagging but England could manage only 215. The visitors rammed the advantage home in the second innings and went on to win by over 400 runs, partly because England insisted on dropping several important catches; it was something they did frequently that summer. In the third Test, though, England actually had the upper hand. They scored 363 thanks to another century from Compton, batting with two stitches in his forehead after mishooking a no-ball early in his innings, and then they got Australia out for 221. After which, Yardley being Yardley, they lost a day and a half to rain and had no chance to press home their advantage.

England also had the upper hand for a fair part of the fourth match. On a good pitch they made 496 and reduced Australia to 68 for 3, riches scarcely dreamed of. Then came nineteen-year-old Neil Harvey, in his first Test against England, making a fine century, and Australia's deficit was only 38 runs; once again England's lack of a fast bowler was highlighted. England scored well again in the second innings, making 365 before Yardley declared. He wrote that he wanted a win, and the only way to achieve it was to give Australia time to get the runs if they could – 404 of them in 344 minutes. It was a good declaration, but it did not come off; England lacked the bowlers to do the business and, generally fielding poorly, they gave Morris and Bradman a life each. It was a historic day as Australia became the first team to score 400 in the last innings to win a Test, with 182 from Morris and 173 not out from the captain, his last Test century.

Two things distinguish the Oval Test – England's lowest total of the century and Bradman's second-ball dismissal by Hollies in his last match, when he needed only four runs for a Test average of one hundred. England had no excuse on a lifeless pitch to succumb to Lindwall for 52; Bradman's excuse was the highly emotional reception given him by the crowd, who sang *For he's a jolly good fellow* as he came out to bat. Only Hutton of the Englishmen gave any account of himself, and Arthur Morris exceeded England's second-innings total by himself. It was another crushing defeat to give Australia the rubber by four games to nil. Fortunately for Bradman Archie MacLaren was now dead, or one suspects he might have tried to repeat his little bit of history at Eastbourne; he would have been seventy-six so he probably would not have batted, but one can imagine him saying that he 'thought he knew how to beat these Australians' and organising something. As it was, this splendid team was able to go one better than Armstrong's men and go through the whole tour undefeated.

Yardley's jinx dogged him to the end of his Test career, which came two years later at home to the West Indies – when, by way of a change from Lindwall and Miller, he came up against Ramadhin and Valentine in calypso mood. To encounter one pair of world-class bowlers, Lady Bracknell might have said, may be regarded as a misfortune; to encounter two looks like carelessness. Still not satisfied with the punishment he had received he became an England selector, and then, after he retired, he worked as a much-respected radio commentator.

Don Bradman, of course, became Sir Donald. For the great part of his life he has been his country's most famous citizen, as he maintained a prominent role in cricketing affairs for decades after his retirement, serving as Chairman of the Board of Control and Chairman of Selectors. He has also been a fine writer and speaker on cricketing matters, and outside the game has worked as a stockbroker and company director, applying the same determination to his business affairs as to his batting. He is revered above everyone in Australia, and rightly so, for his achievements did, after all, transcend those of everyone else who ever picked up a cricket bat.

One could ask the reader to spare a thought for the man who had to follow Bradman, but in truth he needs no such solicitude. Lindsay Hassett, at 5 feet 6 inches one of the shortest Australian Test cricketers, had an impishness which enabled him to step into the great man's shoes without being overawed. He was, after all, one of the best of batsmen – only four players have had a higher career average than his 58, and only Bradman among Australians scored more centuries – and to this he was able to add many qualities that enabled him to become an excellent captain: a different captain from Bradman, but a fine one in his own right.

He was one of those players for whom batting always seems so easy, with his nimble footwork and his glorious strokes all round the wicket. He loved to attack, but at times after the war he chose, if he felt the situation called for it, to accumulate a lot of runs slowly rather than fewer runs quickly, and he didn't always endear himself to the crowd as a result. He later admitted he had been mistaken in this, and tried to make up for it by encouraging others not to follow suit. Like all the Australians of the time he was overshadowed by Bradman, but the only danger in this is that some of his performances may not be given the recognition they deserve. He scored consistently well in his 43 Tests, making over 3,000 runs at 46.

Hassett's success as a captain stemmed from a very perceptive tactical mind and a very warm and humorous personality. Everything about him suggests that he was one of the most likeable men ever to grace a cricket field, a witty character who always tried to find humour in any situation; after a difficult over from Bedser, for instance, he tried to spike the bowler's foot to the ground with his bat. Keith Miller said that he had more genuine friends in all walks of life than any other cricketer, and he was a splendid ambassador for his country.

He was noted for his thoughtfulness towards younger players, especially for trying to help them over difficult hurdles, and his sportsmanship was of the highest. Examples of his good nature are legion; one of the nicest, as told by Ray Robinson, came when he was playing for the Prime Minister's XI at Canberra. He picked up the nearest bat, scored 18, and when he was surrounded by children asking for autographs gave the bat to one of the boys. It happened to belong to Arthur Morris, and when he tried to look annoyed Hassett said 'What does it matter? You should have seen the look on the kid's face.'

All of this meant, of course, that his team would do anything for him, especially as his tactical acumen was so sound. He missed nothing that happened on the pitch and controlled his men with a minimum of arm-waving, clearly operating a smoothly running machine. His tactics were not usually calculated to produce great excitement, nor was he a member of the win-at-all-costs school; his teams tended therefore to lack some of the aggression they had had under Bradman, but perhaps the cricket was more enjoyable as a result. Without Bradman the side could not touch the heights of 1948, and there was something of a decline in interest among the spectators after the great man had gone, but for all that Hassett was still a very good captain of a very good side.

There were a number of contenders for the England captaincy for the 1950–1 tour, but none of them had been in impressive form with the bat – until in the Gentlemen v Players match F.R. Brown scored a rapid century, took some wickets and was promptly given the job. Although England lost the series heavily it was an inspired appointment; even at the age of forty he performed great deeds, led the team very well, made himself immensely

Freddie Brown, such a popular captain that the Australian crowds began cheering for England.

popular with the Australian crowds and with a bit of luck could even have won the series. It was a rubber which serves as a prime example of the dangers of taking the record books at face value, unsupported by background detail.

Freddie Brown was an all-rounder whose record would have been a formidable one had he been able to devote more time to the game during the 1930s when in his twenties. A large, burly man, he was a powerful striker of the ball, particularly on the drive. He was also a leg-break bowler who, towards the end of his career, would occasionally revert (with good effect) to the medium-pace of his youth. He had been on Jardine's tour without appearing in any Tests, but had played six times before the war (half of which he spent in a prisoner-of-war camp). In 1949 he took over as captain of Northamptonshire, for decades the whipping-boys of the Championship who regularly finished in the bottom two, taking them to sixth place. The challenge rejuvenated his career; he did the double for the first time since

1932, and was rewarded with captaincy against New Zealand and the last match against the 1950 Ramadhin and Valentine-inspired West Indians.

When he was appointed to lead the Australian tour Brown was concerned that at his age his form might not be all that it should be. As it turned out it was the majority of his players who struggled and not him. Hutton and Bedser were glorious exceptions, and Bailey too did well, but there were many disappointments, Compton in particular having by far his worst series. Matters were not helped by what now appear rather odd selections, with Edrich and Laker left behind and some inexperienced players taken along; it was not at all a strong team to confront a still-very-good Australian outfit on home territory.

One of the highlights proved, in fact, to be Brown's captaincy, and the spirit he brought to the task made him so popular with the crowds that they began cheering for England instead of their own team! Tactically he was not flawless, and was criticised for his experiment of moving Hutton down the order for the first two Tests. It was not unreasonable, since he had both two good openers in Washbrook and Simpson and a shaky middle order. Although not a total failure, Hutton's rightful place was undoubtedly number one and Brown soon restored him to it. Generally, however, he handled his team very well and did his best to inspire them in difficult conditions during one of Australia's wettest summers. His was a warm, cheerful, friendly personality and he was as popular with his team as with the crowds; the problem was that they did not have the batsmen to support Hutton against fine bowlers. Interestingly, as a pointer to the future, Brown chose to discuss tactics on the field more with Hutton than with his vice-captain Compton; Hutton was, after all, having his best Australian tour while Compton was having his unhappiest.

The first Test started well enough for England when they bowled Australia out for 228 on a good pitch. A weekend's rain then transformed the pitch into a glue-pot, and Brown declared at 68 for 7 to give Australia a taste of the medicine they were administering. Hassett realised that two could play at that game and declared at 32 for 7, leaving England 193 to get. Brown ordered the heavy roller, but at this time in Brisbane it involved getting the horse out of its stable to pull it. At the end of each roll of the pitch the animal had to be unhitched, the roller adjusted and the horse rehitched, and as a result the pitch got only four rolls. If this sounds as though it were a scene from a pantomime, the result was not so funny; the pitch had nothing like the seven-minutes' rolling on which Brown ought really to have insisted. Consequently, by the close of play, England were 30 for 6 and the match was lost. Hutton was held back to take advantage of what was hoped would be an easier wicket, only for him to run out of partners so that Australia won by 70 runs.

It was in the second Test at Melbourne that the crowd began cheering for England. Bedser and Bailey, exploiting the humid conditions beautifully, bowled Australia out for 194; England soon fell to 61 for 6 when Brown and Evans rescued them and passed the home total by 3 runs. Brown continued the good work by taking four wickets, and by the time England batted again they needed 179. They were without Compton who was injured, and his replacement, Brian Close, the youngest man ever to play for England, had an unhappy time. As it was they crept slowly towards the target, cheered all the time by the crowd; but Hutton's dismissal for 40 signalled the end, and they failed by 28 runs. E.W. Swanton records that Australia 'came in, with Lindsay Hassett at their head in the home state in which he was such a popular figure, to a deafening, disappointed silence. It was eerie.'

After the tension of this game, the third and fourth Tests saw Australia cantering away. In the third game England made 290, but then lost Bailey and Wright to injury, enabling Australia to pile up 426. England's second innings gave Iverson, the so-called 'mystery bowler' who spun the ball by flicking it with his second finger, his best Test figures of 6 for 27, and Australia won by an innings. In the fourth match Morris made his highest Test score of 206 and Hutton became the only English batsman to carry his bat through a completed Test innings twice. Unfortunately for England, Morris's team-mates gave him rather better support and Australia took a first-innings lead of 99. Burke then scored a century on début to help set England a total of over 500, which did not provide for an exciting finish. Brown missed the last day having been involved in a car crash the previous evening and Compton led the team. These two matches saw John Warr enter the record books in one of the least desirable ways: his 1 for 281 means that he is still the most expensive wicket-taker in Test cricket.

The victory that England finally achieved meant that 'history had repeated itself' with an astonishing vengeance. The first similarity is that England won the last Test before both world wars. When they finally gained a victory after each war it came, in both cases, after Australia had won eleven times, as the sole win in a 4–1 tour defeat, and at Melbourne. Most remarkable of all is the fact that the gap between England wins was almost identical in each case: from 1912 to 1925 it was 12 years 180 days, while between 1938 and 1951 the gap was 12 years 188 days . . .

It was a good win, too. They bowled Australia out for 217, Brown taking five wickets, and then Simpson, on his thirty-first birthday, scored his only century against Australia. He had been on 92 when the last man, Tattersall, joined him, but they put on 74 for the tenth wicket and England took a lead of 103. Fine bowling on a good pitch then put Australia out for 197, Bedser taking ten wickets in the match, and the deficit was comfortably achieved.

With two of the cheeriest captains in Test history in charge this could hardly fail to be a good-natured series, and indeed it has gone down as one of the friendliest. Freddie Brown, having finished third in both batting and bowling averages, went on to beat New Zealand 1–0 on the way home and South Africa 3–1 the following summer. In 1953, while Chairman of Selectors, he was persuaded to play at Lord's, where he took four second-innings wickets and ensured that Watson and Bailey's match-saving stand was not wasted at the end of the day. This was his last year in first-class cricket, but he subsequently acted as touring manager (a job that he seemed not to relish), as President of MCC, Chairman of the NCA and Chairman of the Cricket Council at a time when a gentleman named Packer was putting his spanner in the works. Alan Gibson wonders how he would have fared had he played before the First World War, for his approach to the game was more in keeping with that period than with his own. For Gibson, Brown was the last of the Edwardians.

History does not give up. Not content with all the similarities between the events after the two world wars there were more yet to come. The Ashes returned to England in the eighth summer after each war ended, and in 1953, as in 1926, four draws were followed by an England victory at the Oval; the only difference the second time around was that there was no young hero to seize the captaincy and the glory, and the glory went to the man who had done so much for his country for so many years.

The momentous decision to appoint Len Hutton as the first regular professional captain of England – the early professional captains, Lillywhite, Shaw and Shrewsbury, had simply been captains on their own privately-organised tours – was taken by Messrs Yardley, Wyatt, Ames and Brown in 1952 for the home series against India. Had there been an outstanding amateur contender for the job he would almost certainly have got it, but there were many who felt that the old amateur–professional distinction was an anachronism; indeed it was to last only another ten years.

Naturally the appointment did not pass without criticism, and one likes to conjure up a picture of elderly colonels spluttering in their brandy when the news was announced, but for anyone who was not firmly entrenched in the past it was a sound and sensible move. Hutton made a good start against the Indians, beating them 3–0 in the series in which Trueman dramatically announced himself, and it was only right that he should continue against Australia in coronation year. The visitors were led once again by Lindsay Hassett, who had captained his team to home triumphs over West Indies and South Africa since the last Ashes series, and the sides seemed more equally matched than they had been for a long time.

Len Hutton and Denis Compton had, of course, been head and shoulders above the rest of the English batsmen since before the war. Of all the fine batsmen who lost a part of their career to the war, probably these two suffered most; had there been no war Bradman and Hammond would probably have retired in the early 1940s, but Hutton and Compton were in their twenties during the war years and would have scored many thousands more Test runs. Yet their styles and approaches could hardly have been more different. It was the difference between the classical and the romantic: Hutton batted correctly, without unnecessary risk, technically superb, a glorious display of disciplined beauty; Compton was his own genius, sparkling and scintillating, dazzling in his footwork, a glorious display of individual beauty. Such is cricket that it was Hutton who had the higher average, by five or six points.

Sometimes Hutton was criticised for the impersonal nature of his play, for the way in which his batting seemed machine-like, with virtually no risks taken and nothing of his own individual self in it. Such criticism overlooked the Yorkshireness that was so strongly a part of his character. Bradman, after all, had come in for the same kind of criticism, to which he might have replied that he had an insatiable appetite for runs and was scoring them in the way that came naturally to him, and if that reasoning is good enough for Bradman it is good enough for Hutton, too. A fairer criticism, perhaps, is that after the war he persisted in playing slow bowling from the crease; not only did this make him rather vulnerable to off-spin, but it had the effect that many young players copied him, often with unfortunate results.

It was clear from the beginning that he was especially talented. His England début came in 1938 against New Zealand, scoring 0 and 1 in the first game and 100 in the second. The 364 at the Oval in 1938 came when he was twenty-two, an innings that was, somehow, too big – too slow, anyway – for real greatness, especially as the game turned into the monstrosity that it did. After years of Bradman's domination it must have come like an oasis in the desert to the England faithful, but undoubtedly he had many finer innings. During the war an accident in a gymnasium left him, after a number of operations, with his left arm an inch shorter and somewhat weaker than it had been, a cruel blow to such a correct batsman whose off-drive was a thing of such peerless beauty. It was a handicap that he overcame with his customary phlegmatic approach.

The war over, he did well enough in 1946–7, but in the first two Tests of 1948 he seemed unhappy against Miller and Lindwall and was dropped for the third match, the only time he was left out of an England team. This did the trick and thereafter his batting matured to real greatness. Hutton never failed to give his all for England, either as player or captain, and finished with the wonderful average of 56, a point above his career average. He also holds the record for the most runs scored in one calendar month, 1,294 in June 1949.

With the amateur–professional distinction long since gone, it is hard for us now to appreciate the pressures that Hutton faced as the first professional to captain England. Without doubt there were those who wanted him to fail, and he encountered problems that no other captain has had to endure. In particular he was up against a weight of tradition that must have sat heavily on the shoulders of such a sensitive man, tradition that said, simply, he should not be there. Happily, despite his inexperience, he did the job successfully and well, if perhaps unadventurously.

He had a very shrewd cricketing brain, and his great experience meant that he was thoroughly at home with the complexities of tactics. His ability to assess a batsman's weaknesses was second to none. He tended to adopt a mixture of attack and defence, attacking until a batsman showed that he had settled in and was about to start piling up runs, and then switching to the defensive. Like other batsmen-captains he would get annoyed at loose bowling. Even if he were not universally loved – that is if those unfortunate enough to be born outside Yorkshire did not always understand him – he was universally liked and respected.

Matters did not always run smoothly, the biggest problems coming on the 1953–4 tour of the West Indies; but while some said that the troubles which occurred there would not have happened with an amateur captain, others felt that Hutton came through a very trying tour with great courage and dignity. Perhaps, all in all, he did the captain's job too cautiously, although with so many snipers ready to shoot him down, he had reason enough for that. One regrettable product of his caution, though, was slow over-rates; he perceived, rightly enough, that his fast bowlers were his match-winners, and as he wanted to keep them as fresh as he could he tended to slow down the tempo of an innings. He could hardly foresee the extent to which this would be taken.

The 1953 series drew more people than had ever before watched an Ashes rubber in England. Perhaps they felt that the tide was turning

Len Hutton (left) and Lindsay Hassett toss at Old Trafford in 1953.

England's way, perhaps they simply felt patriotic because of the coronation, the conquest of Everest, and so on. They saw some fluctuating fortunes. The first Test was played against a background of damp weather and was notable for fourteen wickets from Bedser. After a century from Hassett the last six Australian wickets went down for five runs, the final total being 249. England managed the collapse, but not the century, and could scrape together only 144. Even more of a collapse from Australia left England needing 229, but they lost all of the fourth day and most of the fifth, finishing at 120 for 1.

At Lord's came one of the most famous of all match-saving stands, invariably referred to as the Watson-Bailey epic. Another century from the Australian captain saw his team to 346, during which innings Bedser became the first English bowler to take two hundred Test wickets. The England captain then replied with a century of his own, a glorious 145 that is reckoned to be one of his very best innings, and England made 372. Then it was Miller's turn for a hundred, after which England's target was 343 with seven hours in which to reach it. By the close on the fourth day three wickets were down and Compton did not last too long next morning. There were still almost five hours left when Bailey joined Watson, but it was a situation tailor-made for Bailey's forward-plunging, bat-and-pad-locked-together type of defence.

There were forty minutes left when they were separated, having put on 163 for the fifth wicket. Watson scored 109 in 346 minutes, Bailey 71 in 257 minutes in a display of concentration and determination that – while perhaps not in the Everest-conquering class – was one of the English glories of coronation year. Perhaps the Australians would disagree; Hassett did everything he could, but it simply wasn't to be his day. The England tail could still have capitulated in a matter of minutes, but Brown and Evans made sure that it was not all wasted. Only slowly did the crowd come to realise that the match could actually be saved, and while there were no reports of deaths or umbrella handles being chewed through, many accounts were written of that day, bringing out to the full the agonies that the spectators suffered.

The Old Trafford match was badly affected by rain. Australia's first-innings lead was 42 after a Harvey century, but in their second innings they collapsed to 35 for 8 before time ran out. At Headingley Australia had cause once again to curse Trevor Bailey. England, put in, managed only 167, and the visitors improved on that by 99 (the last Australian wicket to fall gave Bedser the world record, beating Grimmett's 216 and providing due reward for the man who had shouldered England's strike bowling duties almost single-handed since the war). England, desperately trying to save the game, crawled to 275 off 177.3 overs, with Bailey taking 262 minutes over his 38 and with a crucial 48 from Laker at number nine. Australia had 115 minutes in which to score 177, and they were making a good attempt at it when Bailey bowled six overs of defensive leg-theory which made him less than popular with his opponents.

Twenty-seven years and one day after Chapman had taken his bow at the Oval it was Len Hutton's turn to do the same. Indifferent batting from Australia left them at 275, during which Bedser passed Tate's record of thirty-eight wickets in a series. England replied with 306, Hutton and Bailey, the latter at his customary speed, providing the bulk of the runs; Watson, remarkably, had been dropped. And then Australia capitulated, Lock and Laker spinning them out for 162 – although they were less than happy with the legality of some of Lock's deliveries. It does not take much imagination to picture the thoughts of Sir Donald, sitting in the press box. Without a front-line spinner, and defending only 131, Australia never had a chance, and the honour of the winning hit fell to Denis Compton. When Hassett congratulated Hutton on the balcony afterwards he said 'England deserved to win, if not from the first ball at least from the second-last over.' Both captains had worked hard to make it a happy series, and inevitably Hassett could find some humour, even in defeat.

Hassett was awarded the MBE and later became a radio commentator – and a very good one too, for his knowledge of the game and his sense of humour were an ideal combination. His retirement left another large hole in Australia's batting that helped England to win the next two series, but no doubt by then he felt that he had done enough to be allowed to go off and enjoy the fishing that was his passion.

1946–7	Brisbane	A 645	E 141, 172	A inns 332 runs
	Sydney	E 255, 371	A 659–8d	A inns 33 runs
	Melbourne	A 365, 536	E 351, 310–7	Drawn
	Adelaide	E 460, 340–8d	A 487, 215–1	Drawn
	Sydney	E 280, 186	A 253, 214–5	A 5 wkts
1948	Trent Bridge	E 165, 441	A 509, 98–2	A 8 wkts
	Lord's	A 350, 460–7d	E 215, 186	A 409 runs
	Old Trafford	E 363, 174–3d	A 221, 92–1	Drawn
	Headingley	E 496, 365–8d	A 458, 404–3	A 7 wkts
	Oval	E 52, 188	A 389	A inns 149 runs
1950–1	Brisbane	A 228, 32–7d	E 68–7d, 122	A 70 runs
	Melbourne	A 194, 181	E 197, 150	A 28 runs
	Sydney	A 290, 123	A 426	A inns 13 runs
	Adelaide	A 371, 403–8d	E 272, 228	A 274 runs
	Melbourne	A 217, 197	E 320, 95–2	E 8 wkts

1953	Trent Bridge	A 249, 123	E 144, 120–1	Drawn
	Lord's	A 346, 368	E 372, 282–7	Drawn
	Old Trafford	A 318, 35–8	E 276	Drawn
	Headingley	E 167, 275	A 266, 147–4	Drawn
	Oval	A 275, 162	E 306, 132–2	E 8 wkts

1946–7

England

Batting	Innings	NO	HS	Runs	Average
L. Hutton	9	1	122*	417	52.12
D.C.S. Compton	10	1	147	459	51.00
W.J. Edrich	10	0	119	462	46.20
C. Washbrook	10	0	112	363	36.30
N.W.D. Yardley	10	2	61	252	31.50

Bowling	O	M	R	W	Average
N.W.D. Yardley	114	15	372	10	37.20
D.V.P. Wright	240.2	23	990	23	43.04
W.J. Edrich	115.3	13	483	9	53.66
A.V. Bedser	246.3	38	876	16	54.75
T.P.B. Smith	47	1	218	2	109.00

Australia

Batting	Innings	NO	HS	Runs	Average
D.G. Bradman	8	1	234	680	97.14
K.R. Miller	7	2	141*	384	76.80
S.G. Barnes	6	0	234	443	73.83
A.R. Morris	8	1	155	503	71.85
C.L. McCool	7	2	104*	272	54.40

Bowling	O	M	R	W	Average
R.R. Lindwall	122.1	20	367	18	20.38
K.R. Miller	122.3	15	334	16	20.87
E.R.H. Toshack	178.4	50	437	17	25.70
C.L. McCool	182	27	491	18	27.27
I.W. Johnson	124.6	35	306	10	30.60

Wicket-keepers: D. Tallon (A) 20 dismissals   P.A. Gibb (E) 1 dismissal
T.G. Evans (E) 9 dismissals

Captains: D.G. Bradman – batting 187; 234; 79, 49; 0, 56*; 12, 63
W.R. Hammond – batting 32, 23; 1, 37; 9, 26; 18, 22
N.W.D. Yardley – batting 2, 11   bowling 0–7

In the first match D.G. Bradman and A.L. Hassett put on 276 for the third wicket, which is still the record for that wicket in England v Australia Tests. In the second match Bradman and S.G. Barnes put on 405 for the fifth wicket, still the record for that wicket in all Tests. T.G. Evans did not concede a bye in Australia's 659, still the highest total in which no bye was conceded. In the fourth match A.R. Morris and D.C.S. Compton scored a century in each innings, the only time in Tests that a player from each team has scored two centuries in one game.

1948

England

Batting	Innings	NO	HS	Runs	Average
D.C.S. Compton	10	1	184	562	62.44
C. Washbrook	8	1	143	356	50.85
L. Hutton	8	0	81	342	42.75
W.J. Edrich	10	0	111	319	31.90
T.G. Evans	9	2	50	188	26.85

Bowling	O	M	R	W	Average
N.W.D. Yardley	84	22	204	9	22.66
A.V. Bedser	274.3	75	688	18	38.22
R. Pollard	102	29	214	5	42.80
J.C. Laker	155.2	42	472	9	52.44
J.A. Young	156	64	292	5	58.40

Australia

Batting	Innings	NO	HS	Runs	Average
A.R. Morris	9	1	196	696	87.00
S.G. Barnes	6	2	141	329	82.25
D.G. Bradman	9	2	173*	508	72.57
R.N. Harvey	3	1	112	133	66.50
E.R.H. Toshack	4	3	20*	51	51.00

Bowling	O	M	R	W	Average
R.R. Lindwall	222.5	57	530	27	19.62
K.R. Miller	138.1	43	301	13	23.15
W.A. Johnston	309.2	92	630	27	23.33
E.R.H. Toshack	173.1	70	364	11	33.09
S.J. Loxton	63	10	148	3	49.33

Wicket-keepers: T.G. Evans (E) 12 dismissals   D. Tallon (A) 12 dismissals
R.A. Saggers (A) 3 dismissals

Captains: N.W.D. Yardley – batting 3, 22; 44, 11; 22; 25, 7; 7, 9
bowling 2–32; 2–35, 2–36; 0–12; 2–38, 1–44; 0–7
D.G. Bradman – batting 138, 0; 38, 89; 7, 30*; 33, 173*; 0

In the fourth match Australia's 404 was at the time the highest second innings to win a Test, D.G. Bradman and A.R. Morris putting on 301 for the second wicket.

1950–1

England

Batting	Innings	NO	HS	Runs	Average
L. Hutton	10	4	156*	533	88.83
R.T. Simpson	10	1	156*	349	38.77
F.R. Brown	8	0	79	210	26.25
W.G.A. Parkhouse	4	0	29	77	19.25
T.G. Evans	9	1	49	144	18.00

Bowling	O	M	R	W	Average
T.E. Bailey	75.1	18	198	14	14.14
A.V. Bedser	195	34	482	30	16.06
F.R. Brown	109	12	389	18	21.61
D.C.S. Compton	11.6	1	43	1	43.00
D.V.P. Wright	103	6	500	11	45.45

Australia

Batting	Innings	NO	HS	Runs	Average
K.R. Miller	9	1	145*	350	43.75
J.W. Burke	4	1	101*	125	41.66
A.L. Hassett	9	0	92	366	40.66
G.B. Hole	2	0	63	81	40.41
R.N. Harvey	9	0	74	362	40.22

Bowling	O	M	R	W	Average
J.B. Iverson	138.2	29	320	21	15.23
K.R. Miller	106.6	23	301	17	17.70
W.A. Johnston	153.7	28	422	22	19.18
R.R. Lindwall	98.3	11	344	15	22.93
I.W. Johnson	111.6	23	311	7	44.42

Wicket-keepers: D. Tallon (A) 8 dismissals T.G. Evans (E) 11 dismissals

Captains: A.L. Hassett – batting 8, 3; 52, 19; 70; 43, 31; 92, 48
F.R. Brown – batting 4, 17; 62, 8; 79, 18; 16; 6
bowling 2–63; 1–28, 4–26; 4–153; 0–24, 1–14; 5–49, 1–32

In the fourth match L. Hutton became the only Englishman to carry his bat through a completed Test innings twice.

1953

England

Batting	Innings	NO	HS	Runs	Average
L. Hutton	9	1	145	443	55.37
W.J. Edrich	5	1	64	156	39.00
W. Watson	5	0	109	168	33.60
D.C.S. Compton	8	1	61	234	33.42
T.E. Bailey	7	0	71	222	31.71

Bowling	O	M	R	W	Average
A.V. Bedser	265.1	58	682	39	17.48
G.A.R. Lock	61	21	165	8	20.62
J.C. Laker	58.5	11	212	9	23.55
J.H. Wardle	155.3	57	344	13	26.46
T.E. Bailey	143	33	387	8	48.37

Australia

Batting	Innings	NO	HS	Runs	Average
A.L. Hassett	10	0	115	365	36.50
R.N. Harvey	10	0	122	346	34.60
A.R. Morris	10	0	89	337	33.70
G.B. Hole	10	0	66	273	27.30
K.R. Miller	9	0	109	223	24.77

Bowling	O	M	R	W	Average
R.R. Lindwall	240.4	62	490	26	18.84
J.C. Hill	66	18	158	7	22.57
R.G. Archer	69.3	27	95	4	23.75
A.K. Davidson	125	42	212	8	26.50
K.R. Miller	186	72	303	10	30.30

Wicket-keepers: T.G. Evans (E) 15 dismissals D. Tallon (A) 2 dismissals
G.R.A. Langley (A) 9 dismissals

Captains: L. Hutton – batting 43, 60*; 145, 5; 66; 0, 25; 82, 17
A.L. Hassett – batting 115, 5; 104, 3; 26, 8; 37, 4*; 53, 10

In the second match W. Watson and T.E. Bailey saved the game for England with a fifth-wicket stand of 163. A.V. Bedser became the first England bowler to take 200 Test wickets. In the fourth match he passed C.V. Grimmett's Test record of 216 wickets, and finished with a record 39 wickets in a series against Australia.

10

Suspect Pitches and Suspect Actions

The question of who should replace Hassett as captain caused much argument in Australia when Hutton took his team there in 1954–5. The three candidates were Miller, Morris and Johnson, of whom the last-named was the least certain of his place in the team. He had captained Victoria the previous season without distinguishing himself, but he was considered to be the best diplomat of the three. Also in his favour, at least in the eyes of the cynics, were the facts that his father had been a selector, he was the son-in-law of Dr Roy Park, who had played in one Test, and he had been to the same college as the Prime Minister, Robert Menzies, a great devotee of the game. When Johnson's appointment was announced there was plenty of noise from the press.

Ian Johnson was the slowest bowler to play in post-war Test cricket. He also gave the ball greater flight than probably any other spinner since the war, so that he was most dangerous when bowling into the wind; a heavily-spun ball produced an enigmatic delivery that accounted for many fine batsmen. He had come into the Test side immediately after the war and had played in most series since, except the 1953 England tour. In fact he was essentially a hard-wicket bowler, doing well in South Africa and the West Indies but being unconvincing in England, where in nine games he took only thirteen of his 109 Test wickets. He was a useful lower-middle-order batsman with six fifties and exactly 1000 Test runs to his name, and a splendid slip fielder. In all he played in forty-five Tests, seventeen as captain, and had the honour of leading the first Australian teams to the West Indies, where he won handsomely, to Pakistan and to India.

He was unlucky to come to the captaincy at a time when the great team of a few years earlier was in decline. Yet his leadership was not the inspi-rational sort that will lift a team when times are rough; he was solid and dependable, but unoriginal, rarely one for taking a gamble. Too often he was unable to adjust his thinking to the developments of a match, tending to plough on with the tactics he had worked out beforehand, sometimes with disastrous results. This meant that he did not have the respect of his team to the extent that a captain should, especially as there were players in it who felt themselves capable of doing a better job – and whom other players believed would do a better job.

There was also the problem that his performances, especially in 1956, could not always justify his place, and a captain must be very special if he is to be played principally for his leadership qualities; Johnson was a sound captain, but he was no Mike Brearley. Keith Miller, who was doing great things with New South Wales, would almost certainly have made a more inventive and inspiring captain than Johnson, but the selectors were never able to grasp the nettle and forgive Miller for the playboy exploits of his youth. The English usually believe that they have a monopoly on 'holier-than-thou' attitudes, but clearly they do not.

Ian Johnson, Australian captain who came up against Tyson in 1954–5, and Laker in 1956.

Yet the need for the captain to be a diplomat is always important, and at this Johnson excelled. It was because of this that he continued as leader on the tour to the West Indies after Hutton's team had left Australia. The troubles that had occurred both on and off the pitch on England's West Indian tour the year before had made the Australians very wary, and Johnson had to ensure that there was no repeat of these on what was his country's first visit there. He discharged his duties well, and the tour was a cordial one. Since he was a naturally friendly man his two series against England were played in a good spirit too, for he managed to stay cheerful in defeat. The 1956 tour was a difficult one for the Australians, especially as they believed – not without justification – that the pitches were being prepared to suit the English bowlers, but Johnson ensured that relations were not soured. In cricketing terms his appointment as captain for that tour was a puzzling one; his record in 1948 was poor and he had not been selected in 1953. Maybe Miller's leadership would have made sufficient difference to the team for some of the problems not to have arisen, but it may also have caused some friction. Johnson took the line that the interests of the game are best served by the losing team accepting their defeat with good grace.

The 1954–5 series began well for the home team. Expecting the first day to see the pitch at its sharpest, Hutton put Australia in; the result is still the record Test defeat for any captain putting the opposition in. For only the second time ever England went into a game without a spinner, but their four-pronged pace attack could make nothing of a dead pitch, and big centuries from Morris and Harvey saw Australia to 601.

Matters could not have gone more wrong for Hutton; Compton broke a finger while fielding and he himself failed twice with the bat as England subsided to defeat by an innings and 154 runs. This is the game which is invariably cited by anyone who believes that insertion of the opposition is utterly unjustifiable lunacy. Of course Hutton made a major mistake, but one does feel that it would be nice if the critics were as ready to mention the way he made up for it.

This was Bedser's last Test against Australia, for Hutton decided he would concentrate his attack on real speed rather than Bedser's medium-pace guile. This proved to be good strategy, but unfortunately Hutton told him of his decision only at the last moment before the next game. Since Hutton was the most sensitive of men this was a sure sign of the strain he was under.

Both Johnson and Miller then missed the second Test through injury, and the leadership went to Arthur Morris. Morris was one of the greatest of

Arthur Morris, captain once against England, seen here at Leeds in
1948 when he scored 182 to help Australia to a historic win.

left-handers, and had announced himself by becoming the first cricketer to score two centuries on his first-class début. It was a habit he took with him wherever he went, for he scored hundreds in his first matches in England, South Africa and the West Indies, seeming to have no trouble in adapting to the unfamiliar conditions. He was a most elegant batsman, whose back-foot play concentrated on hooks, pulls and on-drives, and with dazzling footwork that took him down the pitch to the spinners. His one weakness seemed to be against the swinging ball around the leg-stump, something that Bedser exploited to the full, taking his wicket no fewer than eighteen times.

In fact Bedser and Morris were good friends, and the story goes that when Morris, on his twenty-ninth birthday, yet again lost his wicket to Bedser the Englishman gave him a parcel that evening which contained a copy of *Better Cricket* by Lindsay Hassett and Ian Johnson, with a passage on batting marked for his attention. In his next Test innings Morris scored 206, after which he returned the book to Bedser with a mark against a passage on bowling. He was a cheerful, friendly character, much liked by everyone, who enjoyed his cricket and refused to accept that it was a matter of life and death.

He became captain of New South Wales in 1947–8 and the following year the state won the Sheffield Shield. Overall his captaincy record is a good one, but he was criticised for over-caution and in one match when he put together two slow-scoring batsmen the crowd expressed their displeasure in the time-honoured way. After some controversy Keith Miller was given the job and told to produce a brighter image, which he did. Morris, though, was often vice-captain of the national team, and when Hassett was injured in the series against West Indies in 1951–2 he took over for one match. He was given a team with a lot of pace bowlers and not many batsmen, and as leaky covers had ruined the pitch a great many wickets fell on the first day and Australia duly lost – a defeat that came, incidentally, on the first Christmas Day on which Test cricket had ever been played.

In the second Test against England he was brave enough, after Hutton's disaster in the previous match, to put England in on a grassy wicket and in sultry conditions. Lacking Miller and with Lindwall below par with a liver complaint, he realised that England had the stronger bowlers and reasoned that in conditions suited to fast bowling it could have been suicidal for Australia to bat first. He was proved right when England were all out for 154, after which Australia put on 228. England were in big trouble at 55 for 3 in their second innings, but May and Cowdrey pulled the innings round and they reached 296. Australia's target was 223, but it was in this match that they first encountered Tyson, having shortened his run, at his most typhoon-like. Earlier in the game he had been knocked out by a bouncer from Lindwall, but now with the wind behind him he tore the heart out of the Australians, supported by Statham operating into the wind. England won a pulsating match by 38 runs, plaudits going to the three tail-enders Wardle, Appleyard and Statham who had put on 43 and 46 in crucial tenth-wicket stands. Morris had led his team well enough, but there was little that any captain could have done against Tyson in that mood. Hutton's captaincy was much praised, especially for the handling of his bowlers.

The third Test was played out against one of the hottest spells that Melbourne had ever known, with a midnight temperature of thirty-six degrees Celsius being recorded. It saw Cowdrey's maiden century for England, yet the team could total only 191, Miller having reduced them to 41 for 4 before Cowdrey came to the rescue. Australia moved to 231 thanks mainly to their tail-enders after the principal batsmen had collapsed. However, it was an innings noted for the slowness with which England bowled their overs – partly because of the heat, but mostly to upset the rhythm of the batsmen. The heat had cracked the pitch so much, though, that it was apparently (illegally) watered during the rest day to stop it disintegrating altogether, and this gave England the best surface of the match for their second innings, enabling them to set a target of 240. After Tyson's performance in the last match when he had been lethal despite being hit on the head, the Australians may have wondered what he would do when he hadn't – and he showed them, taking 6 for 16 in 51 balls, and finishing with 7 for 27, again with fine support from Statham (and with the aid of a catch behind the wicket to dismiss Harvey which Godfrey Evans rated as one of his finest). Australia's last eight wickets fell for 34, and England won by 128 runs. This was Tyson's supreme moment; even he eased off a little after this.

England retained the Ashes in the fourth Test. After the first innings England had a lead of just 18, but they then dismissed Australia for 111. Needing only 94 to win England lost five wickets in getting there, but as before it was Compton who was in at the kill. The final Test lost three-and-a-half days to rain, but contained some interesting oddities. Graveney's beautiful century made him the hundredth batsman to score a century in England–Australia Tests. England declared at 371, during the course of which Bailey allowed Lindwall – who, it was generally (and wrongly) felt, was playing in his last Test – to bowl him to give him his hundredth Ashes wicket, the first fast bowler to achieve this. When Australia batted they failed by just one run to avert the follow-on, and in the two hours that were left contrived to lose six wickets. Hutton, having lasted only four balls in his final innings against Australia, took a wicket with the last ball of the match, to give him his best Test analysis of 1 for 2. It was only his third Test wicket, and his victim was the man who in a few years time would prove himself one of the greatest captains, Richie Benaud.

Hutton had two successful Tests against New Zealand and was chosen as captain the following summer against South Africa, but did not play because of lumbago, and in due course announced his retirement from Test cricket. He became the first professional to be elected to membership of MCC before his career had finished, and it was not long before he was knighted. Without doubt he had found the responsibility a great strain as well as a great honour, and he had returned from Australia, where his batting had been poor, a sick man who had simply had enough. If his natural caution sometimes annoyed people, his record proved that, once accustomed to the job, he had the shrewdness and character it demanded; indeed he occupies a unique position in English cricket.

After Hutton it was the turn of the amateurs again, in the last few years before the distinction was abolished. There was a school of thought which favoured Bailey for the job, but Hutton's vice-captain in Australia had been Peter May and he duly took over against South Africa in 1955. This was the start of his record England run of thirty-five consecutive Tests, not ending

Peter May, classical batsman who led England a record forty-one times. After England's disastrous summer of 1988, this record seems likely to remain for some time!

until 1959. In all he led England a record forty-one times, of which thirteen were against Australia; twenty-one matches were won and ten were lost, so his record is a good one. The only series which he lost was in Australia in 1958–9, which he managed to do rather dramatically.

May is still widely regarded as the finest English batsman to emerge since the war. At Charterhouse he was coached by George Geary, who was not exactly putting his head on the block when he predicted a rosy future for him, and at Cambridge he became one of the few leading run-scorers to average over sixty. He made his début for Surrey in 1950 and for England in 1951, both while he was still at university, marking his Test call-up with 138 against South Africa. After he left Cambridge only illness would keep him out of the team until his premature retirement in 1961, and in 66 matches he scored over 4,500 runs at an average of nearly 47, with 13 centuries. In 1957 he and Cowdrey set the record Test fourth-wicket partnership with their 411 against West Indies at Edgbaston. Australia nearly always found him troublesome for he had few failures against them, and at least three of his innings were crucial in winning the Ashes. His batting was that of the classical stylist, straight and upright in defence, with any number of perfectly timed strokes all round the wicket. Six feet tall and with very strong shoulders he could hit the ball very hard when he chose to, but it was precision, discipline and timing rather than strength that characterised his batting.

By nature he was quiet and rather reserved, not greatly given to socialising, but kind and friendly all the same. As Michael Davie wrote in the *Observer*, he 'has a kind of English frozen-upness about him. . . The total lack of anecdote about him is significant.' Yet many people have commented on the hard streak that was within him, a toughness and ruthlessness that was not apparent from his normally gentle demeanour; he has been summed up as an amateur captain with a professional approach. Not for nothing was he Hutton's vice-captain, and he learned a great deal from him about both tactics and leadership skills. In Alan Gibson's phrase he was 'Hutton's child', but while he benefited from this he also picked up some of the great man's less desirable characteristics. This especially showed up in a sometimes over-cautious approach to a game, for there were times when he seemed reluctant to press for a victory if that would involve any risk of defeat. The sensitive nature of Hutton's position as the first professional captain of England did at least give him some excuse for his caution, but as Gibson says 'the caution that seemed natural and acceptable to Pudsey and Yorkshire did not sit so easily on Charterhouse and Cambridge.'

Hutton's wisdom was listened to very attentively, and his precepts, by and large, became May's precepts. The slowing of over rates that Hutton had started was continued by May as a useful tactical ploy; someone, after all, was going to persevere with it sooner or later. He also learned much from his Surrey captain, Stuart Surridge, who was taking his county to unprecedented heights in the Championship, and May it was who succeeded Surridge in 1957, winning two more titles before the great team began to break up. From both of his mentors he learned, perhaps more than anything else, how to use his bowlers to best effect for both knew well how to win matches with them. What he did not learn from his county captain, though, was Surridge's generally aggressive approach to captaincy; Hutton's caution obviously suited him better.

For a reserved man his problems with personal relations seemed to be minimal, although not non-existent. His courtesy and friendliness meant that he was not only respected for his playing ability but also liked for himself and, at least until matters began to go wrong on the 1958–9 tour, he was usually able to get the best out of his team. On the field he seemed anything but relaxed, but still he managed to strike a happy medium between autocracy and democracy, being firmly in control without making it too obvious, and working on the basis that anyone good enough to be selected for a Test match ought not to need too many instructions. He also managed to combine fairness with playing the game hard. The latter was essential, for by the 1950s, although the win-at-all-costs brigade had not yet made themselves *total* masters of the universe, there were few captains around who achieved much without including a bit of toughness in their make-up.

The side which Ian Johnson brought to England in 1956 was undoubtedly weaker than the home team's, but not drastically so. Miller and Lindwall were still there, and the former was to have one outstanding match, but the summer was a wet one and it was the English spinners who benefited; Johnson and Benaud took 14 wickets between them while Laker and Lock took 58. There was, however, just the smallest suggestion that the pitches had been prepared to favour the England attack.

Before the Tests started Johnson achieved something which none of his predecessors had done for 44 years, not since the weak team of 1912 – he lost to a county. Admittedly it was to the mighty Surrey, but it was by 10 wickets; his tactics were heavily criticised for their ineptitude and it did not endear him to his players. A strong start might have cemented his authority, but their only victories had been against the universities and this defeat undermined him considerably. Laker, incidentally, took 10 for 88 in the Australians' first innings while Lock took 0 for 100; as good an example of shades of things to come as you would wish to find anywhere, although Lock did take seven in the second innings.

At Trent Bridge over two days were lost to rain. May declared twice to try to force a result, but the weather won. At Lord's, however, Australia pulled off a fine victory. In reply to Australia's 285 England could muster only 171. In the second innings Benaud's 97 helped them set a target of 372 and England managed precisely half that. Miller took five wickets in each innings, while Langley set a new world record by taking nine dismissals in the match. As Evans also made seven dismissals the Wicket-keepers' Union had something to celebrate.

Batting first in the third Test England found themselves at 17 for 3 when Washbrook joined May. He had not played in Tests since the 1950–1 tour and was now forty-one (and one of the selectors), but the feeling had been that he was the man to strengthen the England batting. So it proved, for his 98 and May's 101 took the score to 204 before the next wicket fell, and the total reached 325. And then, in overcast weather and with a foretaste of what was to come, Laker and Lock bowled Australia out twice for an innings victory. At the eleventh attempt England gained their first win over Australia at Headingley.

The events in the fourth Test at Old Trafford are rather famous. After an absence of two years Sheppard proved to be another successful recall and scored a century; Richardson also made his first Test hundred in the same innings. By the second afternoon England had made 459, and when the wicket was brushed it produced what has often been referred to as a dust-storm – certainly the photographs support such a description. Laker and Lock were soon bowling, but for over an hour nothing happened. Then May switched them round; by tea McDonald and Harvey had fallen to Laker, bowling from the Stretford end as he did for the rest of the match, with 62 on the board. Lock got Burke with his first ball after tea, by which time the ball was turning dramatically. Craig and Mackay fell in one over, then Miller and Benaud in another. Then Archer; then Maddocks and Johnson in another over, and Laker had taken 7 for 8 off 22 balls since tea. Australia all out 84, Laker 9 for 37.

Just before 5.30 p.m. they followed on; McDonald went off injured, Harvey came on and Laker got him for his second duck in, officially, two hours and four minutes, whereupon the Manchester weather did its best to spoil Laker's party. Little play was possible on the third and fourth days, just enough to take Burke's wicket. By lunch on the last day Australia were 112 for 2 – and then the sun came out. In nine overs Laker took four more wickets for three runs, after which the sun went in again and the pitch seemed to play more easily. McDonald, who had made 89, finally succumbed, Oakman taking his fifth catch of the match. Laker wheeled remorselessly away, bowling beautifully, while Lock, unable to believe that nothing was going for him, became more and more irate. Benaud fell. Johnson was reduced to appealing at the fact that sawdust was blowing in his eyes. Lindwall went, and then, with an hour left, Maddocks was lbw and the astonishing deed was done.

Laker's figures were 10 for 53 from 51.2 overs, while poor Tony Lock had 0 for 69 from 55 overs, although he had held three catches. This set several records, of course, some of which are unlikely ever to be beaten; that is a dangerous thing to say, but this has always seemed one of the more unsurpassable feats. Undoubtedly the pitch gave him plenty of assistance and his close fieldsmen helped him enormously, but he bowled supremely well and it must always remain one of the most remarkable of sporting achievements. And it clinched the Ashes.

At the Oval rain again caused the loss of over two full days. Compton returned and made a beautiful 94 despite being without his right kneecap, and England reached 247. Australia replied with 202 after being 47 for 5, but May made certain there would be no dramatic win by leaving them only 130 minutes to score 228. The pitch was taking spin and a more aggressive captain might have declared earlier and tried to ram home his advantage. As it was there was time for them to lose five wickets, as Laker took another seven in the match to complete his record series haul of forty-six. Lock did at least take three this time.

As well as suspect pitches Australia had had to contend with many injury problems, and disagreements between players, which Johnson had not been able to stamp out, had not helped their cause. In Ray Robinson's glorious words, 'They had their backs to the wall so often that the writing on it rubbed off on them.' It remains in Australian memories as one of the unhappiest of England tours, but on that score England were to beat them hands down next time around. Johnson's Test career ended a few months later after he had led the first tours to Pakistan and India. The one match against Pakistan was lost, but India were beaten 2–0. The following year he became secretary of Melbourne Cricket Club, and during his term of office the ground was considerably expanded. He was awarded the OBE for his services to the game.

If in 1956 Australia felt that the English pitches left something to be desired, England in 1958–9 felt the same thing could be said of the bowling action of some of the Australians, who themselves had thought for years that Lock's action was sometimes illegal (in fact he was to change it himself after this tour). However, after the events of the second Test the English wrath began to centre on Ian Meckiff. Since he was to head the bowling averages with seventeen wickets (although Benaud and Davidson were to take fifty-five between them) the visitors felt hard done by. The situation was worsened by the fact that three others, Slater, Burke and Rorke, were also on the suspect list. More of this anon.

The England team was regarded as a strong one, at least by some people. Others were not so sure. Crucially, there was no settled pair of openers and there was no Johnny Wardle. He had been included in the party, but was sacked by Yorkshire for disciplinary reasons; his response was a number of newspaper articles criticising everything about Yorkshire cricket, including the captain, the players and the committee. MCC felt they had to withdraw his invitation to tour; more surprisingly, they did not replace him with anyone until John Mortimore went out part way through, by which time the series had slipped away. The team also lacked the young Dexter, and though he was called up as a replacement, he had little chance to acclimatise and so gave a poor account of himself.

The 1958–9 England tour of Australia. Captains Richie Benaud and Peter May shake hands after the last Test – the series was won by Australia.

For their series in South Africa in 1957–8 Australia had given the captaincy to twenty-two-year-old Ian Craig, their youngest ever leader. At first he struggled, but went on to win the rubber 3–0, and it was assumed he would continue against England. Illness forced him to withdraw, however, and the feeling was that Harvey would take over. Somewhat out of the blue, Richie Benaud was appointed, having had virtually no first-class captaincy experience. It proved to be a decisive moment in Australian cricket.

Benaud's father had been a grade cricketer who once took all twenty wickets with his leg-break bowling, so he had a useful pedigree. At eighteen he made his début for New South Wales and at twenty-one he was in the Test team. He played fairly regularly but without really distinguishing himself until the tour of South Africa under Craig. In the Tests he scored two centuries and took thirty wickets, and his career took off from there. He had played in 32 Tests before he was made captain and then led his country 28 times without losing a series; his record was won 12, tied 1 and lost only 4. In his last Test as captain (he also played three more under Simpson) he became the first cricketer to score 2,000 runs and take 200 wickets in Tests, and for years he was Australia's leading wicket-taker. He is arguably Australia's greatest all-rounder – and has few challengers for the title of Australia's greatest captain.

His batting was strong and forceful, particularly his driving. Playing at Scarborough at the end of the 1953 tour he scored eleven sixes in an innings, equalling the world record of the time – this, according to the story, after being teased by Len Hutton because he had started very slowly; 'What's matter, lad? Art playing for average?' His career average was 36, although his Test average, despite three centuries, was lower at 24. However, it was his leg-break bowling that was his glory; he practised it endlessly and although it took him years to become as accurate as he knew he could be, he made himself into an outstanding bowler as a result. With a high, fluent action he was able to bowl leg-break, googly, top-spinner and 'flipper', but he always concentrated more on length than spin, with subtle changes of pace and flight. He was less at home on the softer English wickets than on harder ones, although on his last visit to England it was his bowling that clinched the series. He was also an outstanding close fielder and took many memorable catches; the left-handed one in the gully to dismiss Cowdrey at Lord's in 1956 has gone down as one of the all-time greats.

In his earlier years in the Test team Benaud was not the most sociable of characters, preferring to go off on his own at the end of the day. During the South African tour he realised there was much to be gained from talking over the day's events in the dressing-room, and this change in attitude and improvement in his performance made the selectors start looking at him as a possible captain. There can have been very few captains who have responded to the demands of the job so quickly and so positively. He always seemed to be on top of any situation, always trying different ways of gaining an advantage; always thinking shrewdly, never letting a situation drift along without trying to do something about it, always able to see that a bowler would be better off at the other end. Sometimes he would over-use his best bowlers, but not often, and usually he had something else up his sleeve. He seemed never to miss the least detail, an ability that his television commentaries show he has not lost. Ray Robinson tells how he knew, after just one ball of the first Test, that Australia had found the leader they had been looking for; the delivery from Davidson pitched on a grassy strip and hit Richardson on the shoulder, whereupon Benaud brought mid-on in to close forward leg. 'We were witnessing the emergence of the No.1 opportunist of all national cricket leaders,' says Robinson.

He played his cricket with a boundless enthusiasm that could not fail to rub off on his players; Ray Illingworth wrote that 'half an hour with him and he could persuade you to sell your grandmother'. Good bowling and fielding were always given their praise – he worked his players hard to improve their fielding, and some of the catches taken in the coming series were quite outstanding – while failure was greeted not with condemnation but with sound suggestions for remedying the fault. Everyone was encouraged to offer ideas on tactics and so to feel part of the successful unit. Quietly friendly and open, he was always ready to listen to anyone's problems; morale was sky-high. The one criticism that could be made – and certainly was at the time – is that under his captaincy wicket-takers first found themselves deluged under adoring colleagues, the simple congratulatory handshake a thing of the past. Benaud believed that the adrenalin this created helped improve all-round team performance. Regrettably, C.B. Fry had died a couple of years or so earlier; his observations would have made interesting reading.

Probably the greatest of his contributions to the game, however, was to insist on trying to play attacking cricket. The 1950s had not been a good time for the Australian game, and many fans – and potential young players – were turning more to tennis. Now tennis is a fine game, but . . . Benaud's refusal to provide safe, boring 'entertainment' brought them back in their droves, a policy that reached its zenith in the 1960–1 rubber against West Indies when he and Frank Worrell conspired to produce perhaps the most riveting series of all. There were very few occasions when he resorted to defensive play, and usually there was a good reason for it, such as an injury to a principal bowler. Having said all that, he was not entirely blameless (although not the main culprit), that the 1958–9 series against England was anything but riveting.

As if all this were not enough, he was also good on the public relations side. He had been working for some years as a journalist and so understood the needs and problems of the pressmen who followed him around. In his news conferences he managed to be simultaneously firm, honest and diplomatic, incredible as that may seem to the average cynic. At the time Peter May and his much-vaunted team arrived in Australia in 1958 all of these qualities were waiting to be revealed, but as Ray Robinson said, it did not take long for the *cognoscenti* to realise what they had acquired.

Unfortunately, a fine début innings from Norman O'Neill apart, the only other thing that anyone acquired from the first Test was acute boredom. E.W. Swanton described it as the dullest and most depressing he had ever watched. England struggled to 134 and Australia to 186. When England batted again May sent Bailey in at number three, and he played the slowest half-century in all first-class cricket, taking 458 minutes to score 68 and running out Graveney as well. The fourth day produced the lowest number of runs ever scored in a day in an Australian Test, as England meandered through 106 of them on a pitch that was perfect for batting. There seemed to be not the remotest justification for it and England duly lost by eight wickets – not, however, before Burke had contrived to score even more slowly, taking 250 minutes over 28 runs. The only thing about the match worth repeating was the story from the press-box that someone had asked George Duckworth, England's scorer, when Bailey had last scored and was told 'Twenty past two'. 'Today or yesterday?' was the next question.

Melbourne saw Davidson taking three wickets in his second over. May, though, scored the first century by an England captain in an Australian Test since MacLaren's in 1901, and his side made 259. A big century from Harvey seemed to be setting his team up for a good lead, but Statham took 7 for 57 to restrict Australia to 308. Then came Meckiff, fast left-arm, taking 6 for 38 with what the English Press, unmindful of Lock's action or the pitches of 1956, called blatant throwing. True, Jack Fingleton wrote that he felt that Meckiff should have been called, but he also pointed out that the English batting – they were all out for 87 – had been particularly feeble. Another eight-wicket win.

The third match was rain-affected and drawn, but only May and Cowdrey saved England from defeat, Cowdrey scoring what was at the time the slowest hundred in Ashes Tests. This was due at least in part to Benaud actually going on the defensive for once, persuading Davidson to bowl leg-theory, at a time when Australia seemed to be in the driving seat. It was the only time that Laker and Lock were able to show their skills to any degree, but a pitch that suited them suited Benaud, too. When Laker had to drop out of the fourth game with an injured spinning finger, May decided that his best chance of success was to put Australia in. McDonald was almost bowled first ball, but survived to score 170 as his team reached 476. His dismissal is worthy of note: he was batting with a runner when the umpire was in the wrong position to judge a run-out and gave him not out despite the runner having been clearly short. McDonald's response was to allow himself to be bowled by Trueman straight away. For the second match running Benaud took nine wickets as England followed on, failing only by an hour or so to hold on for a draw. A ten-wicket win this time.

A nine-wicket win rounded off the series 4–0. More dismal batting from England, another century from McDonald, similar dismal batting from England with Cowdrey's dismissal again a doubtful one and Bailey getting a pair in his last Test, and that was that. England had, undoubtedly, had a lot of injury problems, but so had Australia in 1956. They had, too, come up against some distinctly suspect bowlers, but it was not for another five years that Meckiff, who sincerely believed his action was legal, was no-balled for throwing and immediately retired from the game.

Benaud came in for criticism for using suspect bowlers, but took the view that if the umpires were satisfied then that was reasonable enough for him. It is all a matter of optics, as the Americans say – you see things through your own eyes. In due course the Australians were to take steps to stamp out 'chucking' for good, but at the time England were unimpressed. It was, though, the batting that had let them down; only May and Cowdrey, and to a lesser extent Graveney, did anything worthwhile, and the bowlers were simply not left with anything to defend. England have had some grim tours over the years, but this was one of the most miserable.

Statistical records which show that Colin Cowdrey captained England against Australia only six times always look wrong, somehow. He was around for so long, was it really only six? Surely he led a tour there, didn't he? No, he didn't, much to his regret; four tours as vice-captain, but never one in charge, which may well be a record in itself. Of his record 114 Tests twenty-seven were as captain, of which eight were won and four lost.

Cowdrey is remembered as a great batsman who could not always quite convince himself of his own greatness. He had all the attributes of wonderful strokeplay, timing, balance, dedication to hard work and so on, but sometimes just seemed not quite able to believe in himself. At those times his batting could be heavy going to watch, yet, when things went well, his

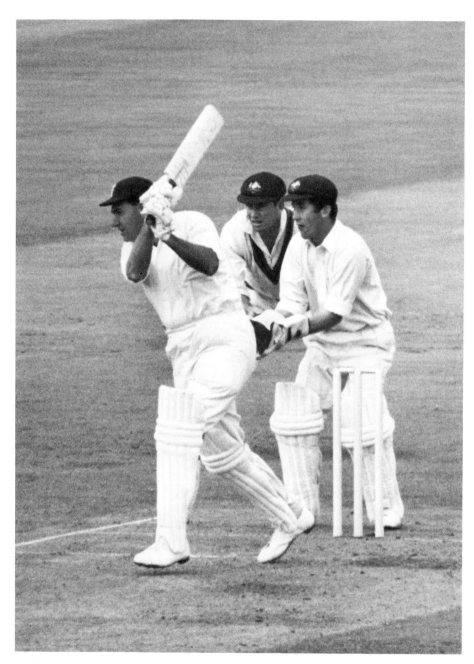

Colin Cowdrey scoring a century in his 100th Test Match, England v Australia at Edgbaston in 1968. Ian Chappell is at slip and Brian Taber is the wicket-keeper.

batting was the personification of natural, polished elegance, with a perfect technique and an easy mastery of the bowling. Few batsmen since the war have brought greater aesthetic pleasure to the spectators, and his best innings are from the very top drawer. He was also one of the outstanding slip fielders, and was for years the leading Test catcher.

At the age of thirteen he became, and remains, the youngest player to appear in a schools match at Lord's, and he went on to captain Oxford. His England début came on the 1954–5 tour, after which he was rarely out of the side until 1971; in 1974–5 came the famous recall to help Denness and Co. stand up to Lillee and Thomson. When he retired he was England's leading run-scorer, with 7,624 at an average of 44 and with 22 centuries to his name.

The name of Cowdrey is synonymous with friendliness, charm, good manners, modesty and any other related virtues you can think of, all underpinned by his religious beliefs. Always courteous with the Press, always willing to put himself out for anyone, the impression he left with most people was that of a gentleman in the best sense of the word. His enthusiasm for life in general and cricket in particular made him very popular, especially in Kent. He was one of the most respected of post-war cricketers for his ability, his sportsmanship and his character as a whole.

He captained Kent from 1957 to 1971, taking them to the Championship in his penultimate year. For all his greatness as a player, though, he is not regarded as an outstanding captain. He knew the game thoroughly, but was not the sort to take a daring gamble. There were times when he seemed to play defensively for no good reason, and was often criticised for not being dynamic enough, for not being able to make quick decisions, and for not letting both the opposition and his own team know who was in charge. For a Test captain he was really too unobtrusive, too unassertive. He was also unfortunate. Against India in 1959 he first became captain, taking over from May for the last two matches and completing a 5–0 win. Two draws followed when he took over from May again on the 1959–60 tour of West Indies, but a match in charge here and there is never a satisfactory way for a captain to stake his claim.

His first full series as captain was against South Africa in 1960 and he won that 3–0, but after May had retired he felt that he needed a winter at home in 1961–2. Dexter led the team that winter, beating Pakistan and losing to India, but the following summer illness lost Cowdrey part of the season and Dexter was appointed for Australia. After him came Smith, then Close, and although Cowdrey led the team in isolated Tests it was 1967–8 before he got another full series in charge. He then missed most of 1969 through injury, lost the job to Illingworth and because the Yorkshireman did it so well Cowdrey never led England again.

The team that Benaud brought to England in 1961 was felt to be a fair batting side but rather short on bowling, especially as Benaud himself had rarely shone in English conditions. Their main strike bowler was Alan Davidson, but they also included young men named McKenzie and Lawry who were to make quite a name for themselves. England appeared to have a team capable of giving them a decent game, with Trueman 'in his pomp' and some useful batting. What they did not have in the first Test was the presence of Peter May, and Cowdrey assumed the captaincy. It was not a distinguished England performance. Batting first they could do no better than 195, to which Australia's response was 516. Unfortunately for them over a day's play was lost to rain, but at the beginning of the last day England were still 215 behind and a wicket down. Dexter had been missed the night before on 1; he went on to make 180, and with a hundred from Subba Row and good support from Barrington the game was saved.

May returned to the team for the second Test but Cowdrey retained the captaincy. Benaud, however, was having trouble with his right shoulder and missed out, the captaincy being taken over by Neil Harvey. Harvey, of course, is one of the greatest batsmen of them all, a left-hander who, when he retired from Test cricket, was second only to Bradman in the Australian listings in terms of aggregate, average and centuries – 6, 149 runs at over 48 with 21 hundreds. A short, stocky man, he had superb technique and strokes all round the wicket; he was an exceptionally strong driver, hooker and cutter, and with his electrifying footwork he delighted in dancing down the wicket to the spinners. He batted for the fun of it, always wanting to take the bowlers on and provide some entertainment by gambling a bit; but he could dig in when his team needed him to. He had made his Test début in 1948 when only nineteen and scored centuries straight away. He was also a superb fielder, either in the deep, in the slips or, best of all, in the covers, from where his fast, deadly returns to the wicket-keeper were legendary.

When Ian Craig dropped out of the captaincy reckoning at the beginning of the 1958–9 tour, Harvey, who had led Victoria in 1956–7 and so had a little more experience than Benaud, was made captain of an Australian XI against May's team. On a damaged pitch matters went wrong for him and the selectors decided on Benaud. Far from feeling hard-done-by Harvey gave Benaud the fullest support and made his job that much easier; more than one writer described him as the ideal vice-captain. On the evidence of this one Test he would have made a pretty good full-time captain, too.

It was the match made famous by the 'ridge' at Lord's, when wickets fell

Neil Harvey led Australia once against England in the Lord's 'ridge' Test of 1961. This photograph was taken in his first Ashes Test in 1948 when he scored a century.

in alarming fashion because of the supposed ridge at the Nursery end. England's 206 seemed not that bad on such a pitch – nor would it have been had it not been for Bill Lawry, playing in only his second Test. He managed 130 when nearly all around were succumbing, a marvellous innings in the circumstances. Then the last two wickets put on over 100 and Australia reached 340. When England batted again, Harvey decided that the young McKenzie, in his first match, would be the most likely one to exploit the ridge, and he duly took 5 for 37 as England subsided for 202. That left Australia only 69 to win, but Statham and Trueman got halfway to their target before Burge got all the way to his. Harvey's captaincy received much praise; Cowdrey handed over to May.

After the third Test England were back on level terms, thanks mainly to Trueman on his home pitch taking 5 for 16 in 6 overs to dismiss Australia for 237. England then made 299, with 93 from Cowdrey. With Australia then on 102 for 4 Trueman, bowling off-cutters, took 5 wickets without conceding a run, 6 for 4 in 7.3 overs, and they were all out for 120. England duly polished off the runs needed. It set up the series for a splendid match at Old Trafford which for much of the time seemed to be England's. Australia could make only 190, to which England replied with 367, including 95 from May. A century from Lawry saw Australia to 334 for 9; just one wicket for England to take and then the rest of the day to polish off the runs. Davidson and McKenzie put on 98 for that last wicket, leaving England 230 minutes to score 256. They made a sound enough start, and then Dexter made a sparkling 76 in almost even time. At 150 for 1 they were ahead of the clock and well set for victory, when Benaud took the stage, ready as usual for a gamble. In nineteen balls he took 4 for 9, continuing after tea as England collapsed still further, and finishing with 6 for 70. Australia won an enthralling match by 54 runs, and the Ashes stayed down under.

The Oval match was a high-scoring, rain-affected draw, centuries from O'Neill and Burge seeing Australia to almost 500, before Subba Row, batting for almost the entire time with a runner, scored a century in his last Test to ensure that his team didn't capitulate again. It was also the last Test for Peter May, who announced his retirement at only thirty-one to concentrate on his business affairs. Perhaps if he had come to the captaincy when a little older he might have stayed on longer, but amid all the regret that was expressed at his decision most people realised that he had been under a great deal of pressure for several years and had not enjoyed the best of health. Among England's post-war captains probably only Illingworth and Brearley, and perhaps Hutton, did the job better than he did. He remained in touch with the administration of the game, becoming President of MCC in 1980; he was also Chairman of Selectors from 1982 until 1988. Like everyone who does that last job he has received a great deal of criticism and very little praise.

1954–5	Brisbane	A 601–8d	E 190, 257	A inns 154 runs
	Sydney	E 154, 296	A 228, 184	E 38 runs
	Melbourne	E 191, 279	A 231, 111	E 128 runs
	Adelaide	A 323, 111	E 341, 97–5	E 5 wkts
	Sydney	E 371–7d	A 221, 118–6	Drawn
1956	Trent Bridge	A 217–8d, 188–3d	E 148, 120–3	Drawn
	Lord's	A 285, 257	E 171, 186	A 185 runs
	Headingley	E 325	A 143, 140	E inns 42 runs
	Old Trafford	E 459	A 84, 205	E inns 170 runs
	Oval	E 247, 182–3d	A 202, 27–5	Drawn
1958–9	Brisbane	E 134, 198	A 186, 147–2	A 8 wkts
	Melbourne	E 259, 87	A 308, 42–2	A 8 wkts
	Sydney	E 219, 287–7d	A 357, 54–2	Drawn
	Adelaide	A 476, 36–0	E 240, 270	A 10 wkts
	Melbourne	E 205, 214	A 351, 69–1	A 9 wkts

1961	Edgbaston	E 195, 401–4	A 516–9d	Drawn
	Lord's	E 206, 202	A 340, 71–5	A 5 wkts
	Headingley	A 237, 120	E 299, 62–2	E 8 wkts
	Old Trafford	A 190, 432	E 367, 201	A 54 runs
	Oval	E 256, 370–8	A 494	Drawn

1954–5

England

Batting	Innings	NO	HS	Runs	Average
T.W. Graveney	3	0	111	132	44.00
P.B.H. May	9	0	104	351	39.00
D.C.S. Compton	7	2	84	191	38.20
T.E. Bailey	9	1	88	296	37.00
M.C. Cowdrey	9	0	102	319	35.44

Bowling	O	M	R	W	Average
R. Appleyard	79	22	224	11	20.36
F.H. Tyson	151	16	583	28	20.82
J.H. Wardle	70.6	15	229	10	22.90
J.B. Statham	143.3	16	499	18	27.72
T.E. Bailey	73.4	8	306	10	30.60

Australia

Batting	Innings	NO	HS	Runs	Average
I.W. Johnson	6	4	41	116	58.00
C.C. McDonald	4	0	72	186	46.50
R.N. Harvey	9	1	162	354	44.25
P.J.P. Burge	2	1	18*	35	35.00
A.R. Morris	7	0	153	223	31.85

Bowling	O	M	R	W	Average
R.G. Archer	97.6	32	215	13	16.53
I.W. Johnson	111	37	243	12	20.25
W.A. Johnston	141.4	37	423	19	22.26
K.R. Miller	88.4	28	243	10	24.30
R.R. Lindwall	130.6	28	381	14	27.21

Wicket-keepers: G.R.A. Langley (A) 9 dismissals   K.V. Andrew (E) 0 dismissals
                L.V. Maddocks (A) 7 dismissals   T.G. Evans (E) 13 dismissals

Captains: I.W. Johnson – batting 24*; 33*, 4*; 41, 3*; 11
                        bowling 3–46, 2–38; 1–20, 1–25; 2–46; 3–68
        A.R. Morris – batting 12, 10
        L. Hutton – batting 4, 13; 30, 28; 12, 42; 80, 5; 6

F.H. Tyson took 10 for 130 in the second match and 9 for 95 in the third.

1956

England

Batting	Innings	NO	HS	Runs	Average
P.B.H. May	7	2	101	453	90.60
Revd D.S. Sheppard	3	0	113	199	66.33
P.E. Richardson	8	0	104	364	45.50
C. Washbrook	3	0	98	104	34.66
M.C. Cowdrey	8	0	80	244	30.50

Bowling	O	M	R	W	Average
J.C. Laker	283.5	127	442	46	9.60
F.S. Trueman	75	13	184	9	20.44
G.A.R. Lock	237.2	115	337	15	22.46
J.B. Statham	106	35	184	7	26.28
T.E. Bailey	108.5	39	223	6	37.16

Australia

Batting	Innings	NO	HS	Runs	Average
J.W. Burke	10	1	65	271	30.11
R. Benaud	9	1	97	200	25.00
C.C. McDonald	10	0	89	243	24.30
K.R. Miller	10	1	61	203	22.55
R.N. Harvey	10	0	69	197	19.70

Bowling	O	M	R	W	Average
K.R. Miller	205.1	44	467	21	22.23
R.G. Archer	207.4	67	451	18	25.05
A.K. Davidson	20	2	56	2	28.00
R.R. Lindwall	100.1	29	238	7	34.00
R. Benaud	154	48	330	8	41.25

Wicket-keepers: T.G. Evans (E) 9 dismissals   G.R.A. Langley (A) 18 dismissals
L.V. Maddocks (A) 6 dismissals

Captains: P.B.H. May – batting 73; 63; 53; 101; 43; 83*, 37
I.W. Johnson – batting 12; 6, 17; 0, 3; 0, 1*; 12, 10
bowling 1–26, 0–29; 0–3; 1–59; 4–151; 0–28, 0–7

In the second match G.R.A. Langley set a new Test record by making 9 dismissals. In the fourth match J.C. Laker took 9–37 and 10–53, the most wickets in a first-class match and the only instance of 10 wickets in a Test innings. He finished the series with a record 46 wickets.

1958–9

England

Batting	Innings	NO	HS	Runs	Average
M.C. Cowdrey	10	1	100*	391	43.44
P.B.H. May	10	0	113	405	40.50
T.W. Graveney	10	1	54	280	31.11
P.E. Richardson	8	0	68	162	20.25
T.E. Bailey	10	0	68	200	20.00

Bowling	O	M	R	W	Average
J.C. Laker	127.6	24	318	15	21.20
J.B. Statham	104	12	286	12	23.83
P.J. Loader	60.2	10	193	7	27.57
F.S. Trueman	87	11	276	9	30.66
F.H. Tyson	54	2	193	3	64.33

Australia

Batting	Innings	NO	HS	Runs	Average
C.C. McDonald	9	1	170	519	64.87
N.C. O'Neill	7	2	77	282	56.40
R.N. Harvey	9	3	167	291	48.50
L.E. Favell	3	1	54	73	36.50
A.K. Davidson	5	0	71	180	36.00

Bowling	O	M	R	W	Average
I. Meckiff	112.2	24	292	17	17.17
R. Benaud	233.2	65	584	31	18.83
A.K. Davidson	183.5	45	456	24	19.00
G.F. Rorke	70.5	17	165	8	20.62
J.W. Burke	25	9	49	2	24.50

Wicket-keepers: A.T.W. Grout (A) 20 dismissals   T.G. Evans (E) 6 dismissals
R. Swetman (E) 3 dismissals

Captains: R. Benaud – batting 16; 0; 6; 46; 64
bowling 3–46, 4–66; 1–61, 0–4; 5–83, 4–94; 5–91, 4–82; 4–43, 1–14
P.B.H. May – batting 26, 4; 113, 17; 42, 92; 37, 59; 11, 4

In the fifth match R.R. Lindwall broke C.V. Grimmett's Australian record of 216 wickets.

1961

England

Batting	Innings	NO	HS	Runs	Average
R. Subba Row	10	0	137	468	46.80
K.F. Barrington	9	1	83	364	45.50
D.A. Allen	6	3	42*	132	44.00
E.R. Dexter	9	0	180	378	42.00
P.B.H. May	8	1	95	272	38.85

Bowling	O	M	R	W	Average
E.R. Dexter	79.4	16	223	9	24.77
F.S. Trueman	164.4	21	529	20	26.45
D.A. Allen	134	53	354	13	27.23
J.B. Statham	201.4	41	501	17	29.47
J.A. Flavell	82.4	17	231	5	46.20

Australia

Batting	Innings	NO	HS	Runs	Average
W.M. Lawry	8	0	130	420	52.50
P.J.P. Burge	8	1	181	332	47.42
R.N. Harvey	8	0	114	338	42.25
B.C. Booth	3	0	71	126	42.00
N.C. O'Neill	8	0	117	324	40.50

Bowling	O	M	R	W	Average
A.K. Davidson	280.2	86	572	23	24.86
G.D. McKenzie	129	36	323	11	29.36
R. Benaud	214.3	76	488	15	32.53
R.B. Simpson	92.4	37	229	7	32.71
K.D. Mackay	273	87	525	16	32.81

Wicket-keepers: J.T. Murray (E) 18 dismissals   A.T.W Grout (A) 21 dismissals

Captains: M.C. Cowdrey – batting 13, 14; 16, 7
P.B.H. May – batting 26, 8*; 95, 0; 71, 33
R. Benaud – batting 36*; 0, 0; 2, 1; 6
bowling 3–15, 0–67; 1–86, 1–22; 0–80, 6–70; 1–35, 3–113
R.N. Harvey – batting 27, 4

In the second match J.B. Statham took his 200th Test wicket and A.T.W. Grout made his 100th Test dismissal, his 21 dismissals for the series being a new record in England v Australia Tests. In the third match F.S. Trueman took 11 for 88. In the fourth match R. Benaud took 5 for 12 in 25 balls to win the game.

11

Should the Ashes be Abolished?

During the summer of 1962 England had Dexter, Cowdrey and, according to Press speculation, the Reverend David Sheppard vying for the captaincy. Cowdrey was appointed to lead the Gentlemen in the last match against the Players, but when he had to go into hospital Dexter seized his opportunity and was duly given the leadership for the coming Australian tour. On his day he was the most imperious of English batsmen since the war, his haughty approach giving some idea of what it might have been like to watch MacLaren. Tall, handsome and aristocratic in appearance he was often referred to as 'Lord Edward', and in his moody moments, before the years mellowed him, he could behave in a cold and aloof manner.

He could also, let it be stressed, be the most charming and considerate of men. His batting was based on an upright orthodoxy with a sound defence, but with the idea that the best way to deal with any bowling is to attack it whenever possible. When the mood was upon him he appeared to treat the bowler simply as the person whose job it was to propel the ball for him to hit; the thought that the bowler might be trying to get him out never seemed to enter into it. He could be the most glorious striker of the ball, extremely powerful off either foot with strokes all round the wicket, at his best when some challenge, such as a race against time, was on – which may just possibly have something to do with Sussex's success in the first years of the Gillette Cup.

Perhaps he did not quite have the elegance of Cowdrey, but nor was he subject to Cowdrey's occasional temperamental aberrations. In his 62 Tests he scored 4,500 runs at an average of nearly 48, seven points higher than his career average. He was also a useful medium-pace change bowler and took sixty-six Test wickets, although, as so often with a captain who bowls, the way in which he used himself did not please everyone. In fact he was a very fine all-round sportsman, playing golf in particular to a high standard.

He had captained Cambridge in his last year, and in 1960 at the age of twenty-five took over at Sussex. Immediately their fortunes improved as they moved from the doldrums to fourth place, although it was a performance

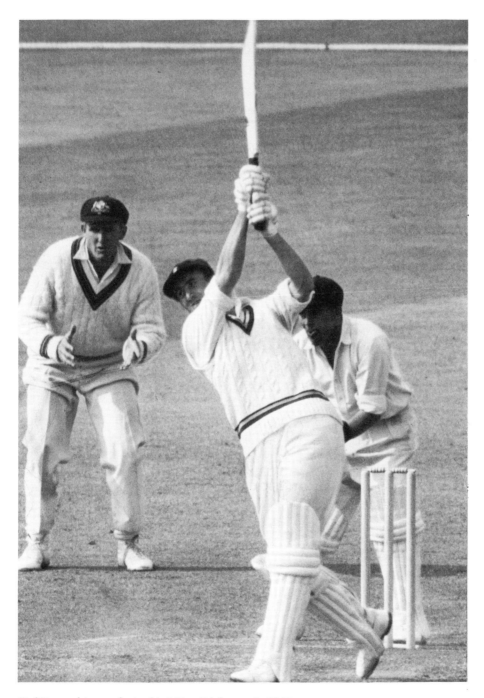

*Ted Dexter hits out during his 180 at Edgbaston in 1961,
despatching Bobby Simpson to the boundary. Davidson and Grout
look on.*

he was not to better in his five other seasons in charge. Not exactly short on self-confidence and charisma, he led by example and inspiration (and often did so successfully), but he was also more than somewhat authoritarian in style. The contrast with Cowdrey could hardly have been more marked, and Cowdrey probably suffered as a result of it.

Dexter was a good captain and was respected by his players, although he could at times be vague and apparently lacking in concentration; he was also a great theorist, and many a crowd must have found some of his ideas rather idiosyncratic. These unconventional moves were not usually just spur-of-the-moment ideas but carefully planned tactics; the problem was that when they didn't work he looked particularly idiosyncratic. Strangely, however, he was not one for gambling on the cricket field – strangely, because he was very fond of gambling off it. Perhaps because of this he had a high proportion of draws as England captain, fourteen out of thirty, with nine wins and seven defeats. Undoubtedly he made some mistakes, including the famous one in 1964 when he tried to polish off the last three Australian wickets by taking the new ball, only for those wickets to add 200 match-winning runs. That was a reasonable move that just went wrong; more relevant are the criticisms that he would over-use some of his bowlers and under-use others, and seemed to be especially suspicious of spinners – although he wasn't exactly alone in that.

The 1962–3 series was notable from an English viewpoint as the first tour to be managed by a duke. The Duke of Norfolk, no less, expressed an interest in the job and was offered it. With Alec Bedser as assistant things generally worked well. E.W. Swanton says that the popular joke of the time was that 'Lord' Ted needed a duke to keep him in hand. Australia were felt to have slightly the stronger team, although not by much; both sides were strong in batting but they probably had the edge in bowling since the English attack lacked variety – all pace and off-spin, and no left-armer for the first time ever on an England trip to Australia.

This impression was confirmed in the first Test when the bat very much dominated the ball. Fourteen fifties were scored, with a century from Booth, 99 from Dexter and 98 from Lawry, but England's target of 378 in six hours proved too steep and they settled for a draw. The second Test saw that rare article in Australia at this period, an English victory. Australia began with 316 and England replied with 331; in the second innings Lawry scored the slowest ever Australian fifty – a mere 275 minutes that Trevor Bailey could beat with his eyes shut – and Booth made another century. Set 234 to win, the final day belonged in particular to David Sheppard, who had scored 0 in the first innings and dropped two catches, producing

Trueman's celebrated comment that this was remarkable in one who should have had more practice than the rest of them in keeping his hands together. Sheppard scored 113 and was run out going for the winning run.

England's grip on the urn did not last long. On a slow Sydney pitch they struggled to 279 as Simpson returned his best Test figures of 5 for 57. Titmus responded by producing his best Test figures, 7 for 79, Australia managing a lead of 40. Davidson and Simpson, the best slip-catcher of them all, then combined to reduce England to shreds and they were all out for 104. It was the only time England's batting really failed, but it was enough to lose the Ashes.

In the next Test it was their catching that let them down. By the time Harvey had scored 26 he had given four chances. Deciding, reasonably enough, that it was his day, he went on to make 154. O'Neill, likewise, was dropped at 2 and made a further 98. Australia totalled 393 and then lost Davidson with a hamstring injury early in England's innings of 331. Handicapped by losing Davidson, Benaud could not gamble on bowling England out and so batted on until well into the last day to ensure a draw. Statham overtook Bedser's record haul of Test wickets in this match.

The romantics must have hoped that this would set up a stirring encounter to decide the series. On the same slow Sydney pitch they were going to be disappointed, as England unhurriedly ground their way to 321. Australia then reached 349, and only in their second innings did England show any urgency, declaring on the last day to leave Australia 241 at a run a minute. At first they seemed to be making an attempt at it, but when wickets fell the curtain came down and the game petered out, the Hillites expressing their feelings in the way that tradition demanded of them.

It had been a well-fought and friendly rubber, the first five-match series in Australia to end all square. Since the home team had started favourites England had obviously put up a decent performance, but there was the belief that with a bit more application and some better catching they could, and really should, have won. Both captains had produced good personal performances, but England were left with the familiar feeling of what might have been.

Benaud played in one more series at home to South Africa, during which he handed over the captaincy to Simpson. On retirement he was awarded the OBE and continued his work as a journalist and writer. He has for many years been the best of the television commentators, possessing the inestimable ability to keep quiet when there is nothing to say, and is very popular as a result. His involvement with Kerry Packer when the 'Great Schism' was upon us did not endear him to many in England, but he took that in his stride and has long since been forgiven. Even the English do not hold grudges against someone as good at his job as Benaud, despite the fact that in his years as captain he insisted on beating them.

For a decade that began with one of the most exciting series of all, Australia v West Indies in 1960–1, the 1960s went on to produce some pretty tedious cricket. Whether the cricket became tedious as a result of declining interest and attendances or whether these declined because the cricket was tedious is a question without a simple answer. This period saw, of course, great changes in the social habits of the western world, and one change that affected cricket attendances considerably was the realisation that, if you want something to do whilst doing nothing, the magic box in the corner of the room provides the ideal answer. But television was only a part of the story: as over-rates had slowed down so too had scoring rates; this coincided with an improvement in fertilisers, so that these could now produce beautiful green outfields which did not roughen up the ball as before but allowed it to keep its shine. The spinner was therefore a less potent force than he had been, and with his decline a good deal of the interest and artistry went out of the game. Medium-pace trundling has altogether less aesthetic appeal, but since the conditions now suited the practitioners of that art-form the clubs duly employed them.

This increase in seam and swing bowling at the expense of spin tended in turn to favour the solid batsman who could steadily accumulate runs rather than the stroke-maker who could entertain the crowd by battling with the spinners, and so the cycle was complete. County cricket had traditionally been watched by three men and a dog, but now, it was said, even the dogs had had enough. Cricket's Leaden Age had arrived, and the only solution was to invent a new game. One-day cricket brought back the crowds well enough, but with the constant switching between two kinds of technique it did little for the players except make it harder to learn either game properly.

Inevitably the increase in tedious uniformity made its way by osmosis up to Test level. There were some splendid matches and some good series but spectators, when they were not rioting, tended on the whole to sigh with nostalgia rather than cheer with delight. Some of the players – Cowdrey, Dexter, Graveney, Sobers, Kanhai, Hall, Graeme Pollock, Benaud, for instance – would have graced any age, but there were plenty more who played regularly for their countries who would scarcely have been considered in another era. Some did well at Test level, but there were plenty of cricket-lovers who felt that that level was no longer what it had been.

Against this background Ted Dexter suggested that it might be no bad thing if the Ashes were abolished. His thinking was that towards the end of a series the team holding the Ashes, if they are not behind in the rubber, need only play to avoid defeat in order to achieve their objective of retaining them. In theory, at least, the attitude of the Ashes-holding captain could be coloured from the beginning of a series, so that he approaches every match with priorities that are not conducive to entertaining cricket. There was more than one match during the 1960s that supported his argument.

When Bobby Simpson brought his team to England in 1964 matters were not improved when the weather produced a very frustrating series, with three matches badly affected by rain. Since one of the others produced the ideal fuel for Dexter's argument for abandonment of the Ashes, few English people were happy when it was all over.

If Benaud had not achieved quite the eminence of Bradman in terms of performance, he had arguably equalled him in stature as a captain. Simpson's task of following him was therefore comparable with Hassett's fourteen years earlier, but the game had toughened up still further in

Bobby Simpson, vigorous and successful defender of the Ashes.

between times and Simpson's approach was rather different from Hassett's. When Benaud retired there had been strong support for Brian Booth to take over, but he had to be content with the understudy's role. Simpson was to go on to lead his country on thirty-nine occasions, ten of which came with his 'reincarnation' at the time of Mr Packer's fireworks, when, at the age of forty-one, he was called out of retirement to lead the squad of youngsters after the senior players had defected.

Only Ian Craig had played for New South Wales at a younger age than Simpson, and at twenty-one he was playing for his country. It took him a while to cement a place in the side as, although he was scoring plenty of attractive runs in Shield matches, he had rather too many Test failures. He moved to Western Australia with the idea of standing out more in a weaker side, and also had a successful season in the Lancashire League. Always very fast on his feet, one of the features of his batting was the speed with which he got into position to play any stroke – and play it hard. He was to finish with over 21,000 runs at 56, of which nearly 4,900 at an average approaching 47 were in Tests. Not until his thirtieth Test did he finally score the magic three figures, but when he did it was with some style (or weight, anyway) and once the barrier had been broken nine more centuries followed.

He also took seventy-one Test wickets with his leg-break bowling that was often under-rated and tended to suffer from living in Benaud's shadow. His slip fielding, however, can claim to have stood clear above the shadow of anyone who has ever played cricket; 110 catches in 62 Tests gives a striking rate among the leading catchers second only to that of Eknath Solkar, a specialist short-leg who took most of his victims from the great Indian spin quartet of the 1970s. Simpson's reflexes and hand–eye co-ordination were such that he still took catches after they had been deflected by the keeper. This wonderful natural ability was backed up by much practice and thought, resulting in some catches that could surely not have been made by anyone else.

He had captained Western Australia in 1960–1, but then returned to take over at New South Wales in 1962–3. Test captaincy came in the 1963–4 series at home to South Africa, by which time he had twenty-three caps. He immediately showed that he was able to appreciate the finer tactical points, and as he grew into the job he tended to make his mind up and stick to his beliefs. There was never any question that he was the one directing the show; everything had to happen through him. He insisted on the highest standards of effort, appearance and attitude from his players, would enforce discipline strongly to ensure that they were maintained, and would very much lead by example.

Perhaps rather oddly, in view of his standards, he was not always able to accept dubious umpiring decisions with the equanimity that tradition demanded, and he had some unhappy times in the Caribbean with umpires who seemed reluctant to agree with him that Charlie Griffith was bowling not only illegally, but in an intimidating fashion. If his tactics sometimes came in for criticism he had his reasons for whatever he did and his tactical soundness was widely acknowledged. His commitment was such that he spent much time improving his speaking voice and manner so that he would be better able to perform the duties of a touring captain. Of his Tests as captain, twelve were won and twelve lost, although nine of these results came in his last ten matches at the end of the 1970s. His proportion of draws was about par for the course in the 1960s, 14 in 29 games.

Some members of the English Press decided to write off the Australians when they arrived in 1964, and Providence saw to it, as Providence will, that this received what it deserved. Probably their team was not as strong as some of its predecessors, but then neither was England's. Once again the batting on both sides seemed stronger than the bowling, as one match (or semi-match) in particular was to bear witness.

Both of the first two Tests were drastically curtailed by rain. The opening match was famous for Wally Grout's sporting action in declining to run out Titmus after he had collided with the bowler. After some low scores Australia were left to make 242 in 195 minutes when the rain closed in yet again. The second match lost even more time to rain, not starting until the third day. John Edrich announced himself with a century, but there was little else of note.

In the third Test at Headingley England could manage only 268 on a good wicket. A middle-order collapse then saw Australia on 178 for 7, at which point Dexter made the most celebrated mistake of his career. Titmus and Gifford had been bowling well and had taken five wickets between them, when Dexter decided, not unreasonably and with a lot of history to back him up, that the new ball was the best means of finishing off the tail. Simpson told Burge, who was on 38 at the time, to counter-attack, Trueman and Flavell bowled poorly, and there were to be another 211 runs scored before the last wicket fell. Burge's 160 was a splendid affair, Hawke and Grout supporting him by scoring 37 each. What should have been a lead was a sizeable deficit, and England seemed demoralised. Only Barrington got a decent score as they left Australia just 109 for victory.

It was now that Dexter's argument for abolishing the Ashes could be seen for its wisdom. The pitch at Old Trafford was perfect for batting, and Simpson did just that for some considerable time, intent on putting the game and the series out of England's reach. He and Lawry opened with 201, and before the day was out he had finally scored his first Test century in his fifty-second innings. Throughout the second day he batted on, at the end of which he was on 265. Only on the third morning did he throw the bat, and after 762 minutes he was finally out for 311, the highest score ever by a Test captain, the longest ever innings against England and the third-longest in first-class cricket. Faced with a total of 656 for 8 declared England could hope for no more than avoiding disgrace; in fact they nearly achieved parity. The substance was provided by Dexter's 174 and Barrington's 256, and when the last wicket fell Test cricket had seen its only instance of both sides scoring over 600 runs in one innings. Veivers bowled a total of 571 balls, only 17 fewer than Ramadhin's record Test number. If you like nonsensical semi-matches it had its attractions, but most people do not. At Old Trafford precisely fifty-five years earlier (both matches finished on the same day, 28 July) Monty Noble, 2–1 up in the series, had been criticised for batting on during the last day rather than declaring earlier and giving England the chance to go for the runs. One imagines that those Edwardian gentlemen would have had apoplexy at the thought of Simpson's innings.

The Oval match was another that lost a great deal of time to rain and ended meaninglessly. But it will always be remembered for one thing, that it was the game in which Fred Trueman became the first bowler through the barrier of 300 Test wickets. Inevitably he did it in dramatic style. Just before lunch he took the ball from Dexter and put himself on – John Arlott records that Dexter was 'in one of his glazed moods' – and with his fifth ball bowled Redpath. The next ball he had McKenzie caught at slip. Further drama had to wait till after lunch, no doubt the only time that every spectator was seated for the resumption of play. The hat-trick did not come but in due course Hawke's wicket did, caught by Cowdrey at slip.

From the English point of view it was probably the most frustrating of all Ashes series, and it can't have been much fun for the Australians either. It marked the end of Dexter's captaincy, although he was to play in nine more Tests before, like May, he retired early from the scene. He went in for a variety of other activities including flying, running a PR company and writing, but he is known chiefly today for his television commentaries. If he didn't manage to win back the Ashes, at least he was the captain who led his team to victory in the first two seasons of the Gillette Cup.

On their tour of India the previous winter England had been led by M.J.K. Smith, and he now took over the captaincy from Dexter once again. Having drawn all the games in India he won in South Africa, beat New Zealand at home and lost to South Africa at home, and was then appointed

Ian Chappell, seen here in his final series as captain against England in 1975, led a very successful Australian team during the early 1970s.

Greg Chappell on his way to 112 at Old Trafford in 1977.

*Tony Greig's colourful personality was always better suited to the
Test arena than to county cricket.*

Mike Brearley, wearing a prototype protective helmet which,
according to Brian Johnston, made him look rather like a spaniel, hits
out at Len Pascoe during the 1977 series.

Graham Yallop had the misfortune to lead a very inexperienced team
in 1978–9, but his own batting was determined and purposeful.

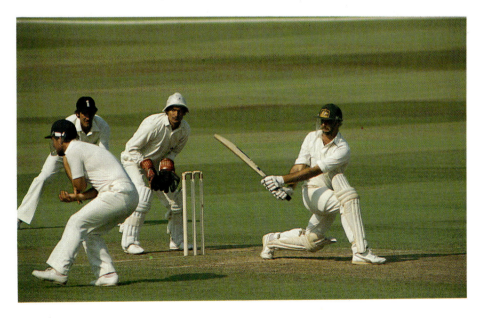

The Australian team for the 1980 Centenary Test.

The England team for the 1980 Centenary Test.

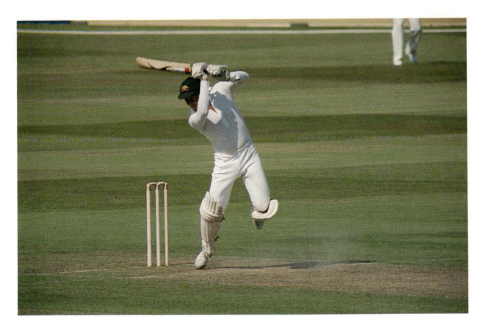

Kim Hughes, star-crossed leader of the 1981 Australians.

Ian Botham may not go down as a great captain, but a Test match against Australia has often been the spur to yet another remarkable performance.

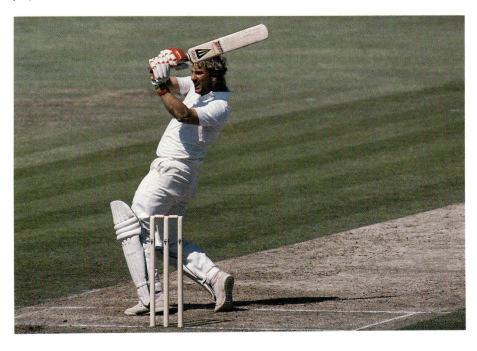

Mike Brearley survives an appeal by Terry Alderman at Headingley in 1981.

Bob Willis on the war-path.

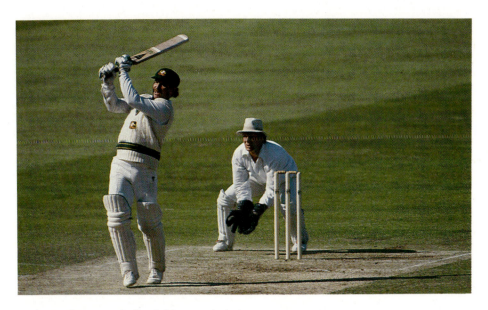

Allan Border enjoyed splendid form with the bat in 1985. Paul Downton watches another ball despatched to the boundary.

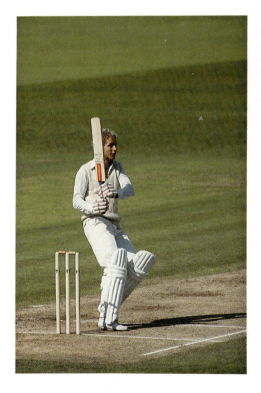

Border was upstaged, however, by David Gower, seen here during his 215 at Edgbaston which left cricket writers racking their brains for fresh superlatives. Between them the two captains scored 1329 runs in six Tests.

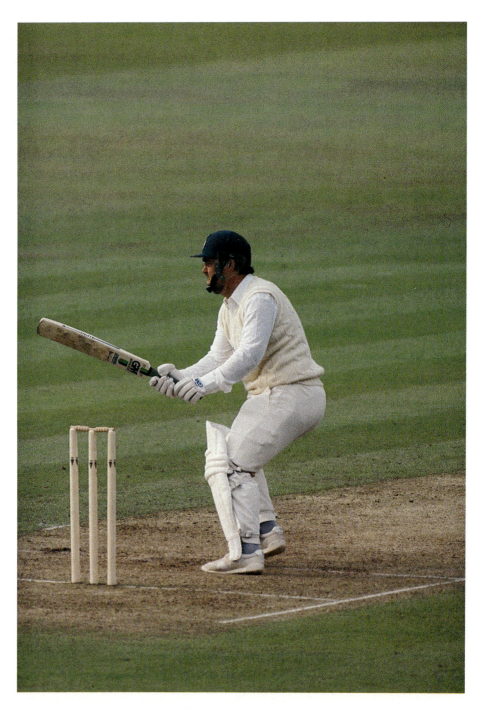

Mike Gatting's captaincy was much praised during England's very successful Australian tour of 1986–7.

*Mike Smith's fielding was one of the features of the 1965–6 tour. Here
he catches David Sincock off Allen's bowling as Barber and Parks
look on.*

to take England to Australia in 1965–6. In all he led his country twenty-five
times, winning five and losing three, leaving one of the highest proportions
of draws of any Test captain. He played in fifty Tests, scoring just under
2,300 runs at the rather low average of less than 32, which was 10 points
below his career average. In part this was because he was never happy
against really fast bowling and tended to be vulnerable until he had played
himself in, but it also reflected the fact that if it was time to take risks to get
some runs he would try and do it himself rather than ask someone else. He
scored prodigiously at Oxford and in his earlier years with Warwickshire,
and totalled in all nearly 40,000 first-class runs, the majority scored on the
leg side. He didn't quite have the class of his three immediate predecessors,
but they were rather exceptional. A brilliant close fielder, he was also a
good enough Rugby player to win an England cap.

Having captained Oxford, he played for Leicestershire for a few years
before moving to Warwickshire; there he took over the leadership in 1957
and challenged for the title for some seasons without quite managing it. He

had a very thorough knowledge of the game, but was not one of nature's gamblers; one of the main criticisms of him was that he was over-inclined to caution, even by the standards of his time. He also seemed unsure of the best way to handle his spinners. As one would expect, he was not a demonstrative leader, but somehow one was aware of his control whereas with the undemonstrative Cowdrey this was less the case.

Of all the England captains since the war Mike Smith was probably the most popular with his players. His glasses gave him something of an academic air that might have counted against him, but his quiet humour and dry wit, his love of deflating conceitedness, his unselfishness, fairness and easily approachable friendliness made him greatly liked; unlike Dexter he was not given to moodiness, and with his all-round straightness, in the best sense of the word, his players would do their utmost for him. He was not the most sociable of people, but neither was he a recluse; he was not the best of interviewees, but neither did he treat the press with the suspicion that some captains have. Strangely though, in view of all this, the press, and therefore the public, were never quite convinced of him as a captain (just as they never really were of Cowdrey), presumably because they are concerned primarily with performances and results on the field rather than with personal characteristics; Smith (and Cowdrey) somehow did not seem to be quite the stuff of which a *real* captain is made, whatever that might be. Perhaps he did not appear assertive enough, perhaps his batting so often did not seem quite good enough, perhaps he simply did not win often enough. For all that, John Woodcock was able to write in *Wisden* when he retired: 'Of how many cricketers may it be said, at the end of a long and distinguished career, that they made no enemies?'

One problem with the 1964 series had been that Simpson and Dexter had never really established a great rapport. Smith's easy-going personality was more in Simpson's line, though, and they were able to produce a friendly and well-contested rubber that contained some good cricket. It was one in which the bat dominated the ball, with four Australians averaging over 68 and seven Englishmen averaging over 40. On neither side was the bowling what it had been a few years before, McKenzie and Hawke having little support and none of the English bowlers making much of an impact. Australia had to be the favourites, but not by much. The home Press had done England the favour of writing them off, just as the English Press had done to the Australians before the previous series. This was, incidentally, the first time England had travelled all the way to Australia by air.

For the first and third Tests Australia were without Simpson, for reasons as diverse as a broken wrist and chickenpox, and Brian Booth duly took

(Left)   *Mike Smith, England captain of the 1965–6 tour to Australia.*   (Right)   *Brian Booth, fine batsman and fine sportsman.*

over. He was a slim, elegant and courageous batsman who made it all look so easy, with lightning footwork and a whole range of strokes. He made his début on the 1961 tour of England and for the next four years was a regular in the side; he was also one of the few Test cricketers to have played serious hockey, having been a member of his country's team in the 1956 Olympics.

Apart from his attractive batting Booth is remembered as a very fine and modest sportsman. He lived his life and played his cricket in accordance with his religious convictions, never making a fuss when things went against him and never making too much of his own achievements. He was invariably a 'walker' if he knew he was out, a practice that had become pretty rare everywhere by the 1960s. His quiet, natural dignity earned him universal respect and enabled him to defuse some tense situations. He had little experience of captaincy, though, and was perhaps just too much of a gentleman, in the same way that Cowdrey was, to do the job really successfully. Having said that, one has the feeling that had he been given an extended run in the job it would have been a very good thing for the game, especially if he had encountered Cowdrey and Smith along the way.

Booth had the better of a rain-affected first Test. Doug Walters made 155 in his first innings, and with 166 from Lawry Australia totalled 443. The follow-on deficit was 150 at the time and England didn't quite make it, though towards the end they had no trouble in saving the game. Simpson then returned for the next match; Australia opened with 358 and with Cowdrey and Edrich both scoring hundreds England passed that by exactly 200. On the last day Australia were still 24 behind when the fourth wicket fell, but when Burge had made 34 Parks missed a stumping chance. Burge went on to 120 and with another century from Walters helped to save the game. This incident is often trotted out by those who believe you should play your best wicket-keeper regardless of his batting ability; the fact that in the next Test Parks made five dismissals in Australia's first innings and so ensured that they followed on is not usually mentioned – nor is his batting average for the series, which was 48.

Simpson's chickenpox left Booth in charge again in the third match. Barber and Boycott put on 234 for the first wicket, with Barber going on to make a chanceless 185, an innings that caught everyone's imagination. Edrich also made a century and England totalled 488. Good pace bowling then bundled Australia out for 221, during the course of which Brown took three wickets in one over with the new ball (Dexter, when he heard that, must have thought back wistfully to Headingley in 1964). In their second innings Titmus and Allen did the damage, and dismissal for 174 gave England their first victory by an innings in Australia since before the war. This caused the selectors' wrath to descend upon poor Booth; he had not done a great deal with the bat in the three games and was dropped, never to return. As well as his teaching career, he has since done much to help young people with social problems, and has been very active in community welfare.

When Simpson returned for the fourth match it became apparent what his team had lacked. England could manage only 241 and he and Lawry then exceeded that on their own, making 244 in almost even time. Simpson went on to 225 and his team to 516, and England had no answer. An innings win for Australia this time, followed by a high-scoring 'bore-draw' to finish with, although it did lose a day to rain. England made 485 with a Barrington century, but then a hundred from Lawry and a significant contribution from Cowper took Australia to 543.

Cowper scored 307, Australia's only triple-century in a home Test. It did not sparkle; at 727 minutes it is the longest innings ever played in Australia, and it broke other records as well. At least the Melbourne crowd had to sit through 35 minutes less of it than the Old Trafford crowd did for

Simpson, but then Simpson did score four more runs . . . This was clearly another game that Simpson was determined not to lose, giving more support to would-be Ashes-abolitionists.

Curiously, both Smith and Simpson retired from cricket for some years and then returned, not just to first-class cricket but to the Test arena. Smith led England for the last time against West Indies in 1966 and retired at the end of 1967; in 1970 he made a comeback that was successful enough to merit three more caps against the 1972 Australians, not finally calling it a day until 1975. Simpson meanwhile continued as captain against South Africa and India before handing over to Lawry; eleven years later it was also against India that he led his team of novices to a 3–2 win at home, and then took them to the West Indies; this series was lost 3–1 and that was the end. He undoubtedly did his country a fine service in a difficult hour.

English cricket fans are likely to recall Bill Lawry with a groan. This is not just because he scored his runs slowly – the nation that gave the likes of Bailey and Tavaré to the cricketing world can hardly complain on that account – but because he scored so many, thwarting England time and again. In all matches against Mike Smith's tourists, for instance, he scored 979 runs in 11 innings spread over 41½ hours. In the context of Test cricket perhaps his scoring rate was not as desperate as the memory recalls, but it was desperate enough for most English fans, at least. His mission in life was to occupy the crease and accumulate runs to enable his team to win matches; it was not his mission in life to entertain the spectators. As missions go he was pretty successful, compiling 5,234 runs in 67 Tests at an average of 47, passing the hundred mark thirteen times; when he retired only Bradman and Harvey had scored more for Australia. The problem for the spectator was that his batting was rarely attractive to watch. Tall and left-handed he could play most of the shots when he wanted to, but not with much elegance or style.

His determination and powers of concentration can be paid no higher compliment than to say that they were the equal of Bradman's, but there is a limit to the number of times people want to see the ball pushed back to the bowler if there is the remotest risk that it might take a wicket. The really annoying thing – as with Tavaré – was knowing that he was quite capable of scoring at a reasonable rate if he put his mind to it; he often seemed to drop anchor simply because he saw himself as the anchor man. A very fine player of fast bowling, he must have been more disheartening to bowl to than almost any other post-war batsman, although he was less happy against the spinners. Undoubtedly he did save his country several times, worthily doing his job – in his own way.

Edgbaston 1968. Colin Cowdrey, in his 100th Test, tosses with Bill Lawry.

He made his début for Victoria the day before his nineteenth birthday, and once he had made the Test team at twenty-four he held his place for ten years. For series after series he and Simpson formed Australia's most dependable opening partnership ever, putting on a string of substantial foundations. Most notable of these was their 382, Australia's record first-wicket partnership, against West Indies in 1965 when both made a double-century against the bowling of Hall, Griffith, Sobers and Gibbs. Lawry's courage, let it be said, was as endless as his patience; over the years he was hit on the head a number of times, but this did nothing to weaken his determination.

Anyone who watched him bat will be surprised to learn that he was quite a practical joker, his schoolboy tricks forming a great contrast with his stolidity on the field. With his team-mates he could be a very humorous man, but the only indication anyone else had of this was in some of the speeches he made as captain. One wonders how much fine cricket he could have played if he had not taken his batting so seriously and let his lighter side come to the fore more often. His serious nature meant that he was not the easiest person for his team-mates to get along with, and he was rarely 'one of the boys'.

Lawry's captaincy tended to match his personality. He led Victoria from 1961–2 to 1970–1, winning the Sheffield Shield three times, and Australia twenty-five times, winning nine and losing eight. Sometimes his hatred of defeat would cause friction when he operated by the letter of the law rather than the spirit of the game, and he seemed to attract more barracking than most captains. Often the advice that the spectators offered so freely concerned his tactics, in particular accusing him of reluctance to use spinners unless the pitch was really suitable. Word had it that he could be over-critical of his bowlers, tending to put them down instead of trying to pick them up. Rather than attack a batsman his policy would often be to stifle him into making a mistake, a course of action that gives the crowd plenty of time to think up more insults. He earned a reputation for melodramatic appealing and for showing his displeasure with umpires. He enraged the population of India by what they saw as his lack of sportsmanship and conciliatory spirit over the dubious dismissal of one of their batsmen, and they duly rioted. Watching Lawry one had the impression that captaincy was an onerous duty which he never actually enjoyed; he was mindful of his great honour and he tried his hardest to win, but there was always the feeling that playing under him or against him had few light moments.

Throughout the 1960s there seemed little to choose between the two teams. Both had a number of dependable batsmen but not many high-class bowlers, so that of twenty-five Tests played during the decade only ten had a definite result, with a 6–4 balance to Australia. With several matches ruined by rain England could never quite do enough to win a series so that history continued to repeat itself; after each war Australia were greatly superior, gave way to England for a while, then re-established themselves. The only difference between the 1960s and the 1930s was that this time there was no Jardine to interrupt the sequence with some bright idea or other. The summer of 1968 saw a continuation of the approximate parity between the teams, more rain-affected matches – and one of the most remarkable of finishes.

Cowdrey by this time was in the middle of his one lengthy spell of captaincy by virtue of having seen off all his rivals of the past few years. He had just returned from the West Indies where he had won the series 1–0, thanks to a sporting declaration from Sobers, and English morale was high. This state of affairs was not destined to last for long. In the first match Lawry so bemused the Englishmen by scoring two sixes that they allowed his team to reach 357 before they replied with 165 in poor batting conditions. By the end of Australia's second innings England needed 413 in a little over nine hours; they made 253.

The Lord's Test was the 200th between the two countries, and it fell to the weather with almost exactly half the time being lost; the first day ended at lunch-time with a violent hailstorm. England made 351 with some fireworks from Milburn, but by the time Australia batted conditions were distinctly difficult. Some fine bowling and catching put them out for 78, but more rain shortened the last day and they were able to hang on for a draw. Rain again at Edgbaston then precluded another result, but did not stop Cowdrey from scoring a century in his hundredth Test, passing 7,000 runs as he did so. England made 409 after which Australia, like England in the first game, only narrowly avoided the follow-on. With more time lost England were unable to press home their advantage.

With Lawry suffering from a broken finger and Cowdrey from a hamstring injury, Headingley saw one of those rare Tests in which both teams are led by deputy captains. For both Graveney and Jarman it was their one taste of Test leadership.

Tom Graveney was one of the supremely elegant batsmen, on his day a glorious stroke-maker who could charm the ball to the boundary with effortless timing and grace, especially off his front foot. His Test career stuttered somewhat from time to time, but in due course he became a pillar of the team, playing 79 Tests and scoring nearly 4,900 runs at over 44.

The elegance of Tom Graveney, here batting for Worcestershire.

Many of his finest knocks were against West Indies, including 258 in 1957 and a number of high scores when he was aged around forty. In all he scored nearly 48,000 runs with 122 centuries, a post-war aggregate exceeded only by Boycott. Always a cheerful, genial man he was very popular with his team-mates and the public, a somewhat rustic air adding to his West Country background, although he was born in Northumberland.

He played for Gloucester from 1948 to 1960, captaining them in the last two years, but after a disagreement moved to Worcestershire, helping them to their first Championship success and captaining them from 1968 to 1970. With all his experience he knew the game thoroughly, but the style he brought to his batting did not extend to his leadership qualities. These were honest and straightforward, but tended to lack inspiration; he was not one for a daring gamble or for driving his team towards an unlikely victory, and he achieved little as a captain. For several years since he retired he has been a television commentator and summariser, his accent conjuring up images of warm, sunny days on the cricket fields of the South-West.

Barry Jarman spent about nine years as understudy to Wally Grout, managing only an occasional Test before he finally became first-choice wicket-keeper when Grout retired. In all he played in nineteen Tests and

Barry Jarman, one of the few wicket-keeper captains of Test history.

made fifty-four dismissals, but at a different period his career could have been long and distinguished. He accepted the number two spot cheerfully, happy to concede that Grout was the best in the business. Unlike Jim Parks in his tussle for the English job with John Murray, Jarman could not point to a superior batting record; he and Grout were about equal, both having a Test average of around 15. Although not tall he was rather heavy for a wicket-keeper at about thirteen and a half stone, but he was still extremely quick and agile. A very animated and humorous man, fond of playing jokes on his team-mates, he was always ready with some quip or other. Highly respected and popular, he had experience of leading South Australia and had shown enterprise and tactical awareness when doing so. Everything about him spoke of a positive approach to life; it was just that when he had the chance to press for Test victory the spectre of the Ashes reared up and he preferred to play for safety.

Australia batted first and ran up 315, to which England responded with 302. By tea on the fourth day Australia were 250 in front with only four wickets down, and everyone assumed they would go for some quick runs to set England a target and then give themselves most of the last day to bowl them out. Instead they meandered on at a funereal pace, and when they were all out England were left with less than five hours to score 326, an impossible target. Some suspected Lawry's influence but Jarman denied it. He said afterwards: 'The Englishmen still had time to win in the last session by having a go. The ball was in their court. If we had needed a win to square the series we would have given it a go. We had come over to retain the Ashes. The name of the game is the Ashes. They had to win to get them. We didn't have to.' At least it proved to be the last time in the 60s that such an attitude stultified a cricket match.

At the Oval England piled up 494 with big centuries from Edrich and D'Oliveira, but a Lawry hundred could get Australia no further than 324 in reply. England then went for some quick runs and managed 181 of them. By lunch on the last day Australia had collapsed to 65 for 5 when a cloudburst completely flooded the ground. Before long, though, the sun came out and the groundstaff set about clearing away the water. Only through the efforts of scores of volunteers from the crowd was the job completed in time for play to begin again, the army of people wielding brooms, spikers and pieces of sacking providing some of cricket's more unlikely photographs.

At 4.45 play was resumed, but for forty minutes nothing much happened. Then D'Oliveira bowled Jarman and Cowdrey brought back Underwood. Mallett and McKenzie fell in his first over; with 12 minutes left Gleeson went, caught by Dexter in his (Dexter's) last Test. And with just five minutes left Inverarity, having batted throughout the innings for 56, was out lbw to Underwood, who finished with figures of 7 for 50. The people who had been mopping the pitch, plus one or two others, ran on to it again to acclaim a new hero. The dreaded Ashes may have remained with Australia but at least the Ashes Tests of the sorry 1960s had ended on a note of splendid excitement.

1962–3	Brisbane	A 404, 362–4d	E 389, 278–6	Drawn
	Melbourne	A 316, 248	E 331, 237–3	E 7 wkts
	Sydney	E 279, 104	A 319, 67–2	A 8 wkts
	Adelaide	A 393, 293	E 331, 223–4	Drawn
	Sydney	E 321, 268–8d	A 349, 152–4	Drawn
1964	Trent Bridge	E 216–8d, 193–9d	A 168, 40–2	Drawn
	Lord's	A 176, 168–4	E 246	Drawn
	Headingley	E 268, 229	A 389, 111–3	A 7 wkts
	Old Trafford	A 656–8d, 4–0	E 611	Drawn
	Oval	E 182, 381–4	A 379	Drawn
1965–6	Brisbane	A 443–6d	E 280, 186–3	Drawn
	Melbourne	A 358, 426	E 558, 5–0	Drawn
	Sydney	E 488	A 221, 174	E inns 93 runs
	Adelaide	E241, 266	A 516	A inns 9 runs
	Melbourne	E 485–9d, 69–3	A 543–8d	Drawn
1968	Old Trafford	A 357, 220	E 165, 253	A 159 runs
	Lord's	E 351–7d	E 78, 127–4	Drawn
	Edgbaston	E 409, 142–3d	A 222, 68–1	Drawn
	Headingley	A 315, 312	E 302, 230–4	Drawn
	Oval	E 494, 181	A 324, 125	E 226 runs

1962–3

England

Batting	Innings	NO	HS	Runs	Average
K.F. Barrington	10	2	132*	582	72.75
E.R. Dexter	10	0	99	481	48.10
M.C. Cowdrey	10	1	113	394	43.77
F.J. Titmus	8	3	59*	182	36.40
Revd D.S. Sheppard	10	0	113	330	33.00

Bowling	O	M	R	W	Average
F.S. Trueman	158.3	9	521	20	26.05
F.J. Titmus	236.3	54	616	21	29.33
E.R. Dexter	95.2	6	373	11	33.90
J.B. Statham	165.2	16	580	13	44.61
L.J. Coldwell	57	5	159	3	53.00

Australia

Batting	Innings	NO	HS	Runs	Average
P.J.P. Burge	6	2	103	245	61.25
B.C. Booth	10	2	112	404	50.50
B.K. Shepherd	3	1	71*	94	47.00
R.B. Simpson	10	1	91	401	44.55
R.N. Harvey	10	0	154	395	39.50

Bowling	O	M	R	W	Average
A.K. Davidson	176.2	30	480	24	20.00
G.D. McKenzie	205.3	25	619	20	30.95
R. Benaud	228	56	688	17	40.47
R.B. Simpson	93	18	369	8	46.12
K.D. Mackay	85.6	19	227	4	56.75

Wicket-keepers: B.N. Jarman (A) 7 dismissals   A.T.W. Grout (A) 9 dismissals
A.C. Smith (E) 13 dismissals   J.T. Murray (E) 1 dismissal

Captains: R. Benaud – batting 51; 36, 4; 15; 16, 48, 57
bowling 6–115, 1–71; 1–82, 0–69; 1–60, 1–29; 1–82, 1–38; 2–71, 3–71
E.R. Dexter – batting 70, 99; 93, 52; 32, 11; 61, 10; 47, 6
bowling 1–46, 2–78; 0–10, 1–18; 0–27; 3–94, 3–65, 1–24, 0–11

In the fourth match J.B. Statham passed A.V. Bedser's Test record of 236 wickets. E.R. Dexter's total of 481 runs is the highest by an England captain in a series in Australia.

1964

England

Batting	Innings	NO	HS	Runs	Average
K.F. Barrington	8	1	256	531	75.85
G. Boycott	6	0	113	291	48.50
E.R. Dexter	8	0	174	384	48.00
M.C. Cowdrey	5	1	93*	188	47.00
J.H. Edrich	4	0	120	161	40.25

Bowling	O	M	R	W	Average
F.S. Trueman	133.3	25	399	17	23.47
N. Gifford	83	35	140	5	28.00
F.J. Titmus	202	92	301	10	30.10
E.R. Dexter	49	7	118	3	39.33
L.J. Coldwell	64	14	158	4	39.50

Australia

Batting	Innings	NO	HS	Runs	Average
R.B. Simpson	8	2	311	458	76.33
P.J.P. Burge	8	1	160	322	46.00
B.C. Booth	8	3	98	210	42.00
T.R. Veivers	5	1	67*	159	39.75
W.M. Lawry	9	1	106	317	39.62

Bowling	O	M	R	W	Average
G.D. McKenzie	256	61	654	29	22.55
N.J.N. Hawke	242.1	80	496	18	27.55
G.E. Corling	193.1	50	447	12	37.25
T.R. Veivers	228.1	73	444	11	40.36
R.B. Simpson	60	19	159	1	159.00

Wicket-keepers: J.M. Parks (E) 6 dismissals   A.T.W. Grout (A) 10 dismissals

Captains: E.R. Dexter – batting 9, 68; 2; 66, 17; 174; 23, 25
            bowling dnb; 2–16, 0–5; 0–40, 0–9; 0–12; 1–36
         R.B. Simpson – batting 50; 0, 15*; 24, 30; 311; 24
            bowling dnb; 0–51; 0–24, 0–11; 0–59; 1–14

R.B. Simpson's 311 in the fourth match is the highest score by a Test captain; his 762-minute innings is the longest against England. In the same match T.R. Veivers bowled 571 balls, the record in England v Australia Tests. In the fifth match F.S. Trueman became the first bowler to take 300 Test wickets. G.D. McKenzie's 29 wickets equalled the record for an Australian bowler in a series in England.

1965–6

England

Batting	Innings	NO	HS	Runs	Average
K.F. Barrington	8	1	115	464	66.28
F.J. Titmus	6	2	60	258	64.50
M.C. Cowdrey	6	1	104	267	53.40
J.M. Parks	6	0	89	290	48.38
J.H. Edrich	8	0	109	375	46.87

Bowling	O	M	R	W	Average
K.F. Barrington	7.4	0	47	2	23.50
B.R. Knight	83.7	10	250	8	31.25
I.J. Jones	129	15	533	15	35.53
D.J. Brown	108	14	409	11	37.18
G. Boycott	23	4	89	2	44.50

Australia

Batting	Innings	NO	HS	Runs	Average
R.B. Simpson	4	0	225	355	88.75
W.M. Lawry	7	0	166	592	84.57
R.M. Cowper	6	0	307	493	82.16
K.D. Walters	7	1	155	410	68.33
G. Thomas	4	0	52	147	36.75

Bowling	O	M	R	W	Average
N.J.N. Hawke	142.7	29	419	16	26.18
G.D. McKenzie	133.4	20	467	16	29.18
K.D. Walters	79	8	283	9	31.44
R.M. Cowper	22	5	76	2	38.00
P.J. Allan	24	6	83	2	41.50

Wicket-keepers: A.T.W. Grout (A) 16 dismissals   J.M. Parks (E) 15 dismissals

Captains: B.C. Booth – batting 16; 8, 27
            R.B. Simpson – batting 59, 67; 225; 4
                           bowling 0–61; dnb; 0–20
            M.J.K. Smith – batting 16, 10*; 41; 6; 29, 5; 0

In the second match K.D. Walters became the second batsman to score a century in each of his first two Tests. In the fourth match R.B. Simpson and W.M. Lawry put on 244 for a record first-wicket partnership against England. In the fifth match R.M. Cowper scored the only triple-century by an Australian in a home Test. A.T.W. Grout ended his Test career with 187 dismissals, the Australian record at the time.

1968

England

Batting	Innings	NO	HS	Runs	Average
B.L. D'Oliveira	4	1	158	263	87.66
J.H. Edrich	9	0	164	554	61.55
K.F. Barrington	4	1	75	170	56.66
T.W. Graveney	9	1	96	337	42.12
C. Milburn	3	0	83	109	36.33

Bowling	O	M	R	W	Average
D.L. Underwood	209.5	103	302	20	15.10
B.L. D'Oliveira	39	20	49	3	16.33
B.R. Knight	40.4	16	85	4	21.25
R. Illingworth	183.2	82	291	13	22.39
P.I. Pocock	58	15	156	6	26.00

Australia

Batting	Innings	NO	HS	Runs	Average
W.M. Lawry	7	1	135	270	45.00
I.M. Chappell	10	2	81	348	43.50
K.D. Walters	9	0	86	343	38.11
I.R. Redpath	10	0	92	310	31.00
R.M. Cowper	8	1	57	191	27.28

Bowling	O	M	R	W	Average
A.N. Connolly	267.1	75	591	23	21.34
R.M. Cowper	103	36	241	8	30.12
E.W. Freeman	67.5	17	186	6	31.00
A.A. Mallett	61	15	164	5	32.80
J.W. Gleeson	193.5	65	417	12	34.75

Wicket-keepers: A.P.E. Knott (E) 15 dismissals   B.N. Jarman (A) 11 dismissals
                H.B. Taber (A) 2 dismissals

Captains: M.C. Cowdrey – batting 4, 11; 45; 104; 16, 35
            T.W. Graveney – batting 37, 41
            W.M. Lawry – batting 81, 16; 0, 28; 6; 135, 4
            B.N. Jarman – batting 10, 4

In the second match M.C. Cowdrey passed W.R. Hammond's record of 110 Test catches. In the third match he became the first to appear in 100 Tests, and scored a century to celebrate, during the course of which he became the second batsman to score 7,000 Test runs. In the last match D.L. Underwood took 7 for 50 to win for England with five minutes to spare.

12

England throw off History and Australia take up Sledging

One good thing about moving into the 1970s was that at long last we were able to throw off the burden of history. For two decades or so the pattern had repeated itself with uncanny faithfulness to the decades after the first war (the hiccup Jardine caused presumably arose because he was outside the domain of Destiny), but now at long last England were free to cast off the shackles, to emerge from the shadow of Father Time and believe that there was no dark force to stop them winning again. They celebrated this new-found 'existential' freedom by appointing, almost by chance, a captain who could go to Australia and return with the Ashes. In ninety or so years only Warner, Douglas (with Warner's help) and Jardine had set off without the Ashes and come back with them. Enter Ray Illingworth.

Perhaps Cowdrey would have done it had he been in charge. But in May 1969 he had snapped an Achilles tendon whilst batting in a Sunday afternoon wallop, and the selectors had decided that Illingworth, and not Graveney, should take over. Only that season he had left Yorkshire after nineteen years to take over as captain of Leicestershire, and perhaps, had he not done so, he would not have been considered for the England job.

He had played in thirty Tests but had never been a regular in the side, contending for a place with several others and often returning figures that did little justice to his bowling. Most of his successes had come at home, and there seemed to be doubts about his bowling overseas. There is a strong parallel with Richie Benaud: both were better at home than abroad, were in the Test team for years before their appointment, represented a gamble by the selectors, and triumphed convincingly. Illingworth began by beating both West Indies and New Zealand 2–0 in three-match series, and when Cowdrey was available again the next season the selectors decided to stick with Illingworth. Cowdrey was offered the vice-captaincy to Australia, for the fourth time. Poor man.

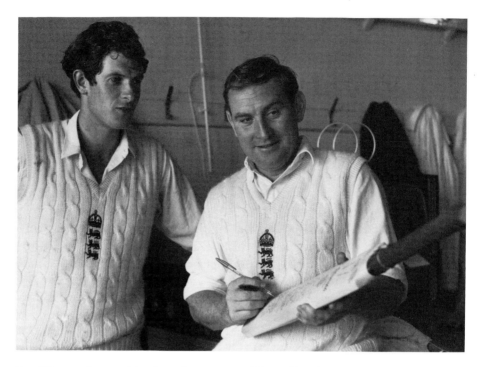

Ray Illingworth, one of the shrewdest captains of them all, with England colleague David Brown.

Illingworth's cricket (he was born in Pudsey, the same town as Len Hutton) had always been played in the best Yorkshire traditions – tough, competitive, thoughtful, determined, unwilling to concede an inch and so on. Year after year he wheeled down hundreds of overs of accurate off-spin, batted soundly and doggedly in the lower middle order, and fielded well, especially in the gully. He was an essential member of seven Championship-winning teams, but it did look for a long time as though he was a high-class county player who had not quite been able to take the last step up the ladder to the very top. But with the move to Leicester and the England appointment it suddenly became clear that he was a natural captain who possessed all the qualifications to be one of the very best. Apart from winning rubbers for England, he took Leicestershire to their first trophy when they won the Benson and Hedges Cup in its inaugural year (beating Yorkshire in the final, which he must have enjoyed), to the Sunday League in 1974 and 1977, and in 1975 not only to the Benson and Hedges again but also to their first Championship win. After he retired in 1978 he was tempted back by Yorkshire at the age of fifty for two seasons in 1982 and 1983; in the second of these they finished bottom of the Championship for the only time in their history yet won the Sunday League, but that is another story.

A dry sense of humour and loyalty to one's friends are important Yorkshire characteristics to which his players could easily respond. He made it his business to talk to his players and find out what made them tick, so that he knew how best to handle them in times of stress and how best to motivate them. Before long, when they saw that he was totally committed to their personal and cricketing interests, they were giving their best for him and he was able to mould a fairly ordinary team into a formidable unit. Having risen from the ranks, as it were, he was no autocrat, but there was never any doubt that he was firmly in charge and that his word was law. The players were able to respect him even more when the responsibility of captaincy caused his batting to emerge as genuine Test class, and he often looked one of the best batsmen in the team, saving them on several occasions. He was to score over 1,800 runs at an average of 23 in 61 Tests with two centuries, and take 122 wickets at 31 – although one criticism of his captaincy, as so often with bowler-captains, was that he under-bowled himself. Of his thirty-one games as captain twelve were won and only five lost. He also led England in the games against the Rest of the World when the South African tour was cancelled.

The real key to his success, though, lay in his tactical shrewdness. Many years in the game under some fine leaders had taught him an enormous amount, and he showed himself to be particularly good at judging the relative merits of the opposition and attacking them on their weak points. He knew just which bowler to pit against which batsman, from which end of the ground and with which field setting. He had, too, the great gift of being able to assess the way in which a match was going and then to know how best to bring it round to the way he wanted it. Everything about the manner in which he did the job showed him to be a tough, experienced, intelligent professional who was rarely in anything other than complete control.

For the 1970–1 series six Tests were scheduled for the first time. The teams, with Lawry still in charge of Australia, were once again fairly evenly matched, with a number of new faces hoping to prove themselves. As before, the batting seemed stronger than the bowling, but this was to be the series in which John Snow emerged as a great bowler, taking thirty-one wickets. It was also a series which was not without its prickly moments; there was a certain amount of friction between Illingworth, Cowdrey and the party's manager, David Clark, and a number of incidents on the field.

Early in the first Test Stackpole, having scored 18, seemed to have been narrowly run out. The umpire, reasonably enough, gave him the benefit of the doubt and he went on to make 207 as Australia totalled 433, their last seven wickets falling for 15. England then batted virtually all the way down the order to exceed this by 31 runs, during the course of which Cowdrey became the leading Test run-scorer. England had taken a bit too long over it, however, and while they managed to bowl the home team out for 214 there was no time left to finish the job. The second Test was the first to be played at Perth, and it produced another stack of runs. A century from Luckhurst helped England to 397 and they then had Australia 107 for 5 before Greg Chappell, in his début innings, joined Redpath to rescue them with a fine hundred. A century from Edrich then saw England out of any danger and another draw entered the record books.

At Melbourne the third Test was washed out completely. The tourists were therefore asked to play an additional Test; to maintain good relations Illingworth and the manager agreed but many of the players were less than pleased. They were happier after the fourth Test. England began with 332 and restricted Australia to 236. A second-innings 142 not out from Boycott allowed Illingworth to declare with over nine hours to bowl Australia out, and this proved to be the finest of Snow's days. Lawry became only the second Australian to carry his bat twice in Tests, but he had no support and Australia crumbled for 116. Snow was unplayable, taking 7 for 40 and breaking McKenzie's nose, and the way in which Illingworth handled his team gained much praise. What should have been the third Test then became the fifth. England marked the Australian first innings by dropping catch after catch, allowing them to make 493 with a hundred from Ian Chappell and 92 not out from Marsh when Lawry declared. Luckhurst, batting with a broken finger, and D'Oliveira both scored centuries in reply, England reached 392 and the match drifted into a draw. There was much short-pitched bowling from Snow which Illingworth seemed to condone, and E.W. Swanton believed that the aggressive Australian attitude of Ian Chappell's team had its roots in England's approach to this series.

England controlled the sixth Test, making 470 with a century from Edrich and a display of annoyance from Boycott (when adjudged run out) that earned him a lot of criticism. The fast bowlers then bundled Australia out for exactly half this total — at which point Illingworth astonished everyone by not enforcing the follow-on. Undoubtedly the quickies were tired — they were playing their third Test in successive weeks — and Illingworth had a reasonable case for batting again, but few people saw it from his point of view. Boycott scored a fairly rapid century as they set Australia a big target, but their batsmen were equal to it.

The Australian selectors then did something unprecedented – they dropped their appointed captain before the rubber had finished, not only from the leadership but from the team. Lawry could consider himself unlucky to go out of the team for he was averaging 40 and indeed finished third in the averages, and he must have been deeply hurt. Although he never played Test cricket again it seemed inevitable, in view of his durability, that cricket fans hadn't heard the last of him, and of course they hadn't – he became a radio commentator.

It was to Ian Chappell that the selectors turned, and his first act on being given the captaincy was to put England in – and bowl them out for 184, Illingworth top-scoring. In reply Australia made 264, but not before the stormiest scene in Ashes history. Snow hit tail-ender Jenner on the head with a bouncer, which resulted in harsh words with the umpire. When he went to field on the boundary his shirt was pulled by a beer-swigging gentleman and there was a scuffle. In moments beer cans were raining down on the pitch.

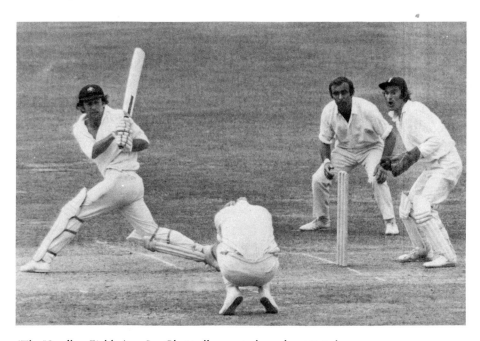

'The Headless Fielder'. . . Ian Chappell seems to have decapitated Bob Woolmer, as the expressions on the faces of Edrich and Knott seem to confirm. The ball went off Woolmer's body to the boundary with nothing more than a bruise for the fielder – England v Australia 1975.

Illingworth's reaction was to march his team off, to be told by the umpires that unless he returned he would forfeit the game. In fact the stoppage lasted only seven minutes, and Illingworth maintained that taking the team away from public view was the best way to ensure that the interruption was a short one. England then batted well in the second innings, almost everyone making a score, and Australia were left with a target of 223. Before long, though, Snow broke his finger on the fence trying to take a catch, leaving the captain without his main strike weapon.

However, Illingworth's leadership now enjoyed one of its great hours as he got the best out of his bowlers and the wickets steadily fell. As the last day began exactly 100 were needed with Greg Chappell and Marsh still there. Illingworth himself struck the vital blow by having Chappell stumped, and at the end Australia fell 62 runs short. Illingworth, 2–0 victor of a rather bad-tempered series, was chaired off the field.

Back in 1935–6 Australia had been captained very successfully in South Africa by Vic Richardson, and now for much of the next decade or so they were to be led by two of his grandsons. And yet early in the fifth Test of this last series Cowdrey had twice dropped Ian Chappell, when he was 0 and 14, and he went on to make 111. Had either chance been taken, he would have had a string of low scores, and Illingworth wrote that he wondered whether he might have been dropped as a result, bearing in mind the funny things that selectors do. As it was he went on to captain Australia thirty times, winning fifteen and losing only five, leading his country through a period of considerable prosperity. A strong team was coming together, with one of the most potent of all spearheads, and the aggressive leadership which he gave made it a good deal stronger. His style of captaincy did not win him universal acclaim, but he would have been the last person to worry about that.

Ian Chappell had played for South Australia as an eighteen-year-old and made his Test début three years later. It took him a while to establish his place in the side, but in due course the centuries began to arrive. An epithet commonly applied to his batting is 'rugged', but if it lacked the polished elegance of some – his brother Greg in particular – it could still be very attractive. The ball was despatched with great power and assurance from a full range of strokes, enabling him to accumulate over 5,300 runs at 42 in 75 Tests, with 14 centuries. His answer to John Snow's bouncers was to practise hooking and then take on the challenge that they offered, rather than duck away from them. Sometimes it caused his downfall, but overall it made him a better batsman – and it had the psychological advantage of showing the bowler that he could not have things too much his own way.

He always made a point of taking no notice of what another batsman said about the pitch or the bowling, preferring to find out for himself what conditions were really like. He was also in the top rank of slip fielders.

His early years in the game had been spent under the adventurous captaincy of Leslie Favell, and he learned a lot from Favell's positive approach. He was made captain of South Australia in 1970–1, but at the time he succeeded Lawry, although he had thirty-six Tests under his belt, he had been captain in only ten first-class games; he had never put the opposition in before, but he was not afraid to do so in his first Test. Before long it was clear that his captaincy reflected his character: relaxed and informal, yet dynamic, forceful, aggressive. The relaxed and informal aspect meant that players were given plenty of opportunity to do things their own way, although there was never any question of who was captain. This easy-going atmosphere was especially important in the dressing-room, where he always tried to keep the tension as low as possible and where everyone was invited to have their say, and have their confidence increased as a result. He worked hard but unobtrusively to build up and maintain friendly relations within the team, and was able to mould them into a fully integrated unit who would have followed him anywhere with complete faith in his leadership.

At the same time Ian Chappell's Australians became the most 'macho' cricket team ever, many sporting moustaches and fashionable clothes, attracting younger crowds and generally giving the impression of revelling in their virility. Their policy was to play their matches to win from the word go, working on the basis that while things may go wrong sometimes the occasional defeat is not the end of the world, and overall they would be more likely to end up in credit. Since this produced positive cricket it was all to the good; what was less attractive was their insistence on 'sledging' (i.e. sledge-hammering) the batsmen, subjecting them to a constant stream of verbal abuse intended to upset their concentration. This was taken to extremes and is a large black mark against Chappell's captaincy.

Under Greg Chappell the 'sledging' eased off and when Bobby Simpson returned he eliminated it, but it is also interesting to note Bradman's observations on the 'tactic', as mentioned by Ray Robinson: 'It's nothing new. The only Tests I've known without verbal aggression were in the bodyline series in 1932–3' – the implication being that these were conducted in a frosty silence. Lindsay Hassett, on the other hand, could say that during his career he never heard players swearing at each other. Obviously England didn't always behave as though they were on a Sunday school outing – Tony Greig's teams certainly did not – but undoubtedly the readiness with which Chappell and his team used strong language to upset opponents was 'unsporting', and the insistence upon 'macho' behaviour gained them only a limited number of fans. From a historical perspective it was inevitable that it would happen sooner or later as the right players found the right captain, but one suspects that there were plenty of opposing players who wished they had not coincided with it.

Chappell's own path to the top had been a fairly tough one and he had had to learn many things the hard way, so that by the time he got there he knew plenty about tactics. The practicalities of a game were always more important than the theorising, and inevitably the central core of his tactical planning was to apply as much pressure – cricketing and psychological – as he could for as much of the time as possible, and he was fortunate to have the players to allow him to do so. Whether Lillee and Thomson would have decimated Denness's team in quite the way they did if, say, Redpath had been captain we can never know, but somehow one has to doubt it. Without question Chappell over-used his fast bowlers, sometimes at the expense of their fitness; like many another batsman-captain he could not quite appreciate the demands that fast bowling makes, and Lillee in particular suffered as a result.

Many feel that Ian Chappell must go down as one of Australia's finest captains. He was lucky to coincide with some strong players, but he must take much of the credit for the strength of the team that emerged and for playing positive and often attractive cricket. His team could probably have won many of their matches without resorting to 'sledging' and posterity would doubtless have ranked him very high indeed, perhaps up with Bradman and Benaud; as it is there will be some who agree with Robin Marlar that 'history will find him to have been one of cricket's barbarians'. If a 'chucker' exists only in the eye of the beholder, perhaps a 'sledger' exists only in the ear of the listener. Perhaps.

When Chappell brought his team to England in 1972 neither side had played a Test since the previous August. On paper England probably looked the stronger team, but only just. The first match was played in cold, damp conditions that cannot have suited the visitors at all, and England made the best of them to go one up. It was a match for the seam bowlers as England were dismissed for 249 and Australia for 142. Needing 342 to win only Stackpole and Marsh made any runs and England, who had started the match on Illingworth's fortieth birthday, won by 89.

Now came the most memorable début since Foster's 287 in 1903, and it was at Lord's to boot. Bob Massie, a twenty-five-year-old from Western Australia, took 8 for 84 off 32.5 overs of swing bowling as England made

272. Greg Chappell's century helped Australia to a lead of 36, but then Massie produced 8 for 53 to skittle England out for 116. Only Laker and Barnes had taken more than his 16 wickets in a Test, and no one had got near that on début. Yet he proved a one-match wonder, taking very few further wickets and soon losing his place; within two years he was even out of the state side. But if you are going to be a one-match wonder, this was, admittedly, a spectacular way to do it. In that remarkable way that cricket has for throwing up curiosities, Narendra Hirwani of India marked his début in 1988 by taking sixteen West Indian wickets for 136, beating Massie's figure by just one run.

At Trent Bridge Illingworth put Australia in, assuming that the pitch would get easier, but a century from Stackpole helped them to 315. England then struggled to 189, after which a big hundred from Edwards enabled Chappell to declare, leaving England nine and a half hours to score 451. Luckhurst made their highest score of the summer with 96, and England played out time. At Headingley, there was much controversy about the pitch. Heavy rain some days earlier had flooded it and being left under covers had allowed a fungal disease to attack it. Underwood in particular enjoyed the result. Australia were all out for 146, while only an eighth-wicket stand between Illingworth and Snow gave England much respectability, seeing them to 263. In their second innings Australia fell to 'Deadly' once again, and England kept the Ashes with a nine-wicket win. Australia were *not* happy.

Their displeasure was shown in the best possible way, by playing some fine cricket in the last Test to give what had been a good series an excellent climax. First they put England out for 284, which would have been much less without Knott's contribution, then the Chappells became the first brothers to score centuries in the same Test innings as they saw their side to 399. England managed to set them a reasonable target of 242, but then lost three bowlers to injury and Australia got home by five wickets to level the rubber. For all of Massie's fireworks it was Lillee who took thirty-one wickets to set a new series record for Australia in England; a few months later in the West Indies, though, he broke down with stress fractures of the back and was out for two years. He returned just in time for the next Ashes series, by which time he had found a new 'cobber'.

Illingworth captained England again the following summer, beating New Zealand and losing to West Indies. His best days with Leicestershire were yet to come, and so too was the CBE and the curious return to Yorkshire. Never exactly effusive in speech, his native pithiness is well suited to the TV commentaries that he now does.

If memory serves, much of the dismay that greeted the appointment of Mike Denness as England captain centred on the fact that he was Scottish. When he was replaced by Tony Greig little was made, if memory still serves, of his South African origins (although by coincidence his father was Scottish). Somehow that seems to encapsulate Denness's fortune, the sort of fortune that not only saw him replacing the very popular Illingworth but also brought him up against one of the most fearsome pairs of fast bowlers in history. His captaincy record overall is in credit, with six wins and five defeats in his nineteen games, but few remember that. Nor do they always remember his drawn series in the West Indies – 'Wasn't that Illingworth?' No, it wasn't.

He had come to Kent in 1962 and established himself as a fine, if unspectacular, batsman with plenty of shots, who could take spinners apart as well as anyone. Against the quicks he was less happy and really fast bowling tended to prove too much for him. In all he totalled nearly 26,000 runs at 33, and it is worth pointing out that his Test average was only just under 40, with 1,667 runs in 28 games. He was also a very high-class fielder, either close to the wicket or in the covers, and was a fine rugby player too. He took over from Cowdrey as captain of Kent in 1972 and in five years led a fine side to six trophies in the one-day competitions and to second place in the Championship. After nine Tests, during most of which he had been Tony Lewis's vice-captain in India and Pakistan, his first series as England captain was in the West Indies in 1973–4 where, in the last game that drew the series, he led the team admirably. The following summer he beat India 3–0 at home and drew all three against Pakistan, so he had done more than enough to deserve to take the team to Australia, even if it appeared that his presence as captain was the reason for Boycott's decision not to join in the fun.

Critics said that his success with the Kent team was not a real guide to his worth as a captain since they were a fine and experienced side who needed a leader much less than most teams do. Perhaps this contained a grain of truth, but there was no doubt that he led them well and they played some very attractive cricket. Yet while he was a friendly enough man he was also by nature quiet and reserved, and he seemed never to be able to relax as one of the boys. His leadership qualities suffered as a result, forming a striking contrast to his opposite number in Australia. He was not helped by the fact that several of his team had played many more Tests than he had, so that he was always in a difficult position which he seemed never entirely to resolve. Tactically he was shrewd and often enterprising, but perhaps being so good at the one-day game made it harder for him to switch to a five-day attitude.

It is possible too that in one way he suffered from having Greig as vice-captain in that his natural reticence contrasted strongly with Greig's extrovert style, and to some people this appeared as a debit against Denness. Certainly Greig was happier with the media than he was, and we all know how easily the media can implant ideas.

The problem with assessing Denness is that the scales in Australia were tipped so heavily against him that he just did not have a chance. A pair of top-class fast bowlers has usually proved the most potent of cricketing weapons, and surely no captain in history could have had much change out of that series – except Bradman who would have seen off Lillee and Thomson single-handed. It is important to remember that when England set off they had little idea about Thomson; he had played one Test a few years earlier and been hammered by the Pakistanis. Admittedly the England batting did not look all that wonderful, certainly not as strong as Australia's, and they seemed to have chosen one fast bowler too many instead of an all-rounder to back up Greig. The home team had to be favourites, and Denness was hardly helped by picking up a virus early on and missing the opening games.

In the first Test Australia made 309 before the carnage began. On a suspect pitch Amiss had his thumb broken and Edrich his hand before Greig's century gave England some respectability at 265. In their second innings, though, after Australia had declared on 288, England capitulated as Thomson took 6 for 46 with speed the like of which the batsmen cannot have seen before, backed up by fine catching. The victory margin was 166 runs. Because of those injuries Cowdrey was summoned from home and played in the second Test only four days after arriving. England were outplayed throughout, managing only 208 runs before allowing Australia to run up 481. Some excellent catching – seven by Greg Chappell – saw them home by nine wickets. Luckhurst and Lloyd were the injured batsmen this time.

The third Test was a very exciting draw, all four innings ending within six runs of each other. England, put in, made 242, Australia replying with one run less. Amiss and Greig were the main contributors to England's 244, which left the home team all of the last day to win. But wickets fell steadily, and as the match entered the final hour they needed fifty-five with four wickets left. Tight bowling from Underwood and Titmus restricted them, then there came a brief flurry against the new ball. Fourteen to win off the last over, but Greig had Lillee caught and at the end Australia needed eight more runs and England two more wickets.

For the fourth Test Denness decided, without any outside pressure, to

(Left) *Mike Denness. Could anyone have done much better against Lillee and Thomson?* (Right) *John Edrich, who batted with broken ribs in his only Test as captain.*

drop himself as he had been in poor form with the bat. John Edrich duly stepped up into the hot seat for the only time, and a very hot one it was. He had been captain of Surrey since 1973 and had led them to second place in the Championship in his first year and to the Benson and Hedges Cup a year later; like Graveney a few years earlier there had been talk of appointing him England captain but it had never materialised. A stocky left-hander, he was one of the most obdurate batsmen of his generation, usually an opener, the scorer of 103 centuries and a fine servant for England. He had plenty of strokes but was not the most attractive batsman to watch, being a strong and steady accumulator rather than a dashing stroke-player or an elegant timer, although in the right mood he could attack with the best. In 77 Tests he scored over 5,100 runs at an average of 43, with 12 hundreds, one of them a triple-century against New Zealand during which he set the record for most boundaries in a Test innings.

His style of captaincy reflected his style of play – sound, determined, grafting rather than adventurous. He was popular enough with his team-mates but was not really a natural leader, generally lacking the ability to inspire a team to a big effort. Tactically he was very knowledgeable, but was too cautious to be really successful, and after his first season Surrey slipped down the table a little. He didn't have a happy time of it in his one Test as captain, but he was hampered by the fact that England's best fieldsmen were not playing. He was also more than slightly hampered by having two ribs broken by the first ball he received in the second innings.

Australia had scored 405 in their first innings, Edrich being criticised for not using his spinners against their wagging tail. The Sydney Hillites were in one of their more aggressive moods when England batted, urging on the fast bowlers who responded with some intimidating deliveries. Chappell was criticised by his own Press for not stopping it, but he took the attitude that it was a matter for the umpires. England reached 295 thanks to Edrich and Knott, and then centuries from Redpath and Greg Chappell left England exactly 400 to get in eight and a half hours after the declaration. As the wickets fell Edrich returned from hospital and battled away for 33 not out, but with a few overs left the last wicket went down and Australia had regained the Ashes.

For the next match Denness returned and as water had seeped under the covers he decided to put Australia in. It worked well for a while, but as the pitch dried out the Australians got back in the game and finished with 304, Underwood taking seven wickets; Denness came in for much criticism for under-using Titmus. Denness then top-scored in England's miserable 172, after which Australia were able to set up another declaration and bowl England out yet again. Knott, having made his 200th dismissal earlier in the match, became the second wicket-keeper after Ames to score a hundred in an Ashes Test. Thomson, having taken thirty-three wickets, injured his shoulder playing tennis on the rest day, and missed the second innings.

For the last match not only were Australia without Thomson but after bowling only six overs Lillee had to drop out with a bruised foot. Before that, however, Lever and Old had bundled Australia out for 152 in humid conditions, and hit Greg Chappell on the jaw as well. Without the speed merchants the home attack was very ordinary, although Walker finished with eight wickets in the innings. Denness scored 188, the highest ever by an England captain in Australia, Fletcher made 146 and England were able to reach 529. Australia's reply was more determined than their first effort but they still fell four runs short of making England bat again. That must have been as sweet a victory as those England players ever experienced.

E.W. Swanton records that he found many people in Australia who were not just happy that England had won the last Test but were especially pleased at Denness's part in it. There was no doubt that, hampered as he was by injuries, he had received a lot of unmerited criticism, for Lillee and Thomson were not only bowling very fast but were often bowling short as well; this was condoned by Chappell and the umpires did nothing about it. Yet the problem for anyone who wants to feel aggrieved is that England had almost certainly been guilty of the same or comparable misbehaviour in the past, and in this case only short memories were required to recall Snow on the previous tour.

Up until this point the series had for decade after decade been played on a regular basis in alternate countries with a couple of years between each. In the late 1970s this pattern went haywire. Only five months after this last Test Australia were in England for a four-match series, the reduction being caused by the first Prudential World Cup which took place in June. The first Test was played at Edgbaston where Denness won the toss and, having first discussed it with his senior players, decided to put Australia in as the weather forecast promised rain. If it was not quite as spectacular an own goal as Hutton's in 1954–5, it was a good imitation. First Australia totalled 359, then, as the England innings began, there came a thunderstorm. When play resumed in damp conditions England collapsed for 101, and second time around they could manage no more than 173. It was the end for Denness, and the captaincy duly passed to Tony Greig.

Greig was one of the most colourful and controversial cricketers since the Second World War, probably second only to Ian Botham. Very tall, blond and handsome he seemed altogether larger than life, with an outgoing, showman's personality that was happiest on the big occasion; his Test average of 40, compared with a career average of 31, shows this clearly. He had first played for Sussex as a twenty-year-old and made 156 in his opening match; when he made his Test début in 1972 he was the top scorer in each England innings and took five wickets as well. Thereafter he was rarely out of the limelight, playing many fine innings at number six and totalling one run short of 3,600 in his 58 consecutive Tests, with 8 centuries. A very strong and courageous batsman, he loved to drive off the front foot and some of his hitting was quite gigantic. He also took 141 wickets at 32 with his fast-medium bowling, although when Denness squared the series against West Indies in 1973–4 Greig took 13 wickets with medium-paced off-spin. He was also one of the great slip-catchers, taking a total of eighty-seven.

Over the years there had been some controversial incidents which did not show him in a flattering light, but these seemed to stem from rashness rather than malice and did not impede his progress to the captaincy. His years as captain of Sussex from 1973 to 1977 were not happy ones for the county,

The charismatic Tony Greig rebuilt the England team after their mauling in 1974–5 – and then sold out to Kerry Packer.

but when he took over from Denness it was clear that the bigger stage suited him better. He realised that the first task was to make the players believe in themselves again after the battering they had received and he set out to inspire them with his own fierce determination. Warmth and charm came out of him with great ease, and with his undoubted charisma he was soon able to create a much better team spirit. This was surely his best achievement. Even on his off-days – and he tended to alternate between extremes more than most – he was always trying to give his best and he insisted that his players did the same. His relations with the Press were good, and off the field he was a fine ambassador. He was to lead England fourteen times, and although he won only three whilst losing five he is still regarded as having done the job fairly well. In 1976 he lost 3–0 against a very strong West Indian team, but the following winter he went to India, won 3–1, and his leadership was widely praised.

The weak spot in his captaincy was his tactical ability. Many captains

Greg Chappell strikes as Tony Greig watches – opposing captains in the first Centenary Test.

have plotted a plan of campaign and then stuck to it too rigidly, but with Greig it seemed that the opposite applied. Often he gave the impression of having little strategy worked out other than broadly attacking or defending, and he sometimes appeared to make his bowling changes and field-placings on a whim rather than on any sound tactical basis. Surprisingly, in view of the way he played the game, he could be unduly defensive in his approach, though by the time of the Indian tour he seemed to have learned from his mistakes, and it appeared he would have the job for the foreseeable future.

Soon afterwards he chose to commit cricketing suicide, but before we reach that point one thing about him should be noted; only after he had left the game was it revealed to the public that he was an epileptic, and anyone who wants to criticise some of his actions should remember the problems this must have caused him.

In the remaining three Tests against Ian Chappell's team he did his best to draw the teeth of Lillee and Thomson, helped by Thomson not taking too readily to English conditions. The new determination which Greig brought to the team was apparent in the second game when after a disastrous start he, Steele and Knott rescued the innings and took it to 315, some fine bowling then putting Australia out for 268. A century from Edrich enabled Greig to declare, but the bowlers couldn't do it again and the game petered out. This match is historic, if that is the right word, for one reason; it saw the début of the Test match streaker in England. Did he deliberately choose a time when John Arlott was commentating, or was this just a happy chance?

From Lord's and streakers the spotlight shifted to Headingley and criminals. England posted 288, whereupon Edmonds, on his début, took 5 for 28 as Australia went for 135. More fine batting from Steele took England to 291, and at the close of the fourth day the match was beautifully poised, Australia needing 225 with seven wickets left, McCosker five runs short of his first Test century. Come the morn and there was much gnashing of teeth when it was discovered that vandals had dug up the pitch and poured oil on it to draw attention to their campaign that 'George Davis is innocent', the said Mr Davis having been convicted of armed robbery. As it happened it rained for much of the day, but poor McCosker lost the chance of his century. This must rank as the most unusual set of circumstances in which the Ashes have ever been retained.

During the last Test Ian Chappell scored 192 and announced his retirement from the captaincy. Since McCosker carried on from where he left off at Headingley and reached his century, Australia were able to declare on 532, and then bowl England out for 191. Yet when they followed on they scored their highest ever second-innings total against Australia, Woolmer compiling the slowest century in Ashes Tests as a big rearguard action was successfully fought and 538 runs were clocked up. It was the longest first-class match ever played in England (six full days), leaving everyone of the opinion that five days was more than enough in future.

After handing over the captaincy to his brother, Ian Chappell played nine more Tests. He was one of the prime movers in setting up World Series Cricket for Kerry Packer and did not endear himself to the establishment as a result, but when the dust settled the rift was patched up and three of those nine games came after his WSC involvement. Many people, at least in England, found Ian Chappell's aggressive approach rather difficult to take, and his alliance with Packer, who was popularly presented as an ogre intent upon destroying the game as it had always existed, seemed especially appropriate. Even if that picture was not an accurate one, at least it gave people the solace of being able to say that they had always known that no good would come of I.M. Chappell.

1970–1	Brisbane	A 433, 214	E 464, 39–1	Drawn
	Perth	E 397, 287–6d	A 440, 100–3	Drawn
	Melbourne	No play		
	Sydney	E 332, 319–5d	A 236, 116	E 299 runs
	Melbourne	A 493–9d, 169–4d	E 392, 161–0	Drawn
	Adelaide	E 470, 233–4d	A 235, 328–3	Drawn
	Sydney	E 184, 302	A 264, 160	E 62 runs
1972	Old Trafford	E 249, 234	A 142, 252	E 89 runs
	Lord's	E 272, 116	A 308, 81–2	A 8 wkts
	Trent Bridge	A 315, 324–4d	E 189, 290–4	Drawn
	Headingley	A 146, 136	E 263, 21–1	E 9 wkts
	Oval	E 284, 356	A 399, 242–5	A 5 wkts
1974–5	Brisbane	A 309, 288–5d	E 265, 166	A 166 runs
	Perth	E 208, 293	A 481, 23–1	A 9 wkts
	Melbourne	E 242, 244	A 241, 238–8	Drawn
	Sydney	A 405, 289–4d	E 295, 228	A 171 runs
	Adelaide	A 304, 272–5d	E 172, 241	A 163 runs
	Melbourne	A 152, 373	E 529	E inns 4 runs
1975	Edgbaston	A 359	E 101, 173	A inns 85 runs
	Lord's	E 315, 436–7d	A 268, 329–3	Drawn
	Headingley	E 288, 291	A 135, 220–3	Drawn
	Oval	A 532–9d, 40–2	E 191, 538	Drawn

1970–1

England

Batting	Innings	NO	HS	Runs	Average
G. Boycott	10	3	142*	657	93.85
J.H. Edrich	11	2	130	648	72.00
B.W. Luckhurst	9	1	131	455	56.87
R. Illingworth	10	1	53	333	37.00
B.L. D'Oliveira	10	0	117	369	36.90

Bowling	O	M	R	W	Average
J.A. Snow	225.5	47	708	31	22.83
R.G.D. Willis	88	16	329	12	27.41
D.L. Underwood	194.6	50	520	16	32.50
P. Lever	143.5	25	439	13	33.76
K. Shuttleworth	75.5	13	242	7	34.57

Australia

Batting	Innings	NO	HS	Runs	Average
K.R. Stackpole	12	0	207	627	52.25
I.R. Redpath	12	2	171	497	49.70
W.M. Lawry	10	2	84	324	40.50
I.M. Chappell	12	0	111	452	37.66
K.D. Walters	12	2	112	373	37.30

Bowling	O	M	R	W	Average
A.R. Dell	42.7	11	97	5	19.40
D.K. Lillee	62.3	5	199	8	24.87
K.D. Walters	61.5	8	181	7	25.85
T.J. Jenner	65.6	15	176	6	29.33
A.A. Mallett	56.7	8	188	6	31.33

Wicket-keepers: R.W. Marsh (A) 13 dismissals   A.P.E. Knott (E) 24 dismissals

Captains: W.M. Lawry – batting 4, 84; 0, 38*; 9, 60*; 56, 42; 10, 21
            I.M. Chappell – batting 25, 6
            R. Illingworth – batting 8; 34, 29; 25, 53; 41; 24, 48*; 42, 29
                bowling 0–47, 1–19; 1–43, 0–12; 1–59, 0–9; 2–59; 1–14, 0–32; 1–16, 3–39

In the first match M.C. Cowdrey became the leading Test run-scorer, passing W.R. Hammond's 7,249 runs. In the fourth match W.M. Lawry became the second Australian to carry his bat through a completed Test innings twice. A.P.E. Knott's 24 dismissals is the England record for any Test series.

1972

England

Batting	Innings	NO	HS	Runs	Average
A.W. Greig	9	1	62	288	36.00
R. Illingworth	8	2	57	194	32.33
B.L. D'Oliveira	9	1	50*	233	29.12
A.P.E. Knott	8	0	92	229	28.62
B.W. Luckhurst	8	1	96	168	24.00

Bowling	O	M	R	W	Average
D.L. Underwood	125	49	266	16	16.62
G.G. Arnold	110.5	25	279	13	21.46
J.A. Snow	205.5	46	555	24	23.12
R. Illingworth	88	28	197	7	28.14
B.L. D'Oliveira	83	23	176	5	35.20

Australia

Batting	Innings	NO	HS	Runs	Average
K.R. Stackpole	10	1	114	485	53.88
G.S. Chappell	10	1	131	437	48.55
R. Edwards	7	1	170*	291	48.50
A.P. Sheahan	4	2	44*	90	45.00
R.W. Marsh	9	2	91	242	34.57

Bowling	O	M	R	W	Average
D.K. Lillee	249.5	83	548	31	17.67
R.A.L. Massie	199.1	58	409	23	17.78
R.J. Inverarity	61	26	90	4	22.50
A.A. Mallett	103	32	269	10	26.90
D.J. Colley	121.3	20	312	6	52.00

Wicket-keepers: A.P.E. Knott (E) 17 dismissals   R.W. Marsh (A) 23 dismissals

Captains: R. Illingworth – batting 26*, 14; 30, 12; 24*; 57; 0, 31
bowling dnb; 1–13; 1–41; 2–32, 2–32; 1–53, 0–26
I.M. Chappell – batting 0, 7; 56, 6; 34, 50; 26, 0; 118, 37

In the second match R.A.L. Massie became the first bowler to take 16 wickets on début, taking 8–84 and 8–53. In the fifth match I.M. and G.S. Chappell became the first brothers to score a century in the same Test innings. D.K. Lillee set an Australian record by taking 31 wickets in the series, and R.W. Marsh's record 23 dismissals included 5 in an innings on two occasions.

1974–5

England

Batting	Innings	NO	HS	Runs	Average
J.H. Edrich	7	1	70	260	43.33
A.W. Greig	11	0	110	446	40.54
A.P.E. Knott	11	1	106*	364	36.40
K.W.R. Fletcher	9	0	146	324	36.00
M.H. Denness	9	0	188	318	35.33

Bowling	O	M	R	W	Average
P. Lever	61	8	214	9	23.77
R.G.D. Willis	140.4	15	522	17	30.70
D.L. Underwood	185	42	595	17	35.00
C.M. Old	51.6	4	210	6	35.00
G.G. Arnold	141.1	23	528	14	37.71

Australia

Batting	Innings	NO	HS	Runs	Average
G.S. Chappell	11	0	144	608	55.27
T.J. Jenner	3	1	74	100	50.00
M.H.N. Walker	8	3	41*	221	44.20
I.R. Redpath	12	1	105	472	42.90
K.D. Walters	11	2	103	383	42.55

Bowling	O	M	R	W	Average
J.R. Thomson	175.1	34	592	33	17.93
A.A. Mallett	140.6	47	339	17	19.94
D.K. Lillee	182.6	36	596	25	23.84
M.H.N. Walker	218.7	46	684	23	29.73
K.D. Walters	56.3	14	175	5	35.00

Wicket-keepers: R.W. Marsh (A) 19 dismissals   A.P.E. Knott (E) 23 dismissals

Captains: I.M. Chappell – batting 90, 11; 25, 11*; 36, 0; 53, 5; 0, 41; 65, 50
M.H. Denness – batting 6, 27; 2, 20; 8, 2; 51, 14; 188
J.H. Edrich – batting 50, 33*

In the second match G.S. Chappell took 7 catches, the Test record for a fielder. In the fifth match A.P.E. Knott became the second wicket-keeper to make 200 Test dismissals and the second to score a century in England v Australia Tests. In the sixth match M.H. Denness's 188 is the highest score by an England captain in Australia. M.C. Cowdrey ended his Test career with a record 120 catches.

1975

England

Batting	Innings	NO	HS	Runs	Average
D.S. Steele	6	0	92	365	60.83
R.A. Woolmer	4	0	149	218	54.50
J.H. Edrich	8	0	175	428	53.40
A.P.E. Knott	8	1	69	261	37.28
A.W. Greig	8	0	96	284	35.50

Bowling	O	M	R	W	Average
J.A. Snow	135.5	29	355	11	32.27
R.A. Woolmer	34	9	72	2	36.00
P.H. Edmonds	81.1	20	224	6	37.33
A.W. Greig	97	23	322	8	40.25
C.M. Old	91	22	283	7	40.42

Australia

Batting	Innings	NO	HS	Runs	Average
R.B. McCosker	7	2	127	414	82.80
I.M. Chappell	6	0	192	429	71.50
D.K. Lillee	4	2	73*	115	57.50
R. Edwards	6	1	99	253	50.60
K.D. Walters	5	1	65	125	31.25

Bowling	O	M	R	W	Average
K.D. Walters	12.5	3	40	5	8.00
G.J. Gilmour	51.2	15	157	9	17.44
D.K. Lillee	207	72	460	21	21.90
J.R. Thomson	175.1	56	457	16	28.56
M.H.N. Walker	204.1	59	486	14	34.71

Wicket-keepers: A.P.E. Knott (E) 4 dismissals   R.W. Marsh (A) 15 dismissals

Captains: M.H. Denness – batting 3, 8
   A.W. Greig – batting 96, 41; 51, 49; 17, 15
         bowling 1–47, 2–82; 0–14, 0–20; 3–107, 1–9
   I.M. Chappell – batting 52; 2, 86; 35, 62; 192

In the third match D.L. Underwood became the fourth bowler to take 200 wickets for England.

13

Two Centenaries, a Jubilee and an Earthquake

If Ian Chappell's path to the top had been tough, his brother Greg had the captaincy handed him on a plate. Having been carefully groomed for the job by Ian, there was never any doubt that there would be any other successor. He was to lead Australia a record forty-eight times, winning twenty-one and losing thirteen, and would have extended this had it not been for Packer and his decision not to tour in 1981. In all he played in 87 Tests and retired as Australia's leading run-scorer with 7,110 at an average of nearly 54, with 24 centuries. His medium-paced back-up bowling brought him 47 Test wickets, and his wonderful slip-catching took him to the world Test record of 122. By a nice little quirk the Chappell brothers both finished with the same 'strike' rate for Test catches; Greg's 122 from 87 games and Ian's 105 from 75 games both work out at 1.4 catches per match.

Greg Chappell was one of the most complete and classically correct batsmen of the post-war period. Tall and upright, graceful and balanced, with a fine technique and an unflappable temperament, he could play every shot in the book with great style, and on his day make Test bowlers look like club players. He favoured the drive through the V from mid-off to mid-wicket, but delicate deflections or thunderous hooks all came the same. Five years younger than his brother, he made his début for South Australia as an eighteen-year-old and also had two seasons as a youngster with Somerset to gain experience. In 1973–4 he moved to Queensland to take over the captaincy, and stayed there until he retired.

A cool, unexcitable, slightly introverted man, his style of captaincy was never as aggressive as his brother's and before he became captain he had managed to keep away from most of the criticism directed at the 'sledging'. Certainly he had a good rapport with his players, but in a less assertive manner than Ian's. Put simply, Ian led by dint of a strong, combative personality backed up by fine and determined playing ability, whereas Greg led by dint of outstanding playing ability backed up by a relaxed personality. This meant that Greg was never able to motivate his men in the way that Ian had; they liked and respected him, and at least part of the time the team was almost as close-knit as it had been under Ian, but the crucial spark that can turn a close game was sometimes missing. He was tough and determined, but again he didn't have these qualities to the extent that Ian did. Tactically Greg was sound enough and certainly thought deeply about the game, but there was not the same adventurous flair.

The Australian journalist Peter McFarline wrote that Chappell's stock pre-Test summing-up was always; 'If we score enough runs and take enough wickets, we should win.' His pep-talk to his team was; 'Come on boys. Wish the bowlers good luck, field well, and tonight will be all that more enjoyable.' Compared with Henry V before Agincourt, perhaps a little tame.

There is no doubt that Greg was the better batsman, but there is, similarly, no doubt that Ian was the better captain. Yet having said that, Greg had problems to contend with that Ian did not, especially on the 1977 tour of England when the Packer bombshell caused much unrest in the Australian ranks. He also has to take the credit for demolishing a strong West Indies team 5–1 in his first series in charge (in the opening game he became the first player to score two centuries in his first Test as captain) although Ian was still in the team to help him. He showed his aptitude against West Indies by changing field-placings that had been successful against England because he felt their style of play called for different tactics, and the results proved him right. Let no one doubt that Greg was a good captain, but he suffers somewhat in comparison with his brother.

Greg Chappell's moment of infamy came when he told his brother Trevor to bowl the last ball of a one-day game against New Zealand under-arm when six runs were needed to win. It was oddly out of character and the pillorying he received should at least ensure that it never happens again. There is no doubt that he regretted it afterwards.

His first game as captain against England was the Centenary Test of March 1977, an idea dreamed up by Hans Ebeling who played once for Australia in 1934. Nearly 200 Test players, some of them in their eighties, gathered in Melbourne for a gala occasion in which the Ashes were not at stake, and a superbly organised festival was crowned with an enthralling match. England under Tony Greig were fresh from a good win in India, and with Australia lacking Thomson and Ian Chappell they had perhaps only just the stronger team.

Greig won the toss, put Australia in and saw them crumble for 138 thanks to poor batting and fine bowling and fielding, Underwood reaching 250 Test wickets and Willis breaking McCosker's jaw along the way. Come England's turn and Lillee and Walker ripped them out for 95, Greig's 18 being top score. Marsh, having passed Grout's record total of dismissals in England's innings, finally achieved the Test century that Lawry's declaration had deprived him of six years earlier, and with good batting from Davis, Hookes and Walters, and a valiant 25 from the bandaged McCosker, Australia declared at 419, leaving England 463 to make in 11 hours. At the end of the fourth day they were 191 for 2, with Randall and Amiss going steadily, and as the last day unfolded the tension mounted. Randall, in his first game against Australia, passed his century and went on to 174 before he fell, but still Greig and Knott carried on the fight. In the end, with Lillee taking eleven wickets, England reached 417, the highest fourth innings in an England–Australia Test, and perhaps the most remarkable of all cricket's coincidences had been achieved – Australia's winning margin of 45 runs was exactly what it had been in the first Test a hundred years earlier. England proved that fighting as they were against history they could not possibly have won, but no one seemed to mind and everyone agreed that it had been a splendid occasion.

A few weeks later came cricket's greatest cataclysm; the news burst that Kerry Packer was setting up his own commercial cricketing series, taking with him many of the world's best players including nearly all the Australian team. When it was learned that one of the leading negotiating roles had been played by Tony Greig when he was in Australia for the Centenary Test, he was vilified in England as not even Botham ever has been and stripped of the captaincy. He held that one of his prime objectives had been to see that all professional cricketers were better paid, and that he had seized this opportunity of making the authorities take notice. His wish was certainly fulfilled and, financially at least, cricketers did benefit from the upheaval. He played for England in the Tests of that summer but no more and, unrepentant at what most people saw as a betrayal of the honour that he had been given, emigrated to Australia where he is still a commentator. Since a bright future had seemed to lie before him as England's captain there was sadness as well as anger and embarrassment.

Out of the furore England managed to produce one of their best captains of all. The bare statistics of Mike Brearley's captaincy are mightily impressive; against Australia 18 Tests (second only to MacLaren), 11 wins, 3 defeats, 4 draws and overall 31 Tests, 18 wins, 4 defeats, 9 draws. Very few others can match that. When we look behind the statistics we find there was a fair amount of good fortune in all this; the Packer upheaval meant that he

Mike Brearley puts his 'degree in people' to good use, encouraging Graham Dilley at Headingley in 1981.

played several Tests against weak sides, he missed out on a series against the mighty West Indies, and when he did meet a full-strength Australian team he came a cropper. Yet England too had lost some important players to Packer, and he achieved what he did with hardly the greatest of England teams. On top of this his own batting performances were scarcely good enough to justify his place in the side, which must have put a great burden on him.

He is the only man to score over 4,000 runs for Cambridge or Oxford, and one of the few to captain either side in two seasons. In 1964 he was chosen Young Cricketer of the Year and began his career with Middlesex. Leading the MCC Under-25 team to Pakistan he became one of the select band to score a triple-century in one day, but over the next few years the demands of academic work took precedence and he played little cricket until 1971, when he took over as captain of Middlesex on a full-time basis. Almost certainly it was this break that hindered his development as a batsman and stopped him from fulfilling his early promise, but by the mid-1970s he was high in the averages and chosen for England as a batsman. In all he scored over 25,000 runs at an average of nearly 38, but in his 39 Tests he totalled only 1442 runs at an average of under 23, and to his great disappointment never managed a century.

Without doubt he was courageous enough and he played plenty of obdurate innings to rescue his team, but somehow he seemed to try too hard and got himself out as a result; more than one observer suggested that what he needed to succeed as a batsman was a captain as sympathetic as himself. It is certainly the case that, had it not been for his captaincy, his Test career would have been a short one, and some felt that his captaincy was hardly sufficient reason for keeping him in the team. However, since the only feasible alternative was Boycott, who was inferior as a captain to a greater degree than he was superior as a batsman, the selectors wisely stayed by Brearley. He himself believed that 'a captain is an all-rounder', and he had a weight of history to back up that view. In domestic cricket he certainly enjoyed his successes, taking Middlesex in 1976 to their first Championship in twenty-seven years. When he retired in 1982 they had won it twice more outright and shared it once, and the Gillette Cup had also been won twice.

In the history of first-class cricket there has been virtually no one who was his intellectual equal; he gained a first in Classics and a high second in Moral Sciences at Cambridge, took top place in the Civil Service entrance examination, and taught philosophy at the Universities of California and Newcastle. With such a background he inevitably became a deep thinker upon the game, but more important to his captaincy was his fascination with and sympathy for the human race, encapsulated in Rodney Hogg's memorable – and rueful – pronouncement 'I reckon Brearley has got a degree in people'. Studying other people and trying to understand what makes them tick has always been an essential part of Brearley's life, so much so that he has studied psychoanalysis and since retiring from cricket has worked in this field. He was therefore better equipped than any captain has ever been to understand his players and the way in which each of them could best be motivated – and he took this aspect of captaincy to new levels.

It was important to him that cricket was never a matter of life and death but something that had to be seen in the context of more serious human activities, and his years outside the game gave him a perspective that few other cricketers have. That, in John Arlott's words, 'enabled him to detach himself mentally from a match in which he was deeply involved and to assess it objectively.' This made it easier for him to remain calm and think clearly in a crisis. Arlott refers, too, to his 'immense mental hunger' which caused him to be thinking, assessing and scheming throughout the course of a game; without the demands of captaincy he would have easily become bored, but with them he was able to keep his brain sharp. This in turn meant that he was able to act decisively when the need arose. Anyone of whom all this can be said is clearly an exceptional person.

If this all sounds too intellectual, it is necessary to stress the *humanity* of Brearley's captaincy. It was essential to his success that he had a quiet, friendly, humorous, sympathetic nature to which most people would readily respond; a serious man, he regarded discipline as important and had a strong will, but was also courteous, considerate, open-minded and fair-minded. Perhaps at first sight he may have seemed something of an establishment man with his public school, Cambridge and Lord's background, but that was never the case; in fact he was in the forefront of those trying to bring about change. He wanted nothing to do with Kerry Packer, but he seemed to be one of the few people in the eye of the storm who remained calm and clear-sighted through it, maintaining that those players who had joined Packer should not be unduly punished, while at the same time trying to strike a balance whereby they could not have their cake and eat it too readily. Being always quick to champion his players' causes made him widely popular and highly respected, and greatly helped him to get the best from his side. He knew the importance of team spirit and when he took over from Greig was careful to ensure its continuity. On the field his leadership was quiet and undemonstrative, and he was always ready to discuss the situation with his senior players and act on their advice.

Having originally been a wicket-keeper he was an outstanding slip fielder, and believed that first slip was the best position from which he could control the team; the concentration needed to stand at slip for hour after hour was all a part of his 'mental hunger'. He worked his players very hard at their fielding, a dedication that paid off handsomely in 1977 when not a catch was dropped before the Ashes were won.

Australia were led in that series by Greg Chappell, and no doubt their morale was undermined by the revelation that most of them would soon be playing World Series Cricket. Some people suggested that this was the main reason for their defeat, but this seems excessive; it was a factor, as was the absence of Lillee, but with two evenly balanced teams it was the English catching that really tipped the scales.

The first Test was played at Lord's and was designated the Jubilee Test in honour of the Queen's twenty-five years on the throne. A combination of Queen Elizabeth II and Lord's meant that it couldn't possibly *not* rain, and sure enough nearly six hours were lost, enough to render it a draw. England opened with 216, and Australia replied with 296, Willis taking 7 for 78; a

*England won the 1977 series principally because of their fielding. Here
Mike Brearley sets an example to his team to dismiss opposing captain
Greg Chappell off the bowling of Mike Hendrick.*

century from Woolmer helped England to 305, and at the close Australia
were on 114 for 6, having made an effort to get the runs in the time but
eventually having been grateful to come off for bad light. The second Test
brought a fine performance by England, bowling Australia out for 297
before running up 437 thanks to another century from Woolmer. Underwood then took 6 for 66 as only Chappell stood firm, and England won by
nine wickets.

Trent Bridge saw the return of Boycott after his three years of taking his
bat away into a corner of the playground so that no one else could use it, as
it were. Some felt that he should be told where to put his bat, but their
opinion did not prevail. It also saw the début of Botham, who took 5 for 74
as Australia were all out for 243. In reply England were 82 for 5 until Knott
joined Boycott and they equalled England's sixth-wicket record against
Australia of 215, during the course of which Knott became the first keeper
to score 4,000 runs in Tests. England reached 364 and then worked through
the visitors' second innings, leaving themselves 189 to win which caused
few problems.

In that match Boycott scored his ninety-eighth century. During the ten-day gap between Tests he hit another, and as the fourth game was at Headingley a full house turned up, willing him to become the first man to score his hundredth in a Test. He duly obliged, going on to 191 and helping England to 436, after which Botham and Hendrick shot Australia out for 103. Following on they could manage no more than 248, and as the last wicket fell and the Ashes had been regained Randall performed the most celebrated cartwheel ever seen on a cricket field. For once history was working in England's favour; they had won the Ashes in 1926, the year the Queen was born, won them again in her coronation year of 1953, and so inevitably won them once more in her jubilee year. Many Englishmen felt it about time the Australians were on the receiving end of a bit of inevitability.

The series ended in anti-climax as the Oval game lost nearly two days to rain. Australia had the better of it, dismissing England for 214 and scoring 385 when England finally dropped a few catches. But there was little time for any more, and there was plenty of sadness about the knowledge that several of the players were ending their Test careers because of their commitment to Packer. At the time no one quite knew what would happen to the game, and English pleasure at regaining the Ashes was tempered with uncertainty about the future. It was clear that cricket was never going to be quite the same again.

Over the years there have been several captains who have drawn a short straw and led a team that was hopelessly outclassed, and in 1978–9 it was Graham Yallop's turn. Mike Denness's sensitive nature must have felt much in sympathy with him as he struggled to do his best with a second-string team, while the players who should have been representing their country were earning a lot of money cavorting about in a meaningless exercise for Mr Packer. Denness and Yallop are in fact quite similar characters, for Yallop is a sensitive, rather introverted man who was given the captaincy after Bobby Simpson had done the job for two series. A side as inexperienced as he had needed firm and inspiring leadership, but he did not quite have the personality to provide it; nor did he have the tactical imagination that might have been sufficient compensation and so given him the opportunity to assert himself. Having said all that he had a fearsomely difficult task that most captains would have found daunting, and coming up against Mike Brearley and a very professionally organised England squad simply compounded his misfortune. The final outcome of 5–1 to England was not a just reflection of the difference between the teams, for there were times when he had England on the run; but few of his players performed consistently and their inexperience often contributed to their own downfall. The fact that six of their twelve opening partnerships ended

The burden of leading the inexperienced Australians in 1978–9 fell on Graham Yallop. There must have been times when he wished it hadn't.

in run-outs is a curious little statistic that somehow says much for Australia's cricket in this series.

Yallop was a fine, orthodox, left-handed batsman who could attack with both determination and style. His 268 against Pakistan in 1983–4 was the high point of a Test career that covered 39 matches and saw him make 2,756 runs at 41 with 8 centuries. Two of those centuries came in this series against England, for at least captaincy seemed not to upset his batting form; his 391 runs were passed only by Gower, which must have salvaged some personal satisfaction for him. He had first tasted international cricket when he toured Sri Lanka with a schoolboy team in 1971–2; he then made his début for Victoria the following season and to gain more experience had spells in the Birmingham League and with Glamorgan 2nd XI. He played three Tests against West Indies in 1975–6 but then lost favour for a while before returning to the team under Simpson. When he took over as captain he had played in only eight Tests, so it should be remembered that he was little more experienced than the team he was leading.

Of those who had played in the previous series, England had lost Greig, Underwood, Knott, Woolmer and Amiss to Packer, so Brearley was leading some youthful players too. It was clear that England were the stronger team, but one or two of Yallop's decisions didn't do his cause much good. Indeed his first decision of the series was ill-advised, for having won the toss on a humid morning at Brisbane he chose to bat and was soon 26 for 6. Australia eventually made 116 to which England replied with 286. Yallop and Hughes then scored centuries (Hughes's was the slowest ever for Australia against England) but the rest contributed little and England were able to chalk up a seven-wicket win. In the second Test Yallop put England in and made an early breakthrough, but Gower and Boycott saw them to 309, after which Australia were dismissed for 190. In England's second innings Hogg took his wickets tally to seventeen in two games, but his batsmen weren't able to back up his efforts and England scored another convincing win.

After three games Hogg had reached twenty-seven wickets and his team were back in contention. The pitch gave the team batting first a distinct advantage, as England found when, having dismissed Australia for 258, they were shot out for 143. Australia's second innings gave England a target of 283 with lots of time, but on an uneven pitch they fell well short. It was Brearley's first defeat in sixteen matches as captain. The fourth Test was a game of changing fortune as England were put out for 152 and Australia took a good lead by scoring 294. Boycott then took his only first-ball dismissal in Tests and England seemed to be in deep trouble. It was Randall, though, who battled against the heat to score the slowest century in Ashes Tests and take the score to 346, leaving the home team to make 205 in four and a half hours. Good bowling from Miller and Emburey, good catching and skilful captaincy that combined the need to attack with the need not to concede too many runs saw England home by 93 runs to retain the Ashes.

In the fifth Test, too, Australia seemed to be in the driving seat but let it slip. After England were all out for 169 Australia fell five short of that total and almost lost Darling for ever when he was hit over the heart by Willis's fifth ball of the innings and collapsed unconscious. Emburey and umpire O'Connell saved him and he was able to bat again next day. In their second innings England were up against it at 132 for 6 when Miller and Taylor, both of Derbyshire, put on 135 for the seventh wicket and England climbed to 360. Taylor's 97 remained his highest Test score, and there can have been few Australians who would have grudged him those extra three runs. That stand seemed to dishearten the young Australians and they batted feebly to lose by 205 runs. They were pretty disheartened during the last Test as well, for without Yallop's century their performance would have been a dismal one. A score of 198 in their first innings and of 143 in their second meant that England had little trouble winning by nine wickets. Hogg took his wickets haul to forty-one, easily an Australian record, but the batsmen had simply not been equal to the England bowlers, especially the off-spinners, and nine of their twelve innings totalled under 200. Brearley conceded that the 5–1 margin flattered England. Meanwhile, Australia plotted revenge.

It was not long in coming. By the following season World Series Cricket had gone the way of all flesh and the problem for the authorities now was to repair the dents that had been made in the image of the official game. With all the banned players restored to possible selection, two concurrent three-match series were organised in Australia, the home team playing alternately against West Indies and England. Because this was seen as something of an artificial arrangement the TCCB decreed that the Ashes were not at stake, an idea at which many Australians blew a raspberry. It fell to Brearley to make it publicly clear that the TCCB would not accept any Packer-style razzmatazz in their sacred Test matches, a job that he should never have had to do and which made him unpopular with the Australian fans. When they treated him to their full repertoire of ocker abuse (which he ignored) the Australian manager, John Edwards, announced that they made him ashamed to be an Australian. This season, incidentally, saw the resumption of the six-ball over in Australia for the first time since the bodyline tour.

Of the England players who had gone to World Series only Underwood was on this 1979–80 tour. Australia had the Chappells back, with Greg captain, together with Marsh, Lillee, McCosker and others, so that the balance of power had now swung back to them. England, significantly in view of the outcome, were not much changed from the previous year. The first Test became famous for Lillee's aluminium bat, an object with which he faced four balls from Botham and scored three runs before the umpires and Brearley persuaded him to change it, causing a fracas that held up the game for ten minutes and ended with him throwing it away in a temper. Australia, put in, made 244 thanks to 99 from Hughes, to which England replied with 228. Border made a century as his team set England 354 to win, but Boycott alone, with Test cricket's only 99 not out, made a decent score, and Australia won easily.

At Sydney for the second Test the pitch had been left exposed to a storm, making it a good toss for Australia to win. England were duly shot out for 123, but fought back well to restrict Australia to 145. England's second innings 237 owed much to 98 not out from Gower, which left Australia quite a tricky target in the conditions, but they made it well enough. One oddity about the match was that Gower and Greg Chappell made identical scores of 3 and 98 not out; there have been very few scores of 98 not out in Test history, and if the chances of two coming in the same match must be long enough, what are the odds against those two batsmen making the same score in their other innings? After the game was won Chappell made it clear that as far as his team were concerned the Ashes had been regained.

The third Test saw the home team's clean sweep. Gooch missed his maiden Test century when he ran himself out on 99, but helped take England to 306. Australia batted doggedly to clock up 477 with a century from Greg Chappell and then reduced England to 92 for 6. Only a hundred from Botham enabled them to set Australia a target and salvage some dignity, but the 103 they needed caused them few problems. Revenge had been complete, and although Brearley led his team well enough and turned in some good innings himself, England had clearly been outclassed.

Then, of course, there had to be another centenary game in England to commemorate the first Test at the Oval, although this one was played at Lord's. After the outstanding success of the first one it was pushing the luck too far to expect things to go well twice; eight hours were lost in all to rain and bad light, the umpires were heavily criticised for not restarting play earlier than they did and were, horror of horrors, actually assaulted by MCC members angered by their tardiness, and England played feebly and unimaginatively. Their captain in particular came in for quite a bit of stick. His name was Ian Botham.

When Brearley announced that he would not be available to tour in the winter of 1980–1 because of his studies in psychoanalysis, it was decided to appoint a new captain at the beginning of the 1980 season for the series against the West Indies. There was no obvious successor and so the England selectors gave the job to their young champion, still only twenty-four, but whose deeds with bat and ball had marked him out as someone special. He had played in twenty-five Tests but had virtually no experience of captaincy, and the selectors were criticised for asking so much more of him at such a young age. The twelve matches in which he led England have passed into history as a disaster, but he was up against the mighty West Indies in nine of those games and one of his three defeats by them was a very close game that England lost by just two wickets. For much of his captaincy he was also handicapped by a back injury that must at least partially explain his poor form. He always insisted that the responsibility did not weigh

Ian Botham during his first-ever innings for England at Trent Bridge in 1977. He scored 25.

heavily on him and affect his performances, but his statistics for those twelve matches are those of an ordinary player rather than an Ian Botham.

His deeds are so well known as to need little elaboration. He was for a while the leading Test wicket-taker with 373 before Richard Hadlee overtook his total in November 1988, on top of which he had scored over 5,000 Test runs; statistically only Sobers, a better batsman but less penetrating bowler, can compete with him. Several records are his, too numerous to list here. He is famed as a very strong batsman who loves to attack from the word go, and as a bowler who in his younger days captured many wickets with swing bowling and who usually tried to bowl imaginatively to keep the batsman guessing. At times his attempts to 'buy' wickets have proved expensive and misguided, and he has undoubtedly had his share of luck in taking wickets with poor balls, but his bowling is normally more intelligent than his critics would have us believe. Despite his attacking, joyful approach to the game, and his extrovert character that leads him into trouble, he is a thoughtful cricketer. Most of the controversy that has surrounded him has been self-induced, but he is a kind and generous man who is widely liked. If he tarnished his image and set a bad example by taking drugs, then he has made up for it by putting his fame to the best possible use and raising enormous amounts for charity with his long-distance walks.

But what of his captaincy? Brearley wrote that Botham would have been his choice to succeed him, as he had been impressed by his natural feel for the game and by his tactical suggestions. While acknowledging his lack of experience he felt that 'Botham offered tremendous hope for a new, vital start.' Yet despite his twenty-five Tests he was still one of the youngest members of the team, and as he is by nature 'one of the boys' it must have been hard for him to assert himself. He was not strong on the psychology that would have helped him to get the best out of his players, and was not good at taking either advice or criticism. While often tactically shrewd, he would sometimes do unintelligent things based on his belief in himself as a great player, and his stubbornness could be exasperating.

Not a natural leader of men by any means, he was the sort of captain who had to lead by example, and when his form declined he was left with few strings to his bow. Had he had the chance to establish himself against anyone but the West Indies things might have been different, but as it was he was always struggling. Quite simply, too much was asked of him at too young an age, just as too much had been asked of Yallop. There ought to be some significance in the fact that even the great Sobers found captaincy a difficult business, and his record, other than as a winner of tosses, is not a distinguished one. Botham's one season in charge of Somerset, when they finished bottom of the table in 1985, confirmed that the demands of the job are better left to others, and one suspects that his captaincy days are over.

The 1980 Centenary Test was his first game as captain against Australia, who were led by Greg Chappell. Three and a half years is a long time in Test cricket, and only Chappell, Lillee and Marsh for Australia and Old for England played in both Centenary games. Chappell won the toss and centuries from Wood and Hughes saw them to 385, in reply to which England could do no better than 205. Australia declared on 189 for 4 to set England a target of 370 in 350 minutes; as it was a celebration game some people actually thought that England might go for it and fail bravely rather than eke out a tedious draw. Their naivety was touching. A combination of the umpires needing a police escort and the England players being relentlessly slow-handclapped meant that it was hardly the happiest of occasions. Lord Harris, England's captain a century earlier, must have looked down on it all with a darkened brow.

1976–7	Melbourne	A 138, 419–9d	E 95, 417	A 45 runs
1977	Lord's	E 216, 305	A 296, 114–6	Drawn
	Old Trafford	A 297, 218	E 437, 82–1	E 9 wkts
	Trent Bridge	A 243, 309	E 364, 189–3	E 7 wkts
	Headingley	E 436	A 103, 248	E inns 85 runs
	Oval	E 214, 57–2	A 385	Drawn
1978–9	Brisbane	A 116, 339	E 286, 170–3	E 7 wkts
	Perth	E 309, 208	A 190, 161	E 166 runs
	Melbourne	A 258, 167	E 143, 179	A 103 runs
	Sydney	E 152, 346	A 294, 111	E 93 runs
	Adelaide	E 169, 360	A 164, 160	E 205 runs
	Sydney	A 198, 143	E 308, 35–1	E 9 wkts
1979–80	Perth	A 244, 337	E 228, 215	A 138 runs
	Sydney	E 123, 237	A 145, 219–4	A 6 wkts
	Melbourne	E 306, 273	A 477, 103–2	A 8 wkts
1980	Lord's	A 385–5d, 189–4d	E 205, 244–3	Drawn

1976–7 Only Test

High scores: Australia – R.W. Marsh 110*, I.C. Davis 68, K.D. Walters 66
              England – D.W. Randall 174, D.L. Amiss 64

Best bowling: Australia – D.K. Lillee 6–26, 5–139, M.H.N. Walker 4–54
              England – D.L. Underwood 3–16, C.M. Old 4–104

Wicket-keepers: R.W. Marsh (A) 5 dismissals   A.P.E. Knott (E) 4 dismissals

Captains: G.S. Chappell – batting 40, 2 bowling 1–29
          A.W. Greig – batting 18, 41 bowling 2–66

D.W. Randall's 174 was the second-highest innings by a batsman playing in his first England v Australia Test. R.W. Marsh became the first Australian wicket-keeper to score a century in England v Australia Tests, and he also passed A.T.W. Grout's Australian record of 187 Test dismissals. D.L. Underwood became the fourth bowler to take 250 Test wickets.

1977

England

Batting	Innings	NO	HS	Runs	Average
G. Boycott	5	2	191	442	147.33
R.A. Woolmer	8	1	137	394	56.28
A.P.E. Knott	7	0	135	255	36.42
G.R.J. Roope	?	0	38	72	36.00
D.W. Randall	8	2	79	207	34.50

Bowling	O	M	R	W	Average
R.G.D. Willis	166.4	36	534	27	19.77
I.T. Botham	73	16	202	10	20.20
M. Hendrick	128.4	33	290	14	20.71
D.L. Underwood	169.1	61	362	13	27.84
A.W. Greig	77	25	196	7	28.00

Australia

Batting	Innings	NO	HS	Runs	Average
K.J. O'Keeffe	6	4	48*	125	62.50
G.S. Chappell	9	0	112	371	41.22
D.W. Hookes	9	0	85	283	31.44
R.B. McCosker	9	0	107	255	28.33
K.D. Walters	9	0	88	223	24.77

Bowling	O	M	R	W	Average
M.F. Malone	57	24	77	6	12.83
J.R. Thomson	200.5	44	583	23	25.34
L.S. Pascoe	137.4	35	363	13	27.92
R.J. Bright	72.1	27	147	5	29.40
M.H.N. Walker	273.2	88	551	14	39.35

Wicket-keepers: A.P.E. Knott (E) 12 dismissals   R.W. Marsh (A) 9 dismissals

Captains: J.M. Brearley – batting 9, 49; 6, 44; 15, 81; 0; 39, 4
      G.S. Chappell – batting 66, 24; 44; 112; 19, 27; 4, 36; 39
            bowling 0–12, 0–24; 0–25; 0–19; 0–25; dnb

In the third match A.P.E. Knott became the first wicket-keeper to score 4,000 Test runs. His 135 is the highest by a wicket-keeper in England v Australia Tests, and his sixth-wicket partnership of 215 with G. Boycott equalled the England record for that wicket against Australia. In the fourth match Boycott became the first batsman to score his hundredth century in a Test match.

1978–9

England

Batting	Innings	NO	HS	Runs	Average
D.I. Gower	11	1	102	420	42.00
D.W Randall	12	2	150	385	38.50
I.T. Botham	10	0	74	291	29.10
R.W. Taylor	10	2	97	208	26.00
G. Miller	10	0	64	234	23.40

Bowling	O	M	R	W	Average
G. Miller	177.1	54	346	23	15.04
M. Hendrick	145	30	299	19	15.73
J.E. Emburey	144.4	49	306	16	19.12
R.G.D. Willis	140.3	23	461	20	23.05
I.T. Botham	158.4	25	567	23	24.65

Australia

Batting	Innings	NO	HS	Runs	Average
A.R. Border	6	2	60*	146	36.50
G.N. Yallop	12	0	121	391	32.58
K.J. Hughes	12	0	129	345	28.75
G.M. Wood	12	0	100	344	28.66
W.M. Darling	8	0	91	221	27.62
Bowling	O	M	R	W	Average
R.M. Hogg	217.4	60	527	41	12.85
A.G. Hurst	204.2	44	577	25	23.08
J.D. Higgs	196.6	47	468	19	24.63
G. Dymock	114.1	19	269	7	38.42
B. Yardley	113.2	12	389	7	55.57

Wicket-keepers: J.A. Maclean (A) 18 dismissals   K.J. Wright (A) 8 dismissals
R.W. Taylor (E) 20 dismissals

Captains: G.N. Yallop – batting 7, 102; 3, 3; 41, 16; 44, 1; 0, 36; 121, 17
J.M. Brearley – batting 6, 13; 17, 0; 1, 0; 17, 53; 2, 9; 46, 20*

R.M. Hogg's 41 wickets was an Australian record for an England v Australia series; although this was a six-match rubber he took only one wicket in the final game.

1979–80

(Over reduced to 6 balls in Australia)

England

Batting	Innings	NO	HS	Runs	Average
G.A. Gooch	4	0	99	172	43.00
G.R. Dilley	4	2	38*	80	40.00
I.T. Botham	6	1	119*	187	37.40
G. Boycott	6	1	99*	176	35.20
J.M. Brearley	6	1	64	171	34.20
Bowling	O	M	R	W	Average
I.T. Botham	173.1	62	371	19	19.52
D.L. Underwood	160.2	48	405	13	31.15
J.K. Lever	60.4	18	129	4	32.25
G.R. Dilley	53	5	143	3	47.66
R.G.D. Willis	98	26	224	3	74.66

Australia

Batting	Innings	NO	HS	Runs	Average
G.S. Chappell	6	2	114	317	79.25
I.M. Chappell	4	1	75	152	50.66
A.R. Border	5	1	115	199	49.75
K.J. Hughes	5	0	99	183	36.60
B.M. Laird	4	0	74	132	33.00
Bowling	O	M	R	W	Average
G. Dymock	130.3	40	260	17	15.29
G.S. Chappell	42	21	66	4	16.50
D.K. Lillee	155.1	41	388	23	16.86
L.S. Pascoe	93.5	17	241	10	24.10
J.R. Thomson	32	6	100	3	33.33

Wicket-keepers: R.W. Marsh (A) 11 dismissals   R.W. Taylor (E) 11 dismissals

Captains: G.S. Chappell – batting 19, 43; 3, 98*; 114, 40*
                    bowling 1–5, 0–6; 1–19, 2–36; dnb
            J.M. Brearley – batting 64, 11; 7, 19; 60*, 10

1980 Only Test

High scores: England – G. Boycott 62, 128* D.I. Gower 45, 35
               Australia – K.J. Hughes 117, 84   G.M. Wood 112   G.S. Chappell 47, 59

Best bowling: England – C.M. Old 3–91, 3–47
               Australia – L.S. Pascoe 5–59   D.K. Lillee 4–43

Wicket-keepers: D.L. Bairstow (E) 3 dismissals   R.W. Marsh (A) 1 dismissal

Captains: I.T. Botham – batting 0   bowling 0–89, 1–43
            G.S. Chappell – batting 47, 59   bowling 0–2

G. Boycott became the fourth batsman to score 7,000 Test runs.

14

History is Replaced with a Wooden Spoon

For English fans the 1981 series provided the kind of cricket that, years hence in old age, one looks back on with a warm glow of satisfaction. Two of the most improbable wins of all came in quick succession to transform a rubber that Australia looked to have under complete control, and to produce a reversal of fortunes about which Kim Hughes will no doubt still have nightmares in his old age.

Poor Hughes was a very fine batsman for whom, as a captain, virtually everything seemed to go wrong. He had taken over in 1979 against Pakistan when Yallop was injured, the first Western Australian to lead his country. Having won that game he retained the job later in the year against India and lost a six-match series 2–0. With the return of the Packer players he handed over to Greg Chappell, and when Chappell declined to tour England in 1981 he was appointed again, despite the presence of the more experienced Marsh and Lillee. It was not a universally popular appointment, but he diplomatically said that while Kim Hughes might not yet be a great captain then Hughes-Marsh-Lillee would prove to be.

He had made his début in the last match of the 1977 series, and with the absence of the Packer players over the next two years he soon had a regular place in the team. His batting was built on a good technique backed up by plenty of concentration, and on his day could be beautiful to watch, with a full range of attractive strokes; yet it was not unknown for him to throw his wicket away through impetuosity, and his Test average of 37 reflects the fact that he had rather too many failures for a top-class batsman. In seventy Tests he totalled over 4,400 runs, scored nine hundreds and saved countless runs through his splendid fielding.

His record as a captain does not make happy reading. Out of twenty-eight matches he won only four, losing thirteen and drawing eleven; only one full series was won when Greg Chappell played under him. He was unlucky in that most of the teams he led were not the strongest Australia had ever fielded, and his own batting often appeared to suffer from the responsibilities of captaincy. He possessed many of the attributes of a good captain, for he was intelligent and perceptive, had a good tactical awareness and a friendly, sympathetic nature that made him popular with his players – yet somehow he seemed ill-fated. His youth – he was twenty-seven in 1981 – and relative lack of experience meant that he did not have the respect of all his team, and also meant that when the tide began to turn against him he seemed not to know what to do to stem it.

To lose the third and fourth Tests in the way he did must indicate poor captaincy, but he was incredibly unlucky suddenly to be confronted with an inspired Botham who turned each game on its head. There seemed an inevitability about Botham's play that no captain could have checked; some of his shots at Headingley were outrageous, and once or twice the ball missed the stumps by the tiniest fraction. Had those matches ended in victory for the tourists, as seemed certain three-quarters of the way through, Hughes would have been an Ashes-winning hero. As it was, he was left as someone who has more cause than most to reflect on the thinness of the dividing line between success and failure.

After an unhappy tour of the West Indies Botham was made England captain for just the first Test. The teams seemed fairly evenly balanced, but neither of them appeared much of a match for some of the sides of the past. The batting was to prove largely undistinguished, prompting one cartoonist as the series unfolded to depict Brian Johnston announcing that 'England have won the toss and have chosen to collapse first.' That was at least partly true of the first Test, in that Australia won the toss and England collapsed first, for 185. Australia then collapsed for six fewer, before England collapsed again for a princely 125. The visitors then did their best to throw the game away, but scraped home, on England's first Sunday of Test cricket, by four wickets. Even with these low scores a string of catches were dropped.

Botham was again appointed for just one more game, which seemed to be simply making life even harder for him. This proved to be a good series for the humorists, for the BBC Radio satirical programme *Weekending* came up with a sketch in which the commentators kept announcing 'And Botham's been made captain until the end of the next over'. The Lord's game, Boycott's 100th Test, was an uninspired affair that saw England make 311 and Australia 345. England then declared on 265, but there was never much question that Australia would save the game. The only excitement centred on whether Botham, who had made a 'pair', would resign before he was sacked. He did, and with dignity.

For Headingley Brearley was summoned and Botham returned to the

Headingley 1981. Ian Botham (6 for 95) bowls to Graham Yallop
(out of picture). Kim Hughes, the captain, is the non-striker, with
Mike Gatting at short leg.

ranks. Australia won the toss and made 401, with a century from Dyson. Botham took 6 for 95. England then made 174, the top-scorer with 50 being, of course, Botham. Following on, they reached 135 for 7 and odds of 500:1 were offered against an England win. Then Dilley joined Botham and they began to swing the bat. This stand made 117 and began the transformation, Old helped Botham add another 67 and Willis pushed out his left leg while Botham farmed the bowling for another 37 runs to finish undefeated on 149. Hughes was criticised for handling his bowlers poorly, especially for bowling Alderman for too long and not using the spinner Bright earlier; but Alderman had been bowling well and taking wickets and it was a criticism that was easily made with hindsight. Perhaps his chief fault was that he appeared not to believe that he could possibly lose, and that it did not much matter what he did, as it was only a question of time before the wickets fell.

In the end Australia's target was only 130, but Willis produced the performance of his life, took 8 for 43, and the unimaginable happened, England winning by eighteen runs to record only the second Test victory made after following on. As one of the most famous cricket matches ever played all these details will be well known, but what of Brearley's captaincy? Richie Benaud wrote that as Brearley must have begun to sense the possibility of setting Australia a target he rightly did not tell Old to play defensively and leave the attacking to Botham but to play his own attacking game and take what runs he could; Benaud felt this was a very brave decision. On the last day, needing to take wickets without giving away runs, he balanced everything beautifully, psyching up Willis for his great achievement, harrying the batsmen relentlessly, not giving up even when they were 56 for 1, changing his bowlers cleverly, setting his field perfectly and inspiring the whole team to play their part with some fine catching. One wonders how many other captains could have done it.

At Edgbaston his captaincy was even better. His 48 in the first innings was the highest score of the match as England stumbled to 189, to which Australia replied with 258. More uninspired batting from England

Edgbaston 1981. David Gower is snapped up by Allan Border. Rod Marsh approves.

produced only 219, Emburey and Taylor putting on a crucial 50 for the ninth wicket, leaving Australia needing 151. Without doubt the luck had gone for England in the previous match but this time they won through playing the better cricket, for they steadily chipped away and wickets fell. Brearley used Emburey particularly cleverly and he took two prize scalps. At 114 for 5 it seemed that Australia must still win. Botham had done little in the match and felt that the pitch had not much to offer him, but Brearley put him on with instructions to keep one end tight for Emburey. Botham's response was to take the last five wickets for one run in 28 balls, to give England victory by 29 runs. The Australian Press began to call their team, who were by now in a state of shock, 'Kim's Kamikaze Kids'. Hughes managed to retain his dignity through all this, not easy in view of the field-day the newspapers were having.

Old Trafford saw a rather more conventional England win. Boycott passed Cowdrey to become England's leading run-scorer, but England could do no better than 231. Australia, however, collapsed dismally for

Trent Bridge 1981. Kim Hughes congratulates Dennis Lillee (8 for 80 in the match) after he has trapped Peter Willey lbw for 13.

130, whereupon England's batting was nothing if not tedious. Enter Botham again, with a glorious century that came from just 86 balls, one fewer than at Headingley, and the match was transformed. Australia were set a target of 506, which they were obviously never going to reach, but they put up a good effort. Yallop made a beautiful century, and Border, batting with a broken finger and limitless determination, scored the slowest Australian Test century as he tried to save the game, to finish on 123 not out. Australia's 402 is their highest fourth innings to lose a Test, so they had at least saved a little face. Brearley's eleventh Ashes win equalled Bradman's record.

A sixth Test was played for the first time in England, and at last the bat was on top of the ball. Brearley put Australia in only to see them chalk up 352, England replying with 314. Hughes's declaration then left England all of the last day to make 383. At 144 for 6 Australia must have been hopeful, but Brearley and Knott put their heads down and the match was saved. Alderman ended his first series with an Australian record of forty-two wickets, with Lillee on thirty-nine. It was Brearley's last Test, and he finished undefeated in his nineteen home matches. The following year he took Middlesex to the Championship in his final season, before retiring to put his 'degree in people' to full professional use.

With a certain amount of relief, one imagines, Kim Hughes handed the captaincy back to Greg Chappell. In due course it came back to him, and after success against Pakistan came several defeats by West Indies. Pressure built up against him from all quarters, including the selectors, some of whom had in their day experienced the same poor form that Hughes was suffering, but who now showed him no mercy. He had little option but to resign, and broke down in tears as he was reading his resignation statement before the television cameras. It was one of the saddest endings for any of the Ashes captains.

The England selectors, having given the captaincy to Keith Fletcher, passed it on to Bob Willis. He had led Warwickshire since 1980 but never tried to pretend he was a natural captain; Gower was felt to be not yet ready and there was no other candidate. Amid Press comment that it was a disastrous appointment – insensitive and self-defeating in the circumstances – Willis accepted the honour and did his best to discharge it. Nor is his record anything to be ashamed of, for in eighteen Tests he won seven and lost five. He came back from Australia without the Ashes, but had it not been for a poor umpiring decision in the last game England *might* have squared the series.

His 90 Tests brought him 325 wickets at 25 – and the record number of

Bob Willis, a fearsome sight for any batsman.

'not outs' in Test cricket, 55 being his grand total. Like John Snow he suffered from not having a partner of comparable pace, and because he had to bear the burden of being England's main strike bowler over many years it seemed several times that his Test career was about to end. That he kept on coming back says much for his character, for the physical and mental effort that he expended must have been huge. His bowling was never elegant and his action was an awkward one that brought much trouble to his knees, but he was immensely strong and determined, taking his wickets through pace rather than subtlety. With the crowd urging him on and the mop of hair billowing, he must have presented an impressive sight to a nervous batsman as he charged in. In fact, he was much more of an England bowler than a county one; those 325 Test wickets were more than one third of his career total of 899.

Few top cricketers have lived on their nerves as much as he did. The tension which he experienced before a big game became such that he resorted to hypnotherapy to try and relieve it, and it was mostly because of this that many felt him unsuitable for the captaincy. The intensity of it all often showed clearly on his face, and the glaring expression in his eyes became a notable feature of an England Test. He would stand for long periods at mid-off apparently withdrawn into his own concentration, the team appearing to be run by the senior players, who were making bowling changes and setting the fields with little involvement from the captain. No doubt that is an exaggeration, but it was how it often seemed to the spectators.

Tactically he was sound enough, if unspectacular; an intelligent, thoughtful man, he was hardly an adventurer. When he was appointed, however, the feeling had been that Willis was precisely the sort of player who needed a sympathetic captain to spur him on, and that he would therefore not perform well himself if he were captain. In the event he proved to be better at motivating his players than many had expected, and as he tried to inspire his men by his own example he turned in some of his best performances during these last two years of his career. Always popular with his teammates for his dry, flat humour, one had the impression that they would try their utmost for him mainly because they realised that he had been given a job that he did not particularly want, but which he was determined to carry out as well as possible.

However, matters began to go wrong near the end of his captaincy. Intensely patriotic, he was saddened when he came to believe that some of the England players were losing their combative edge and were accepting defeat too easily. He never had an easy relationship with the media, and the tabloid stories of goings-on during his last tour caused him much anguish. When, therefore, he missed two Tests in Pakistan through illness and David Gower took over, he was more than happy to play again the following summer under Gower without any rancour that his job had been taken from him. His career ended in anti-climax and disillusionment as he was hammered by the West Indians, a sad finish for a man who made himself into one of the great fast bowlers by sheer will-power and determination.

Willis was unfortunate in that he led England when several of the best players had been banned for three years for touring South Africa, so that his teams were weaker than they might have been. In Australia in 1982–3 he was up against a side that was markedly stronger, Greg Chappell leading them in his last Ashes rubber. The England selectors also made life difficult for him by choosing three off-spinners and no left-armer, a decision which caused widespread public despair. A further problem for Willis was that it was a series that contained several poor umpiring decisions, although he did not criticise the umpires publicly.

The first Test was marred by a bad injury to Terry Alderman. A group of English fans ran on to the pitch as England, having been put in by Chappell, made 400. One of them touched Alderman on the head, at which he gave chase and rugby-tackled the man, but in doing so he injured his shoulder so badly that he was out of cricket for a year. Chappell took his team from the field for a quarter of an hour until order was restored. Australia then replied with 424, including a century from the captain, Botham taking his 250th wicket to add to his 3,000 runs. A hundred from Randall then ensured a good score from England and the match petered out. England were put in again in the second Test but this time managed only 219. Wessels, on début, made 162 as Australia reached 341. England's second innings reached 309, during which Marsh made nine dismissals and passed 300 in Tests, and Lawson took eleven wickets. Needing only 188 Australia won by seven wickets. In the third Test Willis, aware of history but determined to ignore it, put Australia in on a good pitch and paid the penalty as Chappell finally scored a century in his birthplace and his team made 438. Hostile, often short-pitched bowling tumbled England out for 216, and when they followed on they could set Australia only a small target.

Somehow Willis managed to pull his team round to put up a better account of themselves in Melbourne, the 250th Test between the two countries. It proved to be one of the most memorable, another of those rare Tests when all four innings finish within a few runs of each other. England, put in, made 284, and Australia bettered that by three. By the time England had totalled 294 in their second innings the pitch was showing uneven bounce and the home team were clearly going to be pushed to reach their target. When the ninth wicket went down at 218 Thomson joined Border, and Willis soon adopted the tactic of giving Border singles in order to get Thomson on strike. He said afterwards that it had been a team decision; whatever the case, it was a tactic that should have been abandoned when it did not work, but England stuck to it in a way that was positively embarrassing. After thirty-seven of the required runs had been scored on the fourth evening, they still persisted with it next morning to the disbelief of everyone, and as the batsmen neared their target England clearly began to panic. The end came in the most dramatic way, Thomson edging a ball from Botham to Tavaré at second slip; he could only parry it, but Miller, running behind him, lunged forward and caught it. The margin of victory was three runs, equalling the smallest ever margin, in Fred Tate's match in 1902.

This opened the way for a dramatic come-back by England, but at the beginning of the last Test Dyson was ruled not out before he had scored, when it was clear from television that he had failed by some distance to make his ground for a quick single. He went on to score 79 to give Australia a foundation for their 314. England's reply was 237, whereupon a century from Hughes helped take Australia to 382. England's second innings owed much to night-watchman Hemmings, who batted steadily, only to fall five short of what would have been his one Test century. The game was drawn, and there was no doubt that the better team had won the series. The old truth that it is bowlers who win matches was proved yet again.

By the next series in 1985 both captains had retired, Chappell to become a selector and Willis a television commentator. Allan Border had succeeded Hughes and David Gower had taken over from Willis, and if Border's team was weak and generally outplayed, the series nonetheless went down as one of the best-natured of all time, reflecting great credit on the captains.

When Hughes resigned in the middle of the 1984–5 series against West Indies there was no question that anyone other than Border would become captain. He had come into the team during Brearley's 1978–9 tour and proved to be one of the few young players of that series to survive the return of the Packer group. Rather on the short side but very strong, he was soon recognised as the world's best left-handed batsman, an accolade that was confirmed when he became the first man to score 150 in each innings of a Test. Endowed with the concentration and determination to match his ability, his batting often seems impregnable; 'gritty' is a frequently used adjective but it hardly begins to do him justice, for he is by no means simply an accumulator. He can be a very attractive batsman with a full range of

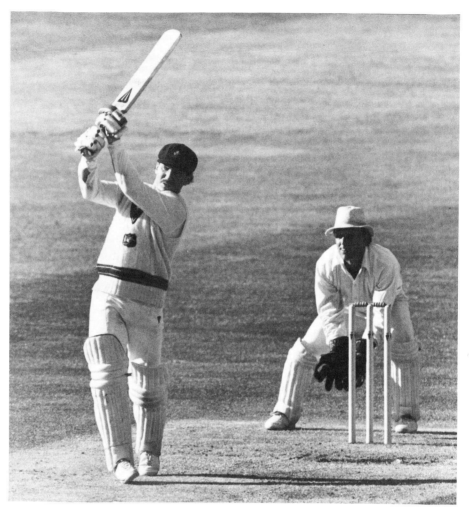

*In 1985 Allan Border was probably the most prolific-scoring captain
since Don Bradman. Paul Downton is behind the stumps.*

glorious strokes, and can score his runs quickly; there might not be the
classical elegance of Greg Chappell about his batting, but there is a
punchiness about it that provides very good entertainment. For years his
has been the prize scalp that bowlers covet, hardly surprising since he has
now overtaken Chappell as Australia's leading run-scorer; by the beginning
of the 1988 English season he had totalled 7,343 runs at an average of 53
from 94 Tests, with 22 centuries to his name.

Before he became captain he had seemed to be rather withdrawn, as tough as they come and fiercely determined to sell his wicket as dearly as possible, but rather lacking in charisma. He seemed too introverted to make a successful captain, and before the 1985 series began the English Press were writing him off, even after Australia had beaten West Indies by an innings in Clive Lloyd's last Test. Border duly produced a surprise, revealing a more outgoing personality than had been seen before. He was popular with his players and was sympathetic to their needs, yet at the same time firm and insisting on total commitment. Since he was, by a wide margin, the best player in the team, he had to lead by example and he did so gloriously, scoring 597 runs in the six Tests and going on to improve his batting average during his years in charge. An intelligent and perceptive man, his tactical acumen has increased as he has grown into the captaincy.

Unfortunately, there has been one major problem; he has had to captain a team which, apart from the weak teams of the Packer years, has been the poorest Australian side since before the First World War. Most writers blame this weakness on the prevalence of one-day cricket that Australia has seen during the 1980s, and the way in which the Australian Cricket Board has allowed itself to be dominated by the marketing men. Whatever the reasons, the fact that one of their finest batsmen should coincide with one of their weakest teams makes one's heart bleed for Border, for he has known some very dark days and the service he has given has deserved a better fate.

His first series win did not come until the eighth attempt, when at the end of 1987 Australia hung on to draw a close game, so beating New Zealand 1–0; soon afterwards he beat Sri Lanka easily at home. After the latter game he had led Australia thirty-one times, winning six, losing nine and being involved, with India, in only the second tied Test. Losing or drawing so many series brought him close to resignation and, having said everything he could in private to his players about their poor performances, he publicly criticised them for the way they kept folding under pressure, not just in Tests but in the relentless one-day internationals. Had there been an obvious successor he said that he would willingly have stood down, but as there was not he was persuaded to soldier on. To his credit he came back from the despair that must have been overwhelming him, and showed that had he been a little luckier with his players he could have proved a more than useful captain; not one of the greats, perhaps, but certainly one who is better than his record suggests. Probably more than any other cricketer of the 1980s Border has suffered from the never-ending pressure that now accompanies top-rank sportspeople.

His opposite number in the 1985 series has known a good deal of pressure too. Like Border, David Gower is a left-hander who has been his country's outstanding batsman of the 1980s; both came into Test cricket within a few months of each other and have played an almost identical number of games, with Border having the better record. In his ninety-six Tests (as at the beginning of the 1988 English season) Gower has totalled 6,789 runs at an average of 44, with fourteen centuries, but he is a very different batsman from Border. Tall, elegant and languid in appearance his batting is all about timing; the ball speeds to the boundary not because it has been bludgeoned there but because it has been pinpointed there with effortless precision. All the strokes are there, but as with most great batsmen it is the cover drive that is the exquisite gem as the bat describes the most graceful of arcs. In a way Gower has not quite fulfilled his potential, for he is clearly as gifted a batsman as has ever picked up the willow; yet he often looks vulnerable early in an innings and has fallen far too often to nibbles outside the off stump. On a bad day his footwork can be non-existent and he can be painful to watch, but on a good day he is, without argument, the most aesthetically pleasing batsman in the world. In the 1985 series he had some good days.

He was fortunate to come into the Leicestershire team under Ray Illingworth, who guided his early years well. His Test début came in 1978 against Pakistan, when he made quite an impact by hooking his first ball for four, and it was clear from his class that he was likely to become captain. His first three games in charge came when Willis was unable to play and at a time when he had little experience of leadership – he did not take over at Leicestershire until 1984 – after which he was appointed in his own right and came up against the 1984 West Indies and their 5–0 'blackwash'. From the depths of that series he came back to beat India in India, a splendid achievement that was followed by his peak against Border's team. A torrid tour of the West Indies followed, a second 'blackwash' on pitches prepared specially for hostile fast bowlers, after which he was appointed for only the first Test against India in 1986. When that was lost he was summarily dismissed, in a way that gained Peter May, the Chairman of Selectors, much criticism for the insensitive way he handled the sacking. There was great sympathy for Gower and his dignity was widely admired. Of his twenty-six Tests as captain five were won and fourteen lost, the legacy of trying to lead a very inferior side against the mighty West Indians. He had been found guilty of failing to do the impossible and he paid the price.

The epithet which must have been most often applied to Gower is 'laid-back'. There is an apparent unconcern about so many of his actions that in a way he has been his own worst enemy. He is a natural athlete who moves with feline grace and is a superb cover fielder, but his languidness when batting and his easy-going approach to press conferences convinced some people that he didn't really care all that much what happened. Moreover, he is one of those players who has been called 'too nice' to be a good captain. Anyone who believed either of those things did not understand him for a moment, for he is a deeply committed cricketer who, as he has shown time and again, can be a real fighter. Yet the image stuck, and as a result he seemed to find little public support when up against the West Indies. He was criticised for not being authoritarian enough, and responded whimsically that he would get a T-shirt with 'I'm in charge' written on it.

An authoritarian approach would never have been his style. His friendly nature has meant that he has always been greatly liked and respected by his team-mates, and if he was tactically weak in his early days he learned quickly and handled the team very well in the 1985 rubber. Arguably he was not strong enough at times, and he did appear to have trouble with Botham occasionally when that gentleman was in one of his stubborn moods. But he saw his role as, in the words of Dirk Wellham, 'quietly directing traffic and allowing his players the opportunity to perform', a reasonable enough way of proceeding against most opposition. Ultimately it was decreed that he had failed, but there were plenty of people who believed that he had been harshly treated.

Most of the leading Australian players of the previous few years having left the scene, there was never any question that England had the stronger team in 1985. It was not long before the visiting bowlers were being called the weakest attack ever to leave Australia, with Lawson unwell and Thomson past his best; the bowlers who had ruled themselves out by going to South Africa were sorely missed. England were to score at over 60 runs per 100 balls, by some margin the highest they had ever achieved against Australia. They were, simply, stronger all round.

The first Test at Headingley was an absorbing affair, with England losing the toss, but then being favoured by the weather. Hilditch scored a century as Australia made 331, but England replied with 533 based on 175 from Robinson, who thus became the second highest scorer on Ashes début. Australia fought well to notch up 324, leaving England to get 123 in 200 minutes with the weather threatening. With everyone vividly aware of what happened the last time the teams played at Headingley, England had a tense time getting there, but made it by 5 wickets. At Lord's, where England have not beaten Australia since 1934, the visitors levelled the series on the one occasion when their bowlers clicked. England were put in and dismissed for 290, whereupon Border made 196 to take his team to 425. Dismissed again for 261, England had to bowl Australia out for less than 126, but there was

*Edgbaston 1985. Phillips c. Gower via Lamb's foot, b. Edmonds.
Umpire Constant at square leg was able to confirm that the catch
was legal.*

no Brearley or Willis this time. They managed six of the wickets all the same.

At Trent Bridge an easy pitch produced a high-scoring draw with three big centuries from Gower, Wood and Ritchie. It was a match that never looked remotely like reaching a conclusion. At Old Trafford it was the weather that won the day, although England undoubtedly missed their chance. Australia's 257 was greeted with 482 from England, Gatting contributing 160. At the beginning of the last day, with Australia needing to bat for hours to save the match, Downton missed a hard chance off Border and he went on to make almost a hundred more and seal the game.

It was in the last two Tests that everything went wrong for Border. At Edgbaston Australia scored 335 and England replied with 595 for 5 declared. Robinson made 148, Gower 215 and Gatting 100 not out, Gower's masterfully elegant innings being the second highest ever by an England captain against Australia, and his stand of 331 with Robinson being the second-highest for any England wicket against Australia. Australia's second innings began with a total collapse, and at the end of the fourth day they were 36 for 5, Ellison having done the damage. But the weather was dull and drizzly on the last day and not till the afternoon did the game restart, when Phillips and Ritchie defended gamely. In the end it was a freak catch that decided it, Phillips clipping a ball down on to Lamb's instep which rebounded for Gower to take a gentle catch. The umpires conferred and gave it out. There were endless television replays of it, and afterwards Border expressed his displeasure about the decision. The rest of the wickets soon tumbled.

The story at the Oval was similar. This time Gooch made 196 and Gower 157, their stand of 351 beating that of the previous match. To England's 464 Australia could reply with only 241, and following on collapsed again for 129 and a second innings defeat. Once again England were striving to win the match against failing weather, and the last Australian pair of Bennett and Gilbert nobly declined to come off for bad light and so deprive England of their deserved win. Soon after the last wicket fell the rain closed in.

Until those last two overwhelming victories, when the Australian bowling disintegrated completely, it had been a closely-fought series. However, it will be remembered in particular for the spirit in which the matches were played, and for the bouquets which the Australians, and especially Border, received for their sportsmanship and friendliness. Both captains were much praised for their part in making it all so amicable.

As David Gower stood on the balcony at the Oval spraying champagne to

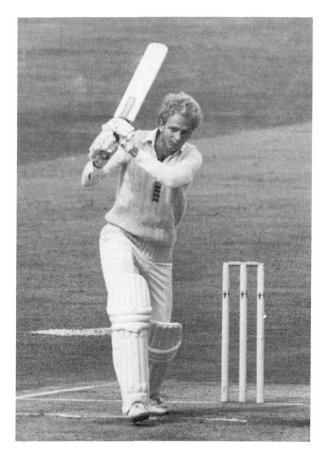

David Gower in gloriously elegant action during his innings of 215 at Edgbaston, 1985.

the heavens, a record 732 runs to his name, there cannot have been many people who thought that in ten months time he would be sacked. Mike Gatting could hardly have thought that in just a year and a half he would be leading England on their most successful tour ever, returning home with three trophies and an OBE to follow. Even after he had been made captain he could not have believed it, for the rest of 1986 was disastrous for England, losing to both India and New Zealand. When England set off for the 1986–7 tour of Australia, it was very much to see who were the holders of Test cricket's 'wooden spoon'.

It had taken Gatting a long time to establish his place in the England team, for he had made his début as far back as 1977–8 as a twenty-year-old. But for years he was never able to reproduce his county form for his country, so often falling lbw without offering a stroke. Because he was scoring so many runs for Middlesex the selectors persevered, and eventually, having been made vice-captain on Gower's tour of India, he scored his first Test century in his thirty-first match and the floodgates opened. By the end of the 1985 series he had raised his average from 23 to 37, and at the beginning of the 1988 English season he had scored 3,810 runs from his sixty-five Tests at an average of 39, with nine hundreds. The comparison with Bobby Simpson, who did not make his first Test century until his thirtieth match and scored freely thereafter, is an obvious one. A solidly-built man, he bats with power, authority, confidence and pugnacity, punching the ball very hard from a full range of strokes. Against the spinners he has few equals, and on his day he can tame the very best bowlers. If he lacks something in elegance he is still very good to watch, and his batting has benefited from the responsibility of captaincy.

He took over at Middlesex in 1983 after Brearley retired and maintained their challenge for the Championship, eventually winning it in 1985 despite losing many players to Test duty. He has also won the Benson and Hedges Cup twice and the Nat West Trophy once. With the exception of the series in Australia, though, his Test record is not an impressive one; after

Mike Gatting led England to victory in the three competitions of the 1987–8 tour and was rewarded with an OBE.

twenty-two matches he had won only two and lost five. Much better is his record in one-day internationals, and in 1987 and 1988 England could reasonably claim to be the best one-day side in the world, despite losing to Australia in the World Cup final. His one-day successes with Middlesex bear out these skills, and he has written a book on the subject called *Limited Overs*.

It is fair to say that, as with Border, his lack of Test success has been due more to an anodyne team than his poor captaincy. Some of his decisions have appeared rather strange and there have been times when he seemed powerless to stop a match from drifting away, but by and large his captaincy has been businesslike and capable. In the language of the 1980s the adjective which several writers used of him on his appointment was 'streetwise'; he knows what the game is all about and gets on with it in a straightforward, uncomplicated manner. He is an energetic leader who has usually got plenty of ideas; not an intellectual, but with a good ability to 'read' a match and sense the right thing to do. Friendly and open by nature, on a good day he can be a truly inspirational captain, weaving subtle schemes in a way perhaps surprising for one so straightforward.

Gatting's emotions on a cricket field are rarely hidden from view, a characteristic that can work to his advantage or disadvantage. Obviously there are times in a match when a display of emotion is a good thing, but there are just as many when it is not. In particular it is not good to indulge in a slanging match with an umpire, however incompetent and biased you believe him to be. Despite all the provocation, virtually none of Gatting's predecessors would have become involved in the way that he did with Shakoor Rana in Pakistan at the end of 1987, and he was rightly condemned for it. In the long run, if it improves the standard of Test umpiring, it might prove to have been a good thing, but that is not really the point; even if you believe he was more sinned against than sinning it still constitutes a black mark on his record.

His sacking from the captaincy after the first Test of 1988, when the tabloids decided it was his turn for their insidious attentions, was one of those situations which will always provoke conflicting views regarding the action that should have been taken. Perhaps the affair reflected more discredit on the authorities for the way they handled it than on Gatting himself; over the years England's cricket administrators have, after all, never been reluctant to strike up a 'holier-than-thou' attitude, and the balance of opinion seemed to be that Gatting was hard done by. Perhaps an appropriate response would be for him to embark upon a long-distance charity walk – or might that be interpreted as a penance?

With the wooden spoon in prospect for the losers of the 1986–7 series, England began their opening tour matches in wretched form and were being written off by every pressman in Australia, of both nationalities, as a joke. Border's team, it appeared, had only to turn up at the right stadium to beat them. And then suddenly in the first Test England clicked; Botham scored his first Test century for three years as England rattled up 456 and then shot Australia out for 248. Despite a century from Marsh they could set England only a small target, and a seven-wicket win made the pressmen start singing a different song. England should have won the second game as well. Centuries from Broad, Gower and Richards and a near miss from Athey took them to 592 (remarkably this total included two ducks from top batsmen), but Border fought hard to avoid the follow-on and this was just achieved. England then scored too slowly as they tried to pile up runs, leaving Australia able to save the game with relative ease. The third match was then a boring, high-scoring draw with several centuries and never a suggestion of a result.

At Melbourne the Ashes were conclusively retained. Gatting put Australia in and Botham and Small shot them out for 141, with five wickets apiece. Broad then became only the third Englishman to score centuries in three consecutive Tests against Australia, propelling himself into the exalted company of Messrs Hobbs and Hammond. England made 349, whereupon Australia collapsed again for 194 and England won by an innings, their first three-day win in Australia since 1901. The last Test at Sydney then turned up a riveting match that was won only right at the end. Australia's 343 included 184 not out from Jones, although England maintained that he had been caught behind when he had made only 5. England totalled 275, after which Australia's second innings amounted to 251, Richards missing a stumping chance off Waugh who then made another 58 runs. England's target was 320, and at 233 for 5 with Gatting on 96 it seemed they would do it. But Gatting fell and there was no one to score the runs in the time. As England tried to shut up shop more wickets fell, and eventually Emburey was bowled off the last ball of the penultimate over. It was Australia's first Test win in over a year.

If one wants to be critical it could not unreasonably be said that England should have won that series 4–0 rather than 2–1. Certainly some of the players thought they should have done. They did, however, win the two one-day competitions on offer, first the Benson and Hedges Challenge in Perth against Australia, West Indies and Pakistan and then the World Series Cup against Australia and West Indies. It was a remarkable achievement for a side that had been written off, but the fact that their next Test win did not come for over eighteen months does imply that Australia were deserving holders of the wooden spoon.

There is one more little story to tell. Early in 1988 the Bicentennial Test was played in Sydney as part of Australia's birthday celebrations. Both captains were still in office, Border fresh from his first series win and Gatting fresh from his avowed last ever visit to Pakistan. England, however, seemed intent on spoiling the party, as Broad made yet another century only to earn himself a fine when he smashed his bat into his stumps as he was out. England's 425 was too much for Australia as they subsided to 214 and the follow-on, but then Boon proved himself the hero of the hour by making 184 not out to save the game – and to save the problem of having to make Broad 'Man of the Match' after he had broken his wicket. Like many another before it, the match expired painlessly, perhaps a fitting epitaph for two teams who only a year before had been trying to establish which one of them was the weakest team, apart from the fledgeling Sri Lanka, in world cricket. That 110 years of supposedly glorious contest had come simply to decide who holds Test cricket's wooden spoon must have left Lillywhite and Gregory, Grace and Murdoch and all their contemporaries turning in anguish in their graves.

It would be unfair to end on a mocking note, poking cheap, wooden-spoon fun at the present teams simply because they happen to be going through a lean period at the same time. If Grace and the others are turning in their graves it is as likely to be at my petty jibes as much as anything. After all, there must still be a great many people for whom an England–Australia game is the only Test match that *really* matters, and for as long as that is the case any talk of wooden spoons is irrelevant and irreverent. The captains and their teams have given us so much entertainment and drama over the years that it would be churlish to bid them farewell with anything other than gratitude.

Forty-four Englishmen and thirty-four Australians have led their countries against each other. Perhaps a few of them wished that they had not, but most did the job at least capably and some did it brilliantly. Yet captaincy is such a complex business that even amongst the successful ones there has been a great variety of personalities; from Jardine insisting that his instructions be obeyed to the letter to the easy-going Chapman, always ready for a drink and a chat; from Bradman's relentless desire for victory to Benaud's shrewd opportunism; from Trott the ex-postman to Brearley the psychoanalyst; from the authoritarian Armstrong and the 'macho' Ian Chappell to the cautious Hutton and the canny Illingworth, and so on and so on. The successful ones have all had the luck to coincide with a decent group of players whom they could mould into a winning team, and some of them had the luck to come up against weak opposition; but they have all possessed outstanding leadership qualities that have allowed them to capitalise on their luck and write their names in the record books as successful captains in the long and, on the whole, glorious tradition of Ashes Tests.

1981	Trent Bridge	E 185, 125	A 179, 132–6	A 4 wkts
	Lord's	E 311, 265–8d	A 345, 90–4	Drawn
	Headingley	A 401–9d, 111	E 174, 356	E 18 runs
	Edgbaston	E 189, 219	A 258, 121	E 29 runs
	Old Trafford	E 231, 404	A 130, 402	E 103 runs
	Oval	A 352, 344–9d	E 314, 261–7	Drawn
1982–3	Perth	E 411, 358	A 424–9d, 73–2	Drawn
	Brisbane	E 219, 309	A 341, 190–3	A 7 wkts
	Adelaide	A 438, 83–2	E 216, 304	A 8 wkts
	Melbourne	E 284, 294	A 287, 288	E 3 runs
	Sydney	A 314, 382	E 237, 314–7	Drawn
1985	Headingley	A 331, 324	E 533, 123–5	E 5 wkts
	Lord's	E 290, 261	A 425, 127–6	E 4 wkts
	Trent Bridge	E 456, 196–2	A 539	Drawn
	Old Trafford	A 257, 340–5	E 482–9d	Drawn
	Edgbaston	A 335, 142	E 595–5d	E inns 118 runs
	Oval	E 464	A 241, 129	E inns 94 runs
1986–7	Brisbane	E 456, 77–3	A 248, 282	E 7 wkts
	Perth	E 592–8d, 199–8d	A 401, 197–4	Drawn
	Adelaide	A 514–5d, 201–3d	E 455, 39–2	Drawn
	Melbourne	A 141, 194	E 349	E inns 14 runs
	Sydney	A 343, 251	E 275, 264	A 55 runs
1988	Sydney	E 425	A 214, 328–2	Drawn

1981

England

Batting	Innings	NO	HS	Runs	Average
A.P.E. Knott	4	1	70*	178	59.33
C.J. Tavaré	4	0	78	179	44.75
G.R. Dilley	6	2	56	150	37.50
I.T. Botham	12	1	149*	399	36.27
G. Boycott	12	0	137	392	32.66

Bowling	O	M	R	W	Average
G.R Dilley	98	24	275	14	19.64
I.T. Botham	272.3	81	700	34	20.58
R.G.D. Willis	252.4	56	666	29	22.96
J.E. Emburey	193.5	58	399	12	33.25
C.M. Old	84	27	175	5	35.00

Australia

Batting	Innings	NO	HS	Runs	Average
A.R. Border	12	3	123*	533	59.22
M.F. Kent	6	0	54	171	28.50
G.M. Wood	12	1	66	310	28.18
G.N. Yallop	12	0	114	316	26.33
K.J. Hughes	12	0	89	300	25.00

Bowling	O	M	R	W	Average
T.M. Alderman	325	76	893	42	21.26
D.K. Lillee	311.4	81	870	39	22.30
G.F. Lawson	106.1	30	285	12	23.75
R.M. Hogg	40.4	8	123	4	30.75
R.J. Bright	191.4	82	390	12	32.50

Wicket-keepers: P.R. Downton (E) 2 dismissals   R.W. Taylor (E) 13 dismissals
A.P.E. Knott (E) 6 dismissals   R.W. Marsh (A) 23 dismissals

Captains: I.T. Botham – batting 1, 33; 0,0
bowling 2–34, 1–34; 2–71, 1–10
J.M. Brearley – batting 10, 14; 48, 13; 2, 3; 0, 51
K.J. Hughes – batting 7, 22; 42, 4; 89, 0; 47, 5; 4, 43; 31, 6

The second match was G. Boycott's 100th Test. In the third match I.T. Botham became the second player after J.M. Gregory to score a century and take five wickets in an innings in England v Australia Tests. R.W. Marsh passed A.P.E. Knott's Test record of 263 dismissals. D.K. Lillee passed H. Trumble's record of 141 wickets in England v Australia Tests. R.G.D. Willis took career-best figures of 8–43, the best for any Headingley Test. In the fourth Test Botham finished the match by taking five wickets for one run in 28 balls. In the fifth Test J.M. Brearley equalled Sir Donald Bradman's record of 11 victories in England v Australia Tests. Boycott became the leading England run-scorer when he passed M.C. Cowdrey's 7,624 runs. Botham reached his century off only 86 balls (one fewer than in the third match), his six sixes being the most in any Test innings in England and the most against Australia. In the sixth match Willis passed W. Rhodes's record of 109 wickets against Australia. Botham took his 200th Test wicket in the record time of 4 years 34 days and at what was then the youngest age of 25 years 280 days. T.M. Alderman's 42 wickets is the record for an Australian in an England v Australia series.

1982–3

England

Batting	Innings	NO	HS	Runs	Average
D.W. Randall	8	0	115	365	45.62
D.I. Gower	10	0	114	441	44.10
A.J. Lamb	10	0	83	414	41.40
G. Fowler	6	0	83	207	34.50
E.E. Hemmings	6	1	95	157	31.40

Bowling	O	M	R	W	Average
R.G.D. Willis	166.3	28	486	18	27.00
G. Miller	171	50	397	13	30.53
N.G. Cowans	107	14	396	11	36.00
I.T. Botham	213.5	35	729	18	40.50
E.E. Hemmings	188.3	59	409	9	45.44

Australia

Batting	Innings	NO	HS	Runs	Average
K.J. Hughes	8	1	137	469	67.00
D.W. Hookes	8	1	68	344	49.14
G.S. Chappell	10	2	117	389	48.62
K.C. Wessels	8	0	162	386	48.25
A.R. Border	9	2	89	317	45.28

Bowling	O	M	R	W	Average
J.R. Thomson	128.4	22	411	22	18.68
G.F. Lawson	230.4	51	687	34	20.20
R.M. Hogg	107.3	26	302	11	27.45
B. Yardley	292.2	91	793	22	36.04
D.K. Lillee	71	25	185	4	46.25

Wicket-keepers: R.W. Marsh (A) 28 dismissals   R.W. Taylor (E) 13 dismissals

Captains: G.S. Chappell – batting 117, 22*; 53, 8; 115, 26*; 0, 2; 35, 11
            bowling 0–11, 1–8; 0–8; dnb; 0–5, 0–6; 0–6
            R.G.D. Willis – batting 26, 0; 1, 10*; 1, 10; 6*, 8*; 1
            bowling 3–95, 2–23; 5–66, 0–24; 2–76, 1–17; 3–38, 0–57; 1–57, 1–33

In the first match I.T. Botham became the only player to score 3,000 runs and take 250 wickets in Tests. In the second match R.W. Marsh became the first wicket-keeper to make 300 Test dismissals; he also set an England v Australia record of six dismissals in an innings and equalled G.R.A. Langley's Australian record of 9 dismissals in a match. His 28 dismissals in the series is a record for all Tests.

1985

England

Batting	Innings	NO	HS	Runs	Average
M.W. Gatting	9	3	160	527	87.83
D.I. Gower	9	0	215	732	81.33
R.T. Robinson	9	1	175	490	61.25
G.A. Gooch	9	0	196	487	54.11
A.J. Lamb	8	1	67	256	36.57

Bowling	O	M	R	W	Average
R.M. Ellison	75.5	20	185	17	10.88
I.T. Botham	251.4	36	855	31	27.58
J.E. Emburey	248.4	75	544	19	28.63
P.H. Edmonds	225.5	59	549	15	36.60
P.J.W. Allott	113	22	297	5	59.40

Australia

Batting	Innings	NO	HS	Runs	Average
A.R. Border	11	2	196	597	66.33
G.M. Ritchie	11	1	146	422	42.20
A.M.J. Hilditch	11	0	119	424	38.54
W.B. Phillips	11	1	91	350	35.00
K.C. Wessels	11	0	83	368	33.45

Bowling	O	M	R	W	Average
C.J. McDermott	234.2	21	901	30	30.03
G.F. Lawson	246	38	830	22	37.72
R.G. Holland	172	41	465	6	77.50
S.P. O'Donnell	145.4	31	487	6	81.16
J.R. Thomson	56	4	275	3	91.67

Wicket-keepers: P.R. Downton (E) 20 dismissals
                  W.B. Phillips (A) 11 dismissals

Captains: D.I. Gower – batting 17, 5; 86, 22; 166, 17; 47; 215; 157
            A.R. Border – batting 32, 8; 196, 41*; 23; 8, 146*; 45, 2; 38, 58
            bowling 0–16; dnb; dnb; dnb; 0–13; 0–8

In the first match R.T. Robinson's 175 was the second-highest score by a batsman playing in his first England v Australia Test. In the second match A.R. Border's 196 was the highest score by an Australian captain at Lord's. In the fifth match D.I. Gower's 215 was the second-highest score by an England captain against Australia, and his partnership of 331 with Robinson was the second-highest for any England wicket against Australia. In the sixth match Gower and G.A. Gooch exceeded this by putting on 351 for the second wicket.

1986–7

England

Batting	Innings	NO	HS	Runs	Average
B.C. Broad	9	2	162	487	69.57
D.I. Gower	8	1	136	404	57.71
M.W. Gatting	9	0	100	393	43.66
C.J. Richards	7	0	133	264	37.71
J.E. Emburey	7	2	69	179	35.80

Bowling	O	M	R	W	Average
G.C. Small	78.4	23	180	12	15.00
G.R. Dilley	176.1	38	511	16	31.93
I.T. Botham	106.2	24	296	9	32.88
P.H. Edmonds	261.4	78	538	15	35.86
J.E. Emburey	315.5	86	663	18	36.83

Australia

Batting	Innings	NO	HS	Runs	Average
D.M. Jones	10	1	184*	511	56.77
G.R.J. Matthews	7	3	73*	215	53.75
A.R. Border	10	1	125	473	52.55
S.R. Waugh	8	1	79*	310	44.28
G.R. Marsh	10	0	110	429	42.90

Bowling	O	M	R	W	Average
P.L. Taylor	55	17	154	8	19.25
B.A. Reid	198.4	44	527	20	26.35
P.R. Sleep	136	43	316	10	31.60
S.R. Waugh	108.3	26	336	10	33.60
C.D. Matthews	70.1	14	233	6	38.83

Wicket-keepers: T.J. Zoehrer (A) 10 dismissals   G.C. Dyer (A) 2 dismissals
C.J. Richards (E) 16 dismissals

Captains: A.R. Border – batting 7, 23; 125, 16; 70, 100*; 15, 34; 34, 49
bowling dnb; 0–6; 0–1; dnb; 1–25
M.W. Gatting – batting 61, 12; 14, 70; 100, 0; 40; 0, 96
bowling 0–2; 0–3; 0–22, 0–4; 0–4; 0–2, 0–0

In the second match I.T. Botham took his 100th catch in his 87th Test. In the fourth match B.C. Broad became the third Englishman after J.B. Hobbs and W.R. Hammond to score a century in three consecutive Tests against Australia.

1988 Only Test

High scores: Australia – D.C. Boon 184*   G.R. Marsh 56   D.M. Jones 56
England – B.C. Broad 139   B.N. French 47   R.T. Robinson 43

Best bowling: Australia – S.R. Waugh 3–51
England – E.E. Hemmings 3–53   G.R. Dilley 3–54

Wicket-keepers: G.C. Dyer (A) 3 dismissals   B.N. French (E) 4 dismissals

Captains: A.R. Border – batting 2, 48*
M.W. Gatting – batting 13

In the second innings A.R. Border set a new Test record, having played 79 consecutive Test innings without failing to score.

Statistical Highlights

Results – Series by Series

	Tests played	Result E	A	D	Ashes held by	Captains England	Australia
1876–7	2	1	1	0	–	James Lillywhite	D.W. Gregory
1878–9	1	0	1	0	–	Lord Harris	D.W. Gregory
1880	1	1	0	0	–	Lord Harris	W.L. Murdoch
1881–2	4	0	2	2	–	A. Shaw	W.L. Murdoch
1882	1	0	1	0	–	A.N. Hornby	W.L. Murdoch
1882–3	4	2	2	0	E*	Hon. Ivo Bligh	W.L. Murdoch
1884	3	1	0	2	E	A.N. Hornby (1st) Lord Harris	W.L. Murdoch
1884–5	5	3	2	0	E	A. Shrewsbury	W.L. Murdoch (1st) T.P. Horan (2nd, 5th) H.H. Massie (3rd) J.M. Blackham (4th)
1886	3	3	0	0	E	A.G. Steel	H.J.H. Scott
1886–7	2	2	0	0	E	A. Shrewsbury	P.S. McDonnell
1887–8	1	1	0	0	E	W.W. Read	P.S. McDonnell
1888	3	2	1	0	E	A.G. Steel (1st) W.G. Grace	P.S. McDonnell
1890	+2	2	0	0	E	W.G. Grace	W.L. Murdoch
1891–2	3	1	2	0	A	W.G. Grace	J.M. Blackham
1893	3	1	0	2	E	A.E. Stoddart (1st) W.G. Grace	J.M. Blackham
1894–5	5	3	2	0	E	A.E. Stoddart	J.M. Blackham (1st) G. Giffen
1896	3	2	1	0	E	W.G. Grace	G.H.S. Trott
1897–8	5	1	4	0	A	A.C. MacLaren (1st, 2nd, 5th) A.E. Stoddart (3rd, 4th)	G.H.S. Trott
1899	5	0	1	4	A	W.G. Grace (1st) A.C. MacLaren	J. Darling
1901–2	5	1	4	0	A	A.C. MacLaren	J. Darling H. Trumble (4th, 5th)
1902	5	1	2	2	A	A.C. MacLaren	J. Darling
1903–4	5	3	2	0	E	P.F. Warner	M.A. Noble
1905	5	2	0	3	E	Hon. F.S. Jackson	J. Darling
1907–8	5	1	4	0	A	F.L. Fane A.O. Jones (4th, 5th)	M.A. Noble
1909	5	1	2	2	A	A.C. MacLaren	M.A. Noble
1911–12	5	4	1	0	E	J.W.H.T. Douglas	C. Hill
1912	3	1	0	2	E	C.B. Fry	S.E. Gregory
1920–1	5	0	5	0	A	J.W.H.T. Douglas	W.W. Armstrong
1921	5	0	3	2	A	J.W.H.T. Douglas (1st, 2nd) Hon. L.H. Tennyson	W.W. Armstrong
1924–5	5	1	4	0	A	A.E.R. Gilligan	H.L. Collins

	Tests played	E	A	D	Ashes held by	Captains England	Australia
1926	5	1	0	4	E	A.W. Carr A.P.F. Chapman (5th)	H.L. Collins W. Bardsley (3rd, 4th)
1928–9	5	4	1	0	E	A.P.F. Chapman J.C. White (5th)	J. Ryder
1930	5	1	2	2	A	A.P.F. Chapman R.E.S. Wyatt (5th)	W.M. Woodfull
1932–3	5	4	1	0	E	D.R. Jardine	W.M. Woodfull
1934	5	1	2	2	A	C.F. Walters (1st) R.E.S. Wyatt	W.M. Woodfull
1936–7	5	2	3	0	A	G.O.B. Allen	D.G. Bradman
1938	+4	1	1	2	A	W.R. Hammond	D.G. Bradman
1946–7	5	0	3	2	A	W.R. Hammond N.W.D. Yardley (5th)	D.G. Bradman
1948	5	0	4	1	A	N.W.D. Yardley	D.G. Bradman
1950–1	5	1	4	0	A	F.R. Brown	A.L. Hassett
1953	5	1	0	4	E	L. Hutton	A.L. Hassett
1954–5	5	3	1	1	E	L. Hutton	I.W. Johnson A.R. Morris (2nd)
1956	5	2	1	2	E	P.B.H. May	I.W. Johnson
1958–9	5	0	4	1	A	P.B.H. May	R. Benaud
1961	5	1	2	2	A	M.C. Cowdrey (1st, 2nd) P.B.H. May	R. Benaud R.N. Harvey (2nd)
1962–3	5	1	1	3	A	E.R. Dexter	R. Benaud
1964	5	0	1	4	A	E.R. Dexter	R.B. Simpson
1965–6	5	1	1	3	A	M.J.K. Smith	B.C. Booth (1st, 3rd) R.B. Simpson
1968	5	1	1	3	A	M.C. Cowdrey T.W. Graveney (4th)	W.M. Lawry B.N. Jarman (4th)
1970–1	+6	2	0	4	E	R. Illingworth	W.M. Lawry I.M. Chappell (7th)
1972	5	2	2	1	E	R. Illingworth	I.M. Chappell
1974–5	6	1	4	1	A	M.H. Denness J.H. Edrich (4th)	I.M. Chappell
1975	4	0	1	3	A	M.H. Denness (1st) A.W. Greig	I.M. Chappell
1976–7	1	0	1	0	–**	A.W. Greig	G.S. Chappell
1977	5	3	0	2	E	J.M. Brearley	G.S. Chappell
1978–9	6	5	1	0	E	J.M. Brearley	G.N. Yallop
1979–80	3	0	3	0	–**	J.M. Brearley	G.S. Chappell
1980	1	0	0	1	–**	I.T. Botham	G.S. Chappell
1981	6	3	1	2	E	I.T. Botham (1st, 2nd) J.M. Brearley	K.J. Hughes
1982–3	5	1	2	2	A	R.G.D. Willis	G.S. Chappell
1985	6	3	1	2	E	D.I. Gower	A.R. Border
1986–7	5	2	1	2	E	M.W. Gatting	A.R. Border
1988	1	0	0	1	–**	M.W. Gatting	A.R. Border
Total	263	88	97	78			
	123	37	30	56	In England		
	140	51	67	22	In Australia		

* Three games were originally scheduled and The Hon. Ivo Bligh was presented with the Ashes after England won 2–1. A fourth game was then played.

+ In 1890 and 1938 the 3rd Tests, both at Manchester, and in 1970–1 the 3rd Test at Melbourne were abandoned without a ball bowled and are excluded.

** The Ashes were not at stake in these games.

Highest Batting Averages – 500 Runs or More

England	M	I	NO	Runs	HS	Ave	100s	50s
E. Paynter	7	11	4	591	216*	84.43	1	3
B.C. Broad	6	10	2	626	162	78.25	4	0
H. Sutcliffe	27	46	5	2741	194	66.85	8	16
K.F. Barrington	23	39	6	2111	256	63.97	5	13
R.T. Robinson	7	10	1	533	175	59.22	2	1
M. Leyland	20	34	4	1705	187	56.83	7	3
L. Hutton	27	49	6	2428	364	56.47	5	14
J.B. Hobbs	41	71	4	3636	187	54.27	12	15
W.R. Hammond	33	58	3	2852	251	51.85	9	7
J.H. Edrich	32	57	3	2644	175	48.96	7	13
Hon. F.S. Jackson	20	33	4	1415	144*	48.79	5	6
G. Boycott	38	71	9	2945	191	47.50	7	14
M.W. Gatting	19	33	4	1366	160	47.10	3	11
D.I. Gower	31	56	3	2479	215	46.77	6	9
P.B.H. May	21	37	3	1566	113	46.06	3	10
Australia								
D.G. Bradman	37	63	7	5028	334	89.79	19	12
S.G. Barnes	9	14	2	846	234	70.50	2	4
A.R. Border	30	57	14	2392	196	55.62	7	11
D.M. Jones	6	12	1	591	184*	53.73	1	4
A.R. Morris	24	43	2	2080	206	50.73	8	8
K.R. Stackpole	13	24	1	1164	207	50.61	3	7
R.B. Simpson	19	31	3	1405	311	50.18	2	9
R.M. Cowper	9	15	1	686	307	49.00	1	3
W.M. Lawry	29	51	5	2233	166	48.54	7	13
S.J. McCabe	24	43	3	1931	232	48.28	4	10
W.H. Ponsford	20	35	2	1558	266	47.21	5	5
G.S. Chappell	35	65	8	2619	144	45.95	9	12
J. Ryder	17	28	4	1060	201*	44.17	2	6
W.M. Woodfull	25	41	3	1675	155	44.08	6	8
C.G. Macartney	26	42	4	1640	170	43.16	5	7
W.A. Brown	13	24	1	980	206*	42.61	3	3
R. Edwards	13	22	3	805	170*	42.37	2	5
G.M. Ritchie	10	19	3	666	146	41.63	1	2
I.M. Chappell	30	56	4	2138	192	41.12	4	16

Batsmen with 1,200 Runs

England	M	I	NO	Runs	HS	Ave	100s
J.B. Hobbs	41	71	4	3636	187	54.27	12
G. Boycott	38	71	9	2945	191	47.50	7
W.R. Hammond	33	58	3	2852	251	51.85	9
H. Sutcliffe	27	46	5	2741	194	66.85	8
J.H. Edrich	32	57	3	2644	175	48.96	7
D.I. Gower	31	56	3	2479	215	46.77	6
M.C. Cowdrey	43	75	4	2433	113	34.27	5
L. Hutton	27	49	6	2428	364	56.47	5
K.F. Barrington	23	39	6	2111	256	63.97	5
A.C. MacLaren	35	61	4	1931	140	33.88	5
D.C.S. Compton	28	51	8	1842	184	42.83	5
T.W. Hayward	29	51	2	1747	137	35.65	2

England	M	I	NO	Runs	HS	Ave	100s
E.H. Hendren	28	48	4	1740	169	39.55	3
W. Rhodes	41	69	14	1706	179	31.02	1
M. Leyland	20	34	4	1705	187	56.83	7
A.P.E. Knott	34	57	6	1682	135	32.98	2
F.E. Woolley	32	51	1	1664	133*	33.28	2
I.T. Botham	34	55	2	1611	149*	30.40	4
P.B.H. May	21	37	3	1566	113	46.06	3
Hon. F.S. Jackson	20	33	4	1415	144*	48.79	5
J.T. Tyldesley	26	46	1	1389	138	30.87	3
M.W. Gatting	19	33	4	1366	160	47.10	3
E.R. Dexter	19	35	0	1358	180	38.80	2
A.W. Greig	21	37	1	1303	110	36.19	1
A. Shrewsbury	23	40	4	1277	164	35.47	3
Australia							
D.G. Bradman	37	63	7	5028	334	89.79	19
C. Hill	41	76	1	2660	188	35.47	4
G.S. Chappell	35	65	8	2619	144	45.95	9
R.N. Harvey	37	68	5	2416	167	38.35	6
A.R. Border	30	57	14	2392	196	55.62	7
V.T. Trumper	40	74	5	2263	185*	32.80	6
W.M. Lawry	29	51	5	2233	166	48.54	7
S.E. Gregory	52	92	7	2193	201	25.80	4
W.W. Armstrong	42	71	9	2172	158	35.03	4
I.M. Chappell	30	56	4	2138	192	41.12	4
A.R. Morris	24	43	2	2080	206	50.73	8
K.D. Walters	36	62	6	1981	155	35.38	4
S.J. McCabe	24	43	3	1931	232	48.28	4
M.A. Noble	39	68	6	1905	133	30.73	1
W.M. Woodfull	25	41	3	1675	155	44.08	6
C.G. Macartney	26	42	4	1640	170	43.16	5
R.W. Marsh	42	68	8	1633	110*	27.22	1
J. Darling	31	55	2	1632	178	30.79	3
A.L. Hassett	24	42	1	1572	137	38.34	4
W.H. Ponsford	20	35	2	1558	266	47.21	5
I.R. Redpath	23	43	4	1512	171	38.77	2
K.R. Miller	29	49	4	1511	145*	33.58	3
K.J. Hughes	22	40	1	1499	137	38.44	3
W. Bardsley	30	49	4	1487	193*	33.04	3
R.B. Simpson	19	31	3	1405	311	50.18	2
G. Giffen	31	53	0	1238	161	23.36	1

Record Partnerships for Each Wicket

England

1st	323	J.B. Hobbs and W. Rhodes	1911–12	Melbourne
2nd	382	L. Hutton and M. Leyland	1938	Oval
3rd	262	W.R. Hammond and D.R. Jardine	1928–9	Adelaide
4th	222	W.R. Hammond and E. Paynter	1938	Lord's
5th	206	E. Paynter and D.C.S. Compton	1938	Trent Bridge
6th	215	L. Hutton and J. Hardstaff (jr)	1938	Oval
	215	G. Boycott and A.P.E. Knott	1977	Trent Bridge
7th	143	F.E. Woolley and J. Vine	1911–12	Sydney
8th	124	E.H. Hendren and H. Larwood	1928–9	Brisbane*
9th	151	W.H. Scotton and W.W. Read	1884	Oval
10th	130	R.E. Foster and W. Rhodes	1903–4	Sydney

* Exhibition Ground

Australia

1st	244	R.B. Simpson and W.M. Lawry	1965–6	Adelaide
2nd	451	W.H. Ponsford and D.G. Bradman	1934	Oval
3rd	276	D.G. Bradman and A.L. Hassett	1946–7	Brisbane
4th	388	W.H. Ponsford and D.G. Bradman	1934	Headingley
5th	405	S.G. Barnes and D.G. Bradman	1946–7	Sydney
6th	346	J.H. Fingleton and D.G. Bradman	1936–7	Melbourne
7th	165	C. Hill and H. Trumble	1897–8	Melbourne
8th	243	R.J. Hartigan and C. Hill	1907–8	Adelaide
9th	154	S.E. Gregory and J.M. Blackham	1894–5	Sydney
10th	127	J.M. Taylor and A.A. Mailey	1924–5	Sydney

Most Runs in a Series

England in England	D.I. Gower	732 (ave 81.33) (6 Tests)	1985
England in Australia	W.R. Hammond	905 (ave 113.12)	1928–9
Australia in England	D.G. Bradman	974 (ave 139.14)	1930
Australia in Australia	D.G. Bradman	810 (ave 90.00)	1936–7

Highest Individual Scores

Name	Score	Year	Ground
England			
L. Hutton	364	1938	Oval
R.E. Foster+	287	1903–4	Sydney
K.F. Barrington	256	1964	Old Trafford
W.R. Hammond	251	1928–9	Sydney
W.R. Hammond	240	1938	Lord's
W.R. Hammond	231*	1936–7	Sydney
E. Paynter	216*	1938	Trent Bridge
D.I. Gower	215	1985	Edgbaston
W.R. Hammond	200	1928–9	Melbourne

+ On début

Australia			
D.G. Bradman	334	1930	Headingley
R.B. Simpson	311	1964	Old Trafford
R.M. Cowper	307	1965–6	Melbourne
D.G. Bradman	304	1934	Headingley
D.G. Bradman	270	1936–7	Melbourne
W.H. Ponsford	266	1934	Oval
D.G. Bradman	254	1930	Lord's
D.G. Bradman	244	1934	Oval
D.G. Bradman	234	1946–7	Sydney
S.G. Barnes	234	1946–7	Sydney
D.G. Bradman	232	1930	Oval
S.J. McCabe	232	1938	Trent Bridge
R.B. Simpson	225	1965–6	Adelaide
D.G. Bradman	212	1936–7	Adelaide
W.L. Murdoch	211	1884	Oval
K.R. Stackpole	207	1970–1	Brisbane
W.A. Brown	206*	1938	Lord's
A.R. Morris	206	1950–1	Adelaide
J. Ryder	201*	1924–5	Adelaide
S.E. Gregory	201	1894–5	Sydney

Fastest Centuries

England

G.L. Jessop	75 mins	104	1902	Oval
J.T. Brown	95 mins	140	1894–5	Melbourne
I.T. Botham	104 mins	118	1981	Old Trafford

Australia

J. Darling	91 mins	160	1897–8	Sydney
V.T. Trumper	94 mins	185*	1903–4	Sydney
D.G. Bradman	99 mins	334	1930	Headingley
G.J. Bonnor	100 mins	128	1884–5	Sydney
D.G. Bradman	105 mins	254	1930	Lord's

Best Bowling Averages – 50 Wickets or More

England	M	Balls	Mdns	Runs	Wkts	Ave	Best	5wi	10wm
G.A. Lohmann	15	3301	326	1002	77	13.01	8–35	5	3
W. Barnes	21	2289	271	793	51	15.55	6–28	3	–
W. Bates	15	2364	282	821	50	16.42	7–28	4	1
R. Peel	20	5216	444	1715	102	16.81	7–31	6	2
J.C. Laker	15	4010	203	1444	79	18.28	10–53	5	2
J. Briggs	31	4941	334	1993	97	20.55	6–45	7	3
S.F. Barnes	20	5749	262	2288	106	21.58	7–60	12	1
W. Rhodes	41	5796	234	2616	109	24.00	8–68	6	1

Australia	M	Balls	Mdns	Runs	Wkts	Ave	Best	5wi	10wm
C.T.B. Turner	17	5179	457	1670	101	16.53	7–43	11	2
R.M. Hogg	11	2629	94	952	56	17.00	6–74	5	2
F.R. Spofforth	18	4185	416	1731	94	18.41	7–44	7	4
H. Trumble	31	7895	448	2945	141	20.89	8–65	9	3
D.K. Lillee	29	8516	361	3507	167	21.00	7–89	11	4
G.E. Palmer	17	4417	452	1678	78	21.51	7–65	6	2
K.R. Miller	29	5717	225	1949	87	22.40	7–60	3	1
R.R. Lindwall	29	6728	216	2559	114	22.45	7–63	6	–
A.K. Davidson	25	5993	221	1996	84	23.76	6–64	5	–
J.R. Thomson	21	4957	166	2418	100	24.18	6–46	5	–
W.A. Johnston	17	5263	224	1818	75	24.24	5–35	3	–
M.A. Noble	39	6895	353	2860	115	24.87	7–17	9	2
J.V. Saunders	12	3268	108	1620	64	25.31	5–28	5	–
W.J. O'Reilly	19	7864	439	2587	102	25.36	7–54	8	3

Bowlers with 75 Wickets

England	M	Balls	Mdns	Runs	Wkts	Ave	Best	5wi	10wm
I.T. Botham	34	7999	278	3852	145	26.57	6–78	9	2
R.G.D. Willis	35	7294	198	3346	128	26.14	8–43	7	–
W. Rhodes	41	5796	234	2616	109	24.00	8–68	6	1
S.F. Barnes	20	5749	262	2288	106	21.58	7–60	12	1
D.L. Underwood	29	8000	408	2770	105	26.38	7–50	4	2
A.V. Bedser	21	7065	209	2859	104	27.49	7–44	7	2
R. Peel	20	5216	444	1715	102	16.81	7–31	6	2
J. Briggs	31	4941	334	1993	97	20.55	6–45	7	3
T. Richardson	14	4497	191	2220	88	25.23	8–94	11	4
J.A. Snow	20	5073	168	2126	83	25.61	7–40	4	–
M.W. Tate	20	7686	330	2540	83	30.60	6–99	6	1
J.C. Laker	15	4010	203	1444	79	18.28	10–53	5	2
F.S. Trueman	19	4361	83	1999	79	25.30	6–30	5	1
G.A. Lohmann	15	3301	326	1002	77	13.01	8–35	5	3

Australia	M	Balls	Mdns	Runs	Wkts	Ave	Best	5wi	10wm
D.K. Lillee	29	8516	361	3507	167	21.00	7–89	11	4
H. Trumble	31	7895	448	2945	141	20.89	8–65	9	3
M.A. Noble	39	6895	353	2860	115	24.87	7–17	9	2
R.R. Lindwall	29	6728	216	2559	114	22.45	7–63	6	–
C.V. Grimmett	22	9164	427	3439	106	32.44	6–37	11	2
G. Giffen	31	6391	434	2791	103	27.10	7–117	7	1
W.J. O'Reilly	19	7864	439	2587	102	25.36	7–54	8	3
C.T.B. Turner	17	5179	457	1670	101	16.53	7–43	11	2
J.R. Thomson	21	4957	166	2418	100	24.18	6–46	5	–
G.D. McKenzie	25	7486	233	3009	96	31.34	7–153	6	–
F.R. Spofforth	18	4185	416	1731	94	18.41	7–44	7	4
K.R. Miller	29	5717	225	1949	87	22.40	7–60	3	1
A.A. Mailey	18	5201	90	2935	86	34.13	9–121	6	2
A.K. Davidson	25	5993	221	1996	84	23.76	6–64	5	–
R. Benaud	27	7284	289	2641	83	31.82	6–70	4	–
G.E. Palmer	17	4417	452	1678	78	21.51	7–65	6	2
W.A. Johnston	17	5263	224	1818	75	24.24	5–35	3	–

Most Wickets in a Series

England in England	J.C. Laker	46 (ave 9.60)	1956
England in Australia	M.W. Tate	38 (ave 23.18)	1924–5
Australia in England	T.M. Alderman	42 (ave 21.26) (6 Tests)	1981
Australia in Australia	R.M. Hogg	41 (ave 12.85) (6 Tests)	1978–9

Best Bowling

England

J.C. Laker	10–53	1956	Old Trafford
J.C. Laker	9–37	1956	Old Trafford
G.A. Lohmann	8–35	1886–7	Sydney
H. Verity	8–43	1934	Lord's
R.G.D. Willis	8–43	1981	Headingley
G.A. Lohmann	8–58	1891–2	Sydney
W. Rhodes	8–68	1903–4	Melbourne
L.C. Braund	8–81	1903–4	Melbourne
T. Richardson	8–94	1897–8	Sydney
B.J.T. Bosanquet	8–107	1905	Trent Bridge
J.C. White	8–126	1928–9	Adelaide

Australia

A.A. Mailey	9–121	1920–1	Melbourne
F. Laver	8–31	1909	Old Trafford
A.E. Trott*	8–43	1894–5	Adelaide
R.A.L. Massie*	8–53	1972	Lord's
H. Trumble	8–65	1902	Oval
R.A.L. Massie*	8–84	1972	Lord's
C.J. McDermott	8–141	1985	Old Trafford
M.H.N. Walker	8–143	1974–5	Melbourne

* On début

Hat-Tricks

England

W. Bates	1882–3	Melbourne
J. Briggs	1891–2	Sydney
J.T. Hearne	1899	Headingley

Australia

F.R. Spofforth	1878–9	Melbourne
H. Trumble	1901–2	Melbourne
H. Trumble	1903–4	Melbourne

Wicket-Keepers with ten Dismissals

England	M	Ct	St	Total
A.P.E. Knott	34	97	8	105
A.F.A. Lilley	32	65	19	84
T.G. Evans	31	64	12	76
R.W. Taylor	17	54	3	57
H. Strudwick	17	37	5	42
L.E.G. Ames	17	33	4	37
G. Duckworth	10	23	3	26
P.R. Downton	7	21	1	22
J.M. Parks	10	17	4	21
J.T. Murray	6	18	1	19
G. MacGregor	7	14	3	17
C.J. Richards	5	15	1	16
R. Pilling	8	10	4	14
A.C. Smith	4	13	–	13
E.J. Smith	7	12	1	13
J. Hunter	5	8	3	11
H. Philipson	5	8	3	11
W. Storer	6	11	–	11
E.F.S. Tylecote	6	5	5	10

Australia	M	Ct	St	Total
R.W. Marsh	42	141	7	148
W.A.S. Oldfield	38	59	31	90
A.T.W. Grout	22	69	7	76
J.M. Blackham	32	35	24	59
J.J. Kelly	33	39	16	55
H. Carter	21	35	17	52
D. Tallon	15	38	4	42
G.R.A. Langley	9	35	2	37
B.N. Jarman	7	18	–	18
J.A. Maclean	4	18	–	18
A.H. Jarvis	9	8	9	17
L.V. Maddocks	5	12	1	13
W.B. Phillips	6	11	–	11

Most Catches

England	Tests	Catches	Australia	Tests	Catches
I.T. Botham	34	54	G.S. Chappell	35	61
W.R. Hammond	33	43	H. Trumble	31	45
M.C. Cowdrey	43	40	A.R. Border	30	40
W.G. Grace	22	39*	W.W. Armstrong	42	37
L.C. Braund	20	37	R. Benaud	27	32
A.W. Greig	21	37	I.M. Chappell	30	31
W. Rhodes	41	36	J.M. Gregory	21	30

England	Tests	Catches	Australia	Tests	Catches
F.E. Woolley	32	36*	C. Hill	41	30
A.C. MacLaren	35	29	R.B. Simpson	19	30
A. Shrewsbury	23	29	I.R. Redpath	23	29
T.W. Graveney	22	24	A.K. Davidson	25	28
L. Hutton	27	22	M.A. Noble	39	26
G.A. Lohmann	15	22	R.N. Harvey	37	25
F.S. Trueman	19	21	V.T. Trumper	40	25
D.I. Gower	31	21	G. Giffen	31	24
J.M. Brearley	19	20	S.E. Gregory	52	24
W. Barnes	21	19	J. Darling	31	23
K.F. Barrington	23	19	K.D. Walters	36	23
W.J. Edrich	21	19	A.C. Bannerman	28	21
A.P.F. Chapman	16	18	S.J. McCabe	24	21
			G.H.S. Trott	24	21

* Includes one catch taken while keeping wicket

Leading Allrounders

The Index is calculated by dividing the batting average by the bowling average.

England	M	Runs	Ave	Wkts	Ave	Index
W. Bates	15	656	27.33	50	16.42	1.66
W. Barnes	21	725	23.39	51	15.55	1.50
W. Rhodes	41	1706	31.02	109	24.00	1.29
F.R. Foster	8	281	28.10	34	21.82	1.29
G. Ulyett	23	901	25.03	48	20.67	1.21
W.R. Hammond	33	2852	51.85	36	44.78	1.16
I.T. Botham	34	1611	30.40	145	26.57	1.14
R.G. Barlow	17	591	22.73	34	22.56	1.01
A.W. Greig	21	1303	36.19	44	37.80	0.96
G. Miller	14	479	20.83	39	21.95	0.95
F.E. Woolley	32	1664	33.28	43	36.16	0.92
R. Illingworth	18	663	26.52	34	32.18	0.82
T.E. Bailey	23	875	25.74	42	32.69	0.79
G.H. Hirst	21	744	24.80	49	32.35	0.77
J.W.H.T. Douglas	17	696	26.77	35	35.06	0.76
F.J. Titmus	19	716	28.64	47	38.17	0.75
J.E. Emburey	21	536	24.36	67	32.93	0.74
L.C. Braund	20	830	25.15	46	38.46	0.65
G.O.B. Allen	13	479	23.95	43	37.28	0.64

Australia						
C.G. Macartney	26	1640	43.16	33	27.52	1.57
K.R. Miller	29	1511	33.58	87	22.40	1.50
M.A. Noble	39	1905	30.73	115	24.87	1.24
W.W. Armstrong	42	2172	35.03	74	30.92	1.13
J.M. Gregory	21	941	34.85	70	33.77	1.03
A.K. Davidson	25	750	24.19	84	23.76	1.02
C. Kelleway	18	874	31.21	37	31.22	1.00
R.R. Lindwall	29	795	22.08	114	22.45	0.98
H.V. Hordern	5	173	21.63	32	24.38	0.89
G. Giffen	31	1238	23.36	103	27.10	0.86
M.H.N. Walker	16	407	23.94	56	33.18	0.72
E.A. McDonald	8	101	20.20	33	32.12	0.63
R. Benaud	27	767	19.67	83	31.82	0.62
C.E. McLeod	17	573	23.88	33	40.15	0.59

The Captains

Name	Age 1st cpt	Tests as cpt	Tests as non-cpt	Won toss	Batted 1st on winng toss	Results			% Wins
						W	D	L	
England									
G.O.B. Allen	34	5	8	2	2	2	0	3	40.00
Hon. I.F.W. Bligh	23	4	0	3	3	2	0	2	50.00
I.T. Botham	24	3	31	0	0	0	2	1	–
J.M. Brearley	35	18	1	8	6	11	3	4	61.11
F.R. Brown	39	5	1	1	1	1	0	4	20.00
A.W. Carr	33	4	0	2	1	0	4	0	–
A.P.F. Chapman	25	9	7	5	5	6	2	1	66.67
M.C. Cowdrey	28	6	37	5	5	1	3	2	16.67
M.H. Denness	33	6	0	2	0	1	1	4	16.67
E.R. Dexter	27	10	9	6	5	1	7	2	10.00
J.W.H.T. Douglas	29	12	5	6	5	4	0	8	33.33
J.H. Edrich	37	1	31	0	0	0	0	1	–
F.L. Fane	32	3	1	1	1	1	0	2	33.33
C.B. Fry	40	3	15	3	3	1	2	0	33.33
M.W. Gatting	29	6	13	3	2	2	3	1	33.33
A.E.R. Gilligan	29	5	0	1	1	1	0	4	20.00
D.I. Gower	28	6	25	4	2	3	2	1	50.00
W.G. Grace	40	13	9	4	4	8	2	3	61.54
T.W. Graveney	41	1	21	0	0	0	1	0	–
A.W. Greig	28	4	17	3	2	0	3	1	–
W.R. Hammond	34	8	25	6	6	1	4	3	12.50
Lord Harris	29	4	0	2	2	2	1	1	50.00
A.N. Hornby	35	2	1	1	1	0	1	1	–
L. Hutton	36	10	17	2	1	4	5	1	40.00
R. Illingworth	38	11	7	6	5	4	5	2	36.36
Hon. F.S. Jackson	34	5	15	5	5	2	3	0	40.00
D.R. Jardine	32	5	5	1	1	4	0	1	80.00
A.O. Jones	35	2	10	1	0	0	0	2	–
James Lillywhite	35	2	0	0	0	1	0	1	50.00
A.C. MacLaren	26	22	13	11	10	4	7	11	18.18
P.B.H. May	26	13	8	9	8	3	4	6	23.08
W.W. Read	32	1	16	0	0	1	0	0	100.00
A. Shaw	39	4	3	4	4	0	2	2	–
A. Shrewsbury	28	7	16	3	3	5	0	2	71.43
M.J.K. Smith	32	5	4	3	3	1	3	1	20.00
A.G. Steel	27	4	9	2	2	3	0	1	75.00
A.E. Stoddart	30	8	8	2	1	3	1	4	37.50
Hon. L.H. Tennyson	31	3	1	2	2	0	2	1	–
C.F. Walters	28	1	4	0	0	0	0	1	–
P.F. Warner	30	5	2	2	2	3	0	2	60.00
J.C. White	38	1	6	1	1	0	0	1	–
R.G.D. Willis	33	5	30	1	0	1	2	2	20.00
R.E.S. Wyatt	29	5	7	4	4	1	2	2	20.00
N.W.D. Yardley	31	6	4	5	5	0	1	5	–
Australia									
W.W. Armstrong	41	10	32	4	4	8	2	0	80.00
W. Bardsley	43	2	28	1	1	0	2	0	–
R. Benaud	28	14	13	6	5	6	6	2	42.86
J.M. Blackham	31	8	27	4	4	3	2	3	37.50
B.C. Booth	32	2	13	1	1	0	1	1	–

312

Name	Age 1st cpt	Tests as cpt	Tests as non-cpt	Won toss	Batted 1st on winng toss	Results W	D	L	% Wins
A.R. Border	29	12	18	5	3	2	5	5	16.67
D.G. Bradman	28	19	18	6	6	11	5	3	57.89
G.S. Chappell	28	15	20	9	4	6	4	5	40.00
I.M. Chappell	27	16	14	8	5	7	5	4	43.75
H.L. Collins	34	8	8	5	5	4	2	2	50.00
J. Darling	28	18	13	5	5	5	9	4	27.78
G. Giffen	35	4	27	3	2	2	0	2	50.00
D.W. Gregory	31	3	0	2	2	2	0	1	66.67
S.E. Gregory	42	3	49	0	0	0	2	1	–
R.N. Harvey	32	1	36	0	0	1	0	0	100.00
A.L. Hassett	37	10	14	9	8	4	4	2	40.00
C. Hill	34	5	36	3	3	1	0	4	20.00
T.P. Horan	30	2	13	1	1	0	0	2	–
K.J. Hughes	27	6	16	3	1	1	2	3	16.67
B.N. Jarman	32	1	6	1	1	0	1	0	–
I.W. Johnson	35	9	13	3	2	2	3	4	22.22
W.M. Lawry	31	9	20	4	3	1	6	2	11.11
P.S. McDonnell	28	6	13	4	2	1	0	5	16.67
H.H. Massie	30	1	8	1	1	1	0	0	100.00
A.R Morris	32	1	23	1	0	0	0	1	–
W.L. Murdoch	25	16	2	7	7	5	4	7	31.25
M.A. Noble	30	15	24	11	10	8	2	5	53.33
J. Ryder	39	5	12	2	2	1	0	4	20.00
H.J.H. Scott	27	3	5	1	1	0	0	3	–
R.B. Simpson	28	8	11	2	2	2	6	0	25.00
G.H.S. Trott	29	8	16	5	5	5	3	0	62.50
H. Trumble	34	2	29	1	1	2	0	0	100.00
W.M. Woodfull	32	15	10	8	8	5	4	6	33.33
G.N. Yallop	26	6	7	5	3	1	0	5	16.67

Captain Most Often

England Tests	W	D	L	Toss won	Australia Tests	W	D	L	Toss won
22 A.C. MacLaren	4	7	11	11	19 D.G. Bradman	11	5	3	6
18 J.M. Brearley	11	3	4	8	18 J. Darling	5	9	4	5
13 W.G. Grace	8	2	3	4	16 I.M. Chappell	7	5	4	8
13 P.B.H. May	3	4	6	9	16 W.L. Murdoch	5	4	7	7
12 J.W.H.T. Douglas	4	0	8	6	15 G.S. Chappell	6	4	5	9
11 R. Illingworth	4	5	2	6	15 M.A. Noble	8	2	5	11
10 E.R. Dexter	1	7	2	6	15 W.M. Woodfull	5	4	6	8
10 L. Hutton	4	5	1	2	14 R. Benaud	6	6	2	6
					12 A.R. Border	2	5	5	5
					10 W.W. Armstrong	8	2	0	4
					10 A.L. Hassett	4	4	2	9

Captains With Most Consecutive Victories

England

6 A.P.F. Chapman	1926 to 1930
4 W.G. Grace	1888 to 1890
4 J.W.H.T. Douglas	1911–12

Australia

8 W.W. Armstrong	1920–1 to 1921
4 G.H.S. Trott	1897–98
4 A.L. Hassett	1950–1

Captains With Most Matches Without Defeat

England			Australia		
7	R. Illingworth	1970–1 to 1972	10	W.W. Armstrong	1920–1 to 1921
7	J.M. Brearley	1977 to 1978–9	10	D.G. Bradman	1946–7 to 1948
			8	R.B. Simpson	1964 to 1965–6
			8	G.S. Chappell	1977 to 1982–3

Centuries by Captains in the Same Test

England		Australia			
A.P.F. Chapman	121	W.M. Woodfull	155	Lord's	1930
W.R. Hammond	240	D.G. Bradman	102*	Lord's	1938
L. Hutton	145	A.L. Hassett	104	Lord's	1953
E.R. Dexter	174	R.B. Simpson	311	Old Trafford	1964

Highest Innings by Captains

England				Australia			
240	W.R. Hammond	Lord's	1938	311	R.B. Simpson	Old Trafford	1964
215	D.I. Gower	Edgbaston	1985	270	D.G. Bradman	Melbourne	1936–7
188	M.H. Denness	Melbourne	1974–5	234	D.G. Bradman	Sydney	1946–7
174	E.R. Dexter	Old Trafford	1964	225	R.B. Simpson	Adelaide	1965–6
173	A.E. Stoddart	Melbourne	1894–5	212	D.G. Bradman	Adelaide	1936–7
166	D.I. Gower	Trent Bridge	1985	211	W.L. Murdoch	Oval	1884
157	D.I. Gower	Oval	1985	196	A.R. Border	Lord's	1985
145	L. Hutton	Lord's	1953	192	I.M. Chappell	Oval	1975
144*	Hon F.S. Jackson	Headingley	1905	187	D.G. Bradman	Brisbane	1946–7

Most Wickets in Innings by Captains

England				Australia			
5–36	G.O.B. Allen	Brisbane	1936–7	7–100	M.A. Noble	Sydney	1903–4
5–46	J.W.H.T. Douglas	Melbourne	1911–2	6–70	R. Benaud	Old Trafford	1961
5–49	F.R. Brown	Melbourne	1950–1	6–115	R. Benaud	Brisbane	1962–3
5–52	Hon F.S. Jackson	Trent Bridge	1905	6–155	G. Giffen	Melbourne	1894–5
				5–26	G. Giffen	Sydney	1894–5
5–66	R.G.D. Willis	Brisbane	1982–3	5–62	H. Trumble	Melbourne	1901–2

Most Wickets in Match by Captains

England				Australia			
8–107	G.O.B. Allen	Brisbane	1936–7	9–173	R. Benaud	Adelaide	1958–9
				9–177	R. Benaud	Sydney	1958–9
				8–40	G. Giffen	Sydney	1894–5
				8–126	H. Trumble	Melbourne	1901–2
				8–140	M.A. Noble	Sydney	1903–4

Best Batting Average While Captain (5 Tests or more)

England	Tests	Inns	NO	Runs	HS	Ave	100s	50s
D.I. Gower	6	9	0	732	215	81.33	3	1
Hon. F.S. Jackson	5	9	2	492	144*	70.29	2	2
P.B.H. May	13	23	3	1091	113	54.55	2	8
E.R. Dexter	10	18	0	865	174	48.06	1	7
W.R. Hammond	8	14	0	571	240	40.79	1	2
M.W. Gatting	6	10	0	406	100	40.60	1	3
L. Hutton	10	18	1	663	145	39.00	1	4
R. Illingworth	10	18	3	527	57	35.13	0	2
A.C. MacLaren	22	36	3	1156	116	35.03	2	6
Australia								
D.G. Bradman	19	32	5	2432	270	90.07	10	6
R.B. Simpson	8	12	2	813	311	81.30	2	3
A.R. Border	12	23	4	1120	196	58.95	4	2
W.W. Armstrong	10	13	2	616	158	56.00	3	1
J. Ryder	5	10	1	492	112	54.67	1	4
G.S. Chappell	15	29	4	1225	117	49.00	4	4
W.M. Lawry	9	17	3	594	135	42.43	1	4
I.M. Chappell	16	30	1	1181	192	40.72	2	9
A.L. Hassett	10	19	0	731	115	38.47	2	4
W.M. Woodfull	15	25	2	878	155	38.17	1	7
M.A. Noble	15	29	3	992	133	38.15	1	7
W.L. Murdoch	16	29	4	877	211	35.08	2	1

Best Bowling Average While Captain (5 Tests or more)

England	Tests	Balls	Mdns	Runs	Wkts	Ave	5wi	10wm
Hon. F.S. Jackson	5	407	8	201	13	15.46	1	0
F.R. Brown	5	872	12	389	18	21.61	1	0
N.W.D. Yardley	6	568	25	219	9	24.33	0	0
R.G.D. Willis	5	999	28	486	18	27.00	1	0
G.O.B. Allen	5	1021	12	526	17	30.94	1	0
R. Illingworth	10	1584	71	546	17	32.12	0	0
J.W.H.T. Douglas	12	1733	46	885	27	32.78	1	0
E.R. Dexter	10	1056	13	491	14	35.07	0	0
Australia								
M.A. Noble	15	2055	101	745	31	24.03	1	0
W.W. Armstrong	10	1379	77	416	17	24.47	0	0
R. Benaud	14	5017	199	1760	63	27.94	4	0
I.W. Johnson	9	1602	69	546	18	30.33	0	0
J. Ryder	5	413	16	180	5	36.00	0	0
G.H.S. Trott	8	786	18	396	11	36.00	0	0

Wicket-Keepers as Captain

England	Australia	Tests	Ct	St	Total
(No instance)	J.M. Blackham	8	11	4	15
	B.N. Jarman	1	3	0	0
	*W.L. Murdoch	1	1	1	2

* J.M. Blackham kept wicket for part of the second innings of this Test

Most Consecutive Tests as Captain

England			Australia		
14 A.C. MacLaren	1899 to 1902		19 D.G. Bradman	1936 to 1948	
14 J.M. Brearley	1977 to 1979–80		16 I.M. Chappell	1971 to 1975	
			15 W.M. Woodfull	1930 to 1934	
			14 W.L. Murdoch	1880 to 1884–5	

Captains Who Sent Opponents In

Name	Ground	Year	Result
England			
A.E. Stoddart	Sydney	1894–5	Lost by inns and 147 runs
A.C. MacLaren	Melbourne	1901–2	Lost by 229 runs
A.O. Jones	Sydney	1907–8	Lost by 49 runs
J.W.H.T. Douglas	Melbourne	1911–2	Won by inns and 225 runs
A.W. Carr	Headingley	1926	Drawn
L. Hutton	Brisbane	1954–5	Lost by inns and 154 runs
P.B.H. May	Adelaide	1958–9	Lost by 10 wkts
E.R. Dexter	Lord's	1964	Drawn
R. Illingworth	Trent Bridge	1972	Drawn
M.H. Denness	Adelaide	1974–5	Lost by 163 runs
M.H. Denness	Edgbaston	1975	Lost by inns and 85 runs
A.W. Greig	Melbourne	1976–7	Lost by 45 runs
J.M. Brearley	Perth	1979–80	Lost by 138 runs
J.M. Brearley	Oval	1981	Drawn
R.G.D. Willis	Adelaide	1982–3	Lost by 8 wkts
D.I. Gower	Old Trafford	1985	Drawn
D.I. Gower	Edgbaston	1985	Won by inns and 118 runs
M.W. Gatting	Melbourne	1986–7	Won by inns and 14 runs
Australia			
P.S. McDonnell	Sydney	1886–7	Lost by 13 runs
P.S. McDonnell	Sydney	1887–8	Lost by 126 runs
G. Giffen	Melbourne	1894–5	Lost by 94 runs
M.A. Noble	Lord's	1909	Won by 9 wkts
A.L. Hassett	Headingley	1953	Drawn
A.R. Morris	Sydney	1954–5	Lost by 38 runs
I.W. Johnson	Sydney	1954–5	Drawn
R. Benaud	Melbourne	1958–9	Won by 9 wkts
W.M. Lawry	Perth	1970–1	Drawn
I.M. Chappell	Sydney	1970–1	Lost by 62 runs
I.M. Chappell	Perth	1974–5	Won by 9 wkts
I.M. Chappell	Melbourne	1974–5	Drawn
G.S. Chappell	Oval	1977	Drawn
G.N. Yallop	Perth	1978–9	Lost by 166 runs
G.N. Yallop	Adelaide	1978–9	Lost by 205 runs
G.S. Chappell	Sydney	1979–80	Won by 6 wkts
K.J. Hughes	Trent Bridge	1981	Won by 4 wkts
K.J. Hughes	Lord's	1981	Drawn
G.S. Chappell	Perth	1982–3	Drawn
G.S. Chappell	Brisbane	1982–3	Won by 7 wkts
G.S. Chappell	Melbourne	1982–3	Lost by 3 runs
A.R. Border	Lord's	1985	Won by 4 wkts
A.R. Border	Brisbane	1986–7	Lost by 7 wkts

Bibliography

Allen, David Rayvern (ed.), *Arlott on Cricket* (Collins)
Arlott, John, *Fred* (Eyre and Spottiswoode)
Bailey, Trevor, *A History of Cricket* (Allen and Unwin)
Benaud, Richie, *On Reflection* (Collins)
Berry, Scyld, *The Observer on Cricket* (Unwin Hyman)
Bose, Mihir, *Keith Miller* (Allen and Unwin)
Bowen, Roland, *Cricket: A History* (Eyre and Spottiswoode)
Brearley, Mike, *Phoenix from the Ashes* (Hodder and Stoughton)
Cardus, Neville, *The Summer Game* (Hart-Davis)
   Days in the Sun (Hart-Davis)
   Good Days (Hart-Davis)
   Australian Summer (Hart-Davis)
Coldham, James D., *Lord Harris* (Allen and Unwin)
Down, Michael, *Archie* (Allen and Unwin)
Engel, Matthew (ed.), *The Guardian Book of Cricket* (Pavilion)
Fingleton, Jack, *Masters of Cricket* (Heinemann)
Frith, David, *England versus Australia: A Pictorial History of the Test Matches since 1877* (Collins)
   The Golden Age of Cricket 1890–1914 (Lutterworth Press)
   My Dear Victorious Stod (Lutterworth Press)
Gregory, Kenneth (ed.), *In Celebration of Cricket* (Pavilion)
Illingworth, Ray, *Captaincy* (Pelham)
   and Gregory, Kenneth, *The Ashes* (Collins)
Johnston, Brian, *It's a Funny Game* (W.H. Allen)
Lemmon, David, *Johnny Won't Hit Today* (Allen and Unwin)
   Percy Chapman (Queen Anne Press)
Mason, Ronald, *Walter Hammond* (Hollis and Carter)
Murphy, Patrick, *The Centurions* (J.M. Dent)
Robinson, Ray, *Between Wickets* (Collins)
Ross, Alan (ed.), *The Cricketer's Companion* (Eyre Methuen)
Swanton, E.W. (ed.), *Swanton in Australia* (Collins)
Thomson, A.A., *Cricket: The Golden Ages* (Stanley Paul)
   Cricket: the Great Captains (Stanley Paul)
Williams, Marcus (ed.), *Double Century – 200 Years of Cricket in The Times* (Collins)
Willis, Ronald, *Cricket's Biggest Mystery: the Ashes* (Lutterworth Press)
Wisden Cricketers' Almanack
Yardley, Norman, *Cricket Campaigns* (Stanley Paul)

Periodicals

The Cricketer
Wisden Cricket Monthly

Index

Note: bold numerals denote entries in statistical sections.